From

Chicago

Here's what the critics say about Frommer's:

"Amazingly easy to use. Very portable, very complete."
—*Booklist*

◆

"The only mainstream guide to list specific prices. The Walter Cronkite of guidebooks—with all that implies."
—*Travel & Leisure*

◆

"Complete, concise, and filled with useful information."
—*New York Daily News*

◆

"Hotel information is close to encyclopedic."
—*Des Moines Sunday Register*

Other Great Guides for Your Trip:

Frommer's Memorable Walks in Chicago

Frommer's Portable Chicago

The Unofficial Guide to Chicago

Frommer's Irreverent Guide to Chicago

Frommer's® 99

Chicago

by Todd A. Savage

MACMILLAN • USA

ABOUT THE AUTHOR

Freelance writer Todd A. Savage has lived in the Chicago area on and off for a decade. He has contributed to numerous local and national magazines and newspapers, including the *Chicago Reader,* the *Chicago Tribune,* and *Chicago* magazine. He is also the author of *Frommer's Chicago By Night* and a contributor to *Frommer's Gay & Lesbian Guide to Europe.*

MACMILLAN TRAVEL

A Simon & Schuster Macmillan Company
1633 Broadway
New York, NY 10019

Find us online at **www.frommers.com**

ISBN 0-02-862347-9
ISSN 1040-936X

Editor: Suzanne Roe Jannetta
Production Editor: Carol Sheehan
Photo Editor: Richard Fox
Design by Michele Laseau
Digital Cartography by Roberta Stockwell
Page Creation by Carrie Allen, Trudy Coler, Toi Davis, Dave Faust, Laura Goetz, Dave Pruett, and Linda Quigley.

SPECIAL SALES

Bulk purchases (10+ copies) of Frommer's and selected Macmillan travel guides are available to corporations, organizations, mail-order catalogs, institutions, and charities at special discounts, and can be customized to suit individual needs. For more information write to Special Sales, Macmillan General Reference, 1633 Broadway, New York, NY 10019.

Manufactured in the United States of America

Contents

List of Maps

DEDICATION

*This book is respectfully dedicated to legendary baseball announcer Harry Caray,
who passed away February 18, 1998, at the age of 83. Harry began his broadcasting
career in 1945 and was the announcer for the St. Louis Cardinals for 25 years and
the Chicago White Sox for 11 before settling into Wrigley Field and the Cubbies in
1982. He was loved by baseball fans across the nation for his signature black glasses,
his legendary seventh-inning stretch renditions of "Take Me Out to the Ballgame,"
and his familiar refrains: "Holy Cow!" and "Cubs win! Cubs win! Cubs win!" Harry
was inducted into the Baseball Hall of Fame in 1989, and for the 1998 season, his
grandson Chip Caray was to join him in the broadcast booth to announce Cubs home
games. Harry was the consummate fan, and he will be missed.*

*Chicago suffered another loss when Harry Caray's predecessor, Jack Brickhouse, died
August 6, 1998, at the age of 82. The hall-of-fame broadcaster, famous for his "Hey!
Hey!", was the Cubs play-by-play announcer for 4 decades, beginning in 1941.*

AN INVITATION TO THE READER

In researching this book, we discovered many wonderful places—hotels, restaurants, shops, and more. We're sure you'll find others. Please tell us about them, so we can share the information with your fellow travelers in upcoming editions. If you were disappointed with a recommendation, we'd love to know that, too. Please write to:

Frommer's Chicago '99
Macmillan Travel
1633 Broadway
New York, NY 10019

AN ADDITIONAL NOTE

Please be advised that travel information is subject to change at any time—and this is especially true of prices. We therefore suggest that you write or call ahead for confirmation when making your travel plans. The authors, editors, and publisher cannot be held responsible for the experiences of readers while traveling. Your safety is important to us, however, so we encourage you to stay alert and be aware of your surroundings. Keep a close eye on cameras, purses, and wallets, all favorite targets of thieves and pickpockets.

WHAT THE SYMBOLS MEAN

✪ Frommer's Favorites

Our favorite places and experiences—outstanding for quality, value, or both.

The following abbreviations are used for credit cards:

AE	American Express	EURO	Eurocard
CB	Carte Blanche	JCB	Japan Credit Bank
DC	Diners Club	MC	MasterCard
DISC	Discover	V	Visa
ER	EnRoute		

FIND FROMMER'S ONLINE

Arthur Frommer's Outspoken Encyclopedia of Travel (www.frommers.com) offers more than 6,000 pages of up-to-the-minute travel information—including the latest bargains and candid, personal articles updated daily by Arthur Frommer himself. No other Web site offers such comprehensive and timely coverage of the world of travel.

The Chicago Experience

A person or a place has only one chance to make a first impression, and you never know what will impress you most about Chicago. It may be the city's brilliant, varied skyline—punctuated by two sky-scraping structures, the Sears Tower and the John Hancock Building. Or, it might be the shimmering, endless waters of Lake Michigan, especially if you approach the city by car via Lake Shore Drive, the famed thoroughfare that hugs the shoreline. Or, maybe after checking into your hotel you'll go out exploring, and you might find yourself rubbing elbows with some locals in a neighborhood hangout or cheering alongside long-suffering Cubs fans in Wrigley Field. In that case you might be most impressed by the no-nonsense, good-natured character of the citizens themselves. Or, maybe you'll be struck by the city's culinary offerings, or its world-class shopping scene, or its venerable cultural institutions.

Not until your arrival, of course, will you know what's going to impress you most about the city, what's going to make "my kind of town," your kind of town. Below is a short list—and believe me, I could go on and on—of my very favorite things to see and do here. Whether you're in town for a weekend getaway with or without the kids, a convention or business meeting, or your cousin's wedding, you'll no doubt leave Chicago with your own list of "favorites."

1 Frommer's Favorite Chicago Experiences

- **Soaking Up Sun at Wrigley Field.** It's a Chicago tradition to play hooky for an afternoon to sit in the bleachers at this most charming of all baseball parks and watch Sammy Sosa and the rest of the Cubbies try to hit 'em onto Waveland Avenue. (See chapter 7 for details.)
- **Listening to Music Under the Stars.** Pack a picnic and take the train (or drive) out to Highland Park's Ravinia, summer home of the Chicago Symphony, or stay in town to enjoy the free concerts presented in the city's front yard, Grant Park. (See chapter 10 for details.)
- **Getting Lost at the Art Institute.** The vast art museum offers myriad places for private meditation on works by all the masters. Take a Sunday stroll in the park courtesy of pointillist painter Georges Seurat, disappear into a lonely night envisioned by the hawklike eye of American Edward Hopper, or reach for Nirvana

Chicago & Vicinity

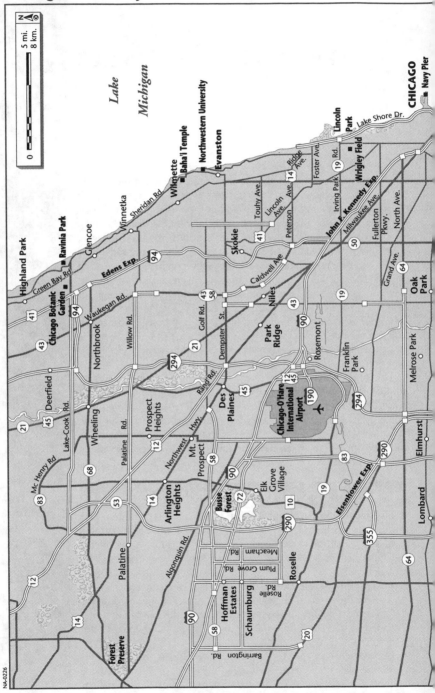

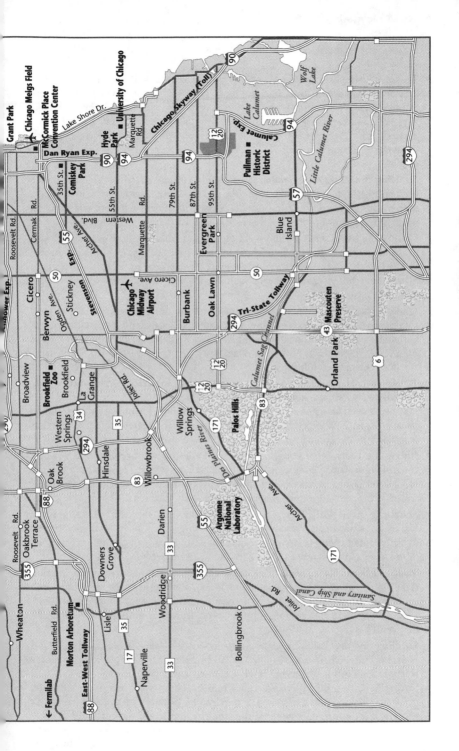

3

drifting among the statuaries of some unknown ancient sculptor. (See chapter 7 for details.)

- **Taking a Taste of Chicago.** The ribs at Carson's are succulent and the stuffed pizza at Gino's East is deservedly hyped, but don't stop there: Chicago is home to an ever-expanding galaxy of sophisticated restaurants whose kitchens are energized by culinary stars. You can sit for a multicourse tasting menu at the incomparable Charlie Trotter's, make the scene at the Chicago outpost of Wolfgang Puck's Spago, or savor the unique Mexican cooking of Rick Bayless at Frontera Grill. (See chapter 6 for details.)

- **Studying the Skyline.** For more than a century Chicago's architectural royals have been putting up buildings that scrape the sky, make peace with the prairie, and do more with less. A good way to ground yourself in the city's history is to take an architectural tour—by foot, bus, bike, or boat. (See chapter 7 for details.)

- **Getting the Blues.** Here in the world capital of the blues, you've got your pick of places to feel them, from the collegiate atmosphere of Kingston Mines in Lincoln Park, where musicians perform continuously on two stages, to the earthy roadhouse New Checkerboard Lounge on the South Side, where neighborhood locals mingle with the tourists, blues lovers all. (See chapter 10 for details.)

- **Walking the Walk.** You notice the most interesting things when you lace up your sneakers and let your curiosity power you. Explore Chicago's diversity with a neighborhood walkabout; it's one of the best ways to get a flavor for how the people here, from Indian immigrants on Devon Avenue to gay couples on Halsted Street, actually live. (See chapter 8 for details.)

- **Taking in a Show.** The stage lights rarely go dark in one of the country's most bustling theater scenes, home to the innovative Steppenwolf (where founders John Malkovich and Gary Sinise got their start), a burgeoning downtown Broadway-style theater district now joined by the refurbished Oriental Theater and droves of other ambitious theater companies on the make. (See chapter 10 for details.)

- **Riding the Rails.** No matter that you have no destination in mind, find out why the Loop is so named by hopping a southbound Brown Line Elevated train (or "the El," for short), and watch the city unfold as the train crosses the Chicago River and screeches through downtown canyons. (See chapter 7 for details.)

- **Shopping the Town.** Chicago may have two baseball teams, but shopping is the national pastime when you're browsing and buying your way up Michigan Avenue or discovering the one-of-a-kind boutiques in River North, along Armitage Avenue, or in one of the city's other trendy enclaves. (See chapter 9 for details.)

- **Taking in Some Cool Jazz at the Green Mill.** This atmospheric Uptown jazz club is the place to go to soak up some smooth sounds from some of the hottest, up-and-coming performers on the jazz scene today. But don't just go for the tunes—the club, a living museum of 1930s Chicago, is an attraction in itself. (See chapter 10 for details.)

- **Strolling by the Lake.** It really is cooler by the lake—meteorologically and metaphorically. There are 29 miles of lakefront for biking, 'blading, or simply being, so get out there and contemplate Chicago's very own ocean.

- **Setting Sail.** To really experience Chicago to its fullest, don't just sit on the shore, get out on the water for a fresh look at the city, one that even many locals have never witnessed. It's surprising how the skyline stretches out across the horizon. Navy Pier is the place to board a boat that's just your speed, from a powerboat to a tall-masted schooner. Or if you feel like putting your own wind in some sails, rent one of the boats from the Chicago Sailing Club in Belmont Harbor. (See chapter 7 for details.)

- **Spying on Sue.** The newest resident of the Field Museum is the mighty T-rex Sue, whose unearthed bones the museum acquired for $8.4 million at auction last year. The dinosaur is being meticulously studied and assembled by researchers at the museum. Visitors can watch scientists at work in a new glass-enclosed laboratory. Their goal is to set the beast loose in the museum in 2000.
- **Playing in the Sand at Oak Street Beach.** If you're staying at a North Michigan Avenue hotel, you can hit the sands at this unique urban beach about as fast as your elevator gets you to the lobby. Of course, you may not want to venture very far into the chilly waters (even in summer), but the crowded boardwalk offers plenty of people-watching to while away a sunny afternoon.
- **Hitting a Matinee at the Music Box.** Head to this venerable, old movie house in Wrigleyville to see classic flicks such as *The Thin Man* or *Meet Me in St. Louis* the way they were meant to be seen. It's a total experience from beginning (an organist keeps the house keyboard in tune before shows) to end (faux clouds float over the ceiling). (See chapter 10 for details.)

2 The City Today

No, Chicago is no longer the "hog butcher to the world"(though you can still get some mighty fine steak here). Nor is it a city of gangsters emptying their tommy guns on the streets (though 1990s versions of gangs certainly exist). Today, the typical visitor will discover that Chicago is more glitz than grit, more Paris than prairie, an exciting and cosmopolitan city.

Visitors have more reasons than ever to visit Chicago, with its impressive new home for the Museum of Contemporary Art; a lively, rehabilitated Navy Pier; the restored downtown Oriental Theater; and steamrollering retail expansion along the city's fabled Magnificent Mile. Come summer, the lake sparkles and draws legions to its shores, slowing traffic on Lake Shore Drive as envious drivers crane their necks to watch the volleyball players cavorting on the beaches. Chicago's domination of the convention business was further solidified recently with the completion of a mammoth new wing at the city's major convention hall, McCormick Place, and that booming trade has sparked another round of hotel construction.

Chicago has a glow about it these days. And it's not just the Bulls bringing home their sixth NBA championship or Sammy Sosa smashing home runs. The city has its well-publicized problems—among them, chronically troubled schools, a beleaguered transit agency, and deplorable public housing conditions—but on many of these fronts the city seems recommitted to repairing its afflictions. A generation ago, people poured out of the city for greener suburban pastures, but today people seem to want to live in the city again. Witness new town houses squeezing into lots in many quarters of the city, and lofts becoming an urban cliché as developers scramble to carve out condos in neighborhoods on the fringes of downtown once thought unfashionable if not downright unsafe. Even fish have returned to the once polluted Chicago River.

It's safe to say that Chicago would be overrun with transplants if it weren't for the fact that summer is followed by fall, and after that, yes, winter. Chicagoans, it seems, can be thankful for that season, too.

Impressions

Hog Butcher for the World, Tool Maker, Stacker of Wheat, Player with Railroads and the Nation's Freight Handler; Stormy, husky, brawling, City of the Big Shoulders.
—Carl Sandburg, "Chicago," from *Chicago Poems* (1916)

3   Chicago History 101

Dateline

- **1673** French explorers Marquette and Jolliet discover portage at Chicago linking the Great Lakes region with the Mississippi River valley.
- **1779** Afro-French-Canadian trapper Jean Baptiste Point du Sable establishes a trading post on the north bank of the Chicago River. A settlement follows 2 years later.
- **1794** Gen. "Mad" Anthony Wayne defeats the British in the Battle of Fallen Timbers; disputed Illinois Territory is finally ceded to the young American Republic by treaty a year later.
- **1803** Garrison of Fort Dearborn is established in Chicago, commanded by the grandfather of artist James McNeill Whistler.
- **1812** Residents of Fort Dearborn are slain by Native Americans trying to reclaim their lost territory.
- **1816** Fort Dearborn manned anew.
- **1818** Illinois Territory admitted to the Union as the 21st state.
- **1833** Town of Chicago officially incorporated, with little more than 300 residents.
- **1850** Chicago's population roughly 30,000.
- **1856** Chicago is chief railroad center in the United States.
- **1860** Republican National Convention in Chicago nominates Abraham Lincoln for the presidency.
- **1865** Chicago stockyards are founded.

continues

By virtue of its location, Chicago became the great engine of America's westward expansion. The particular patch of land where Chicago now stands straddles a key point along an inland water route linking Canada, via Lake Erie, to New Orleans and the Gulf of Mexico by way of the Mississippi River.

The French, busy expanding their own territory in North America throughout the 17th and 18th centuries, were the first Europeans to survey the topography of the future Chicago. The French policy in North America was simple—to gradually settle the Mississippi Valley and the Northwest Territory (modern Michigan, Illinois, Wisconsin, and Minnesota). The policy relied on an alliance between religion and commerce: The French sought a monopoly over the fur trade with the Native American tribes, whose pacification and loyalty they attempted to ensure by converting them to Catholicism.

The team of Jacques Marquette, a Jesuit missionary, and Louis Jolliet, an explorer, personified this policy to perfection. In 1673 the pair found a very short portage between two critically placed rivers, the Illinois and the Des Plaines. One was connected to the Mississippi, and the other, via the Chicago River, to Lake Michigan and then onward to Montréal and Québec.

Chicago owes its existence to this strategic 1½-mile portage trail that the Native Americans had blazed in their own water travels over centuries of moving throughout this territory. Marquette himself was on the most familiar terms with the Native Americans, who helped him make his way over the well-established paths of their ancestral lands. The Native Americans, of course, did not anticipate the European settlers' hunger for such prime real estate.

FIRST SETTLEMENT   Over the next 100 years, the French used this waterway to spread their American empire from Canada to Mobile, Alabama. Yet the first recorded settlement in Chicago, a trading post built by a Frenchman, Jean Baptiste Point du Sable, did not appear until 1781. By this time the British already had conquered the territory, part of the spoils of 70 years of intermittent warfare that cost the French most of their North American holdings. After the American War of Independence, the Illinois Territory was wrested from British/Native American control in a campaign led by the Revolutionary War hero

Gen. "Mad" Anthony Wayne, which ended with a treaty in 1795 ceding the land around the mouth of the Chicago River to the United States.

Between du Sable's day and 1833, when Chicago was officially founded, the land by the mouth of the Chicago River served as a military outpost that guarded the strategic passage and provided security for a few trappers and a trading post. The military base, Fort Dearborn, which stood on the south side of what is now the Michigan Avenue Bridge, was first garrisoned in 1803 under the command of Capt. John Whistler, grandfather of the famous painter. At first the settlement grew slowly, impeded by continued Native American efforts to drive the new Americans from the Illinois Territory. During the War of 1812, inhabitants abandoned Fort Dearborn, and many were slain during the evacuation. But before long the trappers drifted back, and by 1816 the military, too, had returned.

Conflict diminished after that, but even as a civil engineer plotted the building lots of the early town as late as 1830, periodic raids continued, ceasing only with the defeat of Chief Black Hawk in 1832. A year later, the settlement of 300-plus inhabitants was officially incorporated under the name Chicago, said to derive from a Native American word referring to the powerful odors of the abundant wild vegetation in the marshlands surrounding the riverbanks.

COMMERCE & INDUSTRY Land speculation began immediately, as Chicago was carved piecemeal and sold off to finance the Illinois and Michigan Canal that would eliminate the narrow land portage and fulfill the long-standing vision of connecting the two great waterways. Thus the domesticated East would be linked to the pioneer West, with Chicago at midpoint, directing the flow of commerce in both directions. Commercial activity was quick to follow: Within 2 to 3 years, local farmers in the outlying areas were producing a surplus. Chicago grew in size and wealth, shipping grain and livestock to the eastern markets and lumber to the treeless prairies of the West. Ironically, by the time the Illinois and Michigan Canal was completed in 1848, the railroad had arrived, and the water route that gave Chicago its raison d'être was rapidly becoming obsolete. Boxcars, not boats, grabbed the title of principal mode of transportation throughout the region. The combination of the railroad with the emergence of local manufacturing, and later, the Civil War, caused Chicago to grow wildly.

- **1870** City's population numbers almost 300,000, making it perhaps the fastest-growing metropolis in history.
- **1871** Great Chicago Fire burns large sections of the city; rebuilding begins while the ashes are still warm.
- **1882** The 10-story Montauk Building, the world's first skyscraper, is erected.
- **1886** Dynamite bomb explodes during political rally near Haymarket Square, causing a riot in which eight policemen and two civilians are killed; eight anarchists are later convicted in one of the country's most controversial trials.
- **1892** The first elevated train goes into operation.
- **1893** Chicago, completely recovered from the Great Fire, hosts the World's Columbian Exposition.
- **1894** Workers of the Pullman Car Company plant join the American Railway Union in a general strike; President Cleveland sends federal troops to Chicago.
- **1896** William Jennings Bryan delivers "Cross of Gold" speech before delegates of the Democratic National Convention.
- **1900** The flow of the Chicago River is reversed to end the dumping of sewage into Lake Michigan.
- **1903** Theodore Roosevelt is nominated for the presidency by the Republican National Convention.
- **1905** Wobblies, or Industrial Workers of the World (IWW), founded in Chicago.

continues

- **1909** Daniel Burnham's *Plan of Chicago*, the first comprehensive municipal plan ever offered to an American city, is published.
- **1919** "Black Sox" bribery scandal stuns baseball.
- **1919–33** During Prohibition, Chicago becomes a "wide-open town"; rival mobs battle violently throughout the city for control of distribution and sale of illegal alcohol.
- **1932** Franklin Delano Roosevelt is nominated for the presidency by the Democratic National Convention.
- **1945** Chicago Cubs make their last appearance in the World Series—and lose to Detroit.
- **1955** Richard J. Daley begins term as mayor; he is widely regarded as the "last of the big-city bosses."
- **1968** Anti–Vietnam War protests in conjunction with Democratic National Convention end in police riot.
- **1974** The 1,454-foot Sears Tower is completed, becoming the tallest building in the world.
- **1979** Jane Byrne becomes the first woman elected mayor of Chicago.
- **1983** Harold Washington becomes the first African-American mayor of Chicago.
- **1989** Richard M. Daley, the son of the long-serving mayor, is elected mayor.
- **1992** A freight tunnel ruptures; the Loop is flooded underground by water from the Chicago River.
- **1993** Michael Jordan retires from basketball. The city mourns.
- **1995** Jordan returns to the Bulls.

continues

The most revolutionary product of the era sprang from the mind of Chicago inventor Cyrus McCormick, whose reaper filled in for the farmhands who now labored on the nation's battlefields. Local merchants not only thrived on the contraband trade in cotton, but they also secured lucrative contracts from the federal government to provide the army with tents, uniforms, saddles, harnesses, lumber, bread, and meat. By 1870 Chicago's population had grown to 300,000, a thousand times greater than its original population, in the brief interval of 37 years since the city's incorporation.

THE GREAT FIRE   A year later the city lay in ashes. The Great Chicago Fire of 1871 began somewhere on the southwest side of the city on October 8 (legend places its exact origin in the O'Leary shed). The fire jumped the river and continued northward through the night and the following day, when it was checked by the use of gunpowder on the South Side and rainfall to the north and west, just before spreading to the prairie. In its wake, the fire destroyed 18,000 buildings and left 90,000 homeless, taking a toll of 300 lives.

One thing the fire could not destroy was Chicago's strategic location, and on that solid geographic footing the city began to rebuild as soon as the rubble was cleared. By chance, Chicago's railroad infrastructure—factories, grain warehouses, and lumberyards—was also spared, being located beyond the circle of fire on the southern periphery of the city. By 1873 the city's downtown business and financial district was up and running again, and 2 decades later Chicago had sufficiently recovered to host the 1893 World's Columbian Exposition commemorating the 400th anniversary of the discovery of America.

AN AMERICAN ATHENS   The Great Fire gave an unprecedented boost to the professional and artistic development of the nation's architects—drawn by the unlimited opportunities to build, they gravitated to the city in droves. And the city raised its own homegrown crop of architects. Chicago's deserved reputation as an American Athens, packed with monumental and decorative buildings, is a direct by-product of the disastrous fire that nearly brought the city to ruin.

In the meantime, Chicago's population continued to grow as many immigrants forsook the uncultivated farmland of the prairie to join the city's labor pool. Chicago still shipped meat and agricultural commodities around the nation and the world, but the city itself was rapidly becoming a mighty industrial center in its own right, creating finished goods, particularly for the markets of the ever-expanding western settlements.

THE CRADLE OF TRADE UNIONISM Chicago never seemed to outgrow its frontier rawness. Greed, profiteering, exploitation, and corruption were as critical to its growth as hard work, ingenuity, and civic pride. The spirit of reform arose most powerfully from the ranks of the working classes, whose lives, despite the city's prosperity, were plagued by poverty and disease. When the sleeping giant of labor finally awakened in Chicago, it did so with a militancy and commitment that was to inspire the union movement throughout the nation.

■ **1996** The city patches up its turbulent political history by hosting the Democratic National Convention, its first national political gathering in 3 decades. William Jefferson Clinton is nominated for a second term.

By the 1890s, many of Chicago's workers were already organized into the American Federation of Labor. The Pullman Strike of 1894 united black and white railway workers for the first time in common struggle for higher wages and workplace rights. The Industrial Workers of the World, or the Wobblies, which embraced for a time so many great voices of American labor—Eugene V. Debs, Big Bill Haywood, Helen Gurley Flynn—was founded in Chicago in 1905.

AN AFRICAN-AMERICAN CAPITAL The major change in Chicago in the 20th century, however, stems from the enormous growth of the city's African-American population. Coincident with the beginning of World War I, Chicago became the destination for thousands of blacks leaving Mississippi and other parts of the Deep South. Most settled on the South Side. With the exception of Hyde Park, which absorbed the black population into a successfully integrated, middle-class neighborhood, Chicago over the decades gained a reputation as the most segregated city in the United States. Today, though increased black representation in local politics and other institutions has eased some racial tensions, the city remains far more geographically segregated than most of its urban peers.

THE CHICAGO MACHINE While Chicago was becoming a center of industry, transportation, and finance, and a beacon of labor reform, it was also—again by virtue of its location—becoming a powerhouse in national politics. Between 1860 and 1968 Chicago was the site of 14 Republican and 10 Democratic presidential nominating conventions. (Some even point to the conventions as the source of Chicago's "Windy City" nickname, laying the blame on a politician who was full of hot air.) The first of the conventions gave the country one of its most admired leaders, Abraham Lincoln, while the 1968 convention was witness to the so-called Days of Rage, a police riot against demonstrators who had camped out in Grant Park to protest the Vietnam War. As TV cameras rolled, the demonstrators chanted, "The whole world is watching."

And it was; many politicos blame Mayor Richard J. Daley for Hubert Humphrey's defeat in the general election. (Maybe it was a wash; some also say Daley stole the 1960 election for Kennedy.)

A few words about (the original) Mayor Daley: He did not invent the political machine, but he certainly perfected it. As Theodore White writes in *America in Search of Itself,* "Daley ran the machine with a tribal justice akin to the forest Gauls." Daley understood that as long as the leaders of every ethnic and special-interest group had their share of the spoils—the African Americans controlled the South Side, for example, and the Polish-Americans kept their neighborhoods segregated—he could retain ultimate power. His reach extended well beyond Chicago's borders; he

A River Runs Through It

With apologies to the late Norman Maclean for appropriating the title of his wonderful collection of fiction, *A River Runs Through It*, the words here refer to the river in Chicago, not to the one in the writer's native Montana. Chicago owes not only its name but also its existence to its river. Native Americans referred to the land around the river with a word—that to the ears of the early Europeans sounded like "chicago"—meaning "powerful," presumably owing to the strong odors of either the swampy decay or the plant life pervasive along the riverbank. Because the Chicago River provided a crucial link between the Great Lakes and the Mississippi River, the frontier city was destined to grow into the nation's great midcontinental hub of transportation and transshipment, facilitating travel and trade between the eastern settlements and the West.

Today the Chicago River remains one of the most visible yet enigmatic of Chicago's major physical features. It branches into so many neighborhoods that it's almost omnipresent. The effect is similar to that famous revolutionary-era flag of the segmented snake; you see the river only in isolated snatches, each of which usually includes one of the city's 50 some-odd bridges. In fact, Chicago has more movable bridges than any city in the world. An almost mystical moment occurs downtown when all the bridges spanning the main and south branches—connecting the Loop to both the Near West Side and the Near North Side—flap up and then down like the wave of spectators at a ball game. When the drawbridges are raised, allowing for the passage of some ship or barge or contingent of high-masted sailboats, automobile traffic in downtown Chicago grinds to a halt, but only briefly, because the choreography in Chicago is well practiced (after all, it is the city that works).

The Chicago River has long outlived the critical commercial function it once performed for the city that developed along its banks. Most of the remaining millworks that still occupy these banks no longer depend on the river alone for the transport of their materials, raw and finished. The river's main function today is to serve as a fluvial conduit for sewage which, owing to an engineering feat that reversed its flow inland in 1900, no longer pollutes the waters of Lake Michigan. Recently Chicagoans have begun to discover another role for the river, that of leisure resource, providing short cruises on its water, park areas on its banks, and the beginnings of a riverside bike path, which connects to the lakefront route near Wacker Drive. Actually, today's developers aren't the first to wonder why the river couldn't be Chicago's Seine. A look at the early-20th-century Beaux Arts balustrades lining the river along Wacker Drive—complete with comfortably spaced benches—shows that Daniel Burnham knew full well what a treasure the city had.

controlled members of Congress in Washington, and every 4 years he delivered a solid Democratic vote in the November elections. Since his death in 1976, the machine has never been the same. One election produced the city's first female mayor, Jane Byrne, and another, the city's first African-American mayor, Harold Washington. Neither was a novice at politics, but neither could hold the delicate balance of (often conflicting) groups that kept Daley in power for 20 years. Today, Daley's son, Richard M., may have inherited his father's former office, but the estate did not include the Cook County machine. Mayor Richard M. Daley has abandoned his late father's power base of solid white working-class Bridgeport for the newly developed (some would say

Impressions

I have struck a city—a real city—and they call it Chicago. The other places don't count. Having seen it, I urgently desire never to see it again. It is inhabited by savages.
—Rudyard Kipling, *From Sea to Sea* (1889)

It rained and fogged in Chicago and muddy-flowing people oozed thick in the canyon-beds of the streets. Yet it seemed to me more alive and more real than New York.
—D. H. Lawrence, letter to Mrs. Bessie Freeman (August 1923)

yuppie) Central Station neighborhood just south of the Loop. The middle-aged baby boomer appears to be finding himself, but many in the city still enjoy calling him—with more than a hint of condescension—Richie.

The city has ongoing problems. With roughly 2.8 million people total, Chicago's black and white populations are almost equal in size—a rarity among today's urban areas—but the city's residential districts continue to be some of the most segregated in the country. Families are also trying to cope with the school system, which has been undergoing a major restructuring, but whose outlook is still dismal. In 1995 federal government seized control of the city's public housing, pledging to replace the disastrous high-rises with smaller complexes in mixed-income neighborhoods. It is a long-term goal, but authorities have begun the gradual process of tearing down the notorious Cabrini-Green, where then-Mayor Jane Byrne moved briefly to show her support for the crime-victimized residents.

4 Famous Chicagoans

Jane Addams (1860–1935)   Founder of Hull House, Nobel Prize winner, and the leading spirit behind the American Settlement House Movement.

Nelson Algren (1909–81)   The novelist who penned *The Man with the Golden Arm* and *Chicago: City on the Make.*

L. Frank Baum (1856–1919)   He wrote *The Wizard of Oz* while living in Chicago.

Saul Bellow (b. 1915)   Nobel Prize–winning author of *The Adventures of Augie March* and *Humboldt's Gift.* He now lives in Boston.

Gwendolyn Brooks (b. 1917)   The current poet laureate of Illinois, she was the first African-American woman awarded the Pulitzer Prize.

Al Capone (1899–1947)   The most famous mobster of them all, he will be forever linked with Chicago and the dark days of Prohibition.

Nat "King" Cole (1919–65)   The crooner with such hits as "Unforgettable," "Mona Lisa," and "Straighten Up and Fly Right."

Richard J. Daley (1902–76)   The father of the current mayor, he was one of the most powerful political bosses in the United States during his own reign as Chicago's mayor.

Clarence Darrow (1857–1938)   The brilliant defense attorney best known for squaring off against perennial presidential candidate William Jennings Bryan during the famous Scopes Monkey Trial.

Walt Disney (1901–66)   The film producer learned to draw cartoons in Chicago.

Lorraine Hansberry (1930–65)   Chicago-born playwright of *A Raisin in the Sun,* the story of a South Side family and the first play by a black woman produced on Broadway.

Hugh Hefner (b. 1926)   A Chicago native, he founded *Playboy* magazine in his hometown, where the magazine is still published.

Ernest Hemingway (1899–1961)   The great American novelist and Nobel laureate grew up in the Chicago suburb of Oak Park.

Mahalia Jackson (1911–72)   A household name even among those who don't think of themselves as great fans of American gospel music.

Michael Jordan (b. 1963)   He grew up in North Carolina and he lives in a Chicago suburb, but Air Jordan will forever be associated with the city to which he's given six NBA championships.

Ray Kroc (1902–84)   The man who made gold out of the Golden Arches opened his first McDonald's in the suburb of Des Plaines in 1955.

Ann Landers (b. 1918)   Half of the famous sister act of advice givers (Abby is the other), she's still dispensing her column from Chicago.

Mike Royko (1932–97)   Plain-speaking, rapier-sharp newspaper columnist.

Carl Sandburg (1878–1967)   Leading American poet and Lincoln's biographer.

Studs Terkel (b. 1912)   Syndicated radio interviewer and author of oral histories *Division Street: America* and *Working.*

Muddy Waters (1915–83)   The king of Chicago blues.

Oprah Winfrey (b. 1954)   The TV talk show queen and studio head.

5   Rising Like the Phoenix: Chicago's Public Architecture

The Great Fire of 1871 couldn't have come at a better time. As the city began to rebuild from its ashes, gathering to its skirts the best and brightest young architects, it had technology on its side. The construction industry was beginning to experiment with new materials, including steel, which helped make skyscrapers possible; the other invention that enabled architects to build skyward was the elevator. The world's first skyscraper, the Montauk Building, was erected in Chicago in 1882. Coupled with these engineering innovations was an open-mindedness on the part of the civilians that could come only in a frontier town where, less than 60 years earlier, there had stood only a fort and trading post. Chicago was not a Paris or a London; without tradition and history to limit them, the architects of the day were inspired to create the world's first truly modern city.

In the first years after the fire, Daniel Burnham, Louis Sullivan, and Dankmar Adler were among the leading architects to reconstruct the city. While the Sears Tower may awe visitors today, Chicago is home to a number of rather humble structures of no

Impressions

. . . in a few hours we're in that astonishing Chicago—a city where they are always rubbing the lamp and fetching up the genii and contriving and achieving new impossibilities. It is hopeless for the occasional visitor to try to keep up with Chicago—she outgrows his prophecies faster than he can make them. She is always a novelty; for she is never the Chicago you saw when you passed through the last time.
                                              —Mark Twain, *Life on the Mississippi* (1883)

more than 20 stories, such as the Manhattan Building and the Monadnock, that once held the lofty distinction of world's tallest building and were quickly outdone in a flurry of skyscraper building. It was Burnham, from his offices in the Railway Exchange Building he had designed at 224 S. Michigan Ave. (now called the Santa Fe Building), who devised the *Plan of Chicago* in 1909. Nicknamed "Paris on the Prairie," the plan outlined Burnham's vision for the great midwestern city, complete with grand boulevards, parks, and a sacred lakefront. The city today owes the fact that it is so livable to this early urban planning.

Having created its own tradition of nontradition, Chicago fostered the development of Frank Lloyd Wright's "Prairie School," and, still later, of Ludwig Mies van der Rohe's Bauhaus modernism.

Surprisingly, Chicago's protection of its architectural heritage has been spotty. Much of the modern preservation movement can be traced to 1972. That was the year Adler and Sullivan's Stock Exchange Building was demolished, an action that alerted the public to the weakness of the existing preservation laws. Among those other Sullivan buildings that *have* been preserved are the Rookery Building, with its gilded interior by Frank Lloyd Wright, and the Carson Pirie Scott & Co. department store on State Street, with its highly ornamented entrance.

Moving on to architecture of the modern era, the city has a number of examples of work by Mies van der Rohe, founder of the International Style, including his revolutionary steel-and-glass apartment buildings at 860–880 N. Lake Shore Dr. and the Federal Center in the Loop. Designed by the firm of Skidmore, Owings & Merrill, a Chicago favorite is the Inland Steel Building, clad in, of course, a gleaming skin of stainless steel; it was one of the first buildings constructed after World War II.

Chicago's architectural innovation continues to this day. That's not to suggest that every new building, regardless of its wackiness, goes up without criticism. For example, take Hammond, Beeby & Babka's design for the new headquarters of the Chicago Public Library. Built in 1991 and known as the Harold Washington Library Center, it inspired mixed reactions from observers who loved and hated it for much the same reason—the way its classical design so closely looks to Chicago's architectural ancestry for inspiration.

As Chicago has become a virtual open-air museum of architecture, so has it made a commitment to public art, adorning its streets and parks with monumental sculpture by some of the biggest names of the 20th century—Picasso, Calder, Oldenburg, Moore, Chagall, and Miró among them.

The best way to take inventory of Chicago's world-class architecture is to take one of the **Chicago Architecture Foundation's** bus, boat, or walking tours. The Foundation has an army of knowledgeable docents whose enthusiasm for the city and its architectural legacy is sure to get you looking at Chicago in a whole new way. See chapter 7 for details.

6 Chicago in Print & on the Silver Screen

BOOKS   So many great American writers either have come from Chicago, lived here during their productive years, or set their work within the city's confines that it is impossible to recommend a single book that says all there is to say about Chicago. Here are a few suggestions to get you started.

Upton Sinclair's *The Jungle* tells the tale of a young immigrant encountering the filthy, brutal city. Its 1906 publication caused an uproar that led to the passage of the

Pure Food and Drug Act. Theodore Dreiser's *Sister Carrie* is in the same vein of social consciousness at the turn of the century. James T. Farrell's trilogy *Studs Lonigan*, published in the thirties, explores the power of ethnic and neighborhood identity in Chicago.

Other books set (in full or in part) within the city are Willa Cather's *Lucy Gayheart*, Clancy Sigal's *Going Away*, John Dos Passos's *USA*, Philip Roth's *Letting Go*, and Saul Bellow's *The Adventures of Augie March* and *Humboldt's Gift*. Richard Wright spent time in Chicago and wrote about it in *Native Son* and *Cooley High*. Ernest Hemingway was a native son (Oak Park), though he didn't write much about the city. Chicago has had several fabled poets, including Carl Sandburg and Vachel Lindsay, and the brilliant troubadour and popular novelist Nelson Algren wrote *Chicago: City on the Make*. Even Bertolt Brecht set a play, *Saint Joan of the Stockyards*, in Chicago.

The city is a backdrop for a great diversity of fiction writers working today, notably Stuart Dybek (*Childhood and Other Neighborhoods*), Sara Paretksy (inventor of the gutsy detective V. I. Warshawski), and Robert Rodi (farcical gay novels *Drag Queen* and *Kept Boy*).

For a contemporary look at life in Chicago, especially the way the poor live today, take a look at two recent books that give a human face to the city's shameful public housing history: Daniel Coyle's *Hardball: A Season in the Projects*, the true story of youngsters on a Little League baseball team from Cabrini-Green; and Alex Kotlowitz's *There Are No Children Here*, a portrait of children growing up in the Robert Taylor Homes (which Oprah Winfrey also made into a TV movie).

And, of course, no one has given a voice to the people of Chicago as has Mike Royko, the author of perhaps the definitive account of Chicago machine politics, *Boss*, and whose spirited voice as a longtime newspaper columnist was lost when Royko died last year; and the estimable Studs Terkel, whose books *Division Street: America*, *Working*, and his own paean to the city, *Chicago*, reveal much about the place.

FILMS Boosted by a few hit films and the beachhead established here by filmmaker John Hughes (*Home Alone, The Breakfast Club*), Chicago has built a profile in the movie industry. As with books, the movies that take place in Chicago are far too numerous to mention, but a few good ones to rent that give a flavor for the city are *The Blues Brothers*, the John Belushi and Dan Aykroyd comedy about a couple of musicians on a mission from God; Hughes's *Ferris Bueller's Day Off*, starring Matthew Broderick as a high school senior playing hooky to visit many of the same sights you'll probably see on your trip; *While You Were Sleeping*, starring Sandra Bullock and featuring the El; and the recent Julia Roberts vehicle *My Best Friend's Wedding*, which offers views of the city and the northern suburbs (although the movie has a few edits that any Chicagoan would know are pure fiction). Among the several action and suspense movies that capture the feel of Chicago are *The Fugitive*, with Harrison Ford and Tommy Lee Jones; *Backdraft*, with William Baldwin, Kurt Russell, and Robert DeNiro as firefighters; and, for a period gangster flick, *The Untouchables*, with Kevin Costner, Sean Connery, and Robert DeNiro. Right up there at the top of my favorite Chicago flicks list is *Hoop Dreams*, a heartbreaking documentary about two inner-city teens who see basketball as their only way out.

Planning a Trip to Chicago 2

After choosing a destination, most prospective travelers have two fundamental questions: What will it cost and how will I get there? This chapter will answer both of these questions and will resolve other important issues—such as when to go and where to obtain more information about Chicago, before you leave home and once you get here.

The calendar of events will help you plan for (or avoid) festivals, shows, and parades, and the temperature and precipitation chart will help you decide which jacket to bring. If you are traveling with children, or if you're a senior, a student, or have a disability, you will find some special tips and names of organizations that cater to your needs in this chapter, as well.

1 Visitor Information & Money

SOURCES OF INFORMATION

The **Chicago Office of Tourism,** Chicago Cultural Center, 78 E. Washington St., Chicago, IL 60602 (☎ **312/744-2400** or TTY 312/744-2947; www.ci.chi.il.us/Tourism/), will mail you a packet of materials with information on upcoming events and attractions. The **Illinois Bureau of Tourism** (☎ **800/2CONNECT** or TTY 800/ 406-6418; www.enjoyillinois.com) will also send you a packet of information about Chicago and other Illinois destinations.

The **World Wide Web** makes it simple to do additional research before you leave home. Here are a few of the most comprehensive sites providing up-to-date listings on everything from restaurants to blues clubs, as well as valuable links to other sites:

- **www.city.net** (search "Chicago")
- **http://chicago.digitalcity.com**
- **www.sidewalk.chicago.com**
- **www.tezcat.com/web/chicago/html** (a grab bag of resources from current weather to a history of the 1992 Chicago flood)

You can access the exhaustive entertainment and cultural listings of the *Chicago Reader,* the city's alternative weekly, at **www.chireader. com**. Most of the city's major cultural institutions, many hotels, and a few shops and bars have also put up a shingle on the Web. Keep an eye out for relevant Web addresses listed throughout this guide.

What Things Cost in Chicago	U.S. $
Taxi from O'Hare Airport to city center	25.00–30.00
Bus or El fare to any destination within the city	1.50
Double room at The Drake (very expensive)	275.00–365.00
Double room at Hampton Inn & Suites (moderate)	119.00–169.00
Double room at the Park Brompton Inn (inexpensive)	105.00
Lunch for one at the Frontera Grill (moderate)	15.00
Lunch for one at Ed Debevic's (inexpensive)	7.00
Dinner for one, without wine, at the Everest Room (very expensive)	80.00
Dinner for one, without wine, at Zum Deutschen Eck (moderate)	25.00
Dinner for one at Penny's Noodle Shop (inexpensive)	8.50
Glass of beer	2.50
Coca-Cola	1.25
Cup of coffee	1.00
Adult admission to the top of Sears Tower	6.75
Movie ticket	8.25
Theater ticket	10.00–75.00
Local public phone call	.35

MONEY

While most people today depend on their credit or charge cards or ATMs, U.S. dollar traveler's checks are still a safe, negotiable way to carry currency. Most downtown restaurants, hotels, and shops accept traveler's checks, and banks generally exchange them for cash (for a small fee). Once you get away from downtown and the more affluent neighborhoods, however, smaller restaurants and shops may be reluctant to accept traveler's checks. American Express offices are open Monday through Saturday. Call to check for hours. See "Fast Facts: Chicago" in chapter 4 for office locations.

These days, traveler's checks are less necessary because most cities have 24-hour ATMs linked to a national network that most likely includes your bank at home. **Cirrus** (call ☎ 800/424-7787 for locations) and **Plus** (call ☎ 800/843-7587 for locations) are the two most popular networks; check the back of your ATM card to see which networks your bank belongs to. Note, however, that many banks have begun to impose a fee ranging from 50¢ to $3.00 every time you use an ATM in a different city. Your own bank may also charge you a fee for using ATMs from other banks.

2 When to Go

THE CLIMATE

Although not entirely deserved, Chicago has a reputation for being really cold in the winter. In truth, it's about as cold as any other northern city. Still, the February weather does not exactly inspire a leisurely stroll through Lincoln Park Zoo. So most visitors prefer planning trips to Chicago for late spring through early fall.

If you like moderate temperatures, the ideal time to visit is early autumn, when the days are most likely to be consistently pleasant. Chicago's weather is strongly influenced by the proximity of Lake Michigan. At its most humane, the lake cools the city with gentle breezes, particularly welcome during those hours of sweltering humidity that often accompany the dog days of summer, but that same offshore breeze can strengthen to a biting wind throughout the long winter. If you dress properly, however, you certainly can consider Chicago a four-season destination. After all, the city does not curl up and hibernate when the mercury dips below freezing. As an added incentive to "off-season" travelers, hotel rates are rock-bottom during the winter. For current conditions and forecasts, dial ☎ 312/976-1212 or consult the Web: www.ci.chi.il.us/Tourism/Weather/.

Chicago's Average Temperatures & Precipitation

	Jan	Feb	Mar	Apr	May	June	July	Aug	Sept	Oct	Nov	Dec
High °F	20.2	33.9	44.3	58.8	70.0	79.4	85.3	82.1	75.5	64.1	48.2	35.0
Low °F	13.6	18.1	27.6	38.8	48.1	57.7	62.7	61.7	53.9	42.0	31.4	20.3
Rainfall (in.)	1.60	1.31	2.59	3.66	3.15	4.08	3.63	3.53	3.35	2.28	2.06	2.10

CHICAGO CALENDAR OF EVENTS

The best way to stay on top of the city's current crop of special events is to ask the **Chicago Office of Tourism** (☎ 312/744-2400) or the **Illinois Bureau of Tourism** (☎ 800/2CONNECT) to mail you a copy of *Chicago Calendar of Events,* an excellent quarterly publication that surveys special events, including parades and street festivals, concerts and theatrical productions, and museum exhibitions. Also ask to be sent the latest materials produced by the **Mayor's Office of Special Events** (☎ 312/744-3315,** or the Special Events Hot Line ☎ 312/744-3370, TTY 312/744-2964), which keeps current with citywide and neighborhood festivals. The one thing you can count on, whether or not you research the topic in advance, is that you'll be able to choose from a slew of events, regardless of what month you visit Chicago.

Of the annual events, the most lively and unpredictable tend to revolve around the national parades and the street celebrations staged by many of Chicago's numerous ethnic groups. In addition, food, music, art, and flower fairs have their special niches in the city's yearly schedule.

Remember that new events may be added to this list every year and that occasionally special events are discontinued or rescheduled. So, to avoid disappointment, be sure to telephone in advance to either the sponsoring organization, the Chicago Office of Tourism, or the Mayor's Office of Special Events to verify dates, times, and locations.

January

- **New Year's Day 5K Fun Run/Walk,** Lincoln Park (☎ 773/868-3010). This breezy tour through the park is a good way to usher in the new year.
- **Chicago Cubs Convention** (☎ 773/404-CUBS). This annual 3-day confab at the Chicago Hilton and Towers draws thousands of Cubbie fans eager to see their favorite players and coaches and add to their collections of autographs and baseball memorabilia. Cost is $30 for the whole weekend, $5 if you sign up for a package at the hotel. January 15 through 17.
- **Chicago Boat, Sports & RV Show,** McCormick Place, 23rd Street and Lake Shore Drive (☎ 312/946-6262). This extravaganza has been a Chicago tradition for nearly 70 years. All the latest boats and recreational vehicles are on display, plus trout fishing, a climbing wall, boating safety seminars, and big-time entertainment. January 20 through 24.

- **Sports Fishing, Travel, and Outdoor Show,** Rosemont Convention Center, 5555 N. River Rd., Rosemont (☎ 847/692-2220). Held toward the end of the month, it attracts lots of folks in plaid flannel.
- **Azalea and Camellia Flower Shows,** Lincoln Park Conservatory, 2400 N. Stockton Dr. (☎ 312/742-7737), and Garfield Park Conservatory (☎ 312/746-5100), 300 N. Central Park Ave. Featuring spring blooming plants like azaleas, tulips, and hyacinth, both shows are held at a time when you won't see many other (uncut) flowers in the city. January 30 through February 28.

February

- **Black History Month.** It's celebrated with special events at the Chicago Cultural Center, the Museum of Science and Industry, and the Du Sable Museum of African-American History.
- **Chinese New Year Parade,** Wentworth and Cermak streets (☎ 312/326-5320). Join in as the sacred dragon whirls down the boulevard and restaurateurs pass out small envelopes of money to their regular customers. Call to verify the date, which varies from year to year.
- **University of Chicago Folk Festival,** on campus at Mandel Hall, 57th Street and University Avenue. Call (☎ 773/702-9793) for more information. First weekend in February.
- **Chicago Auto Show,** McCormick Place, 23rd Street and Lake Shore Drive (☎ 630/495-2282). More than a thousand cars and trucks, domestic and foreign, current and futuristic, are on display. The event draws nearly a million visitors. Look for special weekend packages at area hotels that include show tickets. February 12 through 21.
- **International Cluster of Dog Shows,** McCormick Place South, 23rd Street and South Lake Shore Drive (☎ 773/237-5100). Come watch as more than 10,000 AKC (American Kennel Club) purebred dogs of all breeds, common and downright peculiar, show their stuff. February 25 to 26.

March

- **Spring Festival of Dance** (☎ 312/629-8696). Most of the city's major dance companies, from the Joffrey Ballet of Chicago to Hubbard Street Dance Chicago, as well as a few touring headliners, take to three big downtown stages for a string of performances over 6 weeks, beginning in early March.
- ✪ **St. Patrick's Day Parade.** Expect the usual enthusiasm and an occasional donnybrook. The Chicago River is dyed kelly green for the occasion. The parade route is along Dearborn Street from Wacker Drive to Van Buren; the best place to view it is around Wacker and Dearborn. Saturday closest to March 17. A second, more neighborhood-like parade is held on the South Side on the following Sunday, on Western Avenue from 103rd to 115th streets.
- ✪ **Medinah Shrine Circus.** The Shriners' annual big-top event to benefit charity, held at the Medinah Temple, 600 N. Wabash Ave. (☎ 312/266-5050) for more than half a century, features all the usual circus suspects: trained chimpanzees, lion acts, and high-flying acrobats. Tickets may be purchased through Ticketmaster or ordered directly from the Shriners. March 5 to 22.
- **Greek-American Parade,** on Halsted Street from Randolph to Van Buren. The parade is part of a weeklong celebration of Greek culture. Call ☎ 312/744-3315 for details. Sunday closest to March 25.
- ✪ **Spring Flower Shows,** Lincoln Park Conservatory, 2400 N. Stockton Dr. (☎ 312/742-7737), and Garfield Park Conservatory, 300 N. Central Park Ave.

(☎ 312/746-5100). Lilies, daffodils, tulips, pansies, and other flowering perennials. March 27 through May 9 (usually opens the week before Easter).

April

- **Opening Day.** For the Cubs, call ☎ 773/404-CUBS; for the White Sox, call ☎ 312/674-1000. Make your plans early to get tickets for this eagerly awaited day. The calendar may say spring, but be warned, Opening Day is usually freezing in Chi-town.

May

- **Festival Cinco de Mayo** is celebrated with a huge weekend celebration of Mexican music, games, food, and family-oriented activities at McCormick Place, 23rd and Lake Shore Drive. There's also a neighborhood parade along Cermak Road from Damen to Kedzie streets. Call ☎ 312/791-7000 for information. Obviously, around May 5.
- ✪ **Buckingham Fountain Color Light Show,** in Grant Park, at Congress Parkway and Lake Shore Drive. The water and the ever-changing colored lights put on their show in the landmark fountain daily from May 1 to October 1, until 11pm nightly.
- **Polish Constitution Day Parade,** along Dearborn Street from Wacker Drive to Congress Parkway (☎ 312/744-3315). The Polish Americans are still a tight-knit community in Chicago. First Saturday in May.
- **Ferris Wheel and Carousel** begin spinning again at Navy Pier, 600 E. Grand Ave. (☎ 312/595-PIER). The rides operate through October. Another seasonal event along the water is the Pier Walk, a temporary installation of more than 150 large-scale sculptures displayed along the pier's South Dock. The sculptures remain on display through mid-October.
- ✪ **Art 1999 Chicago,** one of the country's largest international contemporary art fairs, holds forth at Navy Pier's Festival Hall, 600 E. Grand Ave. (☎ 312/587-3300 or 312/595-PIER). More than 200 art galleries and 2,000 artists participate in the 5-day event. Mother's Day weekend. The event is usually preceded by a bus tour through the city's gallery districts in River North and Wicker Park. For information, call ☎ 312/649-0065.
- **Beverly Hills/Morgan Park Home Tour.** This organized tour of this South Side neighborhood (☎ 773/233-3100) features homes in a range of architectural styles, from 1920s Tudors to Victorian painted ladies. Visitors can take a guided tour or follow the route on their own; the tour starts at the Beverly Art Center, 2153 W. 111th St., or the Metra Rock Island train station, 103rd Street. Sunday after Mother's Day.
- **Wright Plus Tour.** An annual tour of 10 buildings in Oak Park, including Frank Lloyd Wright's home and studio, the Unity Temple, several other Lloyd-designed homes, and several other notable Oak Park buildings in both the Prairie and Victorian styles. Tickets go on sale March 1 and can sell out within 6 weeks. Call ☎ 708/848-1976 (Frank Lloyd Wright Home and Studio) for details and ticket information. Third Saturday in May.
- **International Mr. Leather,** the biggest annual gathering of gay leather lovers in the country, got started in Chicago 2 decades ago. Participants congregate at a series of parties; shop at an eye-opening trade show at the convention headquarters, the Congress Hotel; choose a new title holder; and add to the local color by walking around the city in full leather regalia. Call ☎ 773/878-6360 for more information. Memorial Day weekend.

June

- ✪ **Printers Row Book Fair,** on Dearborn Street from Congress to Polk (☎ 312/ 987-9896). One of the largest free outdoor book fairs in the country, this weekend-long event celebrates the written word with everything from readings and book signings by big-name authors to panel discussions on penning your first novel. Located on the near South Side in a neighborhood named for its association with the printed word, the fair also features more than 150 booksellers displaying new, used, and antiquarian books for sale; a poetry tent; and special activities for children. June 5 to 6.
- • **Summer Tropical Show,** Lincoln Park Conservatory, 2400 N. Stockton Dr. (☎ 312/742-7737), and Garfield Park Conservatory, 300 N. Central Park Ave. (☎ 312/746-5100). Exotics such as palms, flowering banana trees, and ferns are a welcome sight after a long winter. June 5 through September 5.
- ✪ **Ravinia Festival.** Ravinia Park, in suburban Highland Park on the North Shore of Chicago, is the open-air summer home of the Chicago Symphony Orchestra and venue of many first-rate visiting orchestras, chamber ensembles, pop artists, dance companies, and so forth. Call ☎ 847/266-5100 for ticket reservations. See also "Exploring the 'Burbs" in chapter 7. June through September.
- • **Neighborhood Festivals.** Many begin this month at various city locations. The festivals usually entail food, live music, and crafts. Call ☎ 312/744-3315 for more information.
- ✪ **Chicago Blues Festival,** Petrillo Music Shell, at Jackson Drive and Columbus Drive in Grant Park (☎ 312/744-3315). A much-awaited and heavily attended event with dozens of acts, this event is free, but get there in the afternoon to get a good spot on the lawn for the evening show. Usually staged the first full weekend of June.
- • **57th Street Art Fair,** held at 57th and Kimbark streets in Hyde Park, celebrated its 50th anniversary in 1997, making it the oldest juried art fair in the Midwest. Call ☎ 773/493-3247 for details. The first full weekend in June.
- • **Taste of River North,** Dearborn between Kinzie Street and Grand Avenue. Call ☎ 312/645-1047 for more information on this neighborhood festival held in early June.
- ✪ **Chicago Gospel Festival,** Petrillo Music Shell, at Jackson and Columbus drives in Grant Park (☎ 312/744-3315). This free festival features the flip side of the blues and is another huge draw. Second weekend in June.
- ✪ **Boulevard Lakefront Bike Tour.** This 35-mile leisurely bicycle excursion is a great way to explore the city, from the neighborhoods and the lakefront to Chicago's historic link of parks and boulevards. Sponsored by the **Chicagoland Bicycle Federation;** call ☎ 312/42-PEDAL for details. A Sunday morning in early June.
- • **Puerto Rican Day Parade,** along Dearborn Street from Wacker Drive to Van Buren Street (☎ 312/744-3315). One of Chicago's animated Latino street celebrations. Mid-June.
- • **Old Town Art Fair.** This year marks the 50th anniversary of this juried fine art fair, which features the work of 250 artists from the Midwest and around the country (☎ 312/337-1938; www.oldtownartfair.org), as well as an art auction, garden walk, and children's art activities. The street fair is held in the historic Old Town neighborhood, at Lincoln Park West and Wisconsin Street, over the second full weekend in June.
- • **Wells Street Art Festival.** Celebrating its 25th anniversary, this street fair is less prestigious than the nearby Old Town Art Fair, held on the same weekend, but is still lots of fun, with 200 arts and crafts vendors, food, music, and carnival rides.

Wells Street from North Avenue to Division. Call ☎ **312/951-6106** for details. Second full weekend in June.

* **Andersonville Midsommarfest,** along Clark Street from Foster to Balmoral avenues (☎ **773/728-2995**). This event recalls the neighborhood's heyday as Chicago's principal Swedish community. Second weekend in June.
* **Celebrate on State Street Festival,** along State Street from Wacker Drive to Van Buren Street (☎ **312/782-9160**). Outdoor festivities—the usual food, drink, and music—geared to the commercial resuscitation of "that great street" make this event a pleasant distraction if you're passing through the Loop. Third week in June.
* ✪ **Grant Park Music Festival,** Petrillo Music Shell, at Jackson and Columbus drives in Grant Park (☎ **312/742-4763**). The free outdoor musical concerts in the park begin the last week in June and continue through August.
* ✪ **Taste of Chicago,** Grant Park. Ten days of street feasting. Scores of Chicago's restaurants cart their fare to food stands set up throughout the park. Admission is free; you pay for the sampling, of course. Call ☎ **312/744-3315** for information. To avoid the heaviest crowds at this popular event, try going weekdays earlier in the day. Late June and the first week of July.
* **Chicago Country Music Festival,** Petrillo Music Shell, at Jackson and Columbus drives in Grant Park (☎ **312/744-3315**). This free event features big-name entertainers of the country and western genre. The first weekend of the Taste of Chicago, usually the last weekend in June.
* ✪ **Gay and Lesbian Pride Parade.** The parade, which is the colorful culmination of a month of activities by Chicago's gay and lesbian community, runs along Halsted Street, from Belmont Avenue to Broadway, south to Diversey Parkway, and east to Lincoln Park, where a rally and music festival are held. Take up a spot on Broadway for the best view. Call ☎ **773/348-8243** for information. Last Sunday in June, 2pm.
* **Gallery 37.** A summer training program for budding young artists is open to the public with activities and exhibitions, in the tented area along State Street between Washington and Randolph streets. Their original works are for sale here and at a retail shop at 70 E. Randolph. Call ☎ **312/744-8925** for details. Late June through August.
* **Farmers markets** open at two dozen sites all over the city at the end of the month and continue weekly through October. Downtown sites are Daley Plaza (every other Thursday) and Federal Plaza (every Tuesday). For other locations and times, call ☎ **312/744-9187.**

July

* **Independence Day Celebration.** The holiday is celebrated in Chicago on the third of July: Concerts and fireworks are the highlights of the festivities in Grant Park (☎ **312/744-3315**). Expect huge crowds. July 3.
* **Fourth of July Celebration,** Chicago Historical Society grounds, Clark Street and North Avenue (☎ **312/642-4600**). An old-fashioned celebration with color guard, pop concert band, and a children's parade, among other festivities. Free.
* **Sheffield Garden Walk,** which starts at Sheffield and Webster avenues, is a chance to snoop into the lush backyards of Lincoln Park home owners. Call ☎ **773/929-WALK** for details. Mid-July.
* **Chicago Yacht Club's Race to Mackinac Island** has a starting line at the Monroe Street Harbor (☎ **312/861-7777**). The grandest of the inland water races, this 3-day competition is scheduled toward the middle of July. The public is welcome at a Friday night party, and on Saturday you can jockey for a good place to watch the boats set sail.

- **Venetian Night,** from Monroe Harbor to the Adler Planetarium (☎ 312/744-3315). This carnival of illuminated boats on the lake is complete with fireworks. Late July.
- **Fiesta del Sol,** one of the largest street festivals of the summer, fills the streets of the Mexican neighborhood of Pilsen with music and carnival rides. Along Blue Island between 18th and 22nd streets. Call ☎ 312/666-2663 for details. Late July.

August

- **Oz Festival,** Lincoln Park. This popular summer event celebrates "the magical spirit of Frank Baum's book *The Wizard of Oz*," with plenty for kids to enjoy. The festival was recently relocated from Oz Park to a grassy area along Cannon Drive on the east side of the Lincoln Park Zoo. Call ☎ 773/929-8686 for details. First weekend of August.
- ✪ **Northalsted Market Days,** on Halsted Street between Belmont Avenue and Addison Street. The largest of the city's street festivals, held in the heart of this gay neighborhood, Northalsted Market Days offers the best people-watching of the summer, as well as some pretty good music on three stages and hundreds of food and craft vendors. Call ☎ 773/868-3010 for details. Early August.
- **Illinois State Fair,** in Springfield (☎ 217/782-6661). Livestock, homemade pies, carnival rides, the whole bit. Mid-August.
- **Bud Billiken Parade and Picnic.** An African-American celebration; the parade route starts at 39th Street and King Drive and ends at 55th Street and Washington Park. Call ☎ 312/225-2400 for details. Second Saturday in August, beginning at 10am.
- **Ginza Holiday,** Midwest Buddhist Temple, 435 W. Menomonee St. (☎ 312/943-7801). A celebration of Japanese culture, with Japanese food and art vendors; classical dance groups dressed in colorful kimonos; martial art demonstrations; and calligraphers, tapestry makers, and potters on hand. Third weekend of August.
- ✪ **Chicago Air & Water Show,** North Avenue Beach. A hugely popular, perennial aquatic and aerial spectacular. (Even if you don't plan to watch it, you can't help but experience it with jets screaming overhead all weekend.) Free admission. Since the crowds are intense, an alternative viewing spot is Oak Street Beach, along the Gold Coast. Call ☎ 312/744-3315 for details. End of August.

September

- ✪ **Chicago Jazz Festival,** Petrillo Music Shell, Jackson and Columbus drives in Grant Park. The jazz fest is Chicago style, and plenty steamy. The event is free; come early and stay late. Call ☎ 312/744-3315 for details. Labor Day weekend.
- **The art season begins** with galleries holding their season openers in the River North, River West, and Wicker Park/Bucktown gallery districts. Call the River North Gallery District at ☎ 312/649-0064 for details. The first Friday after Labor Day.
- ✪ **Around the Coyote,** marking its 10th year, invites visitors to tour hundreds of artists' studios in the Wicker Park and Bucktown neighborhoods. Music, performances, and fashion shows fill out a week of activity that emanates from the intersection of Milwaukee, Damen, and North avenues, the hub of one of the largest communities of artists in the country. If you miss out, visit the ATC Gallery on the second floor of the Flat Iron Building, 1579 N. Milwaukee Ave. For more information, call ☎ 773/342-6777. Second weekend in September.

- **"Viva! Chicago" Latin Music Festival,** the Petrillo Music Shell, Jackson and Columbus drives in Grant Park. The Latin beat in all its dynamic and sultry variations from mariachi to mambo. Call ☎ 312/744-3315 for details. Second weekend in September.

- **Berghoff's Oktoberfest,** Adams Street between Dearborn and State streets (☎ 312/427-3170). A popular 4-day beer fest with live music is sponsored by one of Chicago's oldest and best-loved restaurants, right down in the Loop at Federal Plaza. Mid-September.

- **Mexican Independence Day Parade,** along Dearborn Street between Wacker Drive and Van Buren Street. Call ☎ 312/744-3315 for more information; Saturday in mid-September. Another parade is held on the next day on 26th Street in the Little Village neighborhood (☎ 773/521-5387).

- **Celtic Fest Chicago,** Petrillo Music Shell, Jackson and Columbus drives in Grant Park. The city's newest music festival celebrates the music and dance of Celtic traditions from around the world. Call ☎ 312/744-3315 for details. Late September.

October

- **Chrysanthemum Shows,** Lincoln Park Conservatory, 2400 N. Stockton Dr. (☎ 312/742-7737), and Garfield Park Conservatory, 300 N. Central Park Ave. (☎ 312/746-5100). Some of the hundreds of varieties of mums on display have been grown for decades at the conservatories. October 2 through 31.

- **Columbus Day Parade,** Dearborn Street from Wacker Drive to Van Buren Street. Italian-American Day by any other name. Call ☎ 312/828-0010 for more information. The closest Monday to October 12.

- **Chicago International Film Festival** (☎ 312/425-9400 or 312/332-FILM for a film schedule). Now in its 4th decade, the festival is screened at various theaters over 2 weeks beginning the first Thursday in October.

- **SOFA Chicago,** Festival Hall, Navy Pier (☎ 800/563-7632). This is a major international exhibition devoted to sculpture and three-dimensional art forms (thus the acronym, which stands for Sculpture Objects Functional Art). Late October or early November.

November

- **The Big Top.** This is the month that Ringling Brothers, Barnum & Bailey comes to Chicago, usually setting up its "tent" at the United Center, 1901 W. Madison St. (☎ 312/455-4000) and the Rosemont Horizon, 6920 N. Mannheim Rd., Rosemont (☎ 773/325-7526). Tickets are available from Ticketmaster (☎ 312/559-1212).

- **47th Annual American Indian Center Powwow,** at the University of Illinois Pavilion. Tribes gather from all over North America to perform traditional dances. Call ☎ 773/275-5871 for more information. Mid-November.

- **Christmas Around the World/Holidays of Light,** at the Museum of Science and Industry, 57th Street and Lake Shore Drive (☎ 773/684-1414). A traditional Christmas exhibit, replete with 90 trees representing various ethnic groups. Opens in late November and stays up until New Year's.

- ✪ **Magnificent Mile Lights Festival.** Beginning at dusk, a colorful parade of Disney characters makes its way south along Michigan Avenue, from Oak Street to the Chicago River, with lights being illuminated block by block as the procession passes. Carolers, elves, and minstrels appear with Santa along the avenue throughout the day and into the evening, and many of the retailers offer hot chocolate and other treats. Call ☎ 312/642-3570 for more information. Saturday before Thanksgiving.

- **Christmas Tree Lighting,** Daley Center Plaza, in the Loop. Call ☎ 312/744-3315 for details. The day after Thanksgiving, around dusk.
- **Winter Flower Shows,** Lincoln Park Conservatory, 2400 N. Stockton Dr. (☎ 312/742-7737), and Garfield Park Conservatory, 300 N. Central Park Ave. (☎ 312/746-5100). The poinsettia show begins November 26 and continues through January 3.

December

- *A Christmas Carol,* Goodman Theatre, 200 S. Columbus Dr. A seasonal favorite performed for more than 2 decades. Call ☎ 312/443-3800 for information and tickets. The show runs from about Thanksgiving through the end of December.
- *The Nutcracker* **ballet,** Joffrey Ballet of Chicago, Auditorium Theatre, 50 E. Congress Pkwy. The esteemed company performs its Victorian-American twist on the holiday classic. For tickets, call ☎ 312/901-1500 (Ticketmaster) or 312/739-0120 (Joffrey office). Production runs 3 weeks from late Thanksgiving to mid-December.
- **Zoo Lights Festival,** Lincoln Park Zoo, 2200 N. Cannon Dr. (☎ 312/742-2000). The zoo is transformed with colorful illuminated displays for the holidays. Another special tradition is the annual Caroling to the Animals, a daylong songfest on a Saturday early in the month.

3 Tips for Travelers with Special Needs

FOR TRAVELERS WITH DISABILITIES

Most of Chicago's sidewalks, as well as major museums and tourist attractions, are fitted with wheelchair ramps. More and more hotels are also providing special accommodations and services for visitors in wheelchairs, such as large bathrooms, ramps, and for the hearing impaired, telecommunications devices; inquire when you make your reservation.

Several of the Chicago Transit Authority's (CTA's) El stations on each line are fitted with elevators. Call the CTA at ☎ 836-7000 (any city or suburban area code) for a list of those that are accessible. All city buses are equipped to accommodate wheelchairs. For other questions about CTA special services, call ☎ 312/432-7025.

For specific information on facilities for people with disabilities, call or write the **Mayor's Office for People with Disabilities,** located at 121 N. LaSalle St., Room 1104, Chicago, IL 60601 (☎ 312/744-6673 for voice; 312/744-4964 for TTY). The office is staffed from 8:30am to 4:30pm Monday through Friday. A free guide assembled for the 1996 Democratic National Convention, entitled *Access to Chicago,* evaluates the accessibility of many local restaurants, hotels, museums, and other attractions (as well as wheelchair repair services).

The **Illinois Relay Center** enables hearing- and speech-impaired TTY callers to call individuals or businesses without TTYs 24 hours a day. Calls are confidential and billed at regular phone rates. Call TTY ☎ 800/526-0844 or voice 800/526-0857. The city of Chicago operates a 24-hour information service for hearing-impaired callers with TTY equipment; call ☎ 312/744-8599. Also, the **Society for the Advancement of Travel for the Handicapped,** 347 Fifth Ave., Suite 610, New York, NY 10016 (☎ 212/447-SATH; fax 212/725-8253; SATHtravel@aol.com), can offer some support.

Many of the major car-rental companies now offer hand-controlled cars for drivers with disabilities. Avis can provide such a vehicle at any of its locations in the

United States with 48-hour advance notice; Hertz requires between 24 and 72 hours of advance reservation at most of its locations. **Wheelchair Getaways** (☎ 800/873-4973; www.blvd.com/wg.htm) rents specialized vans with wheelchair lifts and other features for travelers with disabilities in more than 100 cities across the United States.

FOR SENIORS

Seniors regularly receive discounts at museums, attractions, and entertainment venues. Seniors may also seek discounts at hotels and restaurants, many of which are willing to offer reduced prices, though they may not advertise the fact. Airlines also offer senior discounts, but first compare these fares with any available promotional tickets.

One excellent source of travel information for seniors is the **American Association of Retired Persons (AARP),** 601 E. St. NW, Washington, DC 20049 (☎ 202/434-2277). Members receive discounts on car rentals, hotels, airfares, and even sightseeing. AARP travel arrangements are handled by American Express.

The Mature Traveler, a monthly 12-page newsletter on senior citizen travel, is a valuable resource. It is available by subscription ($30 a year) from GEM Publishing Group, Box 50400, Reno, NV 89513-0400. GEM also publishes *The Book of Deals,* a collection of more than 1,000 senior discounts on airlines, lodging, tours, and attractions around the country; it's available for $9.95 by calling ☎ 800/460-6676. Another helpful publication is *101 Tips for the Mature Traveler,* available from Grand Circle Travel, 347 Congress St., Suite 3A, Boston, MA 02210 (☎ 800/221-2610 or 617/350-7500; fax 617/350-6206).

Seniors also have many resources available to them in Chicago, including discounted fares for public transportation, discounted admission for museums and other attractions, and citywide programs; call the Chicago Park District at ☎ 312/742-PLAY for specific information.

FOR GAY & LESBIAN TRAVELERS

Gay and Lesbian Pride Week (☎ 773/348-8243) is a major event on the Chicago calendar each June, highlighted by a lively parade on the North Side. You may also want to stop by **Unabridged Books,** 3251 N. Broadway (☎ 773/883-9119), an independent bookseller with a large lesbian and gay selection. Here and elsewhere in the Lakeview neighborhood you can pick up several gay publications, including the news weekly *Windy City Times,* which publishes a useful calendar of events. A helpful Web site, with lists of community and social groups, nightlife options, and an events calendar is **www.outchicago.org. Horizon Community Services** (☎ 773/929-HELP or TTY 773/472-1277), a gay social service agency with counseling services, support groups, and an antiviolence project, provides referrals daily from 6 to 10pm; you can also call the main switchboard at ☎ 773/472-6469 during the day with questions.

FOR FAMILIES

Traveling with infants and small children requires some additional planning. Airlines will provide special children's meals with 24 hours' notice, but not baby food, which you must supply. If you will be renting a car in Chicago, inquire about reserving a child safety seat; most major rental-car agencies have these available for a small fee. (Avis, for example charges $5 per day or $25 per week.) Most hotels maintain an active list of baby-sitters. For more on finding a baby-sitter, see "Fast Facts: Chicago" in chapter 4.

Chicago is full of sightseeing opportunities and special activities geared toward children. See "Kid Stuff" in chapter 7 for information and ideas for families.

FOR STUDENTS

Students will find that their valid high school or college ID can mean discounts on travel, theater, and museum tickets, and can be used at some nightspots. Chicago has many fine colleges and universities, all of which are centers of student life and study. The **University of Chicago** (☎ 773/702-1234) is in Hyde Park; the **University of Illinois at Chicago** (☎ 312/996-3000) is near the Loop on the Near West Side; **DePaul University** is located in Lincoln Park (☎ 773/325-7000); **Loyola University of Chicago** (☎ 773/274-3000) is on Sheridan Road in Rogers Park; and **Northwestern University** (☎ 847/491-3741) is in the northern suburb of Evanston. Many of the universities also have downtown campuses that house their professional schools.

Chicago has several hostels offering students and other travelers inexpensive, no-frills lodging. The following hostels are open year-round: **Arlington House International Hostel,** 616 W. Arlington Place, Chicago, IL 60614 (☎ 800/467-8355 or 312/929-5380; fax 312/665-5485), in Lincoln Park; **Chicago International Hostel,** 6318 N. Winthrop Ave., Chicago, IL 60660 (☎ 312/262-1011; fax 312/262-3673) on the north side of the city; and **International House of Chicago,** 1414 E. 59th St., Chicago, IL 60637 (☎ 773/753-2270; fax 773/753-1227; E-mail: jpenner@midway.uchicago.edu), on the University of Chicago campus in Hyde Park. **Hostelling International Chicago Summer Hostel,** 731 S. Plymouth Court, Chicago, IL 60605 (☎ 312/327-5350; fax 312/327-4287; E-mail: hiayhchigo@ aol.com), is a summer-only hostel (open June to Sept) located south of the Loop in the Printers Row area.

4 Getting There

BY PLANE

THE MAJOR AIRLINES   Domestic carriers that fly regularly to O'Hare include **American** (☎ 800/433-7300), **Continental** (☎ 800/525-0280), **Delta** (☎ 800/221-1212), **Northwest** (☎ 800/225-2525), **TWA** (☎ 800/221-2000), **United** (☎ 800/241-6522), and **US Airways** (☎ 800/428-4322). Commuter service is also provided by several regional airlines. Airlines that fly to Chicago's Midway Airport are **America West** (☎ 800/235-9292), **American Trans Air** (☎ 800/225-2995), **Continental** (☎ 800/525-0280), **Frontier** (☎ 800/432-1359), **KIWI** (☎ 800/538-5494), **Northwest** (☎ 800/225-2525), and **Southwest** (☎ 800/435-9792). The toll-free numbers listed are for use in the United States only.

FINDING THE BEST AIRFARE   The easiest, but not necessarily the cheapest, way to purchase an airline ticket is through your local travel agent. A travel agent is a convenience that doesn't cost you anything, but don't expect your travel agent to spend an inordinate amount of time trying to find you the cheapest ticket available—doing so not only will take up his or her time, but will lead to a smaller commission from the airline.

To get the lowest possible fare, you will probably have to do some digging yourself. Call several carriers that fly to Chicago and ask them to quote you the lowest fare available. Airlines have sales, special promotions, and fare wars all the time, so shop

Fun Fact

Ever wonder why bags bound for O'Hare are tagged with the code "ORD"? No, it's not short for "ordeal," it's a holdover from the mega-airport's quaint original name, Orchard Field.

Impressions

At a literary conference at Notre Dame, I . . . ran into a poet who is noted for his verse celebrating the ecology, née Nature. He lives in a dramatic house nailed together completely from uncut pieces of hickory driftwood, perched on a bluff overlooking the crashing ocean. . . . I remarked that this must be the ideal setting in which to write about the ecological wonders. "I wouldn't know," he said. "I do all my writing in O'Hare."
—Tom Wolfe, "The Intelligent Coed's Guide to America,"
in *Mauve Gloves and Madmen, Clutter and Vine* (1976)

around—but remember, in general, the lower the fare, the more restrictions and penalties apply to changing dates and itineraries. The lowest regular economy fares often require that you travel during the week and stay over Saturday night.

Many travelers in recent years have opted to act as their own travel agents, seeking out the lowest possible airfares offered by **consolidators.** Consolidators (also called bucket shops) buy blocks of tickets directly from the airlines. In a sense, they speculate in air-passage futures, and they can sell their "buckets" at prices that are often far below official rates. There are many well-known and legitimate bucket shops, and a number of fly-by-night operations as well. If you have any doubts about a particular company, consult your local branch of the Better Business Bureau. Newspaper travel supplements and the Yellow Pages are good sources for information on the offerings or whereabouts of consolidators.

Many airlines also offer special fares for travelers who register at the Web site to receive **e-mail bulletins** (usually each Wed) listing special fares offered for the upcoming weekend. (I've seen Continental offer $99 round-trip flights to Chicago from New York and $199 round-trip from Los Angeles.) Here's a list of airlines and their Web sites where you can not only get on the e-mailing lists but also book flights directly:

- **American Airlines:** www.americanair.com
- **Continental Airlines:** www.flycontiental.com
- **Northwest Airlines:** www.nwa.com
- **TWA:** www.twa.com
- **US Airways:** www.usairways.com

Epicurious Travel (travel.epicurious.com), another good travel site, allows you to sign up for all of these airline e-mail lists at once. For a complete list of commercial airline Web sites and the latest cyberfares, go to **www.itn.net/airlines**.

CHICAGO'S AIRPORTS   Chicago's **O'Hare International Airport** (☎ 773/ 686-2200) has long held the title of the world's busiest airport. It's located northwest of the city proper, about a 25- to 30-minute drive from downtown, depending, of course, on the traffic. A cab ride into the city will cost you about $25 to $30. You can also ask the taxi stand attendant to arrange a shared ride for you, which will cost about $15 per person.

For $1.50, you can take the El (vernacular for the elevated train), which will efficiently get you downtown in about 40 minutes, regardless of traffic. Trains leave every 6 to 10 minutes during the day, and every half hour in the evening and overnight. O'Hare also has outposts for every major car-rental company (see chapter 4 for details).

O'Hare has information booths in all five terminals, most located on the baggage level. The multilingual personnel, who are outfitted in red jackets, can assist travelers

CyberDeals for Net Surfers

It's possible to get some great deals on airfare, hotels, and car rentals via the Internet. So go grab your mouse and start surfing before you hit the road—you could save a bundle on your trip. The Web sites we've highlighted below are worth checking out, especially since all services are free (but don't forget that time is money when you're on-line).

Microsoft Expedia (www.expedia.com)   The best part of this multipurpose travel site is the "Fare Tracker": You fill out a form on the screen indicating that you're interested in cheap flights to Chicago from your hometown, and, once a week, they'll e-mail you the best airfare deals. The site's "Travel Agent" will also steer you to bargains on hotels and car rentals, and you can book everything, including flights, right on-line. This site is even useful once you're booked: Before you go, log on to Expedia for oodles of up-to-date travel information, including weather reports and foreign exchange rates.

Preview Travel (www.reservations.com and **www.vacations.com)**   Another useful travel site, "Reservations.com" has a "Best Fare Finder," which will search the Apollo computer reservations system for the three lowest fares for any route on any days of the year. Say you want to go from Atlanta to Chicago and back between September 7th and 11th: Just fill out the form on the screen with times, dates, and destinations, and within minutes, Preview will show you the best deals. If you find an airfare you like, you can book your ticket right on-line—you can even reserve hotels and car rentals on this site. If you're in the pre-planning stage, head to Preview's "Vacations.com" site, where you can check out

with everything from arranging ground transportation to getting information about local hotels. The booths also offer a plethora of useful tourism brochures. The booths, labeled "Airport Information," are open daily from 9am to 8pm.

On the opposite end of the city, the Southwest Side, is Chicago's other major airport, **Midway** (☎ 773/838-0600). Although it's smaller than O'Hare, and fewer airlines have routes here, Midway is closer to the Loop and you may be able to get a cheaper fare flying into here. (Always check fares flying into both airports if you want to find the best deal.) Chicago recently extended the El (the Orange Line) to Midway, so now you can make it downtown in about half an hour for $1.50. Please note that the Orange Line stops operating each night at about 11:30pm and resumes service by 5am. Trains leave the station every 6 to 15 minutes. Most major car-rental companies have counters at Midway as well.

You can find the latest information on both airports at the city Department of Aviation's Web site: **www.ci.il.us/worksmart/aviation**.

Continental Air Transport (☎ 800/654-7871 or 312/454-7800) services most first-class hotels in Chicago with its blue and white "Airport Express" vans; ticket counters are located at both airports near the baggage claim (outside Customs at the international terminal at O'Hare). For transportation to the airport, reserve a spot from one of the hotels (check with the bell captain). The cost is $15.50 one-way ($28 round-trip) to/from O'Hare, and $11 one-way ($20 round-trip) to/from Midway. The shuttles operate from 6am to 11:30pm. For limo service from either O'Hare or Midway, call **Carey Limousine of Chicago** (☎ 312/663-1220), or **Chicago Limousine Services** (☎ 312/726-1035). Cost, with tip and tax, is about $75 to $85.

the latest package deals for destinations around the world by clicking on "Hot Deals."

Travelocity (**www.travelocity.com**)   This is one of the best travel sites out there. In addition to its "Personal Fare Watcher," which notifies you via e-mail of the lowest airfares for up to five different destinations, Travelocity will track the three lowest fares for any routes on any dates in minutes. You can book a flight right then and there, and if you need a rental car or hotel, Travelocity will find you the best deal via the SABRE computer reservations system (a huge database used by travel agents worldwide). Click on "Last Minute Deals" for the latest travel bargains, including a link to "H.O.T. Coupons" (**www.hotcoupons.com**), where you can print out electronic coupons for travel in the United States and Canada.

Trip.Com (**www.thetrip.com**)   This site is really geared toward the business traveler, but vacationers-to-be can also use Trip.Com's valuable fare-finding engine, which will e-mail you every week with the best city-to-city airfare deals on your selected route or routes.

Discount Tickets (**www.discount-tickets.com**)   Operated by the ETN (European Travel Network), this site offers discounts on airfares, accommodations, car rentals, and tours. It deals in flights between the United States and other countries, not domestic U.S. flights, so it's most useful for travelers coming to Chicago from abroad.

—Jeanette Foster

With 1 week's notice, **CTA paratransit** offers door-to-door lift services to and from O'Hare for travelers with disabilities. Visitors must be registered with a similar program in their home city. For information, call ☎ **312/432-7025,** 312/917-4357, or 312/917-1338 TTY.

BY CAR

Chicago is serviced by interstate highways from all major points on the compass. I-80 and I-90 approach from the east, crossing the northern sector of Illinois, with I-90 splitting off and emptying into Chicago via the Skyway and the Dan Ryan Expressway. From here I-90 runs through Wisconsin following a northern route to Seattle. I-55 snakes up the Mississippi Valley from the vicinity of New Orleans and enters Chicago from the west along the Stevenson Expressway, and in the opposite direction provides an outlet to the Southwest. I-57 originates in southern Illinois and forms part of the interstate linkage to Florida and the South, connecting within Chicago on the west leg of the Dan Ryan. I-94 links Detroit with Chicago, arriving on the Calumet Expressway and leaving the city via the Kennedy Expressway en route to the Northwest.

Here are a few approximate driving distances in miles to Chicago: from **Milwaukee,** 92; from **St. Louis,** 297; from **Detroit,** 286; from **Denver,** 1,011; from **Atlanta,** 716; from **Washington, D.C.,** 715; from **New York City,** 821; and from **Los Angeles,** 2,034.

BY TRAIN

Rail passenger service, while it may never approach the grandeur of its heyday, has made enormous advances in service, comfort, and efficiency since the creation of

Amtrak in 1971. As in the past, but on a reduced scale, Chicago remains the hub of the national passenger rail system. Traveling great distances by train is certainly not the quickest way to go, nor always the most convenient. But many travelers still prefer it to flying or driving.

For tickets, consult your travel agent or call **Amtrak** (☎ **800/USA-RAIL;** www. amtrak.com). Ask the reservations agent to send you Amtrak's useful travel planner, with information on train accommodations and package tours.

When you arrive in Chicago, the train will pull into **Union Station** at 210 S. Canal between Adams and Jackson streets (☎ **312/655-2385**). Bus nos. 1, 60, 125, 151, and 156 all stop at the station, which is just west across the river from the Loop. The nearest El stop is at Clinton Street and Congress Parkway (on the Blue Line), which is a fair walk away, especially when carrying luggage.

BY BUS

The **Greyhound Bus Station** in Chicago is at 630 W. Harrison (☎ **800/231-2222** travel information, ☎ 312/408-5980 bus station; www.greyhound.com), not far from Union Station. Several city buses (nos. 60, 125, 156, and 157) pass in front of the terminal building, and the nearest El stop is at Clinton Street and Congress Parkway on the Blue Line.

For Foreign Visitors 3

Although American fads and fashions have spread across Europe and other parts of the world, so that America may seem like familiar territory before your arrival, there are still many peculiarities and uniquely American situations that any foreign visitor will encounter.

1 Preparing for Your Trip

ENTRY REQUIREMENTS

DOCUMENT REGULATIONS   Citizens of Canada and Bermuda may enter the United States without visas, but they will need to show proof of nationality, the most common and hassle-free form of which is a passport. The U.S. State Department has a **Visa Waiver Pilot Program** authorized through April 30, 2000, allowing citizens of certain countries to enter the United States without a visa for stays of fewer than 90 days of holiday travel. At press time these countries included Andorra, Argentina, Australia, Austria, Belgium, Brunei, Denmark, Finland, France, Germany, Iceland, Ireland, Italy, Japan, Liechtenstein, Luxembourg, Monaco, the Netherlands, New Zealand, Norway, San Marino, Slovenia, Spain, Sweden, Switzerland, and the United Kingdom. (The program as applied to the UK refers to British citizens who have the "unrestricted right of permanent abode in the United Kingdom," that is, citizens from England, Scotland, Wales, Northern Ireland, the Channel Islands, and the Isle of Man; and not, for example, citizens of the British Commonwealth of Pakistan.)

Citizens from these countries need only a valid passport and a round-trip air or cruise ticket in their possession upon arrival. If they first enter the United States, they may then visit Mexico, Canada, Bermuda, and/or the Caribbean islands and return to the United States without needing a visa. Further information is available from any U.S. embassy or consulate.

Citizens of countries other than those specified above, or those traveling to the United States for reasons or length of time outside the restrictions of the Visa Waiver Program, or those who require waivers of inadmissibility must have two documents:

- **A valid passport,** with an expiration date at least 6 months later than the scheduled end of the visit to the United States. Some countries are exceptions to the 6-month validity rule. Contact any U.S. embassy or consulate for complete information; and
- **A tourist visa,** available from the nearest U.S. consulate.

To obtain a visa, the traveler must submit a completed application form (either in person or by mail) with a 1½-inch square photo and the required application fee. There may also be an issuance fee, depending on the type of visa and other factors.

Usually you can obtain a visa right away or within 24 hours, but it may take longer during the summer rush period (June to August). If you cannot go in person, contact the nearest U.S. embassy or consulate for directions on applying by mail. Your travel agent or airline office may also be able to provide you with visa applications and instructions. The U.S. consulate or embassy that issues your visa will determine whether you will be issued a multiple- or single-entry visa. The Immigration and Naturalization Service officers at the port of entry in the United States will make an admission decision and determine your length of stay.

For more details on applying for a visa as well as a list of U.S. embassies and consulates abroad, consult the U.S. State Department's Web site at **http://travel. state.gov/**.

MEDICAL REQUIREMENTS   No inoculations are needed to enter the United States unless you are coming from, or have stopped over in, areas known to be suffering from epidemics, particularly cholera or yellow fever. If you have a disease requiring treatment with medications containing narcotics or with drugs requiring a syringe, carry a valid, signed prescription from your physician to allay any suspicions that you are smuggling drugs.

CUSTOMS REQUIREMENTS   Every adult visitor may bring in, free of duty: 1 liter of wine or hard liquor; 200 cigarettes or 100 cigars (but no cigars from Cuba) or 3 pounds of smoking tobacco; and $100 worth of gifts. These exemptions are offered to travelers who spend at least 72 hours in the United States and who have not claimed them within the preceding 6 months. It is altogether forbidden to bring into the country foodstuffs (particularly cheese, fruit, and meats) and plants (vegetables, seeds, tropical plants, and so on). Foreign tourists may bring in or take out up to $10,000 in U.S. or foreign currency with no formalities; larger sums must be declared to Customs upon entering or leaving.

For more specific information regarding U.S. Customs, call ☎ **800/697-3662,** or contact the agency's Web site: **www.customs.ustreas.gov/travel**. In Chicago, you can contact the Customs offices at O'Hare International Airport (☎ **773/894-2900**) or downtown at 610 S. Canal St. (☎ **312/353-6100**). The downtown office is open Monday through Friday 8:30am to 5pm.

INSURANCE

Unlike most other countries, there is no national health system in the United States. Because the cost of medical care is extremely high, we strongly advise every traveler to secure health coverage before setting out. You may want to take out a comprehensive travel policy that covers (for a relatively low premium) sickness or injury costs (medical, surgical, and hospital); loss or theft of your baggage; trip-cancellation costs; guarantee of bail in case you are arrested; and costs of accident, repatriation, or death. Such packages (for example, "Europe Assistance" in Europe) are sold by automobile clubs at attractive rates, as well as by insurance companies and travel agencies.

MONEY

CURRENCY   The U.S. monetary system has a decimal base: one American dollar ($1) = 100 cents (100¢). Dollar bills commonly come in $1 ("a buck"), $5, $10, $20, $50, and $100 denominations (the last two are not welcome when paying for small purchases and are not accepted in taxis or at subway ticket booths). There are also $2 bills (seldom encountered). Note that newly redesigned $100, $50, and $20 bills have recently been introduced. (You can spot them easily—they've got really big faces on them.) Despite rumors to the contrary, the old-style bills are still legal tender. There are six denominations of coins: 1¢ (one cent, or a penny), 5¢ (five cents, or a nickel), 10¢ (ten cents, or a dime), 25¢ (twenty-five cents, or a quarter), 50¢ (fifty cents, or a half dollar, seldom encountered), and the rare $1 piece.

TRAVELER'S CHECKS   Though traveler's checks are widely accepted, make sure they are denominated in U.S. dollars, as foreign-currency checks are often difficult to exchange. The three most widely recognized traveler's checks—and the least likely to be denied—are Visa, American Express, and Thomas Cook. Be sure to record the numbers of the checks and keep that information separate from the checks in case they get lost or stolen. Chicago businesses are pretty good about taking traveler's checks, but you're better off cashing them at a bank (in small amounts, of course) and paying in cash. Remember: You'll need identification, such as a driver's license or passport, to change a traveler's check. The foreign-exchange bureaus so common in Europe are rare even at airports in the United States and nonexistent outside major cities.

ATMs   Automated teller machines (ATMs or "cash machines") are so handy— located at banks, shopping centers, transportation terminals, and many hotel lobbies—for replenishing your wallet that they nearly make traveler's checks unnecessary. You may want to contact your bank before you leave on your trip to get a list of ATMs in Chicago that will accept your ATM card.

CREDIT CARDS   The method of payment most widely used is the credit card; the cards most commonly accepted are **Visa** (BarclayCard in Britain), **MasterCard** (Euro-card in Europe, Access in Britain, Chargex in Canada, Diamond in Japan), **American Express, Diners Club, Discover,** and **Carte Blanche.** You can save yourself trouble by using "plastic money" rather than cash or traveler's checks in most hotels, motels, restaurants, and retail stores (a growing number of food and liquor stores now accept credit cards). You must have a credit card to rent a car. It can also be used as proof of identity (often carrying more weight than a passport), or as a "cash card," enabling you to draw money from banks that accept them.

SAFETY

GENERAL SAFETY TIPS   While tourist areas are generally safe, crime is a national problem, and U.S. urban areas tend to be less safe than those in Europe or Japan. This is particularly true of large U.S. cities. Visitors should always stay alert. It is wise to ask the city's or area's tourist office if you're in doubt about which neighborhoods are safe. Avoid deserted areas, especially at night. Don't go into any city park at night unless there is an event that attracts crowds—a concert in the park or the like. Generally speaking, you can feel safe in areas where there are many people and many open establishments.

Avoid carrying valuables with you on the street, and don't display expensive cameras or electronic equipment. Hold on to your pocketbook, and place your billfold in an inside pocket. In theaters, restaurants, and other public places, keep your possessions in sight.

Remember, also, that hotels are open to the public, and in a large hotel, security may not be able to screen everyone entering. Always lock your room door—don't assume that once inside your hotel you are automatically safe and no longer need to be aware of your surroundings. For more about personal safety in Chicago, see "Safety" under "Fast Facts: Chicago" in chapter 4.

Travel Tip

Be sure to keep a copy of all travel papers separate from your wallet or purse, and leave a copy with someone at home should you need it faxed in an emergency.

DRIVING SAFETY Safety while driving is particularly important. Question your rental agency about personal safety, or ask for a brochure of traveler's safety tips when you pick up your car. It's a good idea to ask the agency to show you on a map how to get to your destination.

Recently more and more crime has involved cars and drivers. If you drive off a highway into a doubtful neighborhood, leave the area as quickly as possible. If you have an accident, even on the highway, stay in your car with the doors locked until you assess the situation or until the police arrive. If you are bumped from behind on the street or are involved in a minor accident with no injuries and the situation appears to be suspicious, do not get out of your car. Go directly to the nearest police precinct, or to a well-lighted service station or all-night store to call the police (dial ☎ **911**). If you see someone on the road that indicates a need for help, do not stop. Take note of the location, drive on to a well-lighted area, and telephone the police by dialing ☎ 911.

Park in well-lighted, well-traveled areas if possible. Always keep your car doors locked, whether attended or unattended. Look around you before you get out of your car, and never leave any packages or valuables in sight. If someone attempts to rob you or steal your car, do not try to resist the thief/carjacker—report the incident to the police department immediately.

2 Getting to the U.S.

Travelers from overseas can take advantage of the APEX (Advance Purchase Excursion) fare offered by all the major U.S. and European carriers.

British Airways (☎ 800/247-9297 in the U.S., or 03/4522-2111 in the U.K.) offers direct flights from London's Heathrow Airport to Chicago. Some of the other major international carriers that service Chicago are **Aer Lingus** (☎ 800/223-6537 in the U.S., 01/844-4747 in Dublin, or 061/415-556 in Shannon), **Air Canada** (☎ 800/776-3000 in the U.S., or 888/247–2262 in Canada), **Qantas** (☎ 800/227-4500 in the U.S., or 13-12-11 in Australia), and **Air New Zealand** (☎ 800/926-7255 in the U.S., or 0800/737-000 in Auckland, or 643/379–5200 in Christchurch).

The visitor arriving by air, no matter what the port of entry, should cultivate patience and resignation before setting foot on U.S. soil. Getting through Immigration control may take as long as 2 hours on some days, especially summer weekends. Add the time it takes to clear Customs and you will see that you should make very generous allowances for delay in planning connections between international and domestic flights—an average of 2 to 3 hours at least.

In contrast, for the traveler arriving by car or by rail from Canada, the border-crossing formalities have been streamlined to the vanishing point. And for the traveler arriving by air from Canada, Bermuda, and some places in the Caribbean, you can sometimes go through Customs and Immigration at the point of departure, which is much quicker and less painful.

For further information about travel to and arriving in Chicago, see "Getting There" in chapter 2.

3 Getting Around the U.S.

BY PLANE Flying is the fastest, and most expensive, mode of domestic travel in the United States. For a list of the major carriers that service Chicago from within the U.S., see "Getting There" in chapter 2.

In conjunction with their transatlantic or transpacific flights, some large American airlines offer special discount tickets for any of their U.S. destinations (American Airlines' **Visit USA** program and Delta's **Discover America** program, for example). These cut-rate tickets or coupons are not for sale in the United States, and must, therefore, be purchased before you leave your foreign point of departure. This system is the best, easiest, and fastest way to see the United States at low cost. You should obtain information well in advance from your travel agent or the office of the airline concerned, since the conditions attached to these discount tickets can be changed without advance notice.

BY CAR Travel by car is perhaps the best way to see the United States if you have the time to really wander. After all, the United States is an automobile culture, so the roads here are excellent. But the real adventure is off the interstates and onto the "blue" highways, the secondary roads, along which the small towns of America are strung like beads on a wire. You should arrange to secure an International Driving Permit validating your license before you travel to the United States. For information on car rentals and Chicago driving rules, see "Automobile Rentals" under "Fast Facts: For the Foreign Traveler," below, and "Getting Around" in chapter 4.

BY TRAIN International visitors can also buy a **USA Rail Pass,** good for 15 or 30 days of unlimited travel on **Amtrak** (☎ **800/USA-RAIL;** www.amtrak.com for schedules, bus connections, and on-line booking). An informational brochure about the pass, printed in five languages, is available through many foreign travel agents. At press time, prices for a 15-day pass were $285 off-peak, $425 peak (peak is roughly June 1 through Sept 1); a 30-day pass costs $375 off-peak, $535 peak.

The **North American Rail Pass** is good for up to 30 days of unlimited travel in the United States and Canada on both Amtrak and VIA Rail Canada. At press time, the price of the pass was $450 off-peak, $645 peak (peak is roughly June 1 through October 15). With this pass, your trip must include travel in both Canada and United States.

Regional passes also are an attractive option for the traveler who wants to explore, for example, the Rocky Mountain West or the New England states. (With a foreign passport, you can also buy passes at some Amtrak offices in the United States, including staffed locations in Chicago, San Francisco, Los Angeles, New York, Miami, Boston, and Washington, D.C. Tickets also can be purchased from international Amtrak sales representatives in 48 countries.) Reservations are generally required on all long-distance trains and should be made for each part of your trip as early as possible.

Visitors should also be aware of the limitations of long-distance rail travel in the United States. With a few notable exceptions (for instance, the Northeast Corridor line between Boston and Washington, D.C.), service is rarely up to European standards: Delays are common, routes are limited and often infrequently served, and fares are rarely significantly lower than discount airfares. Thus, cross-country train travel should be approached with caution.

BY BUS The cheapest way to travel the United States is by bus. **Greyhound** (☎ **800/231-2222;** www.greyhound.com), the nationwide bus line, offers an

Ameripass for unlimited travel for 7 days (for $179), 15 days (for $269), and 30 days (for $369). However, bus travel in the United States can be both slow and uncomfortable, so this option is not for everyone.

FAST FACTS: For the Foreign Traveler

Automobile Organizations   Auto clubs will supply maps, suggested routes, guidebooks, accident and bail-bond insurance, and emergency road service. The major auto club in the United States, with 950 offices nationwide, is the **American Automobile Association (AAA).** Members of some foreign auto clubs have reciprocal arrangements with AAA and may enjoy its services with minimal or no charge. If you belong to an auto club, inquire about this before you leave home. In addition, some car-rental agencies now provide these services, so you should inquire about their availability when you rent your car.

Automobile Rentals   To rent a car you need a major credit card. A valid driver's license is required, and you usually need to be at least 25 years old. Some companies rent to younger people but add a daily surcharge. Be sure to return your car with the same amount of gas you started out with; rental companies charge excessive prices for gasoline.

Business Hours   **Banks** are open weekdays from 9am to 3 or 4pm, although there's 24-hour access to the automated teller machines (ATMs) at most banks and other outlets. Generally, **offices** are open weekdays from 9am to 5pm. **Stores** are open 6 days a week, with many open on Sunday, too; department stores usually stay open until 9pm at least 1 day a week.

Climate   See "When to Go" in chapter 2.

Currency   See "Money" in "Preparing for Your Trip," earlier in this chapter.

Currency Exchange   You will find currency exchange services in major airports with international service. Elsewhere, they may be quite difficult to come by. **Thomas Cook Currency Services** offers a wide variety of services: more than 100 currencies; commission-free foreign traveler's checks, drafts, and wire transfers; check collections; and precious metal bars and coins. Rates are competitive and service is excellent. Call ☎ **800/287-7362** for information. Many hotels will exchange currency if you are a registered guest. (Also see "Money" earlier in this chapter.) If you need a foreign-exchange service, the Chicago consumer Yellow Pages lists names and numbers of foreign-exchange services under the heading "Foreign Exchange Brokers." In the Loop, try **World's Money Exchange, Inc.,** 6 E. Randolph St., Suite 204 (☎ **800/441-9634** or 312/641-2151).

Drinking Laws   The legal drinking age in Chicago (and everywhere in the United States) is 21. Depending on the nature of their license and the day of the week, bars may remain open until anywhere from 2 to 5am. It is a serious criminal offense to drink and drive.

Electric Current   The United States uses 110–120 volts, 60 cycles, compared with 220–240 volts, 50 cycles, used in most of Europe. Small appliances of non-American manufacture, such as hair dryers or shavers, will require both a 100-volt converter and a plug adapter with two flat parallel pins. Such converters may be hard to find in the United States; it's better to bring one along from home.

Embassies & Consulates   All embassies are located in the national capital, Washington, D.C.; some consulates are located in Chicago. Most nations have a mission to the United Nations in New York City. Listed here are the embassies (all in Washington, D.C.) and the Chicago consulates of the major English-speaking countries. Travelers from other countries can get telephone numbers for their embassies and consulates by calling directory assistance (☎ 202/555-1212 in Washington, D.C., or 411 in the Chicago area).

The **Australian** embassy is at 1601 Massachusetts Ave. NW, Washington, DC 20036 (☎ 202/797-3000). There is no consulate in Chicago.

The **Canadian** embassy is at 501 Pennsylvania Ave. NW, Washington, DC 20001 (☎ 202/682-1740). The consulate in Chicago is located at 180 N. Stetson Ave., Suite 2400, Chicago, IL 60601 (☎ 312/616-1860).

The **Irish** embassy is at 2234 Massachusetts Ave. NW, Washington, DC 20008 (☎ 202/462-3939). The consulate in Chicago is located at 400 N. Michigan Ave., Suite 911, Chicago, IL 60611 (☎ 312/337-1868).

The **New Zealand** embassy is at 37 Observatory Circle NW, Washington, DC 20008 (☎ 202/328-4800). There is no consulate in Chicago.

The **British** embassy is at 3100 Massachusetts Ave. NW, Washington, DC 20008 (☎ 202/462-1340). The consulate in Chicago is located in the Wrigley Building, 400 N. Michigan Ave., Suite 1300, Chicago, IL 60611 (☎ 312/346-1810).

Emergencies   Call ☎ 911 for fire, police, and ambulance. The non-emergency policy phone number is ☎ 312/746-6000. If you encounter sickness, accident, or lost or stolen baggage, call **Traveler's Aid** (☎ 773/894-2427), an organization that specializes in helping distressed travelers, whether American or foreign. The office, located in Terminal 3 at O'Hare International Airport, is open Monday through Friday from 8:30am to 9pm, Saturday and Sunday from 9am to 9pm.

Gasoline (Petrol)   One U.S. gallon equals 3.75 liters, while 1.2 U.S. gallons equals 1 Imperial gallon. You'll notice there are several grades (and price levels) of gasoline available at most gas stations. And you'll also notice that their names change from company to company. The unleaded ones with the highest octane are the most expensive (most rental cars take the least expensive "regular" unleaded).

Holidays   On the following national legal holidays, banks, government offices, post offices, and many stores, restaurants, and museums are closed: January 1 (New Year's Day); third Monday in January (Martin Luther King, Jr. Day); third Monday in February (Presidents' Day); last Monday in May (Memorial Day); July 4 (Independence Day); first Monday in September (Labor Day); second Monday in October (Columbus Day); November 11 (Veterans Day/Armistice Day); last Thursday in November (Thanksgiving Day); and December 25 (Christmas Day). In addition, many city offices are closed in Chicago for Casimir Pulaski Day, marking the birthday of a Polish-born Revolutionary War hero, which is observed on the first Monday in March. The Tuesday following the first Monday in November is Election Day, which is a legal holiday in presidential-election years.

Information   There are multilingual information desks in all of the terminals at O'Hare Airport, including two at the international terminal. The Chicago

Office of Tourism distributes a brochure entitled "Chicago Map and Guide" in five languages—English, Spanish, French, German, and Japanese.

Legal Aid   The foreign tourist, unless positively identified as a member of the Mafia or of a drug ring, will probably never become involved with the American legal system. If you are pulled over for a minor infraction (for example, of the highway code), never attempt to pay the fine directly to a police officer or you may wind up arrested on the much more serious charge of attempted bribery. Pay fines by mail, or directly into the hands of the clerk of the court. If accused of a more serious offense, it's wise to say and do nothing before consulting a lawyer. Under U.S. law, an arrested person is allowed one telephone call to a party of his or her choice. Call your embassy or consulate.

Mail   If you want your mail to follow you on your vacation and you aren't sure of your address, it can be sent to you, in your name, % General Delivery at the main post office of the city or region where you expect to be. The addressee must pick it up in person and produce proof of identity (driver's license, credit card, passport, etc.). Chicago's new main post office is at 433 W. Harrison St. Generally found at intersections, **mailboxes** are blue with a red-and-white stripe and carry the inscription U.S. MAIL. If your mail is addressed to a U.S. destination, don't forget to add the five-figure postal code, or ZIP (Zone Improvement Plan) code, after the two-letter abbreviation of the state to which the mail is addressed (IL for Illinois, CA for California, FL for Florida, NY for New York, and so on).

Medical Emergencies   If you become ill, consult your hotel concierge or desk staff for a physician recommendation. The best hospital emergency room in Chicago is, by consensus, **Northwestern Memorial Hospital,** right off North Michigan Avenue at 233 E. Superior (☎ 312/908-2000). (When the institution's huge new hospital opens in the spring of 1999, the emergency room entrance will move to Erie Street.) For an ambulance, dial ☎ **911.**

Newspapers/Magazines   National newspapers include the *New York Times, USA Today,* and the *Wall Street Journal.* National news weeklies include *Newsweek, Time,* and *U.S. News & World Report.* The two daily Chicago papers are the *Chicago Tribune* and the *Chicago Sun-Times.* The *Chicago Reader* is a free weekly with extensive entertainment listings, and the monthly *Chicago* magazine is widely read for its restaurant reviews.

Radio & Television   Audiovisual media, with four coast-to-coast networks—ABC, CBS, NBC, and Fox—along with the Public Broadcasting System (PBS) and the Cable News Network (CNN), play a major part in American life. In big cities, televiewers have a choice of about a dozen channels (including the UHF channels), most of them transmitting 24 hours a day, without counting the pay-TV channels showing recent movies or sports events. All options are usually indicated on your hotel TV set. You'll also find a wide choice of local radio stations, each broadcasting particular kinds of talk shows and/or music—classical, country, jazz, pop, gospel—punctuated by news broadcasts and frequent commercials.

Safety   See "Safety" in "Preparing for Your Trip," above.

Taxes   In the United States there is no VAT (Value-Added Tax) or other indirect tax at a national level. Every state, and each city in it, has the right to levy its own local tax on all purchases, including hotel and restaurant checks, airline tickets, and so on. Chicago sales tax is 8.75%. Restaurants in the central part of

Toll-Free Tip

Don't mix up the toll-free **800, 888,** or **877** area codes with numbers with area codes **700** or **900,** which are usually attached to chat lines, phone sex, and the like, all charging oodles per minute.

the city, roughly the 312 area code, are taxed an additional 1%, for a total of 9.75%. The hotel room tax is 14.9%.

Telephone Directory There are two kinds of telephone directories available to you. The general directory is the so-called **White Pages,** in which private and business subscribers are listed. The inside front cover lists the emergency number for police, fire, ambulance, and other vital numbers (such as the Coast Guard, poison-control center, crime-victims hot line, and so on). The first few pages are devoted to community-service numbers, including a guide to long-distance and international calling, complete with country codes and area codes.

The second directory, printed on yellow paper (hence its name, **Yellow Pages**), lists all local services, businesses, and industries by type of activity, with an index at the back. The listings cover not only such obvious items as automobile repairs by make of car, or drugstores (pharmacies), often by geographical location, but also restaurants by type of cuisine and geographical location, bookstores by special subject and/or language, places of worship by religious denomination, and other information that the tourist might otherwise not readily find. The Yellow Pages also include city plans or detailed area maps, often showing ZIP codes and public transportation routes.

Telephone/Fax, Telegraph & Telex The telephone system in the United States is run by private corporations, so rates, especially for long-distance service, can vary widely—even on calls made from public telephones. Local calls made from a public phone cost 35¢. Generally, hotel surcharges on long-distance and local calls are astronomical. You are usually better off using a **public pay telephone,** which you will find clearly marked in most public buildings and private establishments as well as on the street. Outside metropolitan areas, public telephones are more difficult to find. Stores and gas stations are your best bet.

Note that almost all calls to phone numbers in area codes 800, 888, and 877 are toll-free.

Most **long-distance and international calls** can be dialed directly from any phone. For calls to Canada and other parts of the United States, dial 1 followed by the area code and the seven-digit number. For international calls, dial 011 followed by the country code (Australia, 61; Republic of Ireland, 353; New Zealand, 64; United Kingdom, 44), city code, and the telephone number of the person you wish to call.

For **reversed-charge or collect calls, and for person-to-person calls,** dial 0 (zero, not the letter O) followed by the area code and number you want; an operator will then come on the line, and you should specify that you are calling collect, or person-to-person, or both. If your operator-assisted call is international, ask for the overseas operator.

For **local directory assistance** ("information"), dial ☎ **411.** In Chicago you can also get long-distance information by dialing 411. You can also get long-distance information by dialing 1, then the appropriate area code and 555-1212.

Most hotels have **fax machines** available for their guests, usually for a charge in addition to the cost of the call. Some stationery stores and copying centers, such as **Kinko's,** also have public fax machines.

Like the telephone system, **telegraph and telex services** are provided by private corporations such as **ITT, MCI,** and above all, **Western Union.** You can take your telegram to the nearest Western Union office (there are hundreds across the country), or dictate it over the phone (☎ **800/325-6000**). You can also telegraph money, or have it telegraphed to you, very quickly over the Western Union system.

Time   The United States is divided into six time zones. From east to west, these standard time zones are: eastern (EST), central (CST), mountain (MST), Pacific (PST), Alaska (AST), and Hawaii (HST). Always keep time zones in mind if you are traveling (or even telephoning) long distances in the United States. For example, noon in New York City (EST) is 11am in Chicago (CST), 10am in Denver (MST), 9am in Los Angeles (PST), 8am in Anchorage (AST), and 7am in Honolulu (HST). Chicago is on central standard time.

Daylight saving time is in effect from the first Sunday in April through the last Saturday in October (actually, the change is made at 2am on Sunday) except in Arizona, Hawaii, part of Indiana, and Puerto Rico. Remember that timepieces "spring forward" 1 hour ahead with daylight saving time, and "fall back" 1 hour when they return to standard time.

Tipping   The standard rates for tipping are 15% to 20% (before tax) to waiters for a well-served meal; 15% of the fare for a cab ride; $1 to the bellhop for carrying one bag ($1 per additional bag and a minimum of $3 in the first-class hotels); and a couple of dollars for maid service when you check out.

Toilets   Often euphemistically referred to as "rest rooms," public toilets are nonexistent on the streets of Chicago. They can be found, though, in bars, restaurants, hotel lobbies, museums, department stores, and service stations—and will probably be clean (although ones in the service stations sometimes leave much to be desired). Note, however, that some restaurants and bars display a notice that "Toilets are for use of patrons only." You can ignore this sign, or better yet, avoid arguments by paying for a cup of coffee or soft drink, which will qualify you as a patron. The cleanliness of toilets at railroad stations and bus depots may be questionable; some public places are equipped with pay toilets that require you to insert one or two dimes (10¢) or a quarter (25¢) into a slot on the door before it will open. In rest rooms with attendants, leaving at least a 25¢ tip is customary.

4

Getting to Know Chicago

The orderly configuration of Chicago's streets and the excellent public transportation system make this city more accessible than most of the world's other large cities.

This chapter provides an overview of the city's design, as well as some suggestions for how to maneuver within it. The chapter also lists some resources that travelers frequently require, from quick-service eyeglass repair to an all-night pharmacy.

1 Orientation

VISITOR INFORMATION

The **Chicago Office of Tourism** (☎ 312/744-2400 or TTY 312/744-2947) operates three visitor information centers staffed with people who can answer questions and stocked with a ton of brochures on area attractions, including materials on everything from museums and city landmarks to lakefront biking maps and even fishing spots. The main visitor center, located in the Loop and convenient to many places you'll likely be visiting, is on the first floor of the **Chicago Cultural Center,** 77 E. Randolph (at Michigan). The center has a phone that you can use to make hotel reservations and several couches and a cafe where you can study maps and plan your itinerary. The center is open Monday through Friday from 10am to 6pm, Saturday from 10am to 5pm, and Sunday from noon to 5pm. Closed holidays.

A second, smaller center is located in the heart of the city's shopping district, in the **old pumping station, at Michigan and Chicago avenues.** The entrance is on the Pearson Street side of the building, across from the Water Tower Place mall. Its hours are Monday through Friday from 9:30am to 6pm, Saturday from 10am to 6pm, and Sunday from 11am to 5pm. In summer it's open daily 7:30am to 7pm. This location has the added draw of housing a location of Hot Tix, which offers both half-price day-of-performance and full-price tickets to many theater productions around the city, as well as a gift shop.

A third visitor outpost is located at **Navy Pier** in the Illinois Market Place gift shop; it's open Monday through Thursday from 10am to 8pm, Friday and Saturday from 10am to 11pm, and Sunday from 10am to 7pm.

The **Illinois Bureau of Tourism** (☎ 800/2CONNECT or TTY 800/406-6418) can provide general and specific information 24 hours a day. The agency also has staff at the information desk in the lobby of the **James R. Thompson Center,** 100 W. Randolph St., in the Helmut Jahn–designed building at LaSalle and Randolph streets in the Loop. The desk is open from 8:30am to 4:30pm Monday through Friday.

INFORMATION BY TELEPHONE   The **Mayor's Office of Special Events** operates a recorded hot line (☎ 312/744-3370) listing current special events, festivals, and parades occurring throughout the city. The city of Chicago also maintains a 24-hour information line for the hearing impaired; call ☎ 312/744-8599.

PUBLICATIONS   Chicago's major daily newspapers are the *Tribune* and the *Sun-Times.* Both have cultural listings including movies, theaters, and live music, not to mention reviews of the very latest restaurants that are sure to have appeared in the city since this guidebook went to press. The Friday edition of both papers contains a special pullout section with more detailed, up-to-date information on special events happening over the weekend.

In a class by itself is the *Chicago Reader,* a free weekly that is an invaluable source of entertainment listings, classifieds, and well-written articles on contemporary issues of interest in Chicago. Published every Thursday (except the last week of December), the weekly has a wide distribution downtown and on the North Side, and is available in many retail stores, building lobbies, and at the paper's offices, 11 E. Illinois (☎ 312/828-0350), by about noon on Thursday.

Most Chicago hotels stock their rooms with at least one informational magazine, such as *Where Chicago,* that lists the city's entertainment, shopping, and dining locales.

CITY LAYOUT

The **Chicago River** forms a Y that divides the city into its three geographic zones— North Side, South Side, and West Side (Lake Michigan is where the East Side would be). The downtown financial district is called **the Loop.** The city's key shopping street is **North Michigan Avenue,** also known as the **Magnificent Mile.** In addition to department stores and vertical malls, this stretch of property north of the river houses many of the city's most elegant hotels. North and south of this downtown zone, Chicago stretches along 29 miles of Lake Michigan shoreline that is, by and large, free of commercial development, reserved for public use as green space and parkland from one end of town to the other.

Chicago proper today has about three million inhabitants living in an area about two-thirds the size of New York City; another four and a half million make the suburbs their home. But the real signature of Chicago is found between the suburbs and the Loop, where scores of residential neighborhoods give the city a character all its own.

FINDING AN ADDRESS   Having been a part of the Northwest Territory, Chicago is laid out in a **grid system,** with the streets neatly lined up as if on a giant piece of graph paper. Since the city itself isn't rectangular (it's rather elongated), the shape is a bit irregular, but the perpendicular pattern remains. Easing movement through the city are a half dozen or so major diagonal thoroughfares.

One thing that may seem goofy to visitors is that, while the city is divided into four geographical sections, the street numbering does not originate at the city's geographical midpoint. Instead, point zero is nearer to Chicago's historic and commercial center, more north than south, and so far east as almost to border Lake Michigan.

Point zero is located at the downtown intersection of State and Madison streets. **State Street** divides east and west addresses, and **Madison Street** divides north and south addresses. From here, Chicago's highly predictable addressing system begins.

Chicago Neighborhoods

ROGERS PARK

Touhy Ave.

Lincolnwood

Devon Ave.

Lincoln Ave.

Peterson Ave.

Loyola University/
Mundelein College

Northeastern
Illinois University

Foster Ave.

ANDERSONVILLE

Lake
Michigan

Lawrence Ave.

LINCOLN
SQUARE

UPTOWN

Broadway

Irving Park Rd.

Irving Park

Addison St.

WRIGLEYVILLE

Wrigley
Field

Milwaukee

Belmont Ave.

LAKEVIEW

Fullerton Ave.

Pulaski Rd.

Logan
Square

BUCKTOWN/
WICKER PARK

LINCOLN PARK

DePaul
University

Halsted St.

Lincoln
Park

North Ave.

GOLD COAST

NEAR NORTH

Oak Street
Beach

Grand Ave.

Humboldt
Park

RIVER
NORTH

Navy Pier

STREETERVILLE

Chicago Ave.

Garfield
Park

Washington St.

United
Center

NEAR
WEST

La Salle St.

MAGNIFICENT MILE

THE
LOOP

Eisenhower Exp.

Roosevelt Rd.

Cicero Ave.

Chicago River

State St.

Michigan Ave.

Grant Park

Museum
Campus

Ogden Ave.

Douglas
Park

Cermak Rd.

PILSEN

CHINATOWN

Meigs Field

McCormick
Place

31st St.

Sanitary and Ship Canal

31st St.

BRIDGEPORT

35th St.

31st Street
Beach

Stevenson Exp.

CANARYVILLE

Comiskey
Park

Pershing Rd.

Oakwood
Blvd.

Burnham
Park

Archer Ave.

Keeizie Ave.

Western Blvd.

Damen Ave.

Ashland Ave.

47th St.

Halsted St.

Michigan Ave.

Dr. Martin Luther King Jr. Dr.

51st St.

Washington
Park

55th St.

Garfield Blvd.

HYDE PARK

Midway
Plaisance

Midway Airport

NA-2227

0   1 mi.
     1.6 km.

N

43

Making use of this grid, it is relatively easy to plot the distance in miles between any two points in the city.

Virtually all of Chicago's principal north–south and east–west arteries are spaced by increments of 400 in the addressing system—regardless of the number of smaller streets nestled between them. And each addition or subtraction of 400 numbers to an address is equivalent to a half mile. Thus, starting at point zero on Madison Street, and traveling north along State Street for 1 mile, you will come to 800 N. State, which intersects Chicago Avenue. Continue uptown for another half mile and you arrive at the 1200 block of North State at Division Street. And so it goes right to the city line, with suburban Evanston located at the 7600 block north, 9½ miles from point zero.

The same rule applies when traveling south, or east to west. Thus, heading west from State Street along Madison, Halsted Street—at 800 W. Madison—is a mile's distance, while Racine, at the 1200 block of West Madison, is 1½ miles from the center. Madison then continues westward to Chicago's boundary along Austin Avenue, with the near suburb of Oak Park, which at 6000 W. Madison is approximately 7½ miles from point zero.

The key to understanding the grid is that the side of any square formed by the principal avenues (noted in dark or red ink on most maps) represents a distance of half a mile in any direction. Understanding how Chicago's grid system works is of particular importance to those visitors who wish to do a lot of walking in the city's many neighborhoods and who want to plot in advance the distances involved in trekking from one locale to another.

The other ingeniously convenient aspect to the grid is that every major road uses the same numerical system. In other words, the cross street at 1200 N. Lake Shore Dr. is the same as at 1200 N. Clark St., is the same as at 1200 N. LaSalle St., etc. (Division Street).

STREET MAPS A suitably detailed map of Chicago is published by **Rand McNally,** available at many newsstands and bookstores for $2.95 (the smaller, more manageable laminated versions run about $5.95).

NEIGHBORHOODS IN BRIEF

THE LOOP & VICINITY

"Downtown," in the case of Chicago, means the Loop. The Loop refers literally to a core of primarily commercial, governmental, and cultural buildings contained within a corral of elevated subway tracks, but greater downtown Chicago overflows these confines and is bounded by the Chicago River to the north and west, by Michigan Avenue to the east, and by Roosevelt Avenue to the south.

THE NORTH SIDE

Near North/Magnificent Mile North Michigan Avenue is known as the Magnificent Mile, from the bridge spanning the Chicago River to its northern tip at Oak Street. Here Chicago is at its most elegant. Many of the city's best hotels, shops, and restaurants are to be found on and around North Michigan. The area stretching east of Michigan Avenue to the lake is also sometimes referred to as "Streeterville."

River North Just to the west of the Mag Mile's zone of high life and sophistication is an old warehouse district called River North. The area has become increasingly gentrified and is now filled with many of the city's hottest restaurants, nightspots, art galleries, and loft dwellings.

The Gold Coast Some of Chicago's most desirable real estate and historic architecture is found along Lake Shore Drive, between Oak Street and North Avenue and along the adjacent side streets. Despite trendy little pockets of real estate popping up elsewhere, the moneyed class still prefers to live by the lake.

Old Town West of Dearborn, principally on North Wells Street between Division Street and North Avenue, is the nightlife district of Old Town. This area was a hippie haven in the sixties and seventies, and the many comedy clubs here, such as the legendary Second City, have served up the lighter side of life to Chicagoans for more than a generation.

Lincoln Park This fashionable residential neighborhood stretches from North Avenue to Diversey Parkway and is bordered on the east by the huge park of the same name. The triangle formed by Lincoln Avenue, Halsted Street, and Armitage, where many of Chicago's in-spot bars and restaurants are located, is explored in detail in chapter 8.

Lakeview and Wrigleyville Midway up the city's North Side is a one-time blue collar, now semigentrified/bohemian quarter called Lakeview. It's become the neighborhood of choice for many gays and lesbians, recent college graduates, and growing numbers of residents priced out of Lincoln Park. The main thoroughfare is Belmont, between Broadway and Sheffield. Wrigleyville is the name given to the neighborhood in the vicinity of Wrigley Field—home of the Chicago Cubs—at Sheffield Avenue and Addison Street. Many homesteaders have moved into these areas in recent years, and a slew of nightclubs and restaurants has followed in their wake.

Uptown and Andersonville Uptown, along the lake and about as far north as Foster Avenue, is where the latest wave of immigrants—including internal migrants from Appalachia and the Native American reservations—has settled. Vietnamese and Chinese immigrants have transformed Argyle Street between Broadway and Sheridan into a teeming market for fresh meat, fish, and all kinds of exotic vegetables. Slightly to the north and west is the old Scandinavian neighborhood of Andersonville, whose main drag is Clark Street, between Foster and Bryn Mawr. The area has the feel of a small Midwestern village, albeit one with an eclectic mix of Middle Eastern restaurants and a distinct cluster of women-owned businesses.

Lincoln Square West of Andersonville, and slightly to the south, where Lincoln, Western, and Lawrence avenues intersect, is Lincoln Square, the only identifiable remains of Chicago's once vast German-American community. Lincoln Square now also has a distinctly Greek flavor, with several restaurants of that nationality to boot.

Rogers Park Rogers Park, which begins at Devon Avenue, is located on the northern fringes of the city bordering suburban Evanston. It has been a Jewish neighborhood for decades, and now Asians, East Indians, and Russians live among the Orthodox Jews. The food options range from bagels and lox to tandoori.

THE WEST SIDE

Near West On the Near West Side, just across the Chicago River from the Loop, on Halsted Street between Adams and Monroe streets, is Chicago's old "Greek Town," and still the Greek culinary center of the city. Much of the old Italian neighborhood in this vicinity was the victim of urban renewal, but remnants still survive on Taylor Street; the same is true for a few old delis and shops on Maxwell Street, dating from the turn of the century when a large Jewish community lived in the area.

Bucktown/Wicker Park Centered near the confluence of North, Damen, and Milwaukee avenues, where the deco Northwest Tower is the tallest thing for miles, this resurgent area is said to be home to the third-largest concentration of artists in the country. Over the last century, the area has hosted waves of German, Polish, and most recently Spanish-speaking immigrants (not to mention writer Nelson Algren). In recent years it has morphed into a bastion for hot new restaurants, alternative culture, and loft-dwelling yuppies surfing the gentrification wave that's washing over this still somewhat gritty neighborhood.

THE SOUTH SIDE

Pilsen This old bohemian neighborhood, centered at Halsted and 18th streets, is now a largely Mexican neighborhood and a budding artists' colony.

Bridgeport and Canaryville Bridgeport, whose main intersection is 35th and Halsted streets, is the neighborhood of Mayor Daley, both father and son (who up and left in recent years for the new Central Station development in the South Loop area). After the old Comiskey Park was torn down, the Chicago White Sox stayed in Bridgeport, inaugurating their new stadium there. Nearby Canaryville, just south and west, is typical of the "back-of-the-yard" blue-collar neighborhoods that once surrounded the Chicago Stockyards. Neither area offers much to the typical visitor; "outsiders," in fact, aren't all that welcome.

Hyde Park Hyde Park is like an independent village within the confines of Chicago, right off Lake Michigan, and roughly a 30-minute train ride from the Loop. Fifty-seventh Street is the main drag, and the University of Chicago—with all its attendant shops and restaurants—is the neighborhood's principal tenant. Hyde Park's main attraction, however, is the world-famous Museum of Science and Industry.

2 Getting Around

The best way to savor Chicago (or any city) is by walking its streets. Walking is not always practical, particularly when moving between distant neighborhoods and on harsh winter days. In those situations, Chicago's public train and bus systems are efficient modes of transportation.

Walker's Warning

While Chicago is a great city to explore on foot, I must warn people against trying to cross Lake Shore Drive on foot. People have been seriously injured and even killed attempting to dodge the traffic on the Drive. Look for the pedestrian underpasses at Chicago Avenue, Oak Street, and North Avenue, among other locations.

Travel Tip

Visitors may consider buying a **Visitor Pass,** which works like a fare card and allows individual users unlimited rides on the El and CTA buses over a 24-hour period. The cards cost $5 and are sold at airports, hotels, museums, Hot Tix outlets, transportation hubs, and Chicago Office of Tourism visitor information centers. Two-, three-, and four-day passes are also now available. While the passes save you the trouble of feeding the fare machines yourself, remember that they're only economical if you plan to make at least three distinct trips, at least two or more hours apart (you get two additional transfers for an additional 30 cents on a regular fare).

BY PUBLIC TRANSPORTATION

The **Chicago Transit Authority (CTA)** operates an extensive system of trains and buses throughout the city of Chicago. The sturdy system carries about 1.3 million passengers a day. Recently, the CTA has been trying to reverse declining ridership by sprucing up some of the grittier stations and introducing more efficient operating procedures, such as timetables and new fare cards. Subways and elevated trains (known as the El) are generally safe and reliable, though it's advisable to avoid long rides through unfamiliar neighborhoods late at night.

Fares for the bus, subway, and the El are $1.50, with an additional 30¢ for a transfer that allows CTA riders to make two transfers on the bus or El within 2 hours of receipt. Children under 7 ride for free, and those between the ages of 7 and 11 pay 75¢ (15¢ for transfers). Senior citizens can also receive the reduced fare if they have the appropriate reduced-fare permit (☎ 312/836-7000 for details on how to obtain one, though this is probably not a realistic option for a short-term visitor).

Adopting a system used by other urban transit agencies, the CTA recently introduced a new fare card system that automatically deducts the exact fare from a credit-card-size plastic card each time you take a ride. The reusable cards can be purchased with a preset value already stored ($13.50 for 10 rides or $16.50 for 10 rides and 10 transfers), or riders can obtain cards at vending machines located at all CTA train stations and charge them with whatever amount they choose (a minimum of $3 and up to $100). If within 2 hours of your first ride you transfer to a bus or the El, the turnstiles at the El stations and the fare boxes on buses will automatically deduct from your card just the cost of a transfer (30¢). If you make a second transfer within 2 hours, it's free. The same card can be recharged continuously.

Coins (exact change only) and CTA tokens are still accepted on buses (buses are also equipped with fare boxes that accept $1 bills) and the El, but the CTA is pushing everyone to switch to fare cards. You can purchase a 10-pack roll of tokens for $15 at Jewel and Dominick's supermarkets and at hundreds of neighborhood currency exchanges.

CTA INFORMATION   The CTA operates a useful telephone information service (☎ 836-7000 or TTY 836-4949 from any area code in the city and suburbs) that functions daily from 5am to 1am. When you want to know how to get from where you are to where you want to go, call the CTA. Make sure you specify any conditions you might require—the fastest route, for example, or the simplest (the route with the fewest transfers or least amount of walking), and so forth. You can also check out the CTA's Web site at **www.transitchicago.com**. Excellent CTA comprehensive maps, which include both El and bus routes, are usually available at subway or El stations, or by calling the CTA. The CTA also has added a toll-free customer service hot line (☎ **888/YOUR-CTA** or TTY 888/CTA-TTY1 Mon through Fri from 7am to 8pm, with voice mail operating after hours) to field questions and feedback. While the new fare box system has eliminated the need for ticket agents, they have been retrained to offer customer assistance at the subway and El stations.

BY THE EL & THE SUBWAY   The rapid transit system operates five major lines, which the CTA recently began identifying by color (though Chicagoans will often still refer to them by their points of origin): the **Red Line** (also known as the Howard/Dan Ryan Line) runs north–south; the **Green Line** (also known as the Lake Street Line) runs west–south; the **Blue Line** (also known as the O'Hare Line) runs west–northwest to O'Hare Airport; the **Brown Line** (also knows as the Ravenswood Line) runs in a northern zigzag route; and the **Orange Line** runs southwest serving Midway airport.

A separate express line, the **Purple Line,** services Evanston, while a smaller, local line in Skokie (the **Yellow Line,** also known as the Skokie Swift) is linked to the north–south train. Skokie and Evanston are adjacent suburbs on Chicago's northern boundary.

Study your CTA map carefully (there's one printed on the inside back cover of this guide) before boarding any train. While most trains run every 5 to 20 minutes, decreasing in frequency in the off-peak and overnight hours, some stations close after work hours (as early as 8:30pm) and remain closed on Saturday, Sunday, and holidays. The Orange Line train does not operate from about 11:30pm to 5am, the Brown Line operates only north of Belmont after about 9:30pm, the Blue Line's Cermak branch has ceased operating overnight and on weekends, and the Purple Line no longer runs overnight as well.

The CTA recently posted timetables on the El platforms so you can determine when the next train should arrive.

BY BUS   Add to Chicago's gridlike layout a comprehensive system of public buses and there is virtually no place in the city that isn't within close walking distance of a bus stop. Other than on foot or bicycle, the best way to get around Chicago's warren of neighborhoods—the best way to actually see what's around you—is by riding a public bus. (The view from the elevated trains can be pretty dramatic too; the difference is that on the trains you get the backyards, while on the bus you see the buildings' facades and the street life.) Look for the **blue-and-white signs to locate bus stops,** which are spaced about a block or two apart.

A couple of buses that are particularly handy for many visitors are the **no. 146 Marine/Michigan,** an express bus from Belmont Avenue on the North Side that cruises down North Lake Shore Drive (and through Lincoln Park during nonpeak times) to North Michigan Avenue, State Street, and the Grant Park museum campus; the **no. 151 Sheridan,** which passes through Lincoln Park onto inner Lake Shore Drive and then travels along Michigan Avenue as far south as Adams Street, where it turns west into the Loop (and stops at Union Station); and the **no. 156 LaSalle,** which goes through Lincoln Park and then into the Loop's financial district on LaSalle Street.

PACE buses (☎ **836-7000** from any Chicago area code or 847/364-7223, Mon through Fri from 8am to 5pm; www.pacebus.com) cover the suburban zones that surround Chicago. They run every 20 to 30 minutes during rush hour, operating until mid-evening Monday through Friday and early evening on weekends. Suburban bus routes are marked no. 208 and above, and vehicles may be flagged down at intersections since few of the lines have bus stops that are marked.

Downtown El & Subway Stations

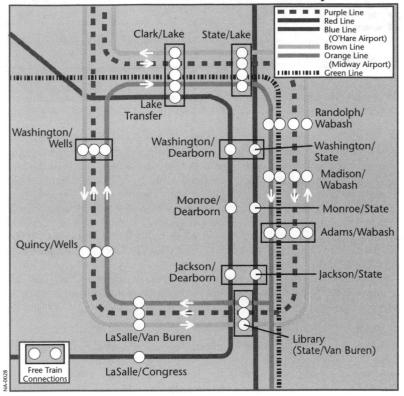

Legend:
- ■ ■ ■ Purple Line
- ─── Red Line
- ─── Blue Line (O'Hare Airport)
- ─── Brown Line
- ─── Orange Line (Midway Airport)
- ▮▮▮ Green Line

Clark/Lake
State/Lake
Lake Transfer
Randolph/Wabash
Washington/Wells
Washington/Dearborn
Washington/State
Madison/Wabash
Monroe/Dearborn
Monroe/State
Adams/Wabash
Quincy/Wells
Jackson/Dearborn
Jackson/State
LaSalle/Van Buren
Library (State/Van Buren)
Free Train Connections
LaSalle/Congress

NA-0028

BY COMMUTER TRAIN

The **Metra** commuter railroad (☎ **312/322-6777** or TTY 312/322-6774 Mon through Fri from 8am to 5pm; at other times call RTA at ☎ 312/836-7000 or TTY 312/836-4949; www.metrarail.com), serves the six-county suburban area around Chicago with 12 train lines. Several terminals are located downtown, including **Union Station** at Adams and Canal, **LaSalle Street Station** at LaSalle and Van Buren, **North Western Station** at Madison and Canal, and **Randolph Street Station** at Randolph and Michigan.

To visit some of the most affluent suburbs in the country, take the **Union Pacific North Line** (previously known as the North Western train), which departs at the North Western Station, and select from among the following destinations: Kenilworth, Winnetka, Glencoe, Highland Park, and Lake Forest.

The **Metra Electric** (once known as the Illinois Central–Gulf Railroad, or the IC) runs close to Lake Michigan on track that occupies some of the most valuable real estate in Chicago. It will take you to Hyde Park and Pullman, both of which are described in this guidebook. You can catch the Metra Electric in the Loop at the Randolph Street Station and at the Van Buren Street Station at Van Buren and Michigan Avenue.

Commuter trains have graduated fare schedules based on the distance you ride. On weekends and holidays and during the summer, Metra offers a family discount that allows up to three children under age 12 to ride for free when accompanying a paid

---

Taxi Trivia

Unlike in New York, where all taxis are painted yellow, Chicago's taxis can come in several colors and still be legitimately licensed.

---

adult. The commuter railroad also offers a $5 weekend pass for unlimited rides on Saturday and Sunday.

BY TAXI

Taxis are a pretty affordable way to get around the Loop and to get to the dining, shopping, and entertainment options found beyond downtown, such as on the Near North Side, in Old Town and Lincoln Park, and on the Near West Side. But for longer distances, the fares will add up.

Taxis are easy to hail in the Loop, on the Magnificent Mile and the Gold Coast, in River North, and in Lincoln Park, but if you go much beyond these key areas, you may need to call. Some cab companies are **Flash Cab** (☎ **773/561-1444**), **Yellow Cab** (☎ **312/TAXI-CAB** or 312/829-4222), or **Checker Cab** (☎ **312/CHECKER** or 312/243-2537).

When this book went to press, the meter in Chicago cabs started at $1.60, and increased $1.40 for each mile, with a 50¢ surcharge for each additional rider age 12 to 65.

BY CAR

Chicago is laid out so logically that it's relatively easy for visitors to get around the city by car. Rush-hour traffic jams are not as daunting as in many other U.S. cities. Traffic runs fairly smoothly at most times of the day. The combination of wide streets and strategically spaced expressways makes for generally easy riding (although construction on the Dan Ryan over the past several years has slowed things down a bit on that particular roadway, with no end in sight).

Great diagonal corridors—such as Lincoln Avenue, Clark Street, and Milwaukee Avenue—slice through the grid pattern at key points in the city and shorten many a trip that would otherwise be tedious on the checkerboard surface of the Chicago streets. **Lake Shore Drive** (also known as the Outer Drive) has to be one of the most scenic and useful urban thoroughfares anywhere. You can travel the length of the city (and beyond), never far from the great lake that is Chicago's most awesome natural feature.

DRIVING RULES   One bizarre anomaly in the organization of Chicago's traffic is the occasional absence of signal lights off the principal avenues, notably in the River North and Streeterville neighborhoods. A block east or west of the Magnificent Mile (North Michigan Avenue)—one of the most traveled streets in the city—you will in some cases encounter only stop signs to control the flow of traffic. Once you've become accustomed to the system, it works very smoothly, with everyone—pedestrians and motorists alike—advancing in their proper turn.

Unless otherwise posted, a right turn on red is allowed after stopping and signaling.

PARKING   Parking regulations are vigorously enforced throughout the city. Read signs carefully: Many neighborhoods have adopted resident-only parking that prohibits others from parking on their streets, usually after 6pm each day (even all day in a few areas, such as Old Town). The neighborhood around Wrigley Field is off-limits during Cubs night games, so look for yellow sidewalk signs alerting drivers about the dozen and a half times the Cubs play under lights. You can park in permit zones if

How to Get to McCormick Place Conference Center

BY PUBLIC TRANSPORTATION   While many trade shows at McCormick Place, 23rd and Lake Shore Drive (☎ 312/791-7000; www.mccormickplace. com), arrange transportation from hotels downtown and along North Michigan Avenue, you can also get there from Michigan Avenue by taking either the **no. 3 King Drive Bus** or the **no. 4 Cottage Grove Bus.** Both buses deposit passengers at the foot of McCormick Place's new South Building, at 23rd Street and Martin Luther King, Jr. Drive. The no. 3 runs from early morning to about 11pm, and the no. 4 runs around the clock.

You can also take a **Metra Electric** commuter train directly to McCormick Place North. Catch the train in the Loop at the Randolph Street Station at Randolph and Michigan Avenue. For more information, call the RTA/CTA Travel Information hot line at ☎ **312/836-7000.**

BY CAR   From the Loop and North Michigan Avenue   Take Lake Shore Drive South and follow the signs to McCormick Place.

From O'Hare Airport   Take the Northwest Tollway (I-90) to the Kennedy/Dan Ryan (I-94) to the Stevenson Expressway North (I-55). Take the Stevenson north to Lake Shore Drive and follow the signs to McCormick Place.

From Midway Airport   Take the Stevenson Expressway (I-55) north to Lake Shore Drive South. Follow the signs to McCormick Place.

PARKING   There are parking lots at 31st Street and Lake Shore Drive; Burnham Harbor; Soldier Field; and across the street from the new South Building, at 2215 S. Prairie Ave.

you're visiting a friend, who can provide you with a pass to stick on your windshield. Beware of tow zones, and, if visiting in winter, make note of curbside warnings regarding snow plowing.

A safe bet is valet parking, which most restaurants provide for $5 or $6. Downtown you might also opt to park in a public garage, but you may have to pay the premium prices common in any metropolitan area. (Several garages connected with malls or other major attractions offer discounted parking with a validated ticket.)

The best deal in town for convenient public parking is the $8 daily rate at **Grant Park Parking,** Michigan Avenue at Van Buren (☎ 312/747-2519), and Michigan at Monroe (☎ 312/742-7530). You'll pay twice that at most other lots, including **MAP Parking** near the Merchandise Mart in River North, 350 N. Orleans (☎ 312/986-6822); **McCormick Place Parking,** 2301 S. Lake Shore Dr. (☎ 312/747-7194); **Midcontinental Plaza Garage,** 55 E. Monroe (☎ 312/986-6821); and **Navy Pier Parking,** 600 E. Grand (☎ 312/595-7437).

RENTALS   Hertz (☎ 800/654-3131), **Avis** (☎ 800/831-2847), **National** (☎ 800/227-7368), and **Budget** (☎ 800/527-0700) all have offices at O'Hare Airport and at Midway Airport. Each company also has at least one office downtown: Hertz at 9 W. Kinzie; Avis at 214 N. Clark; National at 203 N. LaSalle; and Budget at 65 E. Lake St.

BY BOAT

Boat traffic in Chicago has been stirring up a bigger wake these days. **Shoreline Sightseeing** (☎ 312/222-9328) has started ferrying passengers on the lake between Navy

Pier and Shedd Aquarium and on the Chicago River between Navy Pier and the Sears Tower (Adams Street and the river). The **water taxis** operate daily every half hour and cost $6 for adults, $5 for seniors, and $3 for children.

A shuttle boat operated by **Wendella Commuter Boats** (☎ 312/337-1446) floats daily from April through October between a dock below the Wrigley Building (the northwest side of the Michigan Avenue bridge) and North Western Station, a commuter train station across the river from the Loop. The ride, which costs $1.50 each way (or 10 rides for $11) and takes about 8 minutes, is popular with both visitors and commuters. The service operates every 10 minutes in the morning from 7:48 to 8:45am from the station, and in the afternoon from 4:44 to 5:30pm from the bridge.

Several other boat companies have announced plans to begin taxi services and may even allow passengers to request a particular drop-off (within reason).

BY BICYCLE

The city of Chicago has earned kudos for its efforts to improve conditions for bicycling, but it can still be a rough road trying to compete with cars and their drivers, who aren't always so willing to share the road. Make sure you wear a helmet at all times and stick to the lakefront path or area parks if you're nervous about veering into traffic. Designated bikes lanes have been installed on stretches of Wells Street, Roosevelt Road, Elston Avenue, and Halsted Street.

The **Chicagoland Bicycle Federation** (☎ 312/42-PEDAL; www.chibikefed.org), a nonprofit advocacy group, is a good resource for bicyclists. The group publishes several bicycling maps with tips on recommended on-street routes and parkland routes and a guide to safe cycling in the city.

Bike Chicago (☎ 800/915-BIKE) has four locations: Oak Street Beach, Buckingham Fountain in Grant Park (directly east of the fountain, across Lake Shore Drive), Navy Pier, and near the entrance to the Lincoln Park Zoo, at Fullerton Avenue and Cannon Drive. The company rents all sorts of bikes, including tandems, as well as in-line skates. Bikes rent for $8.50 an hour, or $34 a day. It also offers free delivery to hotels for group daily rentals and leads a free lakefront bike tour from Navy Pier at 1:30pm daily. Helmets and pads are free, while locks are extra. The shops are open daily from 10am to about 6pm, weather permitting, with extended hours at Navy Pier.

FAST FACTS: Chicago

American Express Travel service offices are located at the following locations: across from the Art Institute, at 122 S. Michigan (☎ 312/435-2595); across from Crate & Barrel, at 625 N. Michigan (☎ 312/435-2570); and in Lincoln Park, at 2338 N. Clark (☎ 773/477-4000).

Area Codes Like many other urban areas, Chicago has added several new area codes in the last year. The 312 area code long held by the entire city proper now applies to the Loop and the neighborhoods closest to it, including River North, North Michigan Avenue, and the Gold Coast. The rest of the city now has 773 for an area code. Suburban area codes are 847 (northern), 708 (west and southwest), and 630 (far west). Prefixes that have been assigned the new area code are listed in the front of the telephone book.

Baby-sitters Check with the concierge or desk staff at your hotel, who are likely to maintain a list of reliable sitters with whom they have worked in the past. Many of the hotels work with **American Registry for Nurses & Sitters Inc.** (☎ **800/240-1820** or 773/248-8100; fax 773/248-8104), a state-licensed baby-sitting service that can match you with a sitter. The sitters are required to pass background checks, provide multiple child-care references, and be trained in infant and child CPR. It's best to make a reservation 24 hours in advance; the office is open from 9am to 5pm. Rates are about $12 per hour, with a 4-hour minimum.

Business Hours   Shops generally keep normal business hours, opening around 10am and closing by 6pm Monday through Saturday. These days, however, most stores generally stay open late at least one evening a week. And certain businesses, such as bookstores, are almost always open during the evening hours all week. Most shops (other than in the Loop) are now open on Sunday as well, usually from noon to 5pm. Malls, including Water Tower Place at 835 N. Michigan Ave., are generally open until 7pm (Marshall Field's and Lord & Taylor in Water Tower Place stay open until 9pm), and are open Sunday as well. Banking hours in Chicago are normally from 9am (8am in some cases) to 3pm Monday through Friday, with select banks remaining open later on specified afternoons and evenings.

Camera Repair   Central Camera, 230 S. Wabash (☎ **312/427-5580**), has been a Chicago institution since 1899.

Car Rentals   See "Getting Around" in this chapter.

Dentists   The 24-hour **Dental Referral Service** (☎ **630/978-5745**) can refer you to an area dentist. You also might try your hotel concierge or desk staff, who often keep a list of dentists.

Doctors   In the event of a medical emergency, your best bet—unless you have friends who can recommend a doctor—is to rely on your hotel physician or go to the nearest hospital emergency room. **Northwestern Memorial Hospital** also has a **Physician Referral Service** at ☎ **312/908-8400.** See also "Hospitals," below.

Driving Rules   See "Getting Around" in this chapter.

Embassies & Consulates   See chapter 3.

Emergencies   For fire or police emergencies, call ☎ **911.** The nonemergency phone number for the Chicago Police Department is ☎ **312/747-6000.** The city of Chicago proclaims the following policy: "In emergency dial 911 and a city ambulance will respond free of charge to the patient. The ambulance will take the patient to the nearest emergency room according to geographic location." If you desire a specific, nonpublic ambulance, call **Tower Ambulance** (☎ **773/ 561-2308**).

Eyeglass Repair   Pearle Vision Center, 350 N. Michigan (☎ **312/726-8255**), offers 1-hour service in many cases. **Glasses Ltd.** has two locations downtown: 49 E. Oak (☎ **312/944-6876**) and on the fifth level of the 900 N. Michigan shopping mall (☎ **312/751-0073**), and often can provide same-day service.

Faxes   It's pretty standard these days for hotels to be able to assist you in sending or receiving faxes, either with your own in-room fax machine, at the front desk, or through the hotel's business center. In addition, **Kinko's,** a photocopy center with fax service, has several 24-hour locations throughout the city, including 1201 N. Dearborn (☎ **312/640-6100**), 29 S. LaSalle (☎ **312/578-8520**), and a business center with private computer suites for rent that is connected to the downtown Renaissance Hotel (☎ **312/251-0441;** there's also a street entrance at 6 W. Lake).

Hospitals   By consensus, the best emergency room in Chicago is at **Northwestern Memorial Hospital,** 233 E. Superior (☎ **312/908-2000**), right off the Magnificent Mile. When a new hospital building opens in spring of 1999, the new emergency room entrance will be on Erie Street.

Hot Lines   For help with drugs and alcoholism, call ☎ **800/395-3400.** The drug-abuse hot line in Chicago is ☎ **773/278-5015.** There are also two crisis hot lines in Chicago: **Ravenswood Hospital** at ☎ **773/769-6200** or the **Institute of Psychiatry** at ☎ **312/908-8100.**

Libraries   The Chicago Public Library's main branch is the **Harold Washington Library Center** at 400 S. State (☎ **312/747-4300**). The El will drop you practically at the library's front door; take the Loop elevated train (Brown, Orange, or Purple lines) to the new Library/Van Buren station, located on the library's north side.

Liquor Laws   Most bars and taverns have a 2am license, allowing them to stay open until 3am on Sunday ("Saturday night"); some have a 4am license and may remain open until 5am on Sunday.

Lost Property   There is a lost-and-found service at **O'Hare International Airport** (☎ **773/686-2385**).

Maps   See "City Layout" earlier in this chapter.

Newspapers & Magazines   The *Chicago Tribune* (☎ **312/222-3232**) and the *Chicago Sun-Times* (☎ **312/321-3000**) are the two major dailies. The *Chicago Reader* (☎ **312/828-0350**) is a free weekly that appears each Thursday, with all the current entertainment and cultural listings. *Chicago Magazine* is a monthly that is widely read for its restaurant reviews. The *Chicago Defender* covers local and national news of interest to the African-American community. The Spanish-language *La Raza* reports on stories from a Latino point of view. *Windy City Times* publishes both news and feature articles about gay and lesbian issues.

Pharmacies   **Walgreens,** 757 N. Michigan (☎ **312/664-8686**), is open 24 hours. **Osco Drugs** has a toll-free number (☎ **800/654-6726**) that you can call to locate the 24-hour pharmacy nearest you.

Police   For emergencies, call ☎ **911.** For nonemergencies, call ☎ **312/747-6000.**

Post Office   The new main post office is at 433 W. Harrison (☎ **312/654-3895**), with free parking; there are also convenient branches in the Sears Tower, the Federal Center Plaza at 211 S. Clark (designed by Mies van der Rohe no less), the James R. Thompson Center at 100 W. Randolph, and a couple of blocks off the Magnificent Mile at 227 E. Ontario.

Radio   **WBEZ** (91.5 FM) is the local National Public Radio station, which plays jazz in the evenings. **WFMT** (98.7 FM) specializes in fine arts and classical music, and for years was the home of Studs Terkel's syndicated interview show. One of the more special stations anywhere just celebrated its 25th anniversary, **WXRT** (93.1 FM), a progressive rock station whose deejays don't stick to corporate-sanctioned play lists but mix things up with shots of blues, jazz, and local music. On the AM side of the dial, you'll find talk radio on **WGN** (720) and **WLS** (890): two longtime stations that got their names from their immodest owners (respectively, that would be the *Chicago Tribune,* the "World's Greatest Newspaper"; and Sears, the "World's Largest Store"). News junkies should tune to **WBBM** (780) for nonstop news, traffic, and weather reports, and sports fans will find company on the talk station **WSCR** (1160).

Rest Rooms   The **Chicago Historical Society** on Clark Street at North Avenue has a rest room downstairs; it's accessible without entering the museum itself. There's a rest room in the Starbucks cafe on Rush Street that makes a good pit stop for shoppers in the area. The department stores also have public rest rooms, as do the malls.

Safety   Chicago has all of the crime problems of any urban center, so use your common sense and stay cautious and alert. Everyone has a different sense for their own comfort level in unfamiliar terrain, so you'll have to decide for yourself where and when you want to venture. At night you may want to stick to well-lighted streets along the Magnificent Mile, River North, Gold Coast, and Lincoln Park (stay out of the park proper after dark, though), which are all high traffic areas late into the night. Don't walk alone at night, and avoid wandering down dark residential streets, even those that seem perfectly safe. Muggings can happen anywhere, and do.

After dark you may want to avoid the Loop's interior, which gets pretty deserted after business hours, as well as neighborhoods such as Hyde Park, Wicker Park, and Pilsen, which border on areas with more troublesome reputations.

You can also ask the concierge at your hotel or an agent at the tourist visitor center what they would recommend about visiting a particular area of the city.

If you're traveling alone, avoid riding the El after the rush-hour crowds thin out. Of course, it's always smarter to ride with a group. Many of the El stations can be eerily deserted at night—when you'll have to wait around for 15 minutes or longer for the next train. In that case, it's a good idea to spring for a taxi. Buses are a safe option, too, especially nos. 146 and 151, which pick up along North Michigan Avenue and State Street and connect to the North Side via Lincoln Park.

Blue-and-white police cars are a common sight, and officers also patrol by bicycle downtown and along the lakefront and by horseback at special events and parades. There are police stations in busy nightlife areas, such as the 18th District station at Chicago Avenue and LaSalle Street in the hopping restaurant and entertainment mecca of River North, and the 24th District station (known as Town Hall) at Addison and Halsted streets, located in the heart of the gay district and blocks from the busy strip of sports bars and nightclubs in Wrigleyville.

Shoe Repair   Sam the Shoe Doctor has a dozen locations, including one in the Sears Tower (☎ **312/876-9001**), and will do repairs while you wait.

Taxes   The local sales tax is 8.75%. Restaurants in the central part of the city, roughly the 312 area code, are taxed an additional 1%, for a total of 9.75%. The hotel room tax is 14.9%.

Time Zone   All of Illinois, including Chicago, is located in the central time zone, so clocks are set 1 hour earlier than those on the East Coast and 2 hours later than those on the West Coast. Chicago switches to daylight saving time on the first Sunday in April, and back to standard time on the last Sunday in October.

Transit Info   The **CTA** has a useful number to find out which bus or El train will get you to your destination: ☎ **836-7000** (from any area code in the city or suburbs) or TTY **836-4949.**

Traveler's Aid   Travelers in distress can turn to **Traveler's Aid** (☎ **773/894-2427**), which operates an office in Terminal 3 of O'Hare Airport. The office provides food and shelter for stranded travelers, reunites family members who have become separated, locates lost luggage, and even furnishes crisis counseling. The office is staffed from 8:30am to 9pm weekdays and 9am to 9pm weekends.

Weather   For the **National Weather Service's** current conditions and forecast, dial ☎ **312/976-1212** (for a fee), or check the weather on the Web at www.ci.chi.il.us/Tourism/Weather/.

Accommodations

5

Hotels are booming in Chicago. The city was overbuilt in the early years of the decade, but the robust convention trade and tourism market have caught up. Consequently, in the last couple of years developers have made a flurry of announcements about plans for building new hotels as well as updating some of the city's grand old hotels. A few of the newcomers have brought Chicago its first taste of the hip, art-directed hotels that have been all the rage on the East and West coasts. Perhaps a dozen new hotels could enter the scene over the next couple of years, including everything from a luxury Park Hyatt at Michigan and Chicago avenues to a boutique hotel in the historic Reliance Building at State and Washington streets to a budget Red Roof Inn just south on State Street.

While room rates continue to soar at hotels located anywhere near highly desirable North Michigan Avenue, these new lodging options mean that in the near future visitors to Chicago can expect to find a greater range of possibilities to suit their personalities and their pocketbooks.

During the week, Chicago's busy convention market, individual business travelers, and a small minority of tourists fill the city's hotels to capacity. Since Chicago's hospitality industry caters first and foremost to the business traveler, the hotels tend to empty out by Friday. Many hotels are sometimes willing to reduce prices on the weekends to push up their occupancy rates. Still, the hotel industry has been so strong in Chicago in recent years that you won't find reservation agents as willing or able to wheel and deal as they once were. You never know, however, when some huge convention will gobble up all the desirable rooms in the city even on the weekends, so you're wise to book a room well in advance whenever you plan to visit.

If the city has a slow season, it's the depth of winter, when outsiders tend to shy away from the cold and the threat of being snowed in at O'Hare. Serious bargain hunters may choose to visit then. If you'd like to watch your pennies but the idea of sightseeing in a heavy down coat doesn't appeal to you, another option is to stay in a less expensive hotel—perhaps not right on the Magnificent Mile—during the week and move into swell digs for the weekend finale.

The rates given below are per night and do not include taxes, nor do they take into account corporate or other discounts. Prices are always subject to availability and vary seasonally (the lower rates tend to be offered January through March and other off weekends). If you're traveling alone, remember to ask if the hotel has special rates for single occupancy.

RESERVE IN ADVANCE Whatever hotel or hotels you choose, regardless of season, making reservations well in advance will help ensure you get the best rate available. While toll-free phone numbers have been provided for the hotels reviewed below, you may find better rates by calling the hotel's reservations office directly. Most hotels have check-in times somewhere between 3 and 6pm; if you are going to be delayed, call ahead and reconfirm your reservation to prevent cancellation.

CORPORATE DISCOUNTS Most hotels offer discounts of roughly 10% to individuals who are visiting Chicago on business. To qualify for this rate, your company usually must have an account on file at the hotel; in some cases, however, you may only be required to present some perfunctory proof of your commercial status, such as a business card or an official letterhead, to receive the discount. It never hurts to ask.

RESERVATION SERVICES You can check on the latest rates and availability, as well as book a room, by calling the **Illinois Reservation Service** (☎ 800/491-1800). The 24-hour service is free. Another reservation service is **Hot Rooms** (☎ 800/468-3500 or 773/468-7666; www.hotrooms.com), which offers discounts at selected downtown hotels. The 24-hour service is free, but if you cancel a reservation once it's been booked, you're assessed a $25 fee. For a copy of the annual *Illinois Hotel-Motel Directory*, which also provides information about weekend packages, call the **Illinois Bureau of Tourism** at ☎ 800/2CONNECT.

BED & BREAKFAST RESERVATIONS A centralized reservations service called **Bed & Breakfast/Chicago Inc.,** P.O. Box 14088, Chicago, IL 60614 (☎ 800/375-7084 or 312/951-0085; fax 312/649-9243; E-mail: BNBChicago@aol.com), lists more than 70 accommodations in Chicago. The possibilities range from rooms in private homes or apartments to guest houses or inns. Rates generally run from $75 to $125 a night (continental breakfast included), but the service also offers several accommodations that are considerably more pricey. Another service, **Heritage Bed & Breakfast,** 75 E. Wacker, Ste. 3600, Chicago 60601 (☎ 800/431-5546 or 312/857-0800), lists hosted and unhosted private accommodations throughout the area. The staff also will provide "concierge" services for dinner reservations, theater tickets, and car rentals.

ACCESSIBILITY Most hotels are prepared to accommodate travelers with physical disabilities, but you should always inquire when you make reservations to make sure the hotel can meet your particular needs. Older properties, in particular, may not have been able to adapt their structures to meet current requirements or may have limited numbers of specially equipped rooms.

A WORD ABOUT SMOKING Most hotels offer rooms or entire floors for non-smokers. If it's important to you, be sure to specify if you want a smoking or non-smoking room when you make your reservation. Many hotels have now become so sensitive to this issue that the person taking your reservation may ask you which type of room you prefer.

1 Best Bets

- **Best Historic Hotel: The Drake,** 140 E. Walton Place (☎ 800/55-DRAKE), is a master at combining the decorous charm of yesteryear with every modern convenience.

- **Best for Business Travelers:** The attention to detail and level of service you will find at both the **Ritz-Carlton,** 160 E. Pearson St. (☎ **800/621-6906**) and the **Four Seasons,** 120 E. Delaware Place (☎ **800/332-3442**) make them the hotels of choice for discerning business executives.
- **Best for a Romantic Getaway:** Its small size, European flavor, and soft, intimate rooms give the **Tremont,** 100 E. Chestnut St. (☎ **800/621-8133**), an edge in the romance category.
- **Best Trendy Hotel:** The new designer **Hotel Allegro,** 171 W. Randolph St. (☎ **800/643-1500**), has made a splash in the Loop with all the panache of a night-club: black-clad staff, booming pop music in the lobby, and splashes of color in the guest rooms.
- **Best Views:** This one's a toughy, so consider several hotels for their mix of lake and city views—the **Swissôtel,** 323 E. Wacker Dr. (☎ **800/654-7263**); the **Four Seasons, The Drake,** the **Ritz-Carlton,** and the **Holiday Inn—Chicago City Centre,** 300 E. Ohio St. (☎ **800/HOLIDAY**). Peering over the Elevated tracks, the new **Silversmith,** 10 S. Wabash St. (☎ **800/2CROWNE**), in the Loop, offers a distinctly urban vista.
- **Best for Families:** With every room a suite, the **Embassy Suites,** 600 N. State St. (☎ **800/362-2779**), is ideal for families looking for a little more space than the typical hotel room provides. The in-room Nintendo, indoor pool, and location near some popular kid-friendly cats—Michael Jordan's, Planet Hollywood, and the Hard Rock Cafe—should keep junior happy, too.
- **Best Budget Hotels:** Although a little off the beaten path, the **City Suites Hotel,** 933 W. Belmont Ave. (☎ **800/248-9108**); the **Surf Hotel,** 555 W. Surf St. (☎ **800/787-3108**); and the **Park Brompton Inn,** 528 W. Brompton St. (☎ **800/727-5108**), all located on the North Side, are spotless, cheap, and convenient to public transportation.
- **Best Location:** Most visitors will be more than happy with the location of any hotel on the Magnificent Mile of North Michigan Avenue.
- **Best Hotel Restaurant:** Chef Sarah Stegner has won awards and praise for her artfully presented French cuisine in the top-notch **Dining Room at the Ritz-Carlton.**
- **Best Health Club:** The fitness center at the **Four Seasons** is sublime, with dark paneling, a discreet staff, and a columned pool area.
- **Best Hotel Pool:** With its dazzling all-tile junior Olympic-size pool constructed in 1929, the **Inter-Continental,** 505 N. Michigan Ave. (☎ **800/327-0200**), takes this award easily.
- **Best for Travelers with Disabilities:** Despite its age and size, the **Palmer House Hilton,** 17 E. Monroe St. (☎ **800/HILTONS**), has the rooms (25 specially equipped) and the record (a recent convention of 3,000 visually impaired people and 600 Seeing Eye dogs) to top the list.

2 The Loop

Strictly speaking, "downtown" in Chicago means the Loop—the central business district, a six- by eight-block rectangle enveloped by elevated tracks on all four sides. An outer circle beyond this literal loop of tracks is bounded on the north and west by the Chicago River and its south branch, forming an elbow on two sides; on the east by Michigan Avenue running along the edge of Grant Park; and on the south by the Congress Expressway. Within these confines are the city's financial institutions, trading markets, and municipal government buildings, making for, as you might

Central Chicago Accommodations

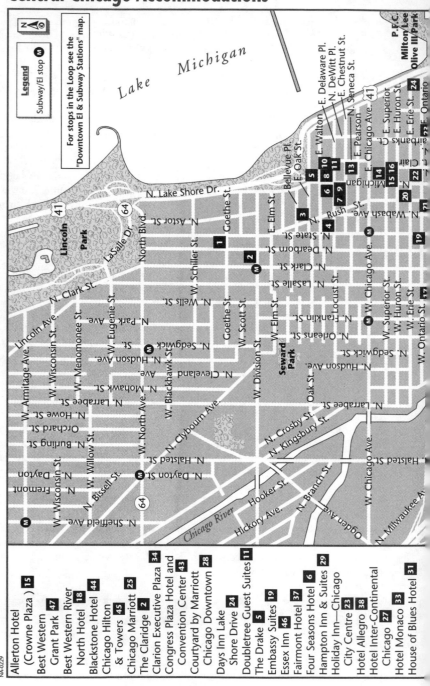

Legend

Ⓜ Subway/El stop

For stops in the Loop see the "Downtown El & Subway Stations" map.

Lake Michigan

Lincoln Park

Seward Park

Chicago River

E. Delaware Pl.
N. DeWitt Pl.
E. Chestnut St.
N. Seneca St.
E. Walton
E. Pearson
E. Chicago Ave.
E. Superior
E. Huron St.
E. Erie St.
E. Ontario
Fairbanks Ct.
N. St. Clair

P.F.C.
Milton Lee
Olive III Park

E. Delaware Pl.
E. Oak St.
Bellevue Pl.
E. Elm St.
E. Scott St.

N. Lake Shore Dr.
N. Astor St.
N. State St.
N. Dearborn St.
N. Clark St.
N. LaSalle St.
N. Wells St.
Rush St.
N. Wabash Ave.
Michigan

Goethe St.
W. Schiller St.
W. Scott St.
W. Elm St.
W. Division St.
Oak St.

N. Sedgwick St.
N. Hudson Ave.
N. Cleveland Ave.
N. Mohawk St.
N. Blackhawk St.
W. North Ave.
W. Eugenie St.
W. Menomonee St.
W. Wisconsin St.
W. Armitage Ave.
Lincoln Ave.

N. Park Ave.
N. Orleans St.
N. Franklin St.
Locust St.
W. Chicago Ave.
W. Superior St.
W. Huron St.
W. Erie St.
W. Ontario Ave.

W. Chicago Ave.
N. Larrabee St.
N. Halsted St.
N. Kingsbury St.
N. Crosby St.
N. Clybourn Ave.
Hooker St.
Hickory Ave.
N. Branch St.
Ogden Ave.
N. Milwaukee Av.

W. Howe St.
N. Larrabee St.
Orchard St.
N. Burling St.
N. Halsted St.
N. Willow St.
N. Bissell St.
N. Dayton St.
N. Wisconsin St.
Fremont
N. Dayton
N. Sheffield Ave.

41
64

Allerton Hotel (Crowne Plaza) **15**
Best Western Grant Park **47**
Best Western River North Hotel **18**
Blackstone Hotel **44**
Chicago Hilton & Towers **45**
Chicago Marriott **25**
The Claridge **2**
Clarion Executive Plaza **34**
Congress Plaza Hotel and Convention Center **43**
Courtyard by Marriott Chicago Downtown **28**
Days Inn Lake Shore Drive **24**
Doubletree Guest Suites **11**
The Drake **5**
Embassy Suites **19**
Essex Inn **46**
Fairmont Hotel **37**
Four Seasons Hotel **6**
Hampton Inn & Suites **29**
Holiday Inn—Chicago City Centre **23**
Hotel Allegro **38**
Hotel Inter-Continental Chicago **27**
Hotel Monaco **33**
House of Blues Hotel **31**

1 2 3 4 5 6 7 8 9 10 11 13 14 15 16 20 21 22 24

60

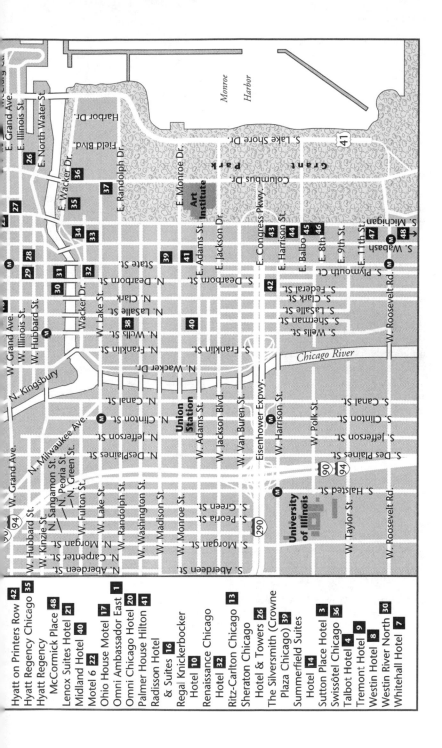

Hyatt on Printers Row 42
Hyatt Regency Chicago 35
Hyatt Regency
McCormick Place 48
Lenox Suites Hotel 21
Midland Hotel 40
Motel 6 22
Ohio House Motel 17
Omni Ambassador East 1
Omni Chicago Hotel 20
Palmer House Hilton 41
Radisson Hotel
& Suites 16
Regal Knickerbocker
Hotel 10
Renaissance Chicago
Hotel 32
Ritz-Carlton Chicago 13
Sheraton Chicago
Hotel & Towers 26
The Silversmith (Crowne
Plaza Chicago) 39
Summerfield Suites
Hotel 14
Sutton Place Hotel 3
Swissôtel Chicago 36
Talbot Hotel 4
Tremont Hotel 9
Westin Hotel 8
Westin River North 30
Whitehall Hotel 7

61

expect, quite a lot of hustle and bustle Monday through Friday. Come Saturday and Sunday, however, the Loop is pretty dead, despite the fact that it is also home to major music and theater venues and is near the Art Institute.

The Loop has an interesting selection of old Chicago hotels, no longer in the first rank perhaps, but with plenty of charm and character, and of undeniable convenience for those who prefer to be at the center of the city.

VERY EXPENSIVE

Renaissance Chicago Hotel. 1 W. Wacker Dr. (at State St.), Chicago, IL 60601. ☎ **800/ HOTELS-1** or 312/372-7200. Fax 312/372-0093. 553 units. A/C MINIBAR TV TEL. $270–$310 deluxe double; $340–$360 Club Level double; $500–$2,500 suite. Weekend rates $179 double. AE, CB, DC, DISC, JCB, MC, V. Subway/El: Brown Line to State/Lake or Red Line to Washington/State. Valet parking $26 with in/out privileges; self-parking $15 with in/out privileges.

Despite several name changes, the Renaissance is still one of the most upscale hotels in the city, located at the top of State Street, just across the bridge from the Magnificent Mile and steps from the Loop's attractions. The hotel embraces its location with bay windows offering stunning views of the river and the towers of North Michigan Avenue. The rooms are tasteful and rather understated—perfectly suited to the business travelers who are the hotel's bread and butter. If you're spending your own hard-earned dollars, however, you can probably find something with a little more pizzazz or charm elsewhere. Hair dryers and a single terry cloth robe (Isn't that just the way to start a squabble?) are placed in every bathroom, along with the usual lotions and fine soaps. Rooms also are furnished with in-room coffeemakers. Club Level rooms, located on the top four floors, are half a room larger and have their own concierge in a private lounge, where complimentary continental breakfast and evening hors d'oeuvres and pastries are served. Because of its proximity to the Loop theater district, the Renaissance frequently offers weekend packages featuring show tickets.

Dining/Diversions: The Great Street Restaurant and Bar, with its contemporary American menu and view over the Chicago River, is the hotel's main dining room and a popular lunch spot for Loop office workers. Another restaurant, Cuisines, specializes in lunches and dinners with a Mediterranean flavor. The Lobby Court serves cocktails and tea—to the sounds of piano music or a live jazz trio most nights.

Amenities: Concierge, 24-hour room service, newspaper delivery, twice-daily maid service, complimentary shoe shine. One nice break: no telephone surcharge for toll-free, collect, or credit-card calls or for incoming faxes. A 24-hour Kinko's Business Center is located in the hotel. Also available is an indoor swimming pool with skylights, plus a fully equipped health club, including sauna and whirlpool, with complimentary chilled water, juices, and fresh fruit.

The Silversmith (Crowne Plaza Chicago). 10 S. Wabash St. (at Madison St.), Chicago, IL 60690. ☎ **800/2CROWNE** or 312/372-7696. Fax 312/372-7320. 143 units. A/C MINIBAR TV TEL. $229–$329 double. Suites start at $329. Special rates from $169. AE, DC, DISC, MC, V. Subway/El: Brown, Green, or Orange Line to Madison/Wabash or Red Line to Washington/State. Valet parking $21 with in/out privileges.

With apologies for the bad pun, you might call the Silversmith something of a hidden gem. The landmark Romanesque Revival building, designed by the celebrated firm of D.H. Burnham and Company, was built in 1897 to serve the jewelry and silver trade on Wabash, still known as the city's Jeweler's Row. Despite an unlikely location fronting the Elevated tracks, the building was completely restored on the outside and gutted and refinished on the inside and turned into a new eight-floor boutique hotel, which opened in 1998.

Rooms come in varying configurations, with 11-foot-high ceilings, large picture windows draped with velvety curtains, handsome Frank Lloyd Wright–inspired fixtures, and homey bedding. For the most part, double-paned glass windows mute the sound of the trains that run directly outside many of the rooms. Each of the oversize bathrooms is equipped with a hair dryer, lighted cosmetic mirror, and a telephone. Business travelers have a nice setup: Rooms have a well-lit work area with an ergonomic chair, a pullout desk drawer to accommodate a laptop, three dual-line speaker phones, dataport connections, and voice mail. Other extras include CD players, irons and ironing boards, in-room safes, and coffeemakers. Nearly half of the rooms are suites, and guests staying in club-level rooms have access to a private lounge.

Dining: On the ground floor of the hotel is an upscale deli called Ada's, and there's also lobby-level lounge with a fireplace.

Amenities: Concierge, limited room service, fitness room, and business center.

EXPENSIVE

Clarion Executive Plaza. 71 E. Wacker Dr. (at Wabash Ave.), Chicago, IL 60601. ☎ **800/ 621-4005** or 312/346-7100. Fax 312/346-1721. 417 units. A/C MINIBAR TV TEL. $169–209 double. Weekend rates $149 double. AE, DISC, MC, V. Subway/El: Brown Line to State/Lake or Red Line to Washington/State. Valet parking $20 with 24-hour in/out privileges.

This hotel is very modern, with a fabulous location on the river, facing the Magnificent Mile. The rooms are furnished in tasteful contemporary detail. Room rates are higher than at comparable Loop hotels, but at the Executive Plaza you are paying extra for the favored location and, perhaps, for the spaciousness of the rooms. The rooms have either a city or a river view. Tower-level rooms, where guests are treated to turn-down service, robes, and complimentary breakfast and cocktails in the restaurant, are priced slightly higher. One nice safety feature: only guests are allowed access to the hotel's guest-room floors. All rooms are equipped with coffeemakers, hair dryers, in-room safes, and irons and ironing boards.

Dining: The Executive Plaza has a restaurant, sidewalk cafe, and lounge.

Amenities: Concierge, fitness center, business center, and room service until midnight.

Hyatt on Printers Row. 500 S. Dearborn St. (at Congress Pkwy.), Chicago, IL 60605. ☎ **800/233-1234** or 312/986-1234. Fax 312/939-2468. 161 units. A/C MINIBAR TV TEL. $200–300 double; $550–$600 suites. Weekend rates (available Fri–Sun) $109 single or double. AE, CB, DC, DISC, ER, JCB, MC, V. Subway/El: Brown Line to Library/Van Buren or Red Line to Harrison/State. Valet parking $23 with in/out privileges; self-parking $16 with in/out privileges.

The Hyatt on Printers Row is in a national historic landmark amid buildings erected in the years immediately following the Great Fire. The hotel actually consists of three joined buildings; guests enter through a turn-of-the century building constructed for the Morton Salt Company. The discreet and tasteful lobby is decorated with Prairie-style light fixtures, mahogany paneling, and richly colored upholstered furniture. All guest rooms, which are generously sized with lofted ceilings, come with two TVs and two phones, hair dryers, coffeemakers, irons, and ironing boards. Live plants in the rooms also give them a homey feel. For business travelers, the Hyatt offers extras such as video cassette players, newspaper delivery, express continental breakfasts, and workstations with computer modem jacks, all for an additional $15 per night. The Hyatt is an easy walk from the Art Institute, Grant Park, Orchestra Hall, the Sears Tower, the Harold Washington Library Center, and the city's financial district.

Dining: The Hyatt's Prairie restaurant is one of the best in the city (see chapter 6, "Dining," for a full review).

Amenities: Limited room service, laundry/valet services, express checkout, complimentary coffee or tea daily for Gold Passport members, and free daily newspapers in lobby. The Hyatt has a small fitness room in the basement; for more extensive offerings, there's a Bally's health club nearby where guests can purchase a day pass for $10. The hotel also has a business center.

Midland Hotel. 172 W. Adams St. (at LaSalle St.), Chicago, IL 60603. ☎ **800/621-2360** outside Illinois, or 312/332-1200. Fax 312/332-5909. 387 units. A/C TV TEL. $195–$259 double; $350–$575 suite. Weekend package $129–$159 per night. AE, CB, DC, DISC, JCB, MC, V. Subway/El: Brown Line to Quincy. Self-parking in a nearby lot about $17.

If you arrive in Chicago by train and are traveling light, you could easily walk to the Midland Hotel, a few short blocks across the river from Union Station. Once a private men's club, the Midland is now primarily a business hotel, though it's also a good base for visitors who wish to concentrate on the many attractions and distractions of the Loop. Architecture buffs will appreciate the cases of artifacts in the lobby and the hotel's location, next door to a Philip Johnson–designed skyscraper and around the corner from the landmark Rookery. The hotel's two-story lobby is narrow but grandiose, designed primarily to speed guests to their rooms or to the public spaces. A number of deluxe rooms with large seating areas and king-size beds are available.

The hotel's meeting facilities are legitimate curios in their own right, worth a detour; each meeting room is designed in the manner of a famous Chicago architect— Wright, Sullivan, and Adler among them.

Dining: The Midland has one restaurant, the Ticker Tape Bar and Bistro, an art-deco dining room.

Amenities: Guests receive complimentary copies of the *Wall Street Journal* at the front desk. The hotel also has limited room service, a concierge, a fitness center, and a 24-hour business center. The Midland offers its regular business clients membership in a corporate travel program called the Lion's Share, which allows members to upgrade their rooms at no added cost (depending on availability) and entitles them to special rates.

Palmer House Hilton. 17 E. Monroe St. (at State St.), Chicago, IL 60690. ☎ **800/ HILTONS** or 312/726-7500. Fax 312/917-1707. 1,639 units. A/C MINIBAR TV TEL. $175–$305 double; $300–$1,200 suite. Weekend rates (including continental breakfast) from $129. AE, CB, DC, DISC, JCB, MC, V. Subway/El: Red Line to Monroe/State. Valet parking $21.25 with in/out privileges; self-parking across the street $15.25.

Guests enter the Palmer House at either Monroe or State street and pass through the hotel's ground-floor arcade of shops and restaurants. Escalators lead to the second-floor lobby, an absolutely cavernous room with a gilded, mural-covered ceiling. The hotel is definitely something out of the past, with furnished elevator landings and wide, spacious hallways (unfortunately the ceilings were lowered to accommodate a sprinkler system). Rooms are large, bright, and well furnished but not especially luxurious, and the smallish bathrooms have been redone in marble. While views are nothing to speak of, the location is ideal for visiting the downtown theaters and museums. With a hotel this enormous, convention business is the lifeblood of the Palmer House. The hotel's top two floors, called the Palmer House Towers, are a private executive area where rooms cost slightly more.

Dining/Diversions: The hotel has four restaurants and bars, including Trader Vic's, and a new theme restaurant called The Big Downtown, which plays up the city's history and even has handmade elevated trains following overhead tracks.

Amenities: Room service and complimentary *USA Today* delivery weekdays. For $8 per day, guests can use the health club, which has an indoor swimming pool and whirlpool, indoor chipping/driving cages, and a golf simulator. The hotel has a business center, shopping arcade, and an airline ticket desk.

MODERATE

○ **Hotel Allegro.** 171 W. Randolph St. (at LaSalle St.), Chicago, IL 60601. ☎ **800/ 643-1500** or 312/236-0123. Fax 312/236-3177. 483 units. A/C MINIBAR TV TEL. $145–$175 double; $185–$295 suite. AE, CB, DC, DISC, MC, V. Subway/El: Washington on all lines. Valet parking $20 with in/out privileges.

The former venerable Bismarck Hotel has been revamped as a hotel you might not expect to find in this town. Under the fashion-forward direction of the Kimpton Group, which operates a small chain of European-style hotels on the West Coast and is developing several other properties in Chicago, the hotel reopened its doors in March 1998, after a $31 million top-to-bottom renovation. It's located in the middle of the financial district, across from City Hall and blocks from the flagship Marshall Field's. Though the hotel may be too much for stuffy types, it's a fun alternative to the sober Chicago hotel scene—plus a good value. Walking into the whimsically designed lobby is like stepping into a cartoon, with its cobalt blue French velvet, Chinese red velour sofas, dark mahogany paneling, and harlequin-patterned carpets. The hotel's sound system pumps jazz and contemporary pop throughout the lobby and elevators. The guest rooms are modest in size and regrettably still retain the building's old plumbing, but they come equipped with two-line phones, voice mail, modem ports, CD players, and fax machines. Suites have terry robes and VCRs. The Allegro has a concierge, limited room service, and a business center. There's a small exercise room, but for $10 guests can use a fitness center across the street. There's a hotel lounge with a nightly complimentary wine service and a full-service Italian restaurant, 312 Chicago.

Hotel Monaco. 225 N. Wabash Ave. (at Wacker Dr.), Chicago, IL 60601. ☎ **800/397-7661** or 312/960-8500. Fax 312/960-1883. 193 units. A/C MINIBAR TV TEL. $125 double; $174 suite. AE, CB, DC, DISC, MC, V. Valet parking available.

Aesthetes now have another alternative when booking a hotel in traditionally conservative Chicago with the late 1998 opening of the Hotel Monaco, another offering from the San Francisco–based Kimpton Group. This stylish yet moderately priced hotel is the result of a total renovation of the former Oxford House. The colorful, French Deco–inspired guest rooms have fax machines and two-line phones with dataports. Amenities include room service, a concierge, and an exercise room. Complimentary morning coffee and evening wine are served, and there's a full-service restaurant and lounge on site.

3 Along South Michigan Avenue

Unlike North Michigan Avenue—the "Mag Mile"—South Michigan Avenue is less about glamour and more about old Chicago. Running the length of Grant Park, South Michigan Avenue is ideal for a long city stroll, passing grand museums, imposing architecture, and the park's greenery and statuary. Two blocks to the west is State Street, address of the giant flagship stores of Marshall Field's and Carson Pirie Scott & Co. The lodging possibilities on the avenue fit all budgets.

EXPENSIVE

Chicago Hilton and Towers. 720 S. Michigan Ave. (at Balbo Dr.), Chicago, IL 60605. ☎ **800/HILTONS** or 312/922-4400. Fax 312/922-5240. 1,543 units. A/C MINIBAR TV TEL.

$185–$345 double. Weekend rates $129–$145 main hotel, $159–$175 Tower. Junior suites start at $245. AE, CB, DC, DISC, JCB, MC, V. Subway/El: Red Line to Harrison/State. Valet parking $21; self-parking $19.

Mammoth it may be, but the Chicago Hilton and Towers is easily the loveliest place to stay in the southern section of the city. From its gray-and-white marble lobby with sweeping staircase to the ubiquitous fresh flower arrangements, the Chicago Hilton takes its job as a luxury hotel seriously. Located 5 blocks from the Art Institute, the Chicago Hilton is only a 10-minute walk from the Shedd Aquarium, Field Museum, and Adler Planetarium. If you're in town for a concert or festival in Grant Park, the location is ideal.

As a result of an astounding $185 million renovation in 1985 that doubled the typical room size, many of the standard rooms have two bathrooms, a real treat when traveling with a companion or family. One of the marble baths has a tub, and the other, a shower. The hotel's Tower section, which was renovated in 1995, consists of three floors of rooms with separate registration area, upgraded amenities (including hair dryers, bathrobes, irons, and ironing boards), and a lounge open from 6am to 11pm, serving complimentary continental breakfast and evening hors d'oeuvres.

Dining/Diversions: The Hilton's four restaurants offer everything from prime aged steaks and an extensive selection of single-malt scotch at Buckingham's to snacks and sandwiches at the Fast Lane Deli. Kitty O'Sheas is an impressively authentic Irish pub with live Irish folk music and sing-alongs. The Sunday buffet brunch is very popular.

Amenities: Concierge, 24-hour room service, complimentary *USA Today* delivery weekdays, and complimentary transportation to the Magnificent Mile. The hotel also has a complete fitness center, featuring a lap pool with glass doors opening to a deck in summer, an indoor track, two hot tubs, a sauna, a steam room, massage, aerobics, and a host of exercise machines (there's an $11 per day fee for the latter). The Chicago Hilton also maintains a boggling amount of convention space, which often handles the overflow from conventions at McCormick Place. There's also a business center. Several shops, including a florist, lease space in the hotel.

MODERATE

Best Western Grant Park. 1100 S. Michigan Ave. (at 11th St.), Chicago, IL 60605. ☎ **800/528-1234** or 312/922-2900. Fax 312/922-8812. 172 units. A/C TV TEL. $118–$125 double. AE, DC, DISC, ER, JCB, MC, V. Subway/El: Red Line to Roosevelt/State. Valet parking $12 with in/out privileges.

Although no longer the bargain it was during its years as a dive called the Ascot, the Best Western Grant Park offers various weekend packages that fit many a traveler's budget. The regular rates are also reasonable. The recently renovated rooms are clean and modern but pretty much your standard roadside lodging variety. Minisuites have kitchenettes, with refrigerators and coffeemakers. The hotel has a fitness room, dry sauna, and a rooftop swimming pool. The Best Western is located on a rather desolate stretch of Michigan Avenue. That said, the location is served by a bus stop and the Roosevelt El station a couple of blocks away. Many of the rooms have wonderful views (especially the 01 and 02 corner rooms) of Navy Pier, Monroe Harbor, and the Museum Campus, which is a short walk away across the street in Grant Park. Room service is available from 7:30am to 9:30pm from the Sunflower Restaurant, which is on the premises.

Blackstone Hotel. 636 S. Michigan Ave. (at Harrison St.), Chicago, IL 60605. ☎ **800/622-6330** or 312/427-4300. Fax 312/427-4736. 250 units. A/C TV TEL. $109 double. Rates include continental breakfast. AE, CB, DC, DISC, JCB, MC, V. Subway/El: Red Line to Harrison/State. Valet parking $15 with in/out privileges; self-parking about $6 half a block away.

When a suitable location was needed for the banquet scene in the movie *The Untouchables,* the Blackstone Hotel was the clear choice. Al Capone once actually holed up at the old Metropole Hotel, a mile or so farther south, but the Blackstone is of the same era. Makers of a host of other films, including *The Hudsucker Proxy, The Package,* and *The Babe,* evidently also found themselves attracted to the Blackstone's period style. A dozen presidents have slept at the hotel, but it's not likely another will visit anytime soon. Most of the rooms are large and comfortable enough, but the hotel has certainly seen better days. Bathrooms are quite small. But you can't beat the price for first-rate views and location. Many rooms look out on Navy Pier and the harbor lighthouse to the north, Grant Park with its fountain and gardens, plus the Field Museum, Shedd Aquarium, and Adler Planetarium. The Blackstone provides guests with a complimentary newspaper and a simple continental breakfast each morning. The hotel also has a game room and a small fitness room.

Congress Plaza Hotel and Convention Center. 520 S. Michigan Ave. (at Congress Pkwy.), Chicago, IL 60605. ☎ **800/635-1666** or 312/427-3800. Fax 312/427-3307. 842 units. A/C TV TEL. $125–$195 double. Special rates start at $99–$129 double. AE, CB, DC, DISC, MC, V. Subway/El: Red Line to Harrison/State. Valet parking $18 with in/out privileges; self-parking in several nearby lots.

Operating since the days of the World's Columbian Exposition, which opened near Hyde Park in 1893, the Congress has a colorful history. The hotel was once a favorite venue for presidential political conventions, at least among candidates named Roosevelt. Teddy opened his Bull Moose convention at the Congress in 1912, and cousin FDR accepted the Democratic nomination here in 1932. Taking a look around, I think it's fair to say the Congress has seen better days. It looks downright shabby today, although it has a few remnants of its former glory (such as the lobby's mosaic ceiling). In parts of the hotel, the hallways are cavernous and dim. Many of the guest rooms appear as though they've been frozen in another era, with furniture that looks like it hasn't been changed since the 1970s. Some rooms have missing tile in the bathroom and spots on the carpet. The hotel has been updating rooms with new carpet and wallpaper, new mattresses, and improved bathrooms. One thing the Congress does have going for it is the clear eastern view of Lake Michigan and Grant Park. The hotel also has a restaurant, bar, game room, and small exercise room.

Essex Inn. 800 S. Michigan Ave. (at 8th St.), Chicago, IL 60605. ☎ **800/621-6909** or 312/939-2800. Fax 312/922-6153. 255 units. A/C MINIBAR TV TEL. $115–$145 double. Weekend rates start at $79. AE, CB, DC, DISC, MC, V. Subway/El: Red Line to Harrison. Valet parking $9 with in/out privileges.

The Essex is far from fancy, but it's a good medium-priced choice, well managed and accommodating. To attract weekend visitors, the Essex often offers particularly imaginative special packages that might include tickets to a Bears football game or passes to the Art Institute (subject to availability). Rooms are clean and of a decent size, if decidedly no-frills (the closet has no door, just a space in the wall).

4 The East Side

The term East Side is a relatively new one and is used to describe the high-rise/high-rent district that is east of Michigan Avenue, south of the river, and north of Grant Park. Don't be surprised if Chicagoans look at you a little funny when you ask directions to the East Side: It has yet to find its way into the geographical lexicon of the city. Most natives don't seem to have any name for the area at all. Don't expect happening restaurants or great stores; the area is essentially one of elite hotels, residential towers, and office buildings. The East Side is definitely a luxury "privacy zone," and the hotels here make the most of that mandate.

VERY EXPENSIVE

Fairmont Hotel. 200 N. Columbus Dr. (at Lake St.), Chicago, IL 60601. ☎ **800/527-4727** or 312/565-8000. Fax 312/856-1032. 692 units. A/C MINIBAR TV TEL. $279–$329 double. Weekend rates begin at $139. AE, CB, DC, DISC, JCB, MC, V. Subway/El: Brown, Orange, or Green Lines to Randolph. Valet parking $26 with in/out privileges.

The sleek pink-granite outline of the 45-story Fairmont Hotel gives notice of the deluxe environment within. Guest rooms have an upscale residential feel with contemporary furnishings and sitting areas. Special attention has been lavished on the beds, which are covered with 200-count supercale sheets, comforter-thick bedspreads, and feather pillows (alternatives are available for guests who are allergic). Nearly three-quarters of the beds are king or queen beds, and they're extra long so that tall guests won't be left with legs dangling. Every room is furnished with electric shoe polishers and a range of media and hi-tech equipment, including a two-line phone, TV and stereo system, fax machine, and a spread of recent magazines. Bathrooms are marble, with separate vanity areas and shower stalls, two-line telephones, and even a swivel TV. Although the hotel is only a block from the river and not far from Grant Park, it still feels a little bit lost in this cluster of office towers. You're not completely isolated, however, as the hotel is connected to the city's underground pedway system, through which you can walk all the way to Marshall Field's on State Street without stepping outside.

Dining/Diversions: Entertainment is a specialty of the Fairmont. Among the restaurants and bars are Entre Nous, a fine-dining restaurant with a French-flavored continental cuisine (jacket and tie required); Primavera Ristorante, an informal Italian restaurant featuring the Primavera Singers and a cute children's menu fashioned by youngsters; and Metropole, an art-deco lounge considered one of the top spots on the city's jazz and cabaret circuit. The Lobby Bar serves afternoon tea.

Amenities: Concierge, 24-hour room service, 1-hour pressings, fur vaults, and on-site florist, who does all of the lovely arrangements in the hotel. One of the top health clubs in the city, Athletic Club Illinois Center, is connected to the hotel, offering aerobics, racquet sports, lap pool, rock-climbing wall, European spa, and basketball court (where you might catch Michael Jordan, one of the club's more famous members, working out); hotel guests can use the facilities for a $10 fee. The nine-hole Illinois Center golf course is across the street.

Hyatt Regency Chicago. 151 E. Wacker Dr. (east of Michigan Ave.), Chicago, IL 60601. ☎ **800/233-1234** or 312/565-1234. Fax 312/565-2966. 2,019 units. A/C MINIBAR TV TEL. $295–$320 double; $295 Regency Club double. Special weekend rates $139. AE, CB, DC, DISC, JCB, MC, V. Subway/El: Brown, Orange, or Green Lines to Randolph. Valet parking $26 with in/out privileges.

Occupying two tall modern towers connected by a glass skyway, the Hyatt Regency is a convention hotel on a mega scale. In fact, it's the largest hotel in the city and the biggest Hyatt in the world. On the upside, if you're desperate to find a room, it's hard to believe this place is ever completely sold out. But on the downside, the walk from the front desk to your room may seem more like a trek across the Himalayas. The lobby, in the east tower, covers half an acre and rises three stories to a greenhouse roof. At the center, a moat surrounds one of the hotel's restaurants.

In 1996, the Hyatt completed the final phase of a $21 million renovation of everything from the ballrooms and corridors to the guest rooms in both towers. The healthy-size rooms are contemporary and fresh and decorated nicely with black-and-white photos of Chicago landmarks and contemporary cherry wood furniture. Bathrooms have been upgraded with new ceramic tile. All rooms are equipped with

---

① Family-Friendly Hotels

Chicago has plenty of options for families on the go. The new **Hampton Inn & Suites** *(p. 83)* keep the kids in a good mood with a pool, Nintendo, and proximity to Michael Jordan's Restaurant. Parents like the fact that children under 18 stay for free. Kiddies also stay for free at the **Holiday Inn–Chicago City Centre** *(p. 79)*, which also has a large outdoor pool and is near Navy Pier and the beach.

When you want a little extra room to spread out, both the **Doubletree Guest Suites** *(p. 75)* and **Embassy Suites** *(p. 81)* offer affordable ways to travel en masse (and keep your sanity).

All of the guest rooms at **Summerfield Suites** *(p. 80)* come equipped with VCRs, and the hotel maintains a video library with children's selections. Both Summerfield and the Hampton Inn provide a complimentary breakfast each morning that offers a simple, budget-conscious way to start the day.

Location is the strong suit of the **Radisson Hotel & Suites** *(p. 79)*, situated just off Michigan Avenue and around the corner from Niketown. The hotel also has an outdoor rooftop pool.

Of course, a luxury hotel like the **Four Seasons** *(p. 72)* can afford to be friendly to all of its guests, and kids are indulged, too, with little robes, balloon animals, Nintendo, and milk and cookies. The hotel also has a wonderful swimming pool.

---

hair dryers, irons and ironing boards, and in-room safes. FedEx boxes are stored in the closets in case you have an immediate shipping need. The hotel also has a plan called "Perfect Stay" that guarantees delivery of any request within 15 minutes. The Hyatt's special "Business Plan" rooms have a workstation, a telephone line with no extra access charge that is also PC compatible, and an in-room fax machine. On the top two floors of the west tower, 72 rooms are reserved for the Regency Club, with its private lounge serving a complimentary continental breakfast in the morning and cocktails and hors d'oeuvres at the end of the workday.

Dining/Diversions: The Hyatt has six restaurants and cafes, including the Big Brasserie and Bar, with views of the Wrigley Building and Tribune Tower across the river, and Stetson's steak house.

Amenities: Concierge, 24-hour room service, video checkout, newspaper delivery service, and nightly turndown and coffeemakers upon request. A shopping arcade, beauty salon, and business center are on the premises. In addition, the hotel is connected by an underground tunnel to the Illinois Center office and retail complex. The Illinois Athletic Club is a half block away ($10 fee for adults) with Olympic-size swimming pool.

EXPENSIVE

✪ **Swissôtel Chicago.** 323 E. Wacker Dr. (at Columbus Dr.), Chicago, IL 60601. ☎ **800/654-7263** or 312/565-0565. Fax 312/565-9930. 632 units. A/C TV TEL. $165–$229 double; from $325 suite. Weekend rates begin at $79. AE, CB, DC, DISC, JCB, MC, V. Subway/El: Brown, Orange, or Green Lines to Randolph. Valet parking $26 with in/out privileges.

Attention, all you golf nuts out there. If you stay at the Swissôtel Chicago, you're virtually an elevator ride away from a round of golf. That's right, the nine-hole, par-three Illinois Center Golf awaits you next door to this modern Swiss-owned hotel, smack-dab in the middle of town. For those of you who prefer your greens in your salad, the

Swissôtel also has plenty to offer. The views from the guest rooms—either of the lake or of Grant Park—are out of this world, and the fitness center atop the triangular tower has just about every gizmo you could possibly want. The hotel was recently freshened up with bold, contemporary furnishings and artwork (Mapplethorpe and Matisse prints adorn the corridors and guest rooms). The guest rooms are lovely and generously sized, with coffeemakers and marble bathrooms that have separate glass showers, scales, and terry robes. The hotel's location is equally convenient to the Loop, North Michigan Avenue, and River North. The rooms are well-equipped for business travelers, too, with oversize writing desks and ergonomic chairs, separate sitting areas, two-line telephones, and oversize TV monitors with access to financial markets. The hotel also boasts a winning weekend package (at $139), which includes a pair of Art Institute passes, buffet breakfast, complimentary valet parking, and free use of the hotel health club.

An underground pedestrian concourse links the hotel to the Illinois Center's shops, restaurants, and office and residential buildings.

Dining/Diversions: The hotel has three restaurants and bars, including the newly ensconced Palm Restaurant, a steak-and-lobster house famed for its caricatures of local and national celebs.

Amenities: Multilingual concierge, 24-hour room service, complimentary turndown service, newspaper delivery on request, complimentary shoe shine. Guests can use the health club, which has a full-size pool and exercise classes, all with sweeping views, for an $8 daily fee. There's also a full business center.

5 Near North & the Magnificent Mile

Along the Magnificent Mile—a stretch of Michigan Avenue running north of the Chicago River to Oak Street—is where you'll find most of the city's premium hotels. The location can't be beat.

VERY EXPENSIVE

✪ **The Drake.** 140 E. Walton Place (at Michigan Ave.), Chicago, IL 60611. ☎ **800/ 55-DRAKE** or 312/787-2200. Fax 312/787-1431. 535 units. A/C MINIBAR TV TEL. $275–$365 double; $335–$450 executive floor; from $595 suite. Weekend rates start at $219 with continental breakfast. AE, CB, DC, DISC, ER, JCB, MC, V. Subway/El: Red Line to Chicago/State. Valet parking $25 with in/out privileges.

The Drake telegraphs elegance. Fronting East Lake Shore Drive with a prominent rooftop marquee that's a signature on the city's skyline, the landmark building recently celebrated its 75th anniversary as Chicago's favorite hotel. The Drake looks over a quiet park and the sands of Oak Street Beach. Touches such as the padded benches in the elevators and the abundant fresh flowers make it clear the Drake is an eminently civilized hotel. Some of the other special details are the extravagantly wide hallways, the new marble floors in the guest bathrooms, and the polished woodwork throughout. For all its old-time glamour, the hotel seems a bit dowdy when placed next to brash newcomers such as the glitzy Four Seasons, but this, of course, is part of the Drake's charm.

The typical bedroom, styled with a few Oriental touches, is generous in size and furnished comfortably with a king-size bed; a sitting area with a well-stuffed settee, armchair, and coffee table; and a bathroom stocked with robes. The 51 rooms and suites on the two slightly more expensive "executive floors" provide such additional amenities as personalized stationery, a generous continental breakfast in a private lounge, free cocktails and hors d'oeuvres, plus a daily newspaper and valet assistance

Near North & River North Accommodations

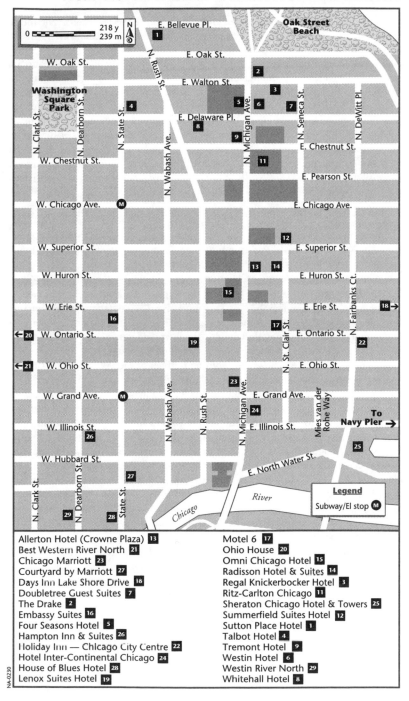

Allerton Hotel (Crowne Plaza) **13**
Best Western River North **21**
Chicago Marriott **23**
Courtyard by Marriott **27**
Days Inn Lake Shore Drive **18**
Doubletree Guest Suites **7**
The Drake **2**
Embassy Suites **16**
Four Seasons Hotel **5**
Hampton Inn & Suites **26**
Holiday Inn — Chicago City Centre **22**
Hotel Inter-Continental Chicago **24**
House of Blues Hotel **28**
Lenox Suites Hotel **19**

Motel 6 **17**
Ohio House **20**
Omni Chicago Hotel **15**
Radisson Hotel & Suites **14**
Regal Knickerbocker Hotel **3**
Ritz-Carlton Chicago **11**
Sheraton Chicago Hotel & Towers **25**
Summerfield Suites Hotel **12**
Sutton Place Hotel **1**
Talbot Hotel **4**
Tremont Hotel **9**
Westin Hotel **6**
Westin River North **29**
Whitehall Hotel **8**

NA-0230

for polishing shoes, packing and unpacking, and securing theater tickets. The fourth and fifth floors have a lounge open to all guests, where soft drinks and fresh-brewed coffee and tea are available without charge.

Dining/Diversions: Even if you don't stay at the hotel, visit the Palm Court for afternoon tea ($15.50) or an after-dinner drink. The hotel's restaurants include the Oak Terrace, a large dining room serving up American fare and some great views of the lake and Michigan Avenue; the Cape Cod Room, a local favorite for seafood; and Coq d'Or, a piano bar featuring local legend Buddy Charles and an eclectic menu.

Amenities: All rooms are provided with fresh fruit, Swiss chocolates at turndown, and newspapers each morning. Other services include 24-hour room service, laundry valet, and express checkout. Facilities include fitness center, meeting rooms, business center, shopping arcade including the recently relocated Chanel boutique, barbershop, and airline ticket office.

○ **Four Seasons Hotel.** 120 E. Delaware Place (at Michigan Ave.), Chicago, IL 60611. ☎ **800/332-3442** or 312/280-8800. Fax 312/280-9184. 343 units. A/C MINIBAR TV TEL. $395–$435 double; $430–$3,000 suite. Weekend rates from $325. AE, CB, DC, DISC, JCB, MC, V. Subway/El: Red Line to Chicago/State. Valet parking $25 with in/out privileges; self-parking $8.25–$14.25. Pets are accepted.

If you're serious about seeing the sights in Chicago, you may not want to book a room at the Four Seasons, one of the top hotels in the country, if not the world. The swanky hotel pampers guests so much that you may not feel inclined to leave the building (not a bad idea when you're staying at the priciest place in town). It's a kick to see what new luxuries hotels will come up with: Guests arriving at the Four Seasons after long-haul flights are greeted with special jet-lag tea steeping in their rooms.

The hotel is ensconced above the shops and offices of the 900 N. Michigan Ave. building, the city's most upscale vertical mall. An atmosphere of elegance pervades the lobby and public spaces. My only objection is the smallness of the front desk and the concierge station, a situation that can create minor mayhem during the busier times.

The snazzy guest rooms have English furnishings, custom-woven carpets and tapestries, and dark-wood armoires. Everything is oh-so-tasteful. Each room has three phones, a VCR, and windows that open to let in the fresh air. The marble bathroom is equipped with a hair dryer, a lighted makeup mirror, oversize towels, scales, and other indulgences from cotton balls to terry robes. Kid-friendly services include little robes, balloon animals, Nintendo, and milk and cookies. The hotel has kept up its sky-high standards with a recent $5.2 million renovation that brightened up the soft goods in many of the rooms. Being the tallest hotel in Chicago, the Four Seasons also boasts spectacular views.

Dining/Diversions: An 18-foot-high white marble fountain marks the entrance to the opulent Seasons Restaurant, which serves elegantly presented American and continental fare for lunch and dinner. Sunday brunch is a favorite at the hotel. A piano player is usually on duty in the Seasons Lounge, where afternoon tea is served. The English study–style bar is equipped with a humidor.

Amenities: Concierge, 24-hour room service, dry cleaning, newspapers at the front desk each morning, twice-daily maid service, complimentary shoe shine, and express checkout. Guests receive shopping cards good for discounts and special services at the mall's stores. A video library is available through the concierge. The hotel's health spa is exquisite. The 50-foot indoor pool is framed by Roman columns and sheltered by a skylight, and the whirlpool accommodates 20 people. The fitness center also has a sundeck, the city's only outdoor jogging track, a steam room, and a sauna, in addition to all the standard equipment. The staff can arrange for a massage and personal trainers. Squash and tennis are available nearby. The hotel also has a business center and beauty salon.

Omni Chicago Hotel. 676 N. Michigan Ave. (at Huron St.), Chicago, IL 60611. ☎ **800/ 843-6664** or 312/944-6664. Fax 312/266-3015. 347 units. A/C MINIBAR TV TEL. $179–$199 suite. Weekend rates $169–$189. AE, DC, DISC, MC, V. Subway/El: Red Line to Grand/State. Valet parking $25 with in/out privileges.

With its large domed chandeliers, marble floors, and beautiful flower arrangements, the Omni Chicago, a business hotel with a fresh, modern interior, is a lovely place to stay. All the rooms are suites with one king-size or two double beds. Each suite, tastefully decorated in deep greens and burgundies, has a living room with a sitting area, a dining table, a wet bar, and a refrigerator, all of which is divided from the bedroom by a set of French doors. About a third of the suites have pullout sofas. Nice extras in the rooms include a phone in the bathroom, two TVs, coffeemakers, safes, and umbrellas. All rooms have fax machines. While they're on the small side, bathrooms have lots of counter space and come with the niceties you'd expect from a luxury hotel: hair dryers, makeup mirrors, and robes. You can request a corner suite with lots of light and views looking down Michigan Avenue, for $20 extra. One drawback can be the lobby, located three floors up from the street, which can get jammed as guests attempt to board elevators loaded up with luggage.

Dining: Off the lobby, overlooking Michigan Avenue with floor-to-ceiling windows, is the American/Mediterranean restaurant Cielo. There's live music on weekends. The attractive bar is stocked with cigars.

Amenities: Concierge, 24-hour room service, and courtesy car available for trips within the downtown area. Executive service offers complimentary newspaper, breakfast, and shoe shine. The Omni has a full health club, including a lap pool and a whirlpool.

✪ Ritz-Carlton Chicago. 160 E. Pearson St., Chicago, IL 60611. ☎ **800/621-6906** or 312/266-1000. Fax 312/266-1194. 435 units. A/C MINIBAR TV TEL. $355–$425 double; $475–$3,500 suite. Weekend rates $245–$355. Subway/El: Red Line to Chicago/State. Valet parking $27 with in/out privileges; self-parking $17.50 with no in/out privileges. Pets are accepted.

Perched high atop Water Tower Place, the Ritz-Carlton casts a soothing presence on guests as they're deposited into the airy 12-floor lobby. Everything is so civilized. Even the lobby rest rooms are furnished with cloth hand towels, a coat rack, and fresh flowers. The Ritz often stacks up against the best hotels in the world (*Condé Nast Traveler* readers recently named it third best in the world), and, as you might expect, the quality of the accommodations is of the highest caliber. The standard guest rooms, which just underwent a $6 million spruce up, have a king-size bed and a bright, bold color scheme. The furnishings—a love seat, a cherry armoire concealing the TV, and a desk—are traditional without being heavy. All rooms are equipped with fax machines. The generously sized marble bathroom is stocked with a robe and a hair dryer. Suites have an additional living area furnished with a nice sofa and chair, a writing desk, a second TV and VCR, and a stereo. Lake views cost more but are spectacular. Guests staying in Premiere Suites, a new level of service that opened last year on the 30th floor, are treated to a gratis wardrobe pressing upon arrival, personalized stationery, and daily deliveries of fresh flowers.

Whether or not you stay here, the Ritz-Carlton is an elegant place for afternoon tea, served at 2:30 and 4:30pm in the lobby. At one end of the lobby is the Greenhouse restaurant, designed with a glass roof and wall that seems to jut out over the city. By the way, this particular Ritz-Carlton is part of the Four Seasons chain, not the Ritz-Carlton one.

Dining: Among the hotel's four restaurants is The Dining Room, one of the best restaurants in Chicago, if not the country, serving French cuisine in an elegant atmosphere, under the direction of chef Sarah Stegner. A cigar bar is equipped with a humidor. The Sunday brunch includes a special buffet for children replete with M&Ms, macaroni and cheese, and pizza.

Amenities: Concierge, 1-hour pressing, overnight dry cleaning and shoe shine, 24-hour business services. Dog walking can be arranged through the concierge. Complimentary coffee is served in the lobby and complimentary newspapers are available on request. Guests also receive a discount card offering savings at many retailers in Water Tower Place, which is an elevator ride away. The skylit indoor lap pool and complete health and exercise facility are free of charge to Carlton Club members, $10 for other guests. An extensive range of spa services and body treatments, including herbal wraps and aroma therapy massage, is also available.

✪ **Whitehall Hotel.** 105 E. Delaware Place (west of Michigan Ave.), Chicago, IL 60611. ☎ **800/323-7500** or 312/944-6300. Fax 312/944-8552. 221 units. A/C MINIBAR TV TEL. $259–$349 double; from $459 suite. Weekend packages from $245. AE, CB, DC, DISC, JCB, MC, V. Subway/El: Red Line to Chicago/State. Valet parking $24 with in/out privileges.

Built in 1928 as a residential building, the Whitehall was converted to a hotel in 1972. After a full renovation, the Whitehall officially reopened in 1994, and has since won accolades as a favored small luxury hotel. The hotel has a traditional ambiance; the cozy lobby is filled with paintings of horses and dogs and embroidered pillows on the couches. The front desk is rather small but adds to the feel of staying at an English manor. Guest rooms are furnished in the style of 18th-century England, with Oriental accents, and include such niceties as in-room safes, scales and makeup mirrors in the marble bathrooms, terry robes, and shopping bags, a nice way to consolidate your purchases from an excursion on North Michigan Avenue, which is only half a block east. The Whitehall has joined the pack of Chicago hotels catering to the business crowd. Its top four floors, called the Club Floors, house a business center and a private lounge. The rooms on those floors as well as all suites have four-poster beds, irons and ironing boards, umbrellas, and fax machines, and guests receive complimentary breakfast.

Dining/Diversions: Whitehall Place, an American bistro, occasionally features live piano entertainment. Pluses include sidewalk dining and afternoon tea.

Amenities: Concierge, 24-hour room service, courtesy sedan drop-off at downtown locations, overnight shoe shine, exercise room, business center (for upper floors).

EXPENSIVE

Chicago Marriott. 540 N. Michigan Ave. (at Ohio St.), Chicago, IL 60611. ☎ **800/228-9290** or 312/836-0100. Fax 312/836-6938. 1,172 units. A/C MINIBAR TV TEL. $199–$349 double; $625 suite. Weekend rates $149–$179. AE, CB, DC, DISC, MC, V. Subway/El: Red Line to Grand/State. Valet parking $25 with in/out privileges; self-parking within 1 block $16.

The Marriott has taken a lot of knocks for its immense size (almost 1,200 rooms) and dreary facade on the Magnificent Mile, but the hotel has been taking some strides to present a friendlier face with a $20 million renovation scheduled to wrap up in early 1999. When the construction crews clear out of the neighboring lots, the Marriott will be abutted by a new Nordstrom department store and adjoining retail mall, a Disney-Quest entertainment center, and several other hotels and retail projects. The makeover began in the lobby, where the old atrium has been eliminated to give the hotel's entryway a more intimate feel and better flow; mahogany wainscoting and marble accents have been added. Of course, none of these changes may matter to you if you're not a fan of hotels this large.

Although many of the guest rooms were still looking pretty fresh, with only a few of the signs of wear and tear, they're also getting refurbished, particularly the smallish bathrooms, which will be brightened up and retiled. All rooms are equipped with coffeemakers, irons and ironing boards, and hair dryers. High-tech amenities include voice mail and dataport connections for laptop computers. Views from the 20th floor and higher are superb, with floor-to-ceiling windows looking onto the lake.

Dining/Diversions: Two restaurants and two bars add to the hotel's self-contained environment.

Amenities: Concierge, room service (6am to midnight), same-day valet service, complimentary newspaper delivery. The fitness center has two outdoor platform basketball courts, a sliver-size indoor swimming pool with whirlpool and exercise facilities, and a sundeck. The Marriott also has a Kinko's copy shop, ample meeting space, and a beauty salon.

Doubletree Guest Suites. 198 E. Delaware Place (at Seneca St.), Chicago, IL 60611. ☎ **800/424-2900** or 312/664-1100. Fax 312/664-9881. 345 units. A/C MINIBAR TV TEL. From $265 double suite. Weekend and summer promotional rates start at $169. Children under 18 stay free in parents' room. AE, CB, DC, DISC, JCB, MC, V. Subway/El: Red Line to Grand/State. Valet parking $23.50 with in/out privileges.

The Doubletree, a full-service all-suite hotel spread over 25 floors, last year put the finishing touches on a top-to-bottom renovation. Each suite features a separate living room and bedroom, deluxe bath, refrigerator, two telephones (with dataports), and two TVs. Living rooms are furnished with pullout sofas. The price of the suite depends on bed size, floor (some have spectacular lake views for $10 extra), and furnishings. The rooms here aren't huge, but the hotel is spotless, and the Doubletree has not skimped on some of those little extras that can make a big difference, such as warm chocolate chip cookies presented to arriving guests, fresh flowers in the lobby, in-room coffeemakers, and complimentary newspaper every morning. The hotel is convenient to Water Tower Place, Bloomingdale's, and the Museum of Contemporary Art.

Dining: Among its restaurants is the outstanding Park Avenue Cafe, the Chicago outpost of a New York original, and Mrs. Park's Tavern, a casual American bistro with a sidewalk cafe.

Amenities: Concierge, valet service, express checkout, business center, laundry room, check cashing, health club with sauna, whirlpool, and pool on the 30th floor with great views (a great perch to view fireworks at Navy Pier).

✪ Hotel Inter-Continental Chicago. 505 N. Michigan Ave. (at Grand Ave.), Chicago, IL 60611. ☎ **800/327-0200** or 312/944-4100. Fax 312/944-1320. 844 units. A/C MINIBAR TV TEL. $189–$299 double. AE, DC, DISC, JCB, MC, V. Subway/El: Red Line to Grand/State. Valet parking $26.50 with in/out privileges.

Rivaling the best hotels in Chicago, the Hotel Inter-Continental is installed in two adjoining buildings at the foot of the Magnificent Mile. The Inter-Continental truly shines in the south tower, a landmark built in 1929 as a luxury men's club. The feeling here is both elegant and intimate, with perhaps six rooms to a floor, each one spacious, comfortable, and attractively decorated in muted tones. The bathrooms have sleek pedestal sinks, and separate tubs and glass-enclosed showers. Each room also has a refrigerator, three dual-line phones, a thick terry robe, coffeemaker, hair dryer, iron and ironing board, and a large desk.

The recently updated guest rooms in the more modern north tower (formerly the Forum), are clean and pleasant and have similar amenities, but are more standard. North tower rooms also don't have the views that the other structure offers.

Dining/Diversions: The Inter-Continental has both a casual restaurant, Cafe 525, and a fine Mediterranean one, The Boulevard. The Salon lobby lounge serves tea by day, and cocktails by night, with jazz entertainment.

Amenities: Concierge, 24-hour room service, business services, twice-daily maid service, weekday newspaper, complimentary overnight shoe shine. The hotel has a health club on the premises, with a spectacular all-tile, junior Olympic-size indoor pool, a gymnasium, an aerobics room, saunas, whirlpools, and steam and massage rooms. Use of the pool is complimentary for guests, but the hotel charges $10 per day or $13.50 for the entire stay for use of the fitness center. Even if you don't have occasion while at the Inter-Continental to throw a party for 200 of your closest friends, take a peek at the richly decorated ballrooms; they're some of the most beautiful around.

Regal Knickerbocker Hotel. 163 E. Walton St. (half a block east of Michigan Ave.), Chicago, IL 60611. ☎ **800/621-8140** or 312/751-8100. Fax 312/751-9663. www.regal-hotels.com/chicago. 305 units. A/C MINIBAR TV TEL. $235–$275 double; Club rooms from $275; $305–$1,100 suite. Weekend packages from $165. AE, DC, DISC, MC, V. Subway/El: Red Line to Chicago/State. Valet parking $24 with in/out privileges; self-parking $16.25.

Built in 1927 and at one time part of Hugh Hefner's Playboy empire, the Knickerbocker is an old Chicago hotel famed for its illuminated ballroom floor. It has a superb location, across the street from the Drake and a block from Oak Street Beach. A recent $16 million renovation has given all the guest rooms a well-deserved fresh look. While the rooms aren't especially spacious, they are warm and homey. Bathrooms are small but nicely done with marble floors, glass shelving, and pedestal sinks, and are furnished with a robe. Rooms have a pair of dual-line phones with dataport links. Views are often rather dismal, but you can catch a glimpse of the lake in all rooms ending in 18, and corner rooms (ending in 17, 28, or 35) look onto Michigan Avenue. Club-level rooms are furnished with marble entries and chaise lounges and have CD players. Club-level guests are served complimentary breakfast, coffee, and munchies in a second-floor lounge.

Dining/Diversions: The hotel restaurant serves up eclectic fusion cuisine, and the lobby bar specializes in 40 different blends of martinis. A live pianist performs in the bar Wednesday through Saturday.

Amenities: Concierge, 24-hour room service, newspaper delivery, express checkout, fitness room.

Sheraton Chicago Hotel & Towers. 301 E. North Water St. (at Columbus Dr.), Chicago, IL 60611. ☎ **800/325-3535** or 312/464-1000. Fax 312/329-6929. 1,204 units. A/C MINIBAR TV TEL. $199–$289 double. Tower rates $229–$409 double. Weekend rates start at $129. AE, CB, DC, DISC, MC, V. Subway/El: Brown, Orange, or Green Line to State/Lake. Valet parking $24 with in/out privileges.

A major convention center during the workweek, the Sheraton Chicago is a full-service leisure hotel on the weekends. Being the newcomer, the Sheraton had last pick of locations, and for that reason, it's a little out of the way compared with its peers—east of North Michigan Avenue along the Chicago River. Enormous only begins to define the Sheraton, and I acknowledge a certain wariness on my part of mega-hotels. That said, the guest rooms are a nice size. A room with a king-size bed, for example, has a sitting area with a love seat and a chair. The views are pretty, and there's access to a riverfront promenade from the lower level. The bathrooms, on the other hand, are of the no-frills variety, with claustrophobically low ceilings. Each room is stocked with an iron and ironing board, a coffeemaker, and a hair dryer. The 34-story building also has 75 tower rooms. Guests in the tower rooms receive perks such as a separate check-in, nightly turndown, terry robes, and an optional butler service. They also have access to a courtesy lounge, where a complimentary continental breakfast and cocktail hour are offered daily.

Dining/Diversions: The Streeterville Grille and Bar features steaks and seafood with an Italian flavor. The Riverside Café is more informal, and the Spectator Sports Bar provides a club atmosphere for sports fans. At ground level, along the river promenade both inside and out, is the Esplanade Express Café.

Amenities: Concierge, 24-hour room service, complimentary newspaper delivery. Nintendo is available, as is a fully equipped health club, indoor pool and sundeck, boat-docking facilities, and a complete business center with all services.

Talbott Hotel. 20 E. Delaware Place (between Rush and State sts.), Chicago, IL 60611. ☎ 800/621-8506 or 312/944-4970. Fax 312/944-7241. 146 units. A/C MINIBAR TV TEL. $220 double; $325–$395 suite. Rates include continental breakfast. AE, DC, DISC, MC, V. Subway/El: Red Line to Chicago/State. Self-parking $14.75 across the street in the Bloomingdale's building.

The family-owned Talbott is another one of those small, European-style gems that seem to thrive in Chicago, despite the city's reputation as a convention town. Constructed in the 1920s as an apartment building, the Talbott was converted to a hotel in 1989 (and was just treated to a $4 million freshening up). Rooms are spacious, modern, and up-to-date with voice mail and modem hookups. Bathrooms have phones and hair dryers. All of the suites and about a quarter of the guest rooms are equipped with kitchens. The wood-paneled lobby, decorated with leather sofas and velvety arm chairs, two working fireplaces, and numerous French horns used for fox hunts, is inviting. Superstitious types may want to note that the hotel does have a 13th floor.

Dining/Diversions: The cozy bar and complimentary evening coffee and cookies in the winter create an intimate, collegial atmosphere. A sidewalk cafe peps up the hotel during the summer months.

Amenities: Concierge, room service daily until 10pm, nightly turndown, and complimentary newspaper delivery. On rainy days, umbrellas are set out in the lobby for the use of guests. Guests have access to a nearby health club for $11 per visit.

✪ Tremont Hotel. 100 E. Chestnut St. (1 block west of Michigan Ave.), Chicago, IL 60611. ☎ 800/621-8133 or 312/751-1900. Fax 312/280-1304. 130 units. A/C MINIBAR TV TEL. $185–$225 double; from $355 suite. AE, CB, DC, DISC, MC, V. Subway/El: Red Line to Chicago/State. Valet parking $24.

If you're looking for a small European-style hotel, the Tremont has great appeal. Built in 1921 as an apartment building and converted to a hotel in the late 1970s, the Tremont possesses an intimacy that most of its competitors lack. The cozy lobby with a fireplace sets the mood from the start. While almost every other hotel seems to be going with a color scheme of burgundy and forest green, the Tremont in its recent renovations opted for a very cheery yellow and green, a nice complement to the bright sunshine that fills many rooms. The furnishings are tasteful without being somber; the striped duvets and shower curtains are especially nice. Every room comes with a fax machine, VCR, and CD player, and guests are furnished with robes. About a dozen rooms have kitchenettes.

Dining: The new steak-and-chops restaurant off the lobby, the memorabilia-filled Iron Mike's Grille, is co-owned by legendary former Chicago Bears football coach Mike Ditka.

Amenities: 24-hour room service and small fitness center (as well as access to nearby health club for $12 a day).

Westin Hotel. 909 N. Michigan Ave. (next door to the Hancock Center), Chicago, IL 60611. ☎ **800/228-3000** or 312/943-7200. Fax 312/943-9347. 751 units. A/C MINIBAR TV TEL. $195–$279 double; $500–$1,200 suite. AE, CB, DC, JCB, MC, V. Subway/El: Red Line to Chicago/State. Valet parking $26 with in/out privileges.

For the price you could probably do better than the Westin, but renovations may make it a more attractive option. The lobby and public spaces have been given a fresh look, and the hotel continues to renovate its rather modest and dated guest rooms, which pale in comparison to the Westin's Magnificent Mile neighbors. Rooms have been given marble entryways, as have the recently expanded bathrooms. The hotel has an ideal location, at the top of North Michigan Avenue across the street from the John Hancock Building and Bloomingdale's and a short walk to Oak Street Beach. The rooms here are well proportioned with contemporary furnishings, including king-size beds with dressing benches and sitting chairs and small desks with chairs. For an extra $30, you may want to spring for one of the Tower rooms, with high ceilings that offer a roomier feel and views of Oak Street Beach or Michigan Avenue. With the business traveler in mind, the Westin offers "office" rooms, which are equipped with a larger desk, fax machine, and ergonomic chair.

    Dining/Diversions: Food and drink options include the full-service Chelsea Restaurant and a lobby cafe.

    Amenities: Concierge, 24-hour room service, valet service, fitness room with sauna, business center.

MODERATE

Allerton Hotel (Crowne Plaza). 701 N. Michigan Ave. (at Huron St.), Chicago, IL 60611. ☎ **800/621-8311** outside Illinois or 312/440-1500. Fax 312/440-1819. www. crowneplaza.com. 383 units (will increase to 420 units after renovation is completed). A/C TV TEL. Before renovation: $129–$149 double; $170–$250 suite. After renovation: $209–$309 double; from $295 suite. AE, CB, DC, DISC, JCB, MC, V. Subway/El: Red Line to Chicago/State. Valet parking $24; self-parking $14; both with in/out privileges.

The Allerton has seen better days. The lobby is a little dingy, the furniture a little worn, and the halls a little dark. The service is not the most genteel (in place of a bell or buzzer, the front desk clerk simply yells to the bellhop). On the other hand, the location can't be beat. With the entrance on Huron, around the corner from Michigan Avenue, the Allerton is at the center of it all. Things should improve here, however, after a $39 million overhaul is completed in the spring of 1999. The hotel is being converted into the flagship hotel of the upscale Crowne Plaza chain. After the renovation (and name change) guests can expect to find an utterly new luxury hotel that intends to compete with the top-of-the-line hotels in town. As part of its transformation, the new Crowne Plaza will get central air (replacing those eyesore window units), a new lobby, and a new restaurant and bar. The guest rooms and suites will give a homey, European-style feel. Decorator touches in the rooms (some of them pretty small) will give the appearance of having your own apartment in the city: antiquish furniture that's a blend of English and Indian styles, potted plants, crown moldings, white shutters on the windows, and pedestal sinks and oversize mirrors in the marble bathrooms. A few of the 57 suites are furnished with working fireplaces. Guests can expect all the perks of a first-rate hotel: 24-hour room service, terry robes, and fancy bath products. For business types, the hotel will offer club-level concierge rooms and a business center. A fitness center will be installed on the hotel's 25th floor.

Days Inn Lake Shore Drive. 644 N. Lake Shore Dr. (at Ontario St.), Chicago, IL 60611. ☎ **800/541-3223** or 312/943-9200. Fax 312/255-4411. 578 units. A/C TV TEL. $149–$239 double. Weekend rates from $109. AE, CB, DC, DISC, JCB, MC, V. Subway/El: Red Line to Grand/State. Self-parking $22 with in/out privileges.

Changes are in store for the Days Inn. New owners are readying a $16 million renovation project, a name change, and a more upscale direction. By early summer 1999, the hotel is scheduled to get an expanded lobby, totally new guest rooms, and an upgraded cafe with alfresco seating. Until then, the lakefront location continues to set the Days Inn apart from the city's other hotels. A large hotel, the Days Inn's more expensive rooms overlook the lake. The hotel is 3 blocks from the newly redeveloped Navy Pier with its Children's Museum, Ferris wheel, and boat cruises. The hotel has a complete fitness center along with an outdoor pool.

❂ **Holiday Inn—Chicago City Centre.** 300 E. Ohio St. (at Fairbanks Ct.), Chicago, IL 60611. ☎ **800/HOLIDAY** or 312/787-6100. Fax 312/787-6238. 500 units. A/C MINIBAR TV TEL. $175 double. Weekend and promotional rates $109–$159. Children under 18 stay free in parents' room. AE, CB, DC, DISC, JCB, MC, V. Subway/El: Red Line to Grand/State. Valet parking $18.50.

Another hotel favored by conventioneers is the Holiday Inn, located north of the Chicago River in an area east of the Magnificent Mile, close to the Ohio Street beach and Navy Pier. Right next door to the hotel is the McClurg Court Sports Complex, where guests may enjoy the facilities—including tennis and racquetball courts, aerobics, indoor pool and whirlpool, and basketball court—free of charge. The hotel also has its own spacious fifth-floor outdoor pool and sundeck. The views are also excellent, with northern views of the Hancock Building and Monroe Harbor. Ever since a $10 million renovation in 1995, the hotel has continued to add amenities to its guest rooms (coffeemakers, hair dryers, and irons and ironing boards), which are clean and up-to-date though pretty basic. The Holiday Inn is a good bet for the budget-conscious family: Kids under 18 stay for free. The hotel has several dining options, including the full-service Centre Cafe, a sports bar, and a bakery deli.

There's a second Holiday Inn in the area, the **Holiday Inn Chicago Mart Plaza,** at 350 N. Orleans St. (☎ 312/836-5000; fax 312/222-9508) in River North. The 528-room hotel is adjacent to the Merchandise Mart and features an eight-story atrium and an indoor pool. Room rates begin at $139.

Lenox Suites Hotel. 616 N. Rush St. (at Ontario St.), Chicago, IL 60611. ☎ **800/ 44-LENOX** or 312/337-1000. Fax 312/337-7217. 325 units. A/C TV TEL. $149 studio; $159–$169 double; $179–$209 junior suite. AE, CB, DC, DISC, JCB, MC, V. Subway/El: Red Line to Grand/State. Valet parking $18.50 with in/out privileges.

Lenox Suites is well suited for business travelers on an extended stay, but its spacious living areas and location halfway between the glossy shops of North Michigan Avenue and the theme restaurant gulch on Ontario Street give it an added appeal to vacationers. Built in the 1920s as an apartment building, the hotel has a mix of room sizes and types, and some of the bedrooms are pretty compact. The hotel was said to have received a renovation in 1995, but the furnishings still look somewhat dated: The rolling TVs are pretty ancient, and while air-conditioning is undeniably a must during humid Chicago summers, the ugly window units are unfortunate. Some nice amenities are the kitchens in all of the rooms and the complimentary muffin, orange juice, coffee, and newspaper delivered each morning. The hotel has a concierge on duty at night, 24-hour room service, a new business center, and a small exercise room. Two restaurants are in the building, Houston's and the Andrews coffee shop.

Radisson Hotel & Suites. 160 E. Huron St. (half a block east of Michigan Ave.), Chicago, IL 60611. ☎ **800/333-3333** or 312/787-2900. Fax 312/787-5158. 341 units. A/C MINIBAR TV TEL. $149–$209 double; from $189 suite. Weekend rates $149–$169. AE, CB, DC, DISC, JCB, MC, V. Subway/El: Red Line to Chicago/State. Valet parking $24.

Recent renovations have improved the Radisson: the lobby has been updated with contemporary furnishings and jazz-age murals; guest rooms have gotten new beds, case goods, and carpeting; and marble bathrooms have been installed. Because sleeping rooms begin on the 14th floor, the Radisson boasts some truly beautiful views of the lake and city. Since the building was built as a condominium, the rooms are spacious. Some of the corner suites have pullout sofas. In-room amenities include a hair dryer, iron and ironing board, coffeemaker, two phones and two lines, a computer modem hookup (built into the lamp for an easy connection), and voice mail. For an additional $30, a guest can upgrade to one of 96 suites, some of which feature microwave ovens. Red Rock Grill is the new Southwestern-style restaurant located off the lobby. The hotel also has a concierge, 24-hour room service, business center, valet service, express checkout, gift shop, fitness center, and outdoor pool.

Summerfield Suites Hotel. 166 E. Superior St. (half a block east of Michigan Ave.), Chicago, IL 60611. ☎ **800/833-4353** or 312/787-6000. Fax 312/787-6133. 120 units. A/C MINIBAR TV TEL. $159 studio suite; $179 executive parlor suite; $199 1-bedroom suite. Weekend rates $149–$169 per night with a 2-night minimum. AE, DC, DISC, MC, V. Subway/El: Red Line to Chicago/State. Valet parking $27 with in/out privileges; self-parking $15 with in/out privileges.

Summerfield Suites completed a $7 million renovation in 1996. What the Summerfield lacks in grand public spaces it makes up for in room size. All of the rooms are suites, and 80% of them have full kitchens, making the Summerfield a good place to consider for long-term stays. All rooms come with coffeemakers, hair dryers, irons and ironing boards. A complimentary full breakfast buffet is served in a seventh-floor dining room. Every suite has a VCR. In addition to hotel valet services, there's also a laundry room where guests can do their own wash. Although the hotel does not have its own restaurant, Benihana of Tokyo is located on the premises; Gino's East pizzeria provides room service. A stairwell from the paneled lobby leads downstairs to the appealing Bookmark Lounge, open from 4:30pm to about 1am. Stocked bookcases line the walls, and complimentary hors d'oeuvres are available during the cocktail hours. The staff is efficient and attentive. Nice extras include the basket of fresh fruit on the reception counter and the small rooftop pool and sundeck. The hotel's biggest convenience may be its location, steps from North Michigan Avenue and 2 blocks from Water Tower Place.

INEXPENSIVE

Motel 6. 162 E. Ontario St. (half a block east of Michigan Ave.), Chicago, IL 60611. ☎ **800/466-8356** or 312/787-3580. Fax 312/787-1299. 191 units. A/C TV TEL. $89 double. AARP discounts available. AE, CB, DC, DISC, MC, V. Subway/El: Red Line to Grand/State. Valet parking $16 with no in/out privileges; self-parking $14.

Just east of North Michigan Avenue, Motel 6 is practically spitting distance from Crate & Barrel and the Tribune Tower. Formerly the Richmont Hotel, its rooms are on the small side, but they're comfortable. The service isn't the Ritz, but then again, neither are the prices. The lobby is clean and bright, and there's a northern Italian restaurant in the building with a sidewalk cafe serving continental breakfast, lunch, and dinner.

6 River North

The name "River North" designates a vast area parallel to the Magnificent Mile. The zone is bounded by the river to the west and south and roughly by Clark Street to the east and by Chicago Avenue to the north. The earthy red-brick buildings that characterize the area were once warehouses of various kinds and today form the core of Chicago's art gallery district. The neighborhood also has spawned many of the city's trendiest restaurants. The hotels here span every price range, from the budget Ohio House Motel all the way up to the luxurious Westin River North.

VERY EXPENSIVE

Westin River North. 320 N. Dearborn St. (at the river), Chicago, IL 60610. ☎ **800/ WESTIN1** or 312/744-1900. Fax 312/527-2664. 424 units. A/C MINIBAR TV TEL. $295–$330 double; $325–$360 river-view room; $650–$2,500 suite. Weekend rates $189–$219. AE, DC, DISC, JCB, MC, V. Subway/El: Brown, Orange, or Green Line to State/Lake. Valet parking $25 with in/out privileges; self-parking $11.

On the northern bank of the Chicago River, the Westin River North has continued to evolve since it ceased being the Hotel Nikko a couple of years ago. Though changes (to the tune of $9 million) in the works have de-emphasized the hotel's unique aesthetic in the guest rooms, the hotel's Japanese sensibility, for the time being, is still apparent from the moment one enters the lobby. In the back of the lobby is a small Japanese garden that separates the Westin from its Riverfront Park, a 300-foot-long landscaped strip between Dearborn and Clark streets. Rooms are getting all new furniture and artwork designed to give them a residential feel. They come with fax machines, three two-line speaker phones with voice mail, coffeemakers, and hair dryers. Bathrooms are furnished with terry robes, makeup mirrors, and upscale bath products. For those who feel like splurging, a suite on the 19th floor more than satisfies, with three enormous rooms, including a huge marble bathroom, black leather couches in the living room, and a large window offering a side view of the river.

Dining/Diversions: The Hana Lounge, sunken in the center of the lobby, is open for drinks and appetizers. Live jazz is offered in the early evening. The excellent Benkay restaurant and its sake bar have been phased out, but a portable sushi counter is open for nibbling at lunch and early evening. The Westin still plays host to an elaborate brunch every Sunday from 10:30am to 2:30pm in its Celebrity Café restaurant.

Amenities: Concierge, 24-hour room service, complimentary shoe shine, business center. The fitness center costs $8 per session (includes shorts, shirt, and socks).

EXPENSIVE

✪ **Embassy Suites.** 600 N. State St. (at State St.), Chicago, IL 60610. ☎ **800/ 362-2779** or 312/943-3800. Fax 312/943-7629. 358 units. A/C MINIBAR TV TEL. $159– $359 king suite; $169–$379 double suite. AE, DC, DISC, JCB, MC, V. Subway/El: Red Line to Grand/State. Valet parking $25 with in/out privileges.

Although it bills itself as a business hotel and does a healthy convention business, the Embassy Suites is also a family-friendly hotel. All 358 suites have two rooms: a living room furnished with a sleeper sofa, a round table, and four chairs, and a bedroom with either a king-size or two double beds. Each room has a TV with video games and a phone with two lines. The suites also have a minikitchen outfitted with a refrigerator, microwave, coffeemaker, and minibar. For an extra $30, guests staying on the newly refurbished VIP floor get nightly turndown service and in-room fax machines and robes. The suites all surround an expansive garden atrium where, at one end, the hotel serves a complimentary cooked-to-order breakfast in the morning and, at the other end, supplies complimentary cocktails and snacks in the evening.

Dining: Off the lobby is an excellent restaurant, Papagus Greek Taverna, and next door, a Starbucks outlet with outdoor seating.

Amenities: Concierge, room service, valet laundry, complimentary *USA Today* delivery weekdays, express checkout. The hotel has an indoor pool along with sauna, whirlpool, and workout room.

House of Blues Hotel, a Loews Hotel. 333 N. Dearborn Ave. (at the river), Chicago, IL 60610. ☎ 800/23-LOEWS or 312/245-0333. Fax 312/245-0504. 367 units. A/C TV TEL. $175–$225 double; $275–$325 suites. AE, DC, DISC, MC, V. Subway/El: Red Line to Grand/State. Valet parking $26.

The House of Blues Hotel, an extension of the blues-themed music venue that opened in Chicago a few years ago, is the first of its kind. Carved out of an office building in Marina Towers, the hotel carries over the arty decor of the nightclub. The decor in the public spaces—by Cheryl Rowley, who also designed the new Hotel Allegro—blends Gothic, Moroccan, and East Indian influences, and includes interesting architectural artifacts, such as ancient panels from an Indian temple. Guest rooms and suites will also feature original artwork. House of Blues creator Isaac Tigrett is a big high-tech believer, so it's no surprise that guest rooms come with two-line phones, CD players, VCRs, fax machines, and Internet access. Other standard amenities are robes and hair dryers. The hotel plans to offer some entertainment-oriented packages that no doubt will be among the hippest in the city.

Dining/Diversions: When it is completed, the House of Blues development will contain a new 26-lane bowling alley; a jazz club; four restaurants, including Smith & Wollensky steak house and the House of Blues restaurant; and a marina with boat rentals.

Amenities: Guests will have access to a huge, new state-of-the-art health club. There is also a business center.

MODERATE

Best Western River North Hotel. 125 W. Ohio St. (at LaSalle St.), Chicago, IL 60610. ☎ 800/528-1234 or 312/467-0800. Fax 312/467-1665. 148 units. A/C TV TEL. $109–$141 double; $173–$295 suite. Weekend rates from $99. AE, CB, DC, DISC, JCB, MC, V. Subway/El: Red Line to Grand/State. Free parking for guests.

This hotel is one of few that is right in the midst of one of the busiest nightlife and restaurant zones in the city. Theme restaurants such as Michael Jordan's and Ed Debevic's are within easy walking distance, as are interesting shops on Wells Street and numerous other more upscale restaurants and art galleries. The rooms are modern and large but no-frills; if you're looking for a reasonably priced place to lay your head, this should do. Rooms come with four pillows and coffeemakers. The hotel also has a (somewhat dingy) all-season rooftop pool and sundeck with sweeping views, a small fitness room, and a ground-floor restaurant called Pizzeria Ora. There's room service from 6am to 10pm.

Courtyard by Marriott Chicago Downtown. 30 E. Hubbard St. (at State St.), Chicago, IL 60611. ☎ 800/321-2211 or 312/329-2500. Fax 312/329-9452. 334 units. A/C TV TEL. $139–$219 double; $249–$279 suite. AE, DC, DISC, MC, V. Subway/El: Red Line to Grand/State. Valet parking $20 with in/out privileges; self-parking $19.

The Courtyard is another big place with the business crowd. Sitting a block north of the river, the hotel's location isn't the most visible, but it is only a couple of blocks from both Michigan Avenue and the Loop. Jazz lovers are in luck: Andy's Jazz Club, a favorite of players around the city, where the first set starts at 5pm, is directly across the street and admits hotel guests for free. The Jazz Record Mart, a treasure trove of jazz and blues recordings, is around the corner on Wabash. Guests have their pick of the dozens of restaurants in River North, including the nearby Tucci Milan and Shaw's Crab House, where they can charge the bill to their room. A standard double room is furnished with a double bed, chair and ottoman, TV, oversize work desk, and two-line phone. King rooms have the added bonus of a sofa bed, and suites come with mini-bars. The standard-issue bathrooms have a separate vanity area. Amenities also include iron and ironing board, hair dryer, and extra pillows. Coffee and daily newspapers are complimentary in the lobby, room service operates until midnight, and the hotel recently added a concierge. There's a cafe serving breakfast and lunch and a bistro serving dinner. An exercise room and pool with a sundeck are located on the sixth floor.

Hampton Inn & Suites. 33 W. Illinois St. (at Dearborn St.), Chicago, IL 60610. ☎ **800/ HAMPTON** or 312/832-0330. Fax 312/832-0333. www.hamptoninn-suites.com. 230 units. A/C TV TEL. $119–$169 double; $139–$239 suite. Children under 18 and 3rd and 4th guests are free. Rates include buffet breakfast. AE, CB, DC, DISC, JCB, MC, V. Subway/El: Red Line to Grand/State. Valet parking $20 with in/out privileges.

This new hotel, conveniently located in the thick of River North, is a welcome addition to the increasingly pricey hotel market in Chicago. The Hampton, which opened last year, has a combination of guest rooms, two-room suites, and studios. The decor takes inspiration from the Prairie architectural style, and the two-story woodsy lobby, with slipcovered furniture and a few Chicago architectural artifacts, feels like a friend's great room. Guest rooms are residential and warm, with framed collages of vintage Chicago postcards on the walls. Each room has a VCR, coffeemaker, iron and ironing board, hair dryer, dataports for modem hookup, and voice mail. One nice surprise is the free local calls. Bathrooms are simple and modestly sized, with a separate vanity outside the bathroom. The apartment-style suites feature galley kitchens with refrigerators, microwave ovens, dishwashers, and cooking utensils. Off the lobby is the Fog City Diner, and a second-floor skywalk connects to a steak house next door. The hotel has a business center, free morning newspaper, valet laundry service and coin-operated machines, an indoor swimming pool, whirlpool, dry sauna, and small exercise room.

INEXPENSIVE

Ohio House Motel. 600 N. LaSalle St. (at Ontario St.), Chicago, IL 60610. ☎ **312/ 943-6000.** Fax 312/943-6063. 50 units. A/C TV TEL. $83 double; $90 king; $100 deluxe double. AE, CB, DC, DISC, MC, V. Subway/El: Red Line to Grand/State. Free parking for guests.

The Ohio House Motel is a real bargain, especially considering its location in one of the hottest entertainment and restaurant districts in Chicago. This is a motel, folks— clean and well maintained, but with none of the luxuries of the Magnificent Mile places just east of here. A real plus is free parking. The breakfast at the Ohio House Coffee Shop, served all day, is on the grand scale, however: the "deuces" special gets you two eggs, two strips of bacon, two sausages, and two pancakes for $3.35. The motel has one suite with a kitchenette.

7 The Gold Coast

The Gold Coast refers to the area beginning approximately at Division Street and extending north to North Avenue, bounded on the west by Clark Street and on the east by the lake. The area encompasses a short strip of some of the city's priciest real estate along Lake Shore Drive. From the standpoint of social status, the streets clustered here are among the finest addresses in Chicago. It's a lovely neighborhood for a stroll among the graceful town houses and the several lavish mansions that remain, relics from an even glitzier past. The hotels here tend to be upscale without hitting the peak that some of the nearby Michigan Avenue hotels reach.

VERY EXPENSIVE

Sutton Place Hotel. 21 E. Bellevue Place (at Rush St.), Chicago, IL 60611. ☎ **800/ 606-8188** or 312/266-2100. Fax 312/266-2141. 246 units. A/C MINIBAR TV TEL. $260–$295 double; $350 Junior Suite for 1, $375 for 2. Weekend rate (including breakfast) $219 double. AE, CB, DC, DISC, MC, V. Subway/El: Red Line to Clark/Division. Valet parking $25.

The Sutton Place stands between the pulsing Rush Street entertainment zone and the posh Gold Coast residential district. The art-decoish lobby is small yet sleek with Robert Mapplethorpe photographs and modern furniture. The guest rooms feel like the apartment of a cool urban friend who always has the latest high-tech toys. The rooms are equipped with TVs with built-in VCRs (a video rental machine is stationed on the fifth floor), CD players, and three phones. The hotel provides some sample CDs, mostly jazz and pop. The generously sized king rooms have a down duvet–covered bed, a sitting chair and ottoman, and a desk with a reading lamp. The bathrooms have the nice combination of glass-enclosed showers and separate sunken tubs; other amenities include a dressing stool in the bathroom, robes and slippers, and a scale. Suites come with built-in safes, two-line speaker phones, and a wet bar. Some of the rooms have floor-to-ceiling windows with city and lake views, and a few of the priciest suites have balconies and terraces. In addition, all of the windows open to let in some fresh air. Kids get special treatment too: cookies and milk at turndown, kid-size robes, and Johnson's bath amenities.

Dining/Diversions: The Brasserie Bellevue, the lobby restaurant and popular out-door cafe, is set up for prime people-watching on Rush Street; most nights a pianist provides entertainment.

Amenities: Concierge, 24-hour room service, complimentary shoe shines, twice-daily maid service, morning newspaper delivery, business center. Car service to the Loop is available early weekday mornings. There's a 24-hour exercise room, and the hotel also offers discounted rates at the Gold Coast Multiplex, a full-service health club with an indoor pool and racquetball and tennis courts. Guests can also borrow a video and riser to do step aerobics in the privacy of their rooms.

EXPENSIVE

Omni Ambassador East. 1301 N. State Pkwy. (2 blocks north of Division St.), Chicago, IL 60610. ☎ **800/843-6664** or 312/787-7200. Fax 312/787-4760. 275 units. A/C MINIBAR TV TEL. $205 double; $245–$450 suite. Weekend rates from $189. AE, CB, DC, DISC, MC, V. Subway/El: Red Line to Clark/Division. Valet parking $24.50 with in/out privileges; self-parking $16.

The Omni Ambassador East blends in discreetly on the tree-shaded corner of State Parkway and Goethe Street in this quiet, residential neighborhood. The modest-size lobby has the feel of an earlier time (the hotel is listed on the National Register of Historic Places), with lots of fresh flowers and Japanese screens in the lounge area. Following a decline throughout the sixties and seventies, the hotel has managed to regain some stature, though it's not in the same league as the Ritz-Carltons, Four Seasons, or Drakes of the world. The rooms are clean and neat, but they have been looking a little tired; an $18 million restoration was launched in late 1997 to bring the hotel up-to-date, from fresh carpeting and drapes to new plumbing and marble bathrooms. No two guest rooms seem to be alike, and some are quite spacious. The Ambassador East has the usual amenities, including terry cloth robes, valet stand, irons and ironing boards, and hair dryers.

Dining: For the past 50 years, celebrities who have come to town to mingle with Chicago's Gold Coast society have done so most publicly from a designated booth in the famed Pump Room (see chapter 6 for a full review).

Amenities: Concierge, 24-hour room service, morning newspaper, overnight shoe shine, beauty salon, and barber. The hotel has a small fitness room, a sundeck, and guests have complimentary use of a health-club facility a couple of blocks away.

MODERATE

The Claridge. 1244 N. Dearborn Pkwy. (1 block north of Division St.), Chicago, IL 60610. ☎ **800/245-1258** or 312/787-4980. Fax 312/787-4069. 163 units. A/C MINIBAR TV TEL. $145 for queen-size bed; $190 for king-size or 2 doubles. Rates include continental breakfast. AE, DC, DISC, JCB, MC, V. Subway/El: Red Line to Clark/Division. Valet parking $21 with in/out privileges.

Built in 1922 as a men's club, the Claridge is a small hotel; the lobby is meant only as a funnel to the rooms or to the French-Japanese–flavored restaurant located in the rear of the building. Thanks to the competent desk staff, what could be a bottleneck functions fluidly. The decor is modern and simple though not luxurious compared to the other European-style boutique hotels in the city. The hotel is gradually renovating rooms, so you may want to ask for a room on a newer floor. Coffeemakers have been added to all of the rooms. The hotel offers a few nice touches, including freshly baked cookies at turndown and daily weather forecasts posted on the elevator landings. Rooms above the eighth floor offer the best views; avoid the dark "king superior" rooms, which look onto the fire escape and have another curtain disguising a wall. Some deluxe accommodations have sitting areas, and three executive suites on the 14th floor have working fireplaces. In the lobby, there's a small yet well-furnished sitting area. Here guests can linger over their complimentary morning newspapers and a continental breakfast. In the morning, a courtesy stretch limo will transport guests anywhere within a 2-mile radius of the hotel. But the Claridge is only a brief stroll to the lakefront and the Oak Street Beach, and even closer to the north end of the Magnificent Mile, just across Division and east of Rush Street.

8 Lincoln Park & the North Side

If you prefer the feel of living amid real Chicagoans in a residential neighborhood, several options await you in Lincoln Park and farther north. Not only do these hotels tend to be more affordable than those closer to downtown, but they also provide a different vantage point from which to view Chicago. If you stay at the Park Brompton Inn or the City Suites Hotel, for example, you can join the locals on a pedestrian pilgrimage to Wrigley Field for a Cubs game. The area is flush with restaurants, and public transportation via the El or buses is a snap.

INEXPENSIVE

✪ **City Suites Hotel.** 933 W. Belmont Ave. (at Sheffield Ave.), Chicago, IL 60657. ☎ **800/248-9108** or 773/404-3400. Fax 773/404-3405. www.cityinns.com. 45 units. A/C TV TEL. $105 double; $119 suite. Rates include continental breakfast. AE, DC, DISC, MC, V. Subway/El: Red Line to Belmont. Parking $8 in nearby lot with in/out privileges.

A few doors down from the elevated train stop on Belmont Avenue, not far from the corner of Sheffield, an enterprising team calling themselves Neighborhood Inns of Chicago has turned a former transient dive into a charming small hotel, something along the lines of an urban bed-and-breakfast. Most of the rooms here are suites, with separate sitting rooms and bedrooms, all furnished with first-rate pieces and decorated in a homey and comfortable style. A bonus—or drawback, depending on your point of view—is the hotel's neighborhood setting. Area locals include everybody from young professional families to gay couples to punks in full regalia. Blues bars, nightclubs, and restaurants abound hereabouts, making the City Suites a find for the bargain-minded and adventuresome. Suites have refrigerators and microwave ovens on request. Room service is available from Ann Sather, a neighborhood institution. The hotel is a $5 cab ride from the Belmont stop of the Blue Line to O'Hare Airport.

✪ Park Brompton Inn. 528 W. Brompton St. (at Lake Shore Dr.), Chicago, IL 60657. **☎ 800/727-5108** or 773/404-3499. Fax 773/404-3495. www.cityinns.com. 52 units. A/C TV TEL. $95–$105 double; $119 suite. Rates include continental breakfast. AE, DC, DISC, MC, V. Subway/El: Red Line to Addison; walk several blocks east to Lake Shore Dr. and then 1 block south. Self-parking $7 in nearby garage with no in/out privileges.

Owned by the same group as the City Suites Hotel and Surf Hotel (below), the Park Brompton is the third and latest property that has been converted into a neighborhood hotel. Located right off Lake Shore Drive, the hotel was built in the 1920s as a hotel and reopened in 1996 after extensive renovations. The hotel has the largest rooms of the three properties and is decorated with an English motif—poster beds, for example—befitting its architectural exterior. Some of the larger suites—the most appealing are those with sun porches—offer butler's pantries with a refrigerator, microwave oven, and wet bar. It's ideally suited for enjoying the North Side and is only a short walk from both Wrigley Field and the lake. The hotel has quickly become a favorite of young residents of the Lakeview neighborhood who can't put up (or don't want to put up) visiting family and friends.

✪ Surf Hotel. 555 W. Surf St. (at Broadway), Chicago, IL 60657. **☎ 800/787-3108** or 773/528-8400. Fax 773/528-8483. www.cityinns.com. 55 units. A/C TV TEL. $95–$105 double; $119 suite. Rates include continental breakfast. AE, DC, DISC, MC, V. Bus: 151 from Michigan Ave., State St. or Union Station, or 156 from LaSalle St.; get off at Sheridan and Surf and walk 1 block west. Self-parking $8.75 in either of two nearby garages with no in/out privileges.

The third Neighborhood Inns of Chicago property is the Surf, a former SRO building situated on a quiet, tree-lined street relatively close to Lake Michigan. The developers have preserved and restored many of the building's vintage 1920s architectural details while making the rooms modern and comfortable. The rooms, including the bathrooms, are immaculate, and rates include a complimentary newspaper and a continental breakfast offering the famed cinnamon rolls from the nearby Swedish restaurant Ann Sather. Refrigerators and microwaves are available upon request.

9 Hyde Park

INEXPENSIVE

Ramada Inn Lakeshore. 4900 S. Lake Shore Dr., Chicago, IL 60615. **☎ 800/228-2828** or 773/288-5800. Fax 773/288-5745. 182 units. A/C TV TEL. $99–$130 double. AE, DC, DISC, MC, V. Bus: No. 6 Jeffry Express to 51st St. and Hyde Park Blvd., then walk 2 blocks; or take the Metra Electric to the 53rd St. Station, then walk about 4 blocks. Free parking.

Hyde Park has been described as a city within a city, and quite accurately so. Site of the Columbian Exposition of 1893 and the birthplace of nuclear fission, it's home to the Museum of Science and Industry, the DuSable Museum of African-American History, architecture by Frank Lloyd Wright, and the culture-packed campus of the elite University of Chicago. Hyde Park can also feel like its own city because of its relative isolation from other attractive Chicago neighborhoods. Many adjacent areas have yet to be touched by urban renewal, and Hyde Park is a 20-minute train ride from downtown (half an hour by express bus). If the idea of staying somewhere less glitzy than the Magnificent Mile appeals to you, though, the Ramada Inn Lake Shore is worth checking out. Bright and very modern, the Ramada has many of the accouterments of a resort, including a large outdoor swimming pool and sun patio. All king and double rooms have coffeemakers; the hotel's 15 suites have minibars, and a couple of special rooms have a pair of TVs and a sofa bed. The restaurant boasts a great view of the Chicago skyline and the lake, most dramatic at night. If you do tire of Hyde Park, the Ramada provides a complimentary shuttle bus to the University of Chicago, State Street, and the North Michigan Avenue shopping and dining district.

10 Near McCormick Place

MODERATE

Hyatt Regency McCormick Place. 2233 S. Martin Luther King Dr. (at 22nd St.), Chicago, IL 60616. ☎ **800/233-1234** or 312/567-1234. Fax 312/528-4000. 800 units. A/C TV TEL. $110–$200 double; $300–$1,000 Regency suites. AE, CB, DC, DISC, JCB, MC, V. Valet parking $24 with in/out privileges; self-park $18; $5–$9 in nearby lots.

The newest major hotel in the city, the Hyatt Regency rises 33 stories from Chicago's ever-sprawling convention center. While the hotel is often solidly booked during trade shows and meetings, it has plenty of rooms to spare during less active months of the year (winter and late summer), so vacationers may find bargains if they are willing to sacrifice the convenience of staying downtown. Although the hotel is only minutes from the Museum Campus, the lakefront, and the Loop, getting around is a little tricky without a car or cab. Guests can board the Metra commuter train for the 10-minute trip downtown. Plans call for courtesy van service to the Loop. The average-size rooms are new and fresh with upbeat, contemporary furnishings. Bathrooms are smallish, with the sink and vanity outside the bathroom.

Dining: The hotel has NetWorks restaurant and lounge as well as a coffee bar.

Amenities: Concierge, 24-hour room service, laundry room, after-hours key-card elevators, fitness room (a bit modest considering size of hotel), sauna, two-lane indoor lap pool, and sun deck.

11 Near O'Hare Airport

The stretch of highway leading to and from O'Hare is lined with lodging choices, some of them quite nice, others not so nice. Combined, they account for more than 6,000 rooms in the immediate vicinity of the airport. Business travelers, especially, find these hotels and motels convenient, but so might people visiting friends or relatives in the suburbs. Those folks, though, need not limit themselves to this one section of Chicagoland to find a good hotel. As much of suburbia has evolved from bedroom community to semi–self-sufficient cities, with office parks popping up not far from residential subdivisions, hotels have moved in. For more information on the suburban hotels, including those near O'Hare, call the toll-free numbers of the major chains, such as Embassy Suites, Hilton, Hyatt, Marriott, Radisson, and Ramada, as well as Howard Johnson, Holiday Inn, Quality Inn, and Travelodge. (See the appendix for a list of toll-free numbers.)

If it's location you're looking for, you can't beat the **O'Hare Hilton** (☎ **800/ HILTONS** or 773/686-8000; fax 773/601-2873), which is the only hotel actually on the grounds of the airport. It's connected to the terminals via underground moving sidewalks. (Sound-resistant windows block out the jet noise.) The 858-room hotel has restaurants, a sports bar, and a health club.

VERY EXPENSIVE

Hotel Sofitel Chicago. 5550 N. River Rd., Rosemont, IL 60018. ☎ **800/233-5959** or 847/678-4488. Fax 847/678-9756. 300 units. A/C MINIBAR TV TEL. $225–$245 double. Weekend rate $99. AE, CB, DC, DISC, JCB, MC, V. Valet parking $12; self-parking $9; both with in/out privileges.

Linked by a heated tunnel to the Rosemont Convention Center, the Hotel Sofitel is part of a French-owned chain now making its appearance in the American market. The lobby recalls the monumental, with its marble floor, muraled walls, and bubbling fountain. Hotel Sofitel, which completed a guest room renovation in early 1998, offers visitors one of the more unique touches at turndown: a bottle of Evian and a single rose. Among the hotel's facilities are two restaurants and a bar, a French bakery, and a health club with a swimming pool.

EXPENSIVE

Westin O'Hare. 6100 N. River Rd., Rosemont, IL 60018. ☎ **800/228-3000** or 847/698-6000. Fax 847/698-6452. 525 units. A/C MINIBAR TV TEL. $139–$225 double. Weekend rate $89. AE, CB, DC, DISC, JCB, MC, V. Valet parking $15 with in/out privileges; self-parking $12.

In addition to its downtown branches, the chain has a Westin Hotel directly adjacent to O'Hare. In decorous, sleek surroundings, guests are offered such distractions as aerobics classes, racquetball courts, Nautilus equipment, and a swimming pool. Each guest room is spacious, with an oversize desk, two telephones, and two TVs (one is in the bathroom). Other facilities include two restaurants and two bars furnished with a humidor. The hotel offers a courtesy shuttle every 15 minutes to the airport.

Dining 6

Famously enthusiastic about their sports teams, Chicagoans share a passion for food, too. And not just the steak-and-potatoes variety. Those days have clearly passed. Chicago has developed a reputation as an increasingly sophisticated restaurant town. A flurry of new establishments has opened over the last few years, both homegrown enterprises such as chef Jean Joho's Brasserie Jo, earning plaudits from critics and diners alike, and eagerly embraced out-of-town operations such as Wolfgang Puck's Spago. The city boasts a number of restaurants—Ambria, Charlie Trotter's, and Everest, to name a few—that can hold their own with the nation's best. Like fans penciling score sheets at Wrigley Field, Chicagoans have learned to track the city's changing culinary landscape in search of the hot new scene, the out-of-the-way gem, the reliable standby.

What they find are restaurants that for the most part mirror the city's neighborhoods. Restaurants **downtown** tend to serve the business diner or the pretheater crowd—efficient places that serve a good meal and get you on your way. On the western fringes of the Loop, right on the way to the United Center where the Bulls and Blackhawks play, a hot new restaurant scene has emerged in the **Randolph Street Market District** with trendy spots existing side by side with many of the city's produce vendors.

Along the **Magnificent Mile** and in the **River North** gallery district—the city's premier restaurant row—the restaurants tend to be high-concept, high-profile places, many owned by the city's leading restaurant mogul, Richard Melman of Lettuce Entertain You Enterprises. He has built an empire of more than two dozen establishments that vary in price and formality from the offbeat foodlife food court to the family-style Maggiano's to the elegant Ambria.

In artsy **Wicker Park,** chefs reflect the neighborhood's creative environs with menus that experiment with an unlikely collision of flavors and ingredients. Restaurants in **Lincoln Park** and the rest of the **North Side** tend to be more intimate storefront operations that often serve less as celebratory destinations than as regular hangouts.

Sometimes restaurants turn up in the most unlikely places. Pioneering locations in working-class blocks or warehouse districts, entrepreneurs save on overhead and earn a little cool cash. They survive less on advertising than on the buzz on the street.

1 Best Bets

- **Best Spot for a Romantic Dinner:** Few activities are more intimate than dipping lobster tails in fondue by candlelight at **Geja's Cafe,** 340 W. Armitage Ave. (☎ 773/281-9101), with a classical guitarist playing softly in the background. A strong challenge in this category is being mounted by the newcomer **North Pond Cafe,** 2610 N. Cannon Dr. (☎ 773/477-5845), an Arts and Crafts–styled, Midwestern-flavored restaurant with a postcard-perfect setting in Lincoln Park. Not only does it boast a dramatic vista of the Gold Coast skyline, but the restaurant's out-of-the-way locale requires diners to begin and end their meal with an idyllic stroll through the park.
- **Best Spot for a Business Lunch:** With great food, great service, and a central location in the Loop, **Trattoria No. 10,** 10 N. Dearborn St. (☎ 312/984-1718), tops the list.
- **Best Spot for a Celebration:** You can't beat the bossa nova for a surefire way to set your mood swinging. And the clubby Brazilian restaurant **Rhumba,** 3631 N. Halsted St. (☎ 773/975-2345), in Lakeview, is a nonstop carnival with its amped-up Latin grooves, flavorful food, and nightly floor show from the house Carmen Miranda.
- **Best View:** Forty stories above Chicago, **Everest,** 440 S. LaSalle St. (☎ 312/663-8920), astounds with a spectacular view—and food to match. In the daytime, another winner is **Spiaggia,** 980 N. Michigan Ave. (☎ 312/280-2750), overlooking Lake Michigan's Oak Street Beach. One brilliant view, day or night, is at the **Signature Lounge** atop the John Hancock Building, 875 N. Michigan Ave. (☎ 312/787-7230). It's good for a drink—at the beginning or the end of the evening.
- **Best Value:** At **Carson's,** 612 N. Wells St. (☎ 312/280-9200), a mere $15.95 gets you a full slab of incredible baby-back ribs, accompanied by a bowl of Carson's almost-as-famous coleslaw and a choice of potatoes. The complimentary chopped liver in the bar area eliminates any need for an appetizer.
- **Best for Kids:** A meal at **Michael Jordan's Restaurant,** 500 N. LaSalle St. (☎ 312/644-DUNK), and a trip to Niketown will keep most kids happy for hours.
- **Best American Cuisine: Zinfandel,** 59 W. Grand Ave. (☎ 312/527-1818), offers a refreshing take on hearty American comfort food of all regions, along with an equally interesting, equally American wine list.
- **Best French Cuisine:** For fine French dining, **Ambria,** 2300 Lincoln Park West (☎ 773/472-0076), has few rivals anywhere in the world. Nestled in an elegant Lincoln Park dining room, Ambria's kitchen does not disappoint.
- **Best Italian Cuisine:** Despite its supertrendy ambiance and buzz, **Centro,** 710 N. Wells St. (☎ 312/988-7775), offers truly first-rate cooking, from the pasta to the chicken Vesuvio.
- **Best Steak House: Eli's,** 215 E. Chicago Ave. (☎ 312/642-1393), broils a mean steak, and if that's not enough, its multiple varieties of cheesecake will send you into cholesterol overdrive.
- **Best Pizza:** The crispy crust and fresh ingredients of **Edwardo's,** 1212 N. Dearborn St. (☎ 312/337-4490), win my vote for the best thin pizza in town, while the chewy, gooey deep-dish version of **Gino's East,** 160 E. Superior St. (☎ 312/943-1124), is the best of its kind.
- **Best Pretheater Dinner:** A local favorite, the **Italian Village,** 71 W. Monroe St. (☎ 312/332-7005)—actually three restaurants run by one family under one roof—knows how to get its clientele seated and fed (very well) in time for a show.

A good choice if you're headed for the symphony, opera, or other downtown destination. If you're seeing a play at Steppenwolf or another off-Loop theater on the North Side, try the eclectic French and Japanese–inspired offerings at **Yoshi's Cafe,** 3257 Halsted St. (☎ 773/248-6160).

- **Best Fast Food:** Serving top-notch pasta, pizza, and salads, you would never guess that **Sopraffina Marketcaffé,** 10 N. Dearborn St. (☎ 312/984-0044), is a fast-food place were it not for its lack of a wait staff. Another alternative is **foodlife** in Water Tower Place, 835 N. Michigan Ave. (☎ 312/335-3663), a food court exemplar with everything from Asian noodles to pizza.

2 Restaurants by Cuisine

ALSATIAN

Brasserie Jo (River North, *M*)
Everest (The Loop, *VE*)

AMERICAN

160blue (Randolph Street, *VE*)
312 Chicago (The Loop, *M*)
Ann Sather (Wrigleyville/
  North Side, *I*)
The Berghoff (The Loop, *I*)
Blackbird (Randolph Street, *E*)
Blackhawk Lodge (Magnificent
  Mile/Gold Coast, *E*)
Bongo Room (Wicker Park/
  Bucktown, *I*)
Carson's (River North, *M*)
Crofton on Wells (River North, *E*)
Elaine & Ina's (Magnificent
  Mile/Gold Coast, *I*)
Goose Island Brewing Company
  (Lincoln Park, *I*)
Gordon (River North, *E*)
Hard Rock Cafe (River North, *M*)
Harry Caray's (River North, *M*)
House of Blues (River North, *M*)
Hudson Club (River North, *E*)
Lou Mitchell's (The Loop, *I*)
The Mashed Potato Club (River
  North, *M*)
Michael Jordan's (River North, *M*)
Mity Nice Grill (Magnificent
  Mile/Gold Coast, *M*)
North Pond Cafe (Lincoln Park, *E*)
Northside Tavern and Grill (Wicker
  Park/Bucktown, *I*)
Planet Hollywood (River North, *M*)
Printer's Row (The Loop, *E*)

Pump Room (Magnificent Mile/
  Gold Coast, *VE*)
Rainforest Cafe (River North, *M*)
Toast (Lincoln Park, *I*)
Toque (Randolph Street, *E*)
Zinfandel (River North, *E*)

ASIAN

Amitabul (Wrigleyville/North Side, *I*)
Big Bowl Café (River North, *I*)
Hi Ricky Asia Noodle Shop and
  Satay Bar (Wrigleyville/
  North Side, *I*)
Penny's Noodle Shop
  (Wrigleyville/North Side, *I*)
Saigon Vietnamese Restaurant
  (Chinatown, *I*)

BARBECUE

Carson's (River North, *M*)
Twin Anchors (Lincoln Park, *I*)

BISTRO

Bistrot Zinc (Wrigleyville/
  North Side, *M*)
Cyrano's Bistrot and Wine Bar (River
  North, *M*)
Le Bouchon (Wicker Park/
  Bucktown, *M*)
Mango (River North, *E*)
Marché (Randolph Street, *M*)
Mon Ami Gabi (Lincoln Park, *E*)
Yoshi's Cafe (Wrigleyville/
  North Side, *M*)

BRAZILIAN

Rhumba (Wrigleyville/
  North Side, *M*)

Key to abbreviations: *VE* = Very Expensive, *E* = Expensive, *M* = Moderate, *I* = Inexpensive.

BREAKFAST

Ann Sather (Wrigleyville/
  North Side, *I*)
Billy Goat Tavern (Magnificent
  Mile/Gold Coast, *I*)
Bongo Room (Wicker Park/
  Bucktown, *I*)
Corner Bakery (River North, *I*)
Elaine & Ina's (Magnificent
  Mile/Gold Coast, *I*)
Heaven on Seven (The Loop, *I*)
Lou Mitchell's (The Loop, *I*)
Oo La La! (Wrigleyville/
  North Side, *M*)
Toast (Lincoln Park, *I*)
Wishbone (Randolph Street, *I*)

BURGERS

Billy Goat Tavern (Magnificent
  Mile/Gold Coast, *I*)
Green Door Tavern (River North, *I*)
Mr. Beef (River North, *I*)
Northside Tavern and Grill (Wicker
  Park/Bucktown, *I*)
Rock-N-Roll McDonald's (River
  North, *I*)

CAJUN/CREOLE

Heaven on Seven (The Loop, *I*)
House of Blues (River North, *M*)
Soul Kitchen (Wicker Park/
  Bucktown, *M*)
Wishbone (Randolph Street, *I*)

CALIFORNIAN

Big Bowl Café (River North, *I*)
Spago (River North, *E*)

CARIBBEAN

Soul Kitchen (Wicker Park/
  Bucktown, *M*)

CHINESE

Dee's Restaurant (Lincoln Park, *M*)
Hong Min (Chinatown, *I*)
Keefer Bakery (Chinatown, *I*)
Phoenix (Chinatown, *M*)
Three Happiness (Chinatown, *I*)
Won Kow (Chinatown, *I*)

COLOMBIAN

Las Tablas (Lincoln Park, *I*)

CONTINENTAL

Bistro 110 (Magnificent Mile/
  Gold Coast, *M*)

CUBAN

Cafe Bolero (Wicker Park/
  Bucktown, *I*)

DELI

Mrs. Levy's (The Loop, *I*)

DINER

Ed Debevic's (River North, *I*)
Heaven on Seven (The Loop, *I*)
Lou Mitchell's (The Loop, *I*)
Nookies, Too (Lincoln Park, *I*)

ECLECTIC

Bite (Wicker Park/Bucktown, *I*)
Cafe Absinthe (Wicker Park/
  Bucktown, *E*)
Earth (River North, *E*)
foodlife (Magnificent Mile/
  Gold Coast, *I*)
Pepper Lounge (Wrigleyville/
  North Side, *M*)
Restaurant Okno (Wicker Park/
  Bucktown, *E*)
Spago (River North, *E*)

FONDUE

Geja's Cafe (Lincoln Park, *E*)

FRENCH

Ambria (Lincoln Park, *VE*)
Bistrot Zinc (Wrigleyville/
  North Side, *M*)
Brasserie Jo (River North, *M*)
Café Bernard (Lincoln Park, *M*)
Cyrano's Bistrot & Wine Bar
  (River North, *M*)
Everest (The Loop, *VE*)
Le Bouchon (Wicker Park/
  Bucktown, *M*)
Le Colonial (Magnificent Mile/
  Gold Coast, *M*)
Marché (Randolph Street, *M*)
Mon Ami Gabi (Lincoln Park, *E*)
Oo La La! (Wrigleyville/
  North Side, *M*)
Yoshi's Cafe (Wrigleyville/
  North Side, *M*)

GERMAN

The Berghoff (The Loop, *I*)
Zum Deutschen Eck
   (Wrigleyville/North Side, *E*)

GREEK

Costas (Greektown, *I*)
Greek Islands (Greektown, *I*)
Papagus Greek Taverna
   (River North, *M*)
Parthenon (Greektown, *I*)
Santorini (Greektown, *I*)

HOT DOGS

Gold Coast Dogs (River North, *I*)
Murphy's Red Hots
   (Wrigleyville/North Side, *I*)
The Wieners Circle (Lincoln Park, *I*)

ICE CREAM

Ben & Jerry's (Lincoln Park, *I*)
Ghirardelli Chocolate Shop & Soda
   Fountain (Magnificent Mile/
   Gold Coast, *I*)
Icebox (Wrigleyville/North Side, *I*)
Margie's Candies (Bucktown/
   Wicker Park, *I*)
Mario's Italian Lemonade
   (Little Italy, *I*)
Mrs. Levy's (The Loop, *I*)

INDIAN

Tiffin (Wrigleyville/North Side, *I*)

INTERNATIONAL

Gordon (River North, *E*)

ITALIAN

312 Chicago (The Loop, *M*)
Bella Vista (Wrigleyville/
   North Side, *M*)
Bice (Magnificent Mile/
   Gold Coast, *E*)
Centro (River North, *E*)
Club Lucky (Wicker Park/
   Bucktown, *M*)
Coco Pazzo (River North, *E*)
Francesca's on Taylor (Little Italy, *M*)
Gene & Georgetti (River North, *E*)
Harry Caray's (River North, *M*)
La Cantina Enoteca (The Loop, *M*)

Maggiano's Little Italy
   (River North, *M*)
Mia Francesca (Wrigleyville/
   North Side, *M*)
Mr. Beef (River North, *I*)
Oo La La! (Wrigleyville/
   North Side, *M*)
Ranalli's Pizzeria, Libations &
   Collectibles (Lincoln Park, *I*)
RoseAngelis (Lincoln Park, *I*)
Rosebud on Rush (Magnificent
   Mile/Gold Coast, *E*)
Rosebud on Taylor (Little Italy, *I*)
Scoozi (River North, *M*)
Sopraffina Marketcaffé (The Loop, *I*)
Spiaggia (Magnificent Mile/
   Gold Coast, *E*)
Trattoria No. 10 (The Loop, *M*)
Tucci Benucch (Magnificent Mile/
   Gold Coast, *I*)
Tucci Milan (River North, *M*)
Tuscany (Little Italy, *M*)
The Village (The Loop, *M*)
Vivere (The Loop, *M*)
Vivo (Randolph Street, *M*)

JAPANESE

Hatsuhana (Magnificent Mile/
   Gold Coast, *VE*)

KOREAN

Amitabul (Wrigleyville/
   North Side, *I*)

LATIN AMERICAN

Las Tablas (Lincoln Park, *I*)
Mambo Grill (River North, *M*)
Soul Kitchen (Wicker Park/
   Bucktown, *M*)

MEXICAN

Frontera Grill & Topolobampo
   (River North, *E*)
Hacienda Tecalitlan (Wicker
   Park/Bucktown, *M*)
Nuevo Leon (Pilsen, *I*)

MIDWESTERN

Blackhawk Lodge (Magnificent
   Mile/Gold Coast, *E*)
Prairie (The Loop, *E*)

NOUVELLE

Charlie Trotter's (Lincoln Park, *VE*)
Yoshi's Cafe (Wrigleyville/
North Side, *M*)

PERSIAN

Reza's (River North, *I*)

PIZZA

Edwardo's (Magnificent Mile/
Gold Coast, *I*)
Gino's East (Magnificent Mile/
Gold Coast, *I*)
Leona's Pizzeria (Little Italy and
Wrigleyville/North Side, *I*)
Lou Malnati's Pizzeria (River North, *I*)
Pat's Pizzeria (Wrigleyville/
North Side, *I*)
Pizzeria Due (River North, *I*)
Pizzeria Uno (River North, *I*)
Pompeii (Wrigleyville/North Side, *I*)
Ranalli's Pizzeria, Libations &
Collectibles (Lincoln Park, *I*)

RUSSIAN

Russian Tea Time (The Loop, *M*)

SEAFOOD

Bluepoint Oyster Bar (Randolph
Street, *E*)
Cape Cod Room (Magnificent Mile/
Gold Coast, *VE*)
La Cantina Enoteca (The Loop, *M*)
Nick's Fishmarket (The Loop, *VE*)
Shaw's Crab House and Blue Crab
Lounge (Magnificent Mile/
Gold Coast, *M*)

SOUTHERN

House of Blues (River North, *M*)
Soul Kitchen (Wicker Park/
Bucktown, *M*)
Wishbone (Randolph Street, *I*)

SPANISH/TAPAS

Café Ba-Ba-Reeba! (Lincoln
Park, *M*)
Cafe Iberico (River North, *I*)

STEAK/CHOPS

Eli's, the Place for Steak (Magnificent
Mile/Gold Coast, *E*)
Gene & Georgetti (River North, *E*)
Gibsons Bar and Steakhouse (Magnif-
icent Mile/Gold Coast, *VE*)
The Saloon (Magnificent Mile/
Gold Coast, *E*)

SWEDISH

Ann Sather (Wrigleyville/
North Side, *I*)

THAI

Arun's (Wrigleyville/North Side, *E*)
Hi Ricky Asia Noodle Shop and
Satay Bar (Wrigleyville/North
Side, *I*)
Pasteur (Wrigleyville/North Side, *M*)
Penny's Noodle Shop
(Wrigleyville/North Side, *I*)
P.S. Bangkok 2 (Lincoln Park, *I*)
Thai Borrahn (Magnificent
Mile/Gold Coast, *I*)

VEGETARIAN

Amitabul (Wrigleyville/North Side, *I*)
Blind Faith Café (Wrigleyville/
North Side, *I*)
Earth (River North, *E*)
Reza's (River North, *I*)

VIETNAMESE

Le Colonial (Magnificent Mile/
Gold Coast, *M*)
Pasteur (Wrigleyville/North Side, *M*)
Saigon Vietnamese Restaurant
(Chinatown, *I*)

3 The Loop

In keeping with their proximity to the towers of power, many of the restaurants in the Loop and its environs—namely Printers Row and the tragically trendy Randolph Street Market District—feature expense-account-style prices. But it's still possible to dine here for less than the cost of your hotel room. Keep in mind that several of the best downtown spots are closed on Sunday.

VERY EXPENSIVE

✪ **Everest.** 440 S. LaSalle St. (at Congress Pkwy.). ☎ **312/663-8920.** Reservations required. Main courses $28.50–$34.50; fixed-price meal from $79; 3-course pretheater dinner $44, including complimentary parking. AE, DC, DISC, MC, V. Tues–Thurs 5:30–9pm, Fri–Sat 5:30–10pm. Subway/El: Brown Line to LaSalle/Van Buren. ALSATIAN.

Forty stories above the Chicago Stock Exchange, in the elite La Salle Club, is the lovely dining room of Everest. Its windows overlook the shimmering nightscape of downtown Chicago, and its culinary experience is one of the finest in the world. Chef (and owner) Jean Joho, a baker in his youth in Strasbourg, France, has paired his earthy appreciation of the home-style cookery of the Rhine country with his determination to procure North American foodstuffs, creating a menu with a rare delicacy of touch and imagination.

On a given evening, the *menu degustation* might consist of an appetizer of terrine of foie gras and marinated figs, followed by a creamless watercress soup with Louisiana crayfish. Then comes a crispy Maryland soft-shell crab, red-beet coulis, and fava beans. The main attractions follow: Lake Superior walleye pike with marinated cabbage Alsace style, giving way to a medaillon of Wisconsin veal, wild morels, and green asparagus. The assortment of desserts is more traditional, but equally sublime, and the whole extravaganza is accompanied by a variety of fine American and Alsatian wines. His inspiration as varied as the peasant's pantry and the craggy sea bottom, Chef Joho spins an extraordinary and memorable culinary event.

Nick's Fishmarket. First National Bank Plaza at Monroe and Clark sts. ☎ **312/621-0200.** Reservations recommended. Main courses $19.50–$45.50; fixed-price lunch $21. AE, CB, DC, DISC, JCB, MC, V. Mon–Thurs 11:30am–3pm and 5:30–11:30pm, Fri 11:30am–3pm and 5:30pm–midnight; Sat 5:30pm–midnight. Subway/El: Blue or Red Line to Monroe. SEAFOOD.

Taking the elevator down below street level to Nick's feels a little like plunging underwater in a submarine. Once submerged, you'll find yourself in one of the best fish and seafood places in the city. Known for the Pacific specials flown in daily from Hawaii, Nick offers everything from California abalone, Maine lobster, and Dover sole to Atlantic swordfish, catfish, and salmon. Nick's also serves beluga caviar with frozen vodka. If you're not in the mood for seafood, the menu still offers you more than a dozen choices, such as veal chop with Barolo wine truffle sauce and lamb chops with mint sauce.

The atmosphere at Nick's, though comfortable, is a bit on the stodgy side, but with a piano player tickling the ivories Tuesday through Saturday evenings, it's a lovely choice for an old-fashioned, dressed-up evening of good food and music.

Note: The restaurant moved last year to the other side of the First National Bank Plaza, gaining an atrium with views of the Chagall mosaic at street level and a more modestly priced bar and grill.

EXPENSIVE

Prairie. In the Hyatt on Printers Row, 500 S. Dearborn St. (at Congress Pkwy.). ☎ **312/663-1143.** Reservations required. Main courses $13.50–$21.50; Sun brunch $15. Half portions of many dishes available for lunch. AE, CB, DC, MC, V. Mon–Fri 6:30am–2pm and 5–10pm, Sat 7am–2pm and 5–10pm, Sun 7am–2pm and 5–9pm. Subway/El: Red Line to Harrison/State. MIDWESTERN.

From the light fixtures to the stained glass, the interior of this restaurant in the south Loop neighborhood of Printers Row is inspired by Frank Lloyd Wright. The earth-tone colors and honey-oak wood trim form patterns like those on a Native American blanket. The restaurant offers a view of urban life, looking onto busy Congress Parkway. Celebrating the culinary traditions of the Midwest, the restaurant prepares meals with all the ingredients (as well as all of the wines) originating from the 14 Midwestern states.

Dining In the Loop & Near North

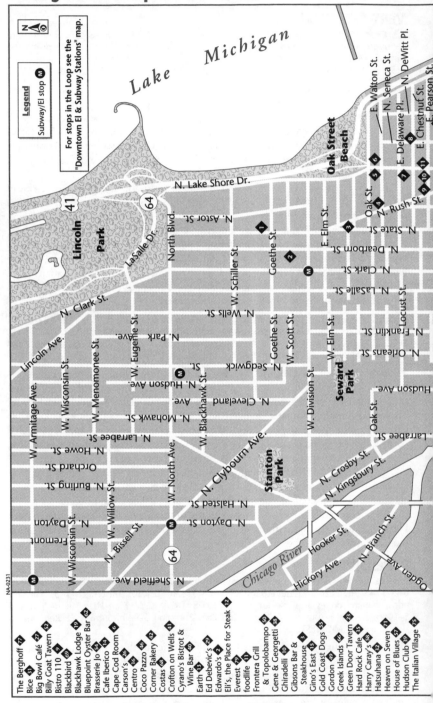

Legend

🔵 Subway/El stop Ⓜ

For stops in the Loop see the "Downtown El & Subway Stations' map.

Lake Michigan

Lincoln Park

N. Lake Shore Dr.

Oak Street Beach

41

64

LaSalle Dr.

N. Clark St.

Lincoln Ave.

N. Park Ave.

W. Armitage Ave.

W. Wisconsin St.

W. Menomonee St.

W. Eugenie St.

N. Hudson Ave.

W. Mohawk St.

N. Mohawk St.

N. Larrabee St.

N. Howe St.

Orchard St.

N. Burling St.

W. Willow St.

N. Halsted St.

N. Dayton St.

W. Wisconsin St.

N. Bissell St.

N. Sheffield Ave.

N. Fremont St.

N. Dayton St.

W. North Ave.

N. Clybourn Ave.

W. Blackhawk St.

N. Blackhawk St.

N. Cleveland Ave.

Ave.

N. Sedgwick St.

W. Schiller St.

W. Scott St.

W. Goethe St.

N. Wells St.

Goethe St.

N. Astor St.

North Blvd.

N. Elm St.

W. Division St.

W. Elm St.

Seward Park

N. Orleans St.

N. Franklin St.

Locust St.

N. LaSalle St.

N. Clark St.

N. Dearborn St.

N. State St.

N. Rush St.

Oak St.

E. Elm St.

Goethe St.

E. Walton St.

N. Seneca St.

N. DeWitt Pl.

E. Delaware Pl.

E. Chestnut St.

E. Pearson St.

Stanton Park

Hudson Ave.

Larrabee St.

Oak St.

N. Crosby St.

N. Kingsbury St.

Hooker St.

N. Branch St.

Hickory Ave.

Ogden Ave

Chicago River

64

Restaurant Index

The Berghoff 🔷47
Bice 🔷51
Big Bowl Café 🔷27
Billy Goat Tavern 🔷52
Bistro 110 🔷7
Blackbird 🔷69
Blackhawk Lodge 🔷42
Bluepoint Oyster Bar 🔷62
Brasserie Jo 🔷54
Cafe Iberico 🔷24
Cape Cod Room 🔷6
Carson's 🔷26
Centro 🔷22
Coco Pazzo 🔷48
Corner Bakery 🔷62
Costas 🔷68
Crofton on Wells 🔷41
Cyrano's Bistrot & Wine Bar 🔷40
Earth 🔷43
Ed Debevic's 🔷29
Edwardo's 🔷2
Eli's, the Place for Steak 🔷12
Everest 🔷
foodlife 🔷
Frontera Grill & Topolobampo 🔷50
Gene & Georgetti 🔷
Ghiradelli 🔷40
Gibsons Bar & Steakhouse 🔷3
Gino's East 🔷15
Gold Coast Dogs 🔷55
Gordon 🔷
Greek Islands 🔷66
Green Door Tavern 🔷23
Hard Rock Cafe 🔷35
Harry Caray's 🔷
Hatsuhana 🔷47
Heaven on Seven 🔷
House of Blues 🔷57
Hudson Club 🔷58
The Italian Village 🔷45

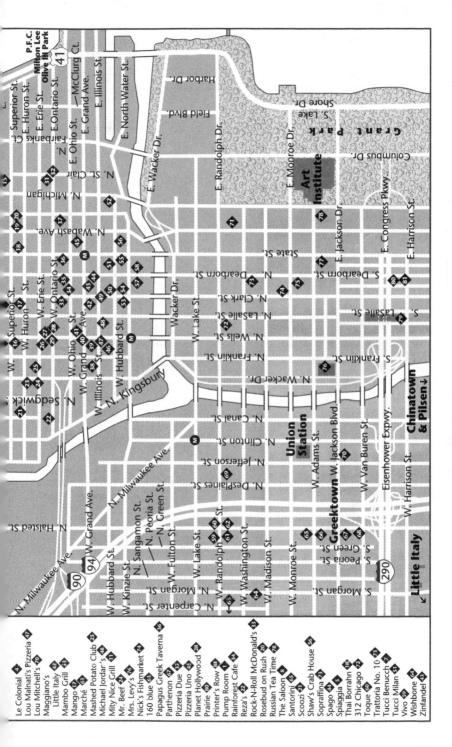

Le Colonial **47**
Lou Malnati's Pizzeria **9**
Lou Mitchell's **70**
Maggiano's **40**
Little Italy **53**
Mambo Grill **34**
Mango **67**
Marché **36**
Mashed Potato Club **48**
Michael Jordan's **37**
Mity Nice Grill **11**
Mr. Beef **24**
Mrs. Levy's **76**
Nick's Fishmarket **72**
160 blue **63**
Papagus Greek Taverna **46**
Parthenon **61**
Pizzeria Due **19**
Pizzeria Uno **42**
Planet Hollywood **28**
Prairie **68**
Printer's Row **71**
Pump Room **4**
Rainforest Cafe **44**
Reza's **22**
Rock-N-Roll McDonald's **43**
Rosebud on Rush **76**
Russian Tea Time **73**
The Saloon **8**
Santorini **65**
Scoozi **21**
Shaw's Crab House **56**
Sopraffina **23**
Spago **44**
Spiaggia **5**
Thai Borrahn **18**
312 Chicago **17**
Toque **66**
Trattoria No. 10 **74**
Tucci Benucch **10**
Tucci Milan **51**
Vivo **64**
Wishbone **64**
Zinfandel **43**

97

Don't expect, however, that anything arriving at the table will look homespun and plain. For starters, Prairie has a multitoned tomato soup, in swirls of yellow, red, and green, with sour cream and sturgeon caviar floating in the center. The sautéed wild mushrooms in a sweet potato basket was quite pleasing and practically a meal itself.

Among the main courses, the must-sample is the buffalo steak, baked in clay over a bed of wild beans and served in its natural juices. Another favorite is the Indiana duck, cooked in a delicious dried cherry port wine sauce. We've also enjoyed the seared chicken breast, served with apple cornmeal stuffing, straw vegetables, and sweet orange chicken jus. Portions are generously sized, and while the food won't disappoint, the fact that the restaurant is ensconced in a hotel means the prices are a bit steep. For dessert, have a great hot-fudge sundae with real bittersweet chocolate or the sweet potato praline cheesecake.

Printer's Row. 550 S. Dearborn St. (at Harrison St.). ☎ **312/461-0780.** Reservations recommended. Main courses $14.95–$21.95. AE, CB, DC, DISC, MC, V. Daily 11:30am–2:30pm; Mon–Thurs 5–10pm, Fri–Sat 5–10:30pm. Subway/El: Red Line to Harrison/State. AMERICAN.

Printer's Row is another citadel of new-wave American cuisine catering to the hip clientele who now live in buildings where Chicago's publishing industry was once centered. But if the neighborhood has lost its ink-stained commercial character, the Loop in general has gained by the return of inner-city dwellers, and the creation of some interesting and innovative restaurants.

Printer's Row has built a solid reputation over the past few years, mostly through chef Michael Foley's imaginative cooking. Among his novelties are his various preparations of New York State foie gras. Venison, Foley's signature dish, is also regularly featured on the menu, as are tasty fish and poultry dishes. All meals are accompanied by a healthy assortment of fresh vegetables. The game, incidentally, is New Zealand farm raised and may be accompanied by a sun-dried blueberry-and-brandy sauce or by a sauce of honey-glazed wheatberries and lemon rosemary. Homemade desserts and ice creams are also first-rate.

MODERATE

312 Chicago. 136 N. LaSalle St. (at Randolph St.). ☎ **312/696-2420.** Reservations recommended. Main courses $9.95–$22.95. AE, CB, DC, DISC, JCB, MC, V. Mon–Thurs 7–10am, 11am–3pm, 5–10pm; Fri 7–10am, 11am–3pm, 5–11pm; Sat 8am–3pm, 5–11pm; Sun 8am–3pm, 5–10pm. Subway/El: Red Line to Washington/State. ITALIAN/AMERICAN.

Downtown is becoming a more lively place as the millennium approaches, with new theaters and hotels debuting in succession, as well as restaurants to serve their patrons looking for some activity in the Loop after dark. One of the latest is 312 Chicago, occupying a prominent window-laden corner across from City Hall/County Building and connected to the snazzy new Hotel Allegro. The restaurant has a clubby jazz-age feel with mahogany wood, antique pieces, and earthy coloring in the two-level dining room, and an exhibition kitchen equipped with a rotisserie directed by Dean Zanella, who has spent time at Charlie Trotter's, Gordon, and the now-closed Grappa. Signature dishes on the Italian-inspired American menu include appetizers such as seared day boat scallops with wild mushrooms and truffle oil and carpaccio of pepper-seared Angus with roasted peppers and arugula, pasta such as rigatoni with veal meatballs poached in tomato sauce and ricotta salata, and entrees like spit-roasted leg of lamb on parsnip puree with grappa-soaked grapes and olive oil–poached sea bass with leeks, fennel, tomatoes, and basil. On weekends, the restaurant has simple brunch offerings distinguished by home-baked breads.

Russian Tea Time. 77 E. Adams St. (between Michigan and Wabash aves.). ☎ **312/ 360-0000.** Reservations recommended. Main courses $15–$27. AE, CB, DC, DISC, JCB, MC, V. Sun–Mon 11am–9pm, Tues–Thurs 11am–11pm, Fri–Sat 11am–midnight. Subway/El: Brown, Purple, Green, or Orange Line to Adams or Red Line to Monroe or Jackson. RUSSIAN.

This restaurant has a been a favorite pre- and posttheater place to dine ever since it opened as the Russian Tea Cafe in 1993. Its customers include both patrons and personnel of the Chicago Symphony, opera-goers, and hosts and guests from the television and radio stations nearby. The atmosphere is old-world and cozy, with lots of woodwork and a friendly staff.

House specialties include blini with Russian caviar, *goriachaya zakuska* (an appetizer platter for two), stuffed quail with pomegranate sauce, and for vegetarians, mushrooms filled with spinach, onion, and cheese. The beef stroganoff and *kulebiaka* (meat pie with ground beef, cabbage, and onions) are great. Roast pheasant is served with a brandy, walnut, and pomegranate sauce and brandied prunes. For dessert try the homemade apricot-plum strudel.

۞ Trattoria No. 10. 10 N. Dearborn St. (between Madison and Washington sts.). ☎ **312/984-1718.** Reservations recommended. Main courses $11.95–$26.95. AE, DC, DISC, MC, V. Mon–Thurs 11:30am–2pm and 5:30–9pm, Fri 11:30am–2pm and 5:30–10pm, Sat 5:30–10pm. Subway/El: Red or Blue Line to Dearborn. ITALIAN.

Trattoria No. 10 is always at the top of my list of Loop restaurants. The burnt orange tones and ceramic floor tiles are straight out of Tuscany, and the food is contemporary Italian, with such touches as sun-dried tomato butter sauce and plenty of pine nuts. A new menu is prepared each day and includes some of the restaurant's core specialties. Each ravioli dish, the house specialty, is better than the next and can be ordered as an appetizer or as a main course. If you're not in the mood for ravioli, there is plenty of other interesting pasta dishes to choose from, such as farfalle with duck confit, asparagus, caramelized onions, and pine nuts and the cannelloni with portobello, crimini, and shiitake mushrooms in a red-wine mushroom reduction. You could also start with grilled octopus with a salad of fresh oranges, watercress, and rosemary or the caramelized soft carrot polenta with roasted vegetables. While it serves lamb, veal, and chicken dishes, Trattoria No. 10's strength is clearly pasta.

۞ THE ITALIAN VILLAGE

The building at 71 W. Monroe St. houses three separate Italian restaurants, collectively known as the Italian Village. The Village was the first to open, back in 1927, followed shortly by La Cantina Enoteca, and, in the early nineties, by Vivere. All three are owned by the Capitanini family, now in its third generation of management. But each has a unique take on Italian ambiance and cooking, and they're all suitable for a pre- or posttheater meal. They also share an exemplary wine cellar and fresh produce grown in a family garden.

La Cantina Enoteca. 71 W. Monroe St. (between Clark and Dearborn sts.). ☎ **312/ 332-7005.** Reservations recommended. Main courses (including soup, salad, dessert, and coffee) $12–$25.50; salads $9.95–$11.95; sandwiches $7.50–$7.95. Lunch prices slightly lower. AE, CB, DC, DISC, JCB, MC, V. Mon–Thurs 11:30am–11pm, Fri 11:30am–midnight, Sat 5pm–midnight, Sun 4:30–8pm (seasonally). Subway/El: Red or Blue Line to Monroe. ITALIAN/SEAFOOD.

La Cantina is the most moderately priced of the three. It makes the most of its basement location by creating the feel of a wine cellar. The restaurant attracts a daily regular clientele of lawyers, judges, and the like, many of whom eat at the bar. Specializing in seafood, La Cantina offers at least five fresh varieties every day.

The dinner menu offers a big-time bargain: à la carte dishes (most of which are under $20) include a salad, and for $2 more you also get soup, dessert, and coffee. As for the cuisine, no surprises where the pasta is concerned—all the reliable standards are here.

The Village. 71 W. Monroe St. (between Clark and Dearborn sts.). ☎ **312/332-7005.** Reservations recommended (accepted for parties of 3 or more). Main courses (including salad) $10.50–$23.75; salads $5.50–$10.25; pizza $11–$14.25; sandwiches $7.95–$14.95. Lunch prices slightly lower. AE, CB, DC, DISC, JCB, MC, V. Mon–Thurs 11am–1am, Fri–Sat 11am–2am, Sun noon–midnight. Subway/El: Red or Blue Line to Monroe. ITALIAN.

Upstairs is The Village, with its charming interpretation of alfresco dining in a small Italian town, complete with a midnight-blue ceiling, twinkling "stars," and banquettes tucked into private cavelike little rooms. It's the kind of pan-Chicago place where you might see one man in a tux and another in shorts. With 200 items, the menu is so big and broad that it's sure to satisfy. Those old-time, hearty southern Italian standards are all here, and at a great value. We're talking chicken Vesuvio (with garlic and herbs), veal marsala (with marsala wine and mushrooms), eggplant parmigiana, tortellini alla bolognese (meat sauce), and, yes, even pizza. The lunch menu is somewhat abbreviated but still offers an enormous selection of salads, pasta, meats, and sandwiches. You can also opt to eat at the bar; if you're pals with the bartender, he may bring back some special off-the-menu selections.

Vivere. 71 W. Monroe St. (between Clark and Dearborn sts.). ☎ **312/332-4040.** Reservations recommended. Main courses $12.95–$24.95. AE, CB, DC, DISC, JCB, MC, V. Mon–Thurs 11:30am–2:30pm and 5–10pm, Fri 11:30am–2:30pm and 5–11pm, Sat 5–11pm. Subway/El: Red or Blue Line to Monroe. REGIONAL ITALIAN.

On the main floor is Vivere, the Italian Village's take on gourmet cooking. Created by Chicago designer Jordan Moser, the chic interior, with rich burgundies, textured walls, spiraling bronze sculptures, and fragmented mosaic floors, complements the modern cuisine. In addition to excellent daily risotto and fresh fish dishes served three ways, Vivere presents interesting preparations of game and a particularly good *petto d'anatra*, a duck breast with escarole sautéed in red wine and balsamic vinegar. Pastas, which at lunch are available either in "primi" appetizer size or as the main course, range from the basic linguine alla bolognese to the slightly daring *agnolottini di fagiano* (pheasant-filled pasta with butter, sage, and Parmesan).

INEXPENSIVE

The Berghoff. 17 W. Adams St. (between State and Dearborn sts.). ☎ **312/427-3170.** Reservations recommended. Main courses $8.25–$10.95 at lunch, $8.95–$17.95 at dinner. AE, MC, V. Mon–Thurs 11am–9pm, Fri 11am–9:30pm, Sat 11am–10pm. Subway/El: Red or Blue Line to Jackson or Monroe. GERMAN/AMERICAN.

Celebrating its centennial in 1998, The Berghoff is a Chicago landmark. The immense 700-seat restaurant is housed in one of the first buildings constructed in the Loop after the Chicago Fire and one of the only remaining buildings in the city with a cast-iron facade. The Berghoff holds Chicago liquor license no. 1, issued at the close of Prohibition, and it still serves its own brand of beer at $3 a stein.

While the menu rotates seasonally, the German standard-bearers are always available. The Berghoff serves hundreds of orders of Wiener schnitzel every day, plus bratwurst, sauerbraten, corned beef, and the like. Because some of us have arteries to worry about, the third generation of family management has added some lighter fare in the form of salads, broiled fish, and vegetarian dishes.

If the food sounds somewhat manly, it's no coincidence. The stand-up bar at The Berghoff didn't even admit women until 1969, when a group of NOW activists staged a protest. The bar, where men used to drink nickel beers and eat free sandwiches, is still overwhelmingly male. The Berghoff also holds a popular Oktoberfest celebration each year in mid-September.

Heaven on Seven. 111 N. Wabash Ave. (at Washington St.), 7th floor. ☎ **312/263-6443.** Reservations not accepted. Menu items $2.75–$9.95. No credit cards. Mon–Fri 8:30am–5pm, Sat 10am–3pm. First and third Fri of month 5:30–9pm. New location at 600 N. Michigan Ave. (☎ **312/280-7774;** entrance at Ohio and Rush sts.) is open for lunch and dinner, and accepts reservations and credit cards. Subway/El: Red Line to Washington/State. CAJUN/COFFEE SHOP.

Don't be scared off by the lunchtime line that extends all the way down the hall of the seventh floor of the Garland Building, just across from Marshall Field's. It moves pretty quickly. And once you're inside you'll be in one of the working locals' favorite joints. Heaven on Seven is loud, it's crowded, and it serves a mean bowl of gumbo for $3.95. The Cajun and Creole specialties, most of which run about $9 or $10 and come with a cup of soup, include such Louisiana staples as red beans and rice, a catfish po' boy sandwich, and jambalaya. If you don't have a taste for tabasco, the enormous coffee-shop-style menu covers all the traditional essentials: grilled cheese sandwiches, omelets, tuna, the works. On the first and third Friday of the month, Heaven on Seven's original location hosts special dinners from 5:30 to 9pm.

Mrs. Levy's. Sears Tower, concourse level, 233 S. Wacker Dr. ☎ **312/993-0530.** Sandwiches $4–$6.99. AE, DC, DISC, MC, V. Mon–Fri 6:30am–3pm. Subway/El: Brown or Orange Line to Quincy. DELI.

To paraphrase the well-known slogan of rye-bread fame, "You don't have to be Jewish to like Mrs. Levy's," an eat-in delicatessen. It's all here at Mrs. Levy's in the Loop: matzoh-ball soup, bagels with lox and cream cheese, gefilte fish, latkes (potato pancakes), pastrami and corned beef, and much, much more. The food is good, not great, and the service is friendly, with no pressure if you want to linger a bit over your meal. Take-out orders are also available.

۞ Sopraffina Marketcaffé. 10 N. Dearborn St. (between Madison and Washington sts.). ☎ **312/984-0044.** Reservations not accepted. Pizza $3.95 for a half portion, $6.95 for a whole; pasta $5.50; sandwiches $4.95–$5.95. AE, CB, DC, DISC, MC, V. Mon–Fri 11am–4pm. Subway/El: Red Line to Monroe/State. ITALIAN.

Leave it to the folks at Trattoria No. 10 to create a first-rate fast-food Italian restaurant. Sopraffina somehow manages to offer low-priced fare without sacrificing creativity. We're not talking simple spaghetti with ketchup impersonating marinara here. Instead, Sopraffina features funky pizzas on tasty thin crusts, including one with chicken, mushrooms, broccoli, provolone, and Parmesan; a lasagna with a choice of Parmesan cream or marinara sauce; and a selection of sandwiches on crusty Italian bread. The antipasti include salad niçoise, marinated green beans, and cucumber and feta salad. Sopraffina does not have table service, but that's where the similarity to any other fast-food joint ends. Sopraffina has added outposts at 222 W. Adams St., with an entrance on Franklin Street (☎ **312/726-4800**), conveniently located near the Sears Tower, and on the lobby level of the Amoco Building, 200 E. Randolph St. (☎ **312/729-9200**).

4 Chic Eats: The Randolph Street Market District

Either that old real estate axiom "location, location, location" has its limits, or the owners of Vivo and Marché, two restaurants that practically define the word hip in Chicago, have proved that the more unexpected, the more out of the way the spot, the more people will want to come. This little stretch of Randolph Street west of the Loop has become a white-hot culinary neighborhood all its own.

Transportation to the Market District is easy, by the way—it's about a $5 cab ride from Michigan Avenue, or a slightly longer trek by bus (no. 8 or 9) or El, with stops at Halsted and Lake, a block from the restaurants. The walk from the Loop is very pleasant and totally secure in the daytime, but at night I'd save my stroll for Michigan Avenue.

Blackbird. 619 W. Randolph St. ☎ **312/715-0708.** Reservations recommended. Main courses $14–$24. AE, DC, DISC, MC, V. Mon–Thurs 11:30am–2pm and 5:30–10:30pm; Fri–Sat 5:30–11:30pm. AMERICAN.

Located on the east side of the expressway apart from all the area's other hot spots farther west, superhip Blackbird fairly glows behind its white facade framing a wall of glass. The narrow 70-seat restaurant is austere with white-washed walls, a gun-metal gray mohair-fitted banquette, and aluminum chairs. A table-hopping cool crowd notches up the volume with animated conversation. The American menu, with a foundation in French cooking, presents some of the more unusual and inventive offerings in town. A good way to start would be with the Maine lobster salad with baby beans, beets, and young greens, or the seared duck with plums, frisee, French green lentils, and walnut oil vinaigrette, or especially one of the wonderful soups, which the waiter will pour steaming over the dish's primary ingredient. Entrees include wood-grilled California sturgeon with couscous, yogurt, cucumber and carrot-ginger sauce; and braised veal cheeks with herbed gnocchi, citrus braising juices, and melted leeks. Unfortunately, the wait for the complicated, artfully presented dishes may require some patience, but the knowledgeable staff keeps things running smoothly.

Bluepoint Oyster Bar. 741 W. Randolph St. ☎ **312/207-1222.** Reservations recommended. Main courses $14.95–$22.95 (lobster and crab market prices higher). AE, CB, DC, DISC, MC, V. Mon–Thurs 11am–10pm, Fri 11:30am–midnight, Sun 5–9:30pm. SEAFOOD.

Bluepoint has the stylings of an art deco 1940s fish house, the nostalgic vision of Roger Greenfield and Ted Kasemir, a team of ambitious restaurateurs whose Restaurant Development Group operates a dozen flashy spots around town from the Saloon to Mambo Grill. This new corner restaurant has a big, handsome dining room with huge comfy booths and tufted banquettes, maroon and black marble floors, and ceiling fans spinning overhead. Oyster lovers will be delighted by the selection of more than a dozen varieties at the raw bar. Other appetizers include clams, sushi and sashimi, seafood cocktails, cold salads, and several specialty items such as baked and stuffed cherrystone clams and steamed Prince Edward mussels. The extensive list of entrees includes a range of fresh fish and seafood items prepared to your liking (broiled, grilled, blackened, and sautéed), and there are some big-ticket items like Maine lobsters, Alaskan king crab legs, and stone crab dinners (October to May). Some of the house specialties are spicy braised catfish shanks, scallion-crusted marlin, grilled tuna Bordelaise, and Bluepoint oyster and wild mushroom ragout. There are a few steak and chicken alternatives, too.

Marché. 833 W. Randolph St. (1 block west of Halsted St.). ☎ **312/226-8399.** Reservations recommended. Main courses $9–$25. AE, DC, MC, V. Mon–Fri 11:30am–2pm, Sun–Wed 5:30–10pm, Thurs 5:30–11pm, Fri–Sat 5:30pm–midnight. FRENCH BISTRO.

The basic idea behind Marché is derivative of the popular and cavernous Paris cafe. The menu is also a by-product of French inspiration, but the execution is pure Americana. Co-owner and furniture designer Jerry Kleiner created an interior that's a visual potpourri of mixed-media materials, favoring the eclectic, the postmodern, and the outrageous. Multilevel seating enhances the effect and suggests a perpetual fiesta.

To ensure that Marché will outlast the impact of its perishable aesthetic, Michael Kornick, a dynamic young chef with some impressive credits already on his resume

(Gordon in Chicago, Four Seasons in Boston) was brought in to create the menu and supervise the kitchen, which is visible to diners from behind a glass barrier along one corner of the building. Chef Kornick seems to handle every idiom, whether the ordinary or the exotic, with equal ease and grace. There's still nothing like a steaming bowl of good onion soup to remove that inner chill on a blustery day. The coriander-crusted tuna with horseradish and arugula is as delicious as it is original, and ditto the seasonal offering of spring morels served with wild leeks.

Though the menu changes frequently, the main courses the night I dined at Marché were divided almost equally between meat and fish, plus two pasta dishes for vegetarians. My grilled veal chop was delicate yet hearty, and my companion chose that old bistro standby, steak with pommes frites. We sated our respective sweet tooths with a chocolate pot de crème and a scoop of vanilla-bean ice cream doused with a compote of rhubarb.

✪ 160blue. 160 N. Loomis St. (at Randolph St. and Ogden Ave.). ☎ **312/850-0303.** Reservations recommended. Main courses $16–$27. AE, DC, MC, V. Mon–Thurs 5–10pm, Fri–Sat 5–11pm. AMERICAN.

160blue has the talented staff and sleek decor, but this ambitious new restaurant also has a mystique about it generating the kind of buzz most restaurants can't afford to buy. For one, there's a certain heavily endorsed professional basketball legend who may even be an owner. And then there's the odd name, a nod to the street address and vibrant blue color of the brick building, a former pickle factory, which is certainly one of the most out-of-the-way high-end restaurants in the country. 160blue has assembled a Dream Team of its own, with a sophisticated interior of subdued lighting and warm surfaces designed by Adam Tihany, who has done hot spots like Le Cirque 2000 and Jean Georges in New York City, and the kitchen directed by Patrick Robertson, who brings his considerable international experience to work in 160blue's exhibition kitchen. A few winners on the "two begin" appetizer menu include slow-roasted beets sandwiching goat cheese and hazelnuts or a crab sandwich with citrus sauce. The "Four dinner" menu features half fish and seafood and the rest selections of lamb, game, and beef, including such items as a grilled T-bone of lamb with Japanese eggplant, red snapper and roasted sea scallop pot-au-feu with poached heirloom tomatoes, and a wood-roasted wild stripe bass. Tables in the spacious restaurant are spread out giving diners plenty of elbow room, and the staff provides gracious service.

Toque. 816 W. Randolph St. ☎ **312/666-1100.** Reservations recommended. Main courses $13.50–$27.50. AE, DC, DISC, MC, V. Mon–Fri 11:30am–11:30pm, Sat 5–11:30pm, Sun 5–10pm. AMERICAN.

One of the newcomers in the block, Toque offers a change-of-pace from the theatrics of many of the high-design restaurants on the row. The pretty two-room restaurant has light wood floors and chairs, soft-colored walls, and an open feel from high ceilings. The French-inspired American menu from Mark Chmielewski (formerly of Ambria and Park Avenue Cafe) is eclectic and appealing, with appetizers such as wood-grilled quail, lobster gazpacho, dungeness Asian crab cake, and a nice mix of game, fish, and beef entrees. Main courses include grilled fillet of beef with shiitake corn home fries and carmelized shallots, bacon-wrapped halibut with sweet pea puree and pearl onions, and vanilla-scented duck breast with sweet corn, sugar snap peas, and herb polenta. Open all day, Toque offers lunch and then a petit menu (2:30 to 4:45pm) to get diners through until dinner.

Vivo. 838 W. Randolph St. (1 block west of Halsted St.). ☎ **312/733-3379.** Main courses $11.95–$17.95. AE, DC, MC, V. Mon–Fri 11:30am–2:30pm, Sun–Wed 5:30–10pm, Thurs 5:30–11pm, Fri–Sat 5:30pm–midnight. SOUTHERN ITALIAN.

Before there was Marché, there was Vivo, pioneer and prototype of the genre, half the size, and hot, hot, hot when it opened in 1991. Vivo's mock-market ambiance is enhanced by fragments of the old warehouse that are allowed to peek through the artsy decor. While the trendies have moved on to other places, you can still get a good meal at Vivo in chic, candlelit surroundings. If you're simply in search of the best Italian fare in town, head to Taylor Street or to Centro (in River North). Go to Vivo for its one-of-a-kind combination of people-watching and filling food.

For starters, the portobello alla griglia and the antipasto della casa are both positively first-rate. I have tried several pasta dishes, each of which is more than satisfying.

✪ **Wishbone.** 1001 W. Washington St. (at Morgan St.). ☎ **312/850-2663.** Reservations accepted only for parties of 6 or more (no reservations on Sun). Main courses $4.75–$13.50; breakfast and lunch $3.75–$8.25. AE, CB, DC, DISC, MC, V. Mon 7am–3pm, Tues–Thurs 7am–10pm, Fri 7am–11pm, Sat 8am–11pm, Sun 8am–2:30pm. CAJUN/SOUTHERN/BREAKFAST.

A giant mural of an ear of corn marks the corner location of Wishbone, a down-home alternative to the scene-making bistros on Randolph Street. Wishbone had rather modest beginnings in a cozy old house on Grand Avenue (the original is still open), but a few years ago it morphed into this cavernous spot that fills up for lunch and weekend brunch. The West Side location, with its loft-high ceilings and hardwood floors, draws a diverse clientele—a mix of suits, families, gallery folk, white, black, Latino, gay, and everything in between, as well as staff from Harpo Studios (Oprah's compound around the corner).

The modest menu is bolstered by a list of daily specials—from pan-fried chicken to jambalaya to chicken etoufee, as well as two or three seafood items. The house special is the Hoppin' Jack, a pairing of peas and beans poured over a bed of brown rice and sprinkled with cheddar cheese, scallions, and tomatoes (carnivores can add grilled chicken or ham if they like for an extra charge). The fun comes from picking a couple of side orders from a list of a dozen fixin's: comfort foods like mashed potatoes, roasted butternut squash, corn on the cob, yams, green beans, sautéed spinach, and sautéed kale. A tasty corn muffin comes with everything. Breakfast is a big draw, too, with an appealing selection of omelets and pancakes, and lunch is served cafeteria style, sit-down, or take-out. There's outdoor seating in nice weather.

5 Ethnic Dining Near the Loop

All of the dining choices below are an easy cab ride from McCormick Place.

CHINATOWN

Chicago's Chinatown, about 20 blocks south of the Loop and about 2 long blocks west of the McCormick Place convention complex, is expanding. For the moment, most of the commerce, which includes approximately 50 restaurants, plus several colorful food-and-vegetable markets and import houses, are strung along two thoroughfares, Cermak Road and Wentworth Avenue as far south as 24th Place. Of course, hailing a cab from the Loop is the easiest way to reach Chinatown, but you can also drive and leave your car in the validated lot near the entrance to Chinatown or take the El to the Cermak stop, a well-lit station located right on the edge of the Chinatown commercial district.

Many shops in Chinatown provide interesting browsing, especially the dry goods and fresh vegetable markets. You might also want to visit a Chinese bakery, such as **Keefer Bakery,** 249 W. Cermak Ave. (☎ 312/326-2289). Chinese baked goods are made with less sugar than is used in Western bakery products, and many pastries are filled with lotus or red-bean paste. The red-bean snowball is a typical pastry. The Keefer Bakery also has a line of dumplings, one filled with pork, another with ham and egg. As for the store's non-Chinese-sounding name, it comes from a street in Hong Kong! It's open daily from 8am to 6pm.

In the mezzanine-level dining room at **Won Kow,** 2237 S. Wentworth Ave. (☎ 312/842-7500), you can enjoy dim sum from 9am to 3pm daily. Most of the dumplings cost between $1.50 and $2 an order. Other house specialties include Mongolian chicken, and Duck with seafood.

MODERATE

Phoenix. 2131 S. Archer Ave. (at Wentworth Ave.). ☎ **312/328-0848.** Reservations recommended on weekends. Main courses $9.95–$25. AE, DC, DISC, MC, V. Daily 8am–1am. Subway/El: Red Line to Cermak. CHINESE.

One of the newest additions to Chinatown is this spacious, casually elegant restaurant with brightly lit dining rooms and a nice skyline view. There's plenty of room for big tables of family or friends to enjoy the Cantonese (and some Szechuan) cuisine served here. It's an especially popular spot for dim sum.

INEXPENSIVE

Hong Min. 221 W. Cermak Rd. (at Archer Ave.). ☎ **312/842-5026.** Main courses $7–$9. MC, V. Daily 10am–2am. Subway/El: Red Line to Cermak. CHINESE.

Hong Min is certainly not fine dining, but the small two-room restaurant is a favorite destination for its inexpensive Cantonese Chinese food dished out until the wee hours.

Saigon Vietnamese Restaurant. 232 W. Cermak Rd. (at Archer Ave.). ☎ **312/808-1318.** Main courses $4.95–$14.95. AE, DISC, MC, V. Daily 11am–3am. Subway/El: Red Line to Cermak. VIETNAMESE/ASIAN.

The food here is eclectic, and there aren't as many authentic Vietnamese dishes as one might wish. You can't blame the restaurant's owners, however; the American dining public simply has never acquired a taste for this very special cuisine. The spring rolls are Vietnamese style, though, and go down nicely with a bottle of Chinese beer. Shabu shabu is a kind of Japanese fondue where you construct a soup: To a steaming bowl of hot broth, you add the shrimp, fish, and veggies. Another soup, rice noodle, is a very generous serving for the price.

Three Happiness. 209 W. Cermak Rd. ☎ **312/842-1964.** Main courses $4.75–$12. AE, DC, DISC, MC, V. Daily 9am–2am. Subway/El: Red Line to Cermak. CHINESE.

Three Happiness has enjoyed a reputation over many years of providing consistently reliable dishes from several regions of China. City residents come back to Three Happiness year after year during their once- or twice-annual visit to Chicago's traditional Chinatown. There is another Three Happiness at 2130 S. Wentworth Ave. (☎ 312/791-1228).

LITTLE ITALY

Convenient to most downtown locations, a few blocks' stretch of Taylor Street is home to a host of traditional hearty Italian restaurants. Italian food, much of it superior to what's found in Little Italy, permeates the city, so you won't really miss much if you don't make a trip to Little Italy. There's not much to see here, and a housing project right on Taylor Street doesn't add to the ambiance. In addition to the options listed below, two popular North Side restaurants (see reviews below under sections 9 and 11, respectively) have outposts in Little Italy: **Francesca's on Taylor,** 1400 W. Taylor St. (☎ 312/829-2828); and **Leona's Pizzeria,** 1419 W. Taylor St. (☎ 312/850-2222).

In the summertime, you may want to pass on dessert and opt instead for a treat of fla-vorful fruit ice at **Mario's Italian Lemonade,** a little stand at 1070 W. Taylor St.

MODERATE

Tuscany. 1014 W. Taylor St. (between Racine Ave. and Halsted St.). ☎ **312/829-1990.** Reservations recommended. Main courses $9.25–$26.95. AE, DC, DISC, MC, V. Mon–Fri 11am–3:30pm, Mon–Thurs 5–11pm, Fri–Sat 5pm–midnight, Sun 2–9:30pm. Subway/El: Blue Line to Polk. NORTHERN ITALIAN.

Tuscany is one of the reliable Italian restaurants on Taylor Street. In contrast to the city's more fashionable Italian spots, family-owned Tuscany has the comfortable feel of a neighborhood gathering place. As you might expect, the extensive menu features the culinary fare of the Tuscany region, including pastas, pizzas, veal, chicken, and a risotto of the day, and the portions are large. There's a second location in Wrigleyville across from Wrigley Field at 3700 N. Clark St. (☎ **773/404-7700**).

INEXPENSIVE

☼ **Rosebud on Taylor.** 1500 W. Taylor St. (1 block east of Ashland Ave.). ☎ **312/942-1117.** Reservations recommended, especially on weekends. Main courses $5.95–$12.95 at lunch, $11–$30 at dinner. AE, DC, DISC, MC, V. Mon–Thurs 11am–10pm, Fri 11am–11pm, Sat 5–11pm, Sun 4–10pm. Subway/El: Blue Line to Polk. ITALIAN.

Expect to wait well beyond the time of your reservation, but fear not: Your hunger will be satisfied. The original Rosebud serves up enormous helpings of pasta in white bowls. Almost everyone walks out with a bag of leftovers. But the portions aren't just large, they're delicious. The deep-dish lasagna ($14.95) is intense, and the fettuccine alfredo defines the word *rich*. Rosebud also offers a tempting selection of "secondi"— meat, fish, and poultry dishes.

GREEKTOWN

A short cab ride across the south branch of the Chicago River will take you to the city's Greektown, basically a row of moderately priced and inexpensive Greek restaurants clustered on Halsted between Van Buren and Washington streets. **Greek Islands,** 200 S. Halsted (☎ **312/782-9855**); **Parthenon,** 314 S. Halsted (☎ **312/726-2407**); and **Costas,** 340 S. Halsted (☎ **312/263-0767**), are all good bets for gyros, Greek salads, shish kebabs, and moussaka, a sort of Greek lasagna. While they all basically offer the same lively atmosphere, one of my favorites is **Santorini,** 800 W. Adams St., at Halsted Street (☎ **312/829-8820**), where my friends and I go for the tasty pan-fried calamari as soon as we're seated.

PILSEN

Not far from McCormick Place and Chinatown, Pilsen is an interesting picture of Chicago's changing neighborhoods. Once a stronghold of Bohemians following the Great Fire, Pilsen today is a solidly Mexican community. Today, the area is also something of an artists' community and boasts a multitude of elaborate murals. The **Mexican Fine Arts Center Museum** is located in Pilsen at 1852 W. 19th St. (☎ **312/738-1503**); it's open Tuesday through Sunday from 10am to 5pm. (See "Other Neighborhoods to Explore," in chapter 8, for a walking tour of the area.)

INEXPENSIVE

Nuevo Leon. 1515 W. 18th St. (½ block east of Ashland Ave.). ☎ **312/421-1517.** Main courses $5–$9.50. No credit cards. Sun–Thurs 7am–midnight, Fri 7am–4am, Sat 7am–5am. Subway/El: Blue Line to 18th. MEXICAN.

Dining Near McCormick Place

McCormick Place is not within walking distance of much of anything, but there are a few ethnic enclaves within a short cab ride where you'll find some good eats. For the most part, you're probably better off heading back to your hotel in the Loop or along North Michigan Avenue to take advantage of the bounty of excellent restaurants concentrated there. I've described each of the restaurants listed below in more detail elsewhere in the chapter, but here, in order of proximity to McCormick Place, is a quick checklist of my top suggestions:

Chinatown: Chicago's growing Chinatown is a short cab ride from the convention center, and probably the closest place to go out for dinner. There are too many restaurants in the area to list, but here are two good bets:

- **Phoenix,** 2131 S. Archer Ave. (☎ 312/328-0848), is a new, large banquet hall with popular dim sum offerings. (*See page 105.*)
- **Three Happiness,** 209 W. Cermak Rd. (☎ 312/842-1964) and 2130 S. Wentworth (☎ 312/791-1228), serves up reliable cooking in two Chinatown locations. (*See page 105.*)

Little Italy: Italian cuisine is abundantly represented all over Chicago, but Taylor Street, the last vestige of the city's Italian neighborhood, has half a dozen pretty good restaurants. Taylor Street is almost a straight shot west by cab from McCormick Place.

- **Francesca's on Taylor,** 1400 W. Taylor St. (☎ 312/829-2828), is the sister restaurant of boisterous, trendy Mia Francesca on the North Side but without the long wait. (*See page 136.*)
- **Rosebud on Taylor,** 1500 W. Taylor St. (☎ 312/942-1117), serves a traditional Italian feast, an especially good choice if you have a refrigerator in your hotel room to store the leftovers. (*See page 106.*)
- **Tuscany,** 1014 W. Taylor St. (☎ 312/829-1990), is a lively, family-owned restaurant serving northern Italian cuisine. (*See page 106.*)

Printers Row: A South Loop neighborhood once home to the city's sizable publishing industry, Printers Row is now a fashionable neighborhood for loft living and has some excellent restaurants.

- **Printer's Row,** 550 S. Dearborn St. (☎ 312/461-0780), features imaginative American cooking in an upscale setting. (*See page 98.*)
- **Edwardo's,** 521 S. Dearborn St. (☎ 312/939-3366), one of the best pizza chains in town, has a convenient outpost in the neighborhood. (*See page 114.*)
- **Prairie,** in the Hyatt on Printers Row, 500 S. Dearborn St. (☎ 312/663-1143), offers Midwestern cuisine amid a subdued Frank Lloyd Wright–esque decor. It's one of Chicago's finest restaurants. (*See page 95.*)

One of the immigrant families to call Pilsen home is the Gutierrez family, who opened a taqueria on 18th Street in 1962 and built it into a three-room restaurant that's now a busy hub of neighborhood activity. Three generations of the family work in the restaurant, including the grandmother who hand wraps the corn-husk tamales. A meal begins with a serving of crisp tortilla chips served with a potent tomatillo sauce, and if that's not hot enough for you, the wait staff will bring an even hotter red sauce with jalapeños and cooked cayenne peppers. Nuevo Leon makes its own flour tortillas each morning and only has to go next door to a tortilla factory to get the corn variety. Steak, a staple of the northern cattle ranching regions of Mexico, dominates the menu, which also offers a wide selection of tacos, enchiladas, flautas, burritos, and tamales. There are a number of more exotic items such as veal brain dipped in egg and pan fried ("for the gourmet," the menu wryly notes). Because Nuevo Leon does not have a liquor license, you are invited to bring your own beverages.

6 The Magnificent Mile & the Gold Coast

A great many tourists who visit Chicago never stray far from the Magnificent Mile and the adjoining Gold Coast area. From the array of restaurants, shops, and pretty streets in the area, it's not hard to see why.

The city's other neighborhoods, however, are home to some culinary curiosities, so if you have at least a couple of nights in the city, venture out to, say, Wicker Park for dinner one evening. But the restaurants listed along or near the Magnificent Mile are undeniably some of the best in the city.

VERY EXPENSIVE

Cape Cod Room. In The Drake Hotel, 140 E. Walton Place (at Michigan Ave.). ☎ 312/787-2200. Reservations recommended. Main courses $20–$42. AE, CB, DC, DISC, ER, JCB, MC, V. Daily noon–11:30pm. Closed Dec 25. Subway/El: Red Line to Chicago/State. SEAFOOD.

The Cape Cod Room is usually filled to capacity even during the middle of the week, underscoring its perennial popularity. The large multilevel room, with tables and booths covered in red-and-white checkerboard cloths, is wood-beamed and stuffed with nautical paraphernalia. Since the fresh seafood catch from Lake Michigan and nearby rivers is minimal, the Dover sole—the dish favored by Paul Newman, who is said to dine here often when in Chicago—is flown in fresh every 2 days from its native channel waters off the coast of England. The sole is broiled to a light, crusty golden brown and served in a superb almond meunière sauce. The waiter performs the delicate surgery of deboning the fish at tableside into four delectable strips. The sole is accompanied by au gratin potatoes and a mixed salad, though the iceberg lettuce is a reminder that there is nothing nouvelle about the Cape Cod Room.

For starters, the delicious, hearty Bookbinder red snapper soup is flavored to taste with dry sherry brought to the table. Or you might order a mixed seafood appetizer of shrimp, crab fingers, clams, and oysters. For the main course, you can choose from pike, Wisconsin largemouth (freshwater) bass, turbot from the coast of France, pompano from Florida, Gulf swordfish, and Pacific salmon. Shellfish include bay and sea scallops, shrimp, and Maine lobster. The menu also offers a small selection of prime meat cuts, steaks, and chops. For dessert, try a simple bowl of fresh red raspberries and cream in season.

Gibsons Bar & Steakhouse. 1028 N. Rush St. (at Bellevue Place). ☎ 312/266-8999. Reservations recommended. Main courses $22–$30. AE, CB, DC, DISC, MC, V. Mon–Sat 5pm–midnight, Sun 4pm–midnight (bar open later). Subway/El: Red Line to Clark/Division. STEAK.

Popular with its Gold Coast neighbors, Gibsons is the steak house you visit when you want to make the scene. There are sporty cars idling at the valet stand, photos of the celebs and near-celebs who've appeared here, and overdressed denizens mingling and noshing in the bar, which has a life all its own. Gibsons evokes a more romantic time, from the sleek art-deco decor to the bow-tied bartenders. Everything is big here. The namesake martinis are served in 10-ounce glasses, and the entrees are outlandishly scaled, from the six-piece shrimp cocktail, so huge you swore you downed a dozen, to the turtle pie that comes with a steak knife. Huge well-aged steaks are the reason you're here. Yes, Gibsons has a clubby atmosphere, but the food deserves some credit for the crowds who show up every night. You can also order from the menu in the bar.

Hatsuhana. 160 E. Ontario St. (1 block east of Michigan Ave.). ☎ **312/280-8808.** Reservations required. Main courses $20–$30. AE, CB, DC, DISC, JCB, MC, V. Mon–Fri 11:45am–2pm and 5:30–10pm, Sat 5–10pm. Subway/El: Red Line to Grand/State. JAPANESE.

Hatsuhana has one of the most popular sushi bars in Chicago. The restaurant also offers tempura and teriyaki dinners, but I recommend sitting at the sushi bar to watch the skilled chefs at work.

If the sushi mood strikes, you could also try **CoCoRo,** located in River North at 668 N. Wells St. (☎ 312/943-2220). In addition to fresh sushi, the cozy spot specializes in tempura and shabu-shabu.

Pump Room. In the Omni Ambassador East Hotel, 1301 N. State Pkwy. (at Goethe St.). ☎ **312/266-0360.** Reservations required. Main courses $21–$34. AE, DC, DISC, MC, V. Mon–Thurs 6:30–10:30am, 11:30am–2:30pm, 6–10pm; Fri–Sat 6:30–10:30am, 11:30am–2:30pm, 5pm–midnight; Sun 6:30am–2:30pm, 5pm–midnight. Subway/El: Red Line to Clark/Division. AMERICAN.

Back when celebrities journeyed by train between Hollywood and New York and stopped in Chicago to court the press, they would come to the Pump Room. Diners at Booth One inevitably showed up in the morning papers. Today the closest the Pump Room gets to most celebrities are the photographs of movie stars lining the walls. But last year a new owner embarked on a $2 million renovation with the hope of restoring the luster of one of Chicago's most famous restaurants. The dining room was returned to its original color scheme of cobalt blue and gold and spruced up with crystal chandeliers, reupholstered banquettes and fresh draperies, and a new granite bar. A new French-inspired menu with Californian, Pacific Rim, and East Coast touches has been introduced by new executive chef Martial Noguier. There's live entertainment in the bar on weekends and Sunday brunch.

EXPENSIVE

Bice. 158 E. Ontario St. (east of Michigan Ave.). ☎ **312/664-1474.** Reservations recommended. Main courses $9.25–$22.75 at lunch, $14–$25 at dinner. AE, DC, DISC, MC, V. Mon–Thurs 11:30am–10:30pm, Fri–Sun 11:30am–11pm. Subway/El: Red Line to Grand/State. NORTHERN ITALIAN.

Direct from Milan comes Bice, which first opened its doors in 1926 as a small hole in the wall, and now has fashionable affiliates in New York and Beverly Hills, where it continues to be one of the hottest lunch spots in town. Bice occupies a lovely two-story building just minutes from North Michigan Avenue. Seating begins with open-air tables on the street level and moves through a series of raised platforms to the more or less formal interior dining room. The Bice menu, which changes regularly, emphasizes northern Italian tastes.

A unique and intriguing appetizer is carpaccio of either tuna or swordfish. I was very satisfied with my misto di pasta della casa main course—a selection of four exquisitely prepared pastas; and likewise the simple scaloppine di vitello—veal scaloppine sautéed with roasted peppers, oregano, and basil. Desserts are all made on the premises, including the ice cream.

✪ **Blackhawk Lodge.** 41 E. Superior St. (at Wabash Ave.). ☎ **312/280-4080.** Reservations recommended. Main courses $15.95–$27.95. Lunch prices slightly lower. AE, CB, DC, DISC, MC, V. Mon–Thurs 11am–3pm and 5–10pm, Fri–Sat 11am–3pm and 5–11pm, Sun bluegrass brunch 11am–3pm and 5–10pm. Subway/El: Red Line to Chicago/State. REGIONAL AMERICAN/MIDWESTERN.

Comfort food with a twist. Blackhawk's regional American menu features treats such as hickory-smoked fried chicken with whipped potatoes and tangy vegetable slaw and herb-crusted Idaho trout over puffed couscous with winter squash and a light basil cream.

The rustic setting of early American furniture and pine-knot paneling is reminiscent of a cabin in the North Woods and includes evergreens and twinkling holiday lights in the winter months. Always a hit is the basket of rolls, cornbread muffins, and buttermilk biscuits placed on the table along with raspberry red-pepper preserves and sweetened butter. From there Blackhawk offers a nice range of appetizers, from terrific crab cakes to roasted corn chowder with smoked bacon. For dessert, look no further than the cranberry and apple crisp. Servings are generously Midwestern in size, and the service is excellent.

✪ **Eli's, the Place for Steak.** 215 E. Chicago Ave. (at Fairbanks Court). ☎ **312/ 642-1393.** Reservations recommended. Main courses $17.95–$30.95. AE, DC, DISC, MC, V. Mon–Fri 11am–3pm and 5–11pm, Sat–Sun 5–11pm. Subway/El: Red Line to Chicago/State. STEAK/CHOPS.

Every big town has its short list of restaurant institutions—Eli's is definitely on Chicago's. But Eli's is much more than a traditional steak joint where an occasional big-name celebrity shows up for a meal and a photo session. The restaurant has some deep roots of its own. The potato pancakes and the sautéed liver and onions are variations on the Central European comfort foods that found their way here by way of a neighborhood delicatessen where the late Eli Schulman got his start in Chicago 50 years ago. Add to this solid pedigree an element of friendly formality, a commitment to quality, and servings generous enough to ensure that you have something left for tomorrow's lunch, and you have in a nutshell the formula that has kept Eli's at the forefront of Chicago eateries since 1966.

The meal begins with a scoop of delicate chopped liver, accompanied by diced eggs and onions, a colorful crudité of fresh vegetables, and a basket of various breads and rolls. The restaurant's signature appetizer is the shrimp de jonghe, baked to succulent perfection with garlic and bread crumbs. Now about those steaks—Eli's does not disappoint. The 20-ounce T-bone ($30.95) is perfect—full-flavored, juicy, and not too rich. And liver connoisseurs will appreciate the calf's liver Eli, a truly delicate and palate-pleasing selection.

Be sure to save some room for a slice of Eli's famous cheesecake.

Rosebud on Rush. 720 N. Rush St. (at Superior St.). ☎ **312/266-6444.** Reservations recommended. Main courses $12.95–$29.95. AE, DC, DISC, MC, V. Mon–Thurs 10am–3pm and 5–10:30pm, Fri 10am–3pm and 5–11:30pm, Sat 11am–3pm and 5–11:30pm, Sun noon–3pm and 4–9:30pm. Subway/El: Red Line to Chicago/State. ITALIAN.

If you don't feel like trekking to the original Rosebud on Little Italy's Taylor Street, this version offers delicious food in a trendier atmosphere. The wait can be long—as in an hour plus—and here's a warning to summer travelers: Rosebud turns away hungry people wearing shorts and baseball caps.

Assuming you swing a table—either in the covered outdoor eating area or inside—you might try the minestrone soup, followed by the scrumptious rigatoni with broccoli in garlic and olive oil. The other pasta dishes fall nicely between boring and unnecessarily complicated. If you're craving protein, Rosebud offers plenty of veal, chicken, and seafood, plus pork and lamb chops. All in all, good food in a great location, if a tinge overpriced. If you want a more watery slant on Italian cooking, Rosebud's owners recently opened **Carmine's Clamhouse** a few blocks north at 1043 N. Rush St. (☎ **312/988-7676**).

---

① Family-Friendly Restaurants

Of course, all of the theme restaurants *(see page 124)*, from **Michael Jordan's** to **Planet Hollywood,** practically exist to coax families into their environs with menus and attractions designed to entertain.

One of the best all-around options, and a homegrown place as well, is the Southern-style restaurant **Wishbone** (1001 W. Washington St., ☎ 312/ 850-2663). It has much to recommend it. You don't need to worry about your kids disturbing the peace here because any noise is covered by the general commotion of the place. Children can be kept busy looking at the large and surrealistic farm life paintings on the walls or reading a special new picture book, *Floop the Fly,* loaned to diners (written and illustrated by the parents of the owners). The food is diverse enough that both adults and kids can find something to their liking, but there's also a new menu geared just to children, too.

A fun breakfast and lunch spot in Lincoln Park, **Toast** (746 W. Webster St., ☎ 773/935-5600), employs an age-old restaurateur's device for keeping idle hands and minds occupied: tables at this neighborhoody spot are covered with blank canvases of butcher-block paper on which kids of all ages can doodle away with crayons.

Of course, the same goes at **Gino's East** (160 E. Superior St., ☎ 312/ 943-1124), the famous Chicago pizzeria, except patrons are invited to scrawl all over the graffiti-strewn walls and furniture.

With its heaping plates of pasta served up family-style, **Maggiano's** (516 N. Clark St., ☎ 312/644-7700) in River North is a good choice for a budget-conscious family.

The Saloon. 200 E. Chestnut St. (at Mies van der Rohe Way). ☎ **312/280-5454.** Reservations recommended. Main courses $11.95–$27.95. AE, DC, DISC, MC, V. Mon–Thurs 11:30am–10:30pm, Fri–Sat 11:30am–11pm, Sun noon–10pm. Subway/El: Red Line to Chicago/State. STEAK.

Forget the prosaic name. The Saloon is no diamond in the rough. Its setting, a few steps below sidewalk level in one of the neighborhood's most elegant apartment buildings, is all tony, with superb food. You wouldn't think there are many spins you could give to a meal of honest meat and potatoes, but The Saloon has managed to turn a corner or two, as it lives up to its claim to be a "steak house for the '90s." The Kansas City Bone-in Strip ($24.95), served "black 'n' blue," was a knockout, rich as butter under its outside crust, and just as tender. The Saloon's bargain taste treat is a thick slab of smokey barbecued meat loaf ($11.95). The menu also has a wide selection of seafood dishes. And let's not forget those potatoes—seven varieties from mashed to hashed. Lunch here, incidentally, is popular and quite reasonable.

✪ Spiaggia. 980 N. Michigan Ave. (at Oak St.). ☎ **312/280-2750.** Reservations required on weekends. Main courses $13.95–$21.95 at lunch, $26.95–$32.95 at dinner. AE, CB, DC, DISC, MC, V. Mon–Thurs 11:30am–2pm and 5:30–9pm, Fri–Sat 11:30am– 2pm and 5:30–10pm, Sun 5:30–9pm. Subway/El: Red Line to Chicago/State. ITALIAN.

Picture a long, narrow room, colored in soft desert pastels and sharply contoured, with a ceiling two stories high. Against the outer wall, a curtain of tall, segmented windows with a spectacular view of Lake Michigan and Oak Street Beach gives the illusion that the entire room is curved and in motion. This is Spiaggia, whose boldness and novelty of design match its innovative cuisine.

Spiaggia recognizes that pizza is a suitable appetizer, no matter how elegant the restaurant, if the dough is treated as pastry. The small pizza with fresh tomato sauce, basil, and mozzarella is thin, crisp, and delicious. It's not unreasonable to make a lunch at Spiaggia exclusively from side dishes, adding to the pizza, say, an order of tender carpaccio (sun-dried beef) or zuppa di gamberi e fagioli (shrimp and white bean soup). The *insalata normale,* an interesting variety of leaves dressed with a light coating of herb vinegar and olive oil, is the best salad I have eaten in any Chicago restaurant.

Among the many pasta dishes are *pappardelle con salsiccia e pollo* (wide pasta with Italian sausage, chicken, mushrooms, tomatoes, and herbs) and *agnolotti di vitello* (veal-filled pasta crescents with tomato-basil sauce). Or if fish appeals, you might select the *mista griglia di pesce* (mixed seafood grill).

Lovers of sweets unite and confront your finest struggle at Spiaggia! Try the hot zabaglione with seasonal fruits or the *cioccolato bianco e nero,* semisweet chocolate layers filled with white-chocolate mousse and seasonal fruits.

Adjacent to the restaurant in a narrow, window-lined space is the **Café Spiaggia** (☎ 312/280-2764), a more informal but equally spiffy trattoria with an updated interior and menu.

MODERATE

Bistro 110. 110 E. Pearson St. (just west of Michigan Ave.). ☎ **312/266-3110.** Main courses $11.95–$28.95. AE, CB, DC, DISC, MC, V. Mon–Thurs 11:30am–11pm, Fri–Sat 11:30am–midnight, Sun 11am–10pm. Subway/El: Red Line to Chicago/State. CONTINENTAL.

One of the few restaurants in Chicago with a year-round sidewalk cafe (alfresco during the warm season and enclosed the rest of the year) is half a block west of North Michigan Avenue. Patrons sitting outdoors have a close-up view of Chicago's historic Water Tower. Inside, Bistro 110 is divided into several environments—the sidewalk enclosure, a bar area, and a large back room where most diners are seated. An activities chalkboard covers one whole side wall near the front of the restaurant, listing such bulletins as the daily news headlines, weather forecasts, movie and theater information, market quotes, and sports results. Neighborhood cronies tend to congregate here, drawn by the familiar faces and the reasonably priced daily specials.

A sample dinner might begin with half a dozen raw oysters and move on to a classic main course such as steak au poivre or fillet of salmon, served with a whole squadron of veggies: a wedge of orange bell pepper, a plum tomato, new potatoes, a section of corn on the cob, carrots, and asparagus.

✪ Le Colonial. 937 N. Rush St. (just south of Oak St.). ☎ **312/255-0088.** Reservations recommended. Main courses $12–$19. AE, DC, MC, V. Mon–Sat noon–2:30pm, Mon–Fri 5–11pm, Sat 5pm–midnight, Sun 5–10pm. Subway/El: Red Line to Chicago/State. FRENCH/VIETNAMESE.

Le Colonial is one of the latest New York restaurants to find a home in Chicago. Here in the tony Oak Street corridor, Le Colonial has quickly become a chic destination, housed in a vintage town house with a pretty terrace and sidewalk cafe. One of the lovelier rooms in the city, the restaurant evokes 1920s Saigon with bamboo shutters, rattan chairs, potted palms and banana trees, and black-and-white photographs of life in French Indochina. The food is delicious and satisfying, and dining for lunch at Le Colonial makes for a special afternoon treat. We started with *chao tom* (grilled puree of shrimp wrapped around sugar cane and served with angel-hair noodles, mint, and peanut sauce that you wrap with lettuce). Next we moved on to the main course, sharing *ga xao cari* (sautéed chicken breast with eggplant, mango, string beans, and cashew nuts in a coconut curry sauce), and then a real delight—one of the house specialties—*ca chien Saigon* (Vietnamese crisp-seared whole red snapper with a spicy mix of chile, garlic, and shallot in a lime sauce). On your way to the rest rooms upstairs, take a look at the bar area, one of the most atmospheric cocktail lounges in the city. We were far too satisfied to overdo it with dessert (naps were already looming), but a selection of ice cream and sorbets, a float of ice cream and chilled espresso, and tempting pastries from the local bakery, Bittersweet, await another visit.

Mity Nice Grill. In Water Tower Place, 835 N. Michigan Ave. ☎ **312/335-4745.** Reservations recommended. Main courses $7.95–$18.95. AE, CB, DC, DISC, MC, V. Mon–Sat 11am–10pm, Sun 11am–9pm. Subway/El: Red Line to Chicago/State. AMERICAN.

Ensconced in the mezzanine of the busy vertical shopping mall at Water Tower Place, Mity Nice is a good place to go for a consolation meal after a frenzied bout of shopping. As a Lettuce Entertain You restaurant, Mity Nice is certainly reliable in the kitchen, but it falls short of exciting. The price of a meal, though, is quite reasonable, making it a more service-oriented alternative to the **foodlife** food court (see below) just outside its doors. Most dinner main courses are in the $10 to $14 range, and the hot lunches rarely exceed $9. One lunchtime treat not on the dinner menu is grilled lemon chicken with capers, a large and lightly breaded fillet of chicken breast. On both menus is the house specialty, a generous slice of meat loaf served with mashed potatoes and green beans ($8.95 at lunch, $11.95 at dinner). Other comfort foods, such as roast turkey and pot roast, rotate daily. Among the Italian selections, the toasted macaroni and cheese, made with penne instead of egg noodles, is terrific.

Shaw's Crab House and Blue Crab Lounge. 21 E. Hubbard St. (between State St. and Wabash Ave.). ☎ **312/527-2722.** Reservations accepted only for the main dining room. Main courses $12.95–$21.95. AE, CB, DC, DISC, MC, V. Mon–Thurs 11:30am–10pm, Fri–Sat 11:30am–11pm, Sun 5–10pm. Subway/El: Red Line to Grand/State. SEAFOOD.

This is a moderately priced to expensive fish house, organized continental style, with plush red banquettes along the walls and linen-covered tables in the center. For business lunches, Shaw's is right up there with any of its downtown rivals (though it's popular for dinner, too). For starters, if you're in luck, there are fresh oysters (based on availability at market prices). Other appetizers include oysters Rockefeller, blue crab fingers, and popcorn shrimp; and for soup there is a house gumbo by the bowl or the cup. Main courses include sautéed scallops and a pound of fresh Texas stone crab claws. Other popular specials are crab cakes and french-fried shrimp. Shaw's menu also offers a number of side dishes, both traditional and exotic, such as broccoli or asparagus, both topped with hollandaise, or Cajun-style four-grain wild rice. Shaw's trademark dessert, key lime pie, suggests the restaurant's subtle Key West/ Papa Hemingway theme, as do the suave strains of such thirties tunes as "Begin the Beguine" playing in the background. Three nights a week there's live jazz and blues from 7 to 10pm in the Blue Crab Lounge.

INEXPENSIVE

Billy Goat Tavern. 430 N. Michigan Ave. ☎ **312/222-1525.** Reservations not accepted. Menu items $3–$6. No credit cards. Mon–Sat 7am–2am, Sat 10am–2am, Sun 11am–2am. BREAKFAST/BURGERS.

"Cheezeborger, Cheezeborger—No Coke . . . Pepsi." Viewers of the original *Saturday Night Live* will certainly remember the classic John Belushi routine, a moment in the life of a crabby Greek short-order cook. The comic got his material from the Billy Goat Tavern, located under North Michigan Avenue near the bridge that crosses to the Loop. Just "butt in anytime" says the sign on the red door with the picture of the billy goat on it. The tavern is a hangout for the newspaper workers and writers who occupy the nearby Tribune Tower and Sun-Times Building. Offering beer and greasy food (of course, "cheezeborgers") in the kind of dive journalists love to haunt, it's a good place to watch a game, chitchat at the bar, and down a few beers.

☉ Edwardo's. 1212 N. Dearborn St. (at Division St.). ☎ **312/337-4490.** Reservations not accepted. Pizzas $9.50–$22; all-you-can-eat pizza and salad served Sat–Sun 11:30am–2pm for $5.25. AE, MC, V. Sun–Thurs 11am–11pm, Fri–Sat 11am–midnight. Subway/El: Red Line to Clark/Division. PIZZA.

Some locals claim that Edwardo's has the best pizza in Chicago. The chain has several locations, including additional locations in Lincoln Park and the South Loop area, and the all-you-can-eat pizza special is the only one in Chicago.

☉ foodlife. In Water Tower Place, 835 N. Michigan Ave. ☎ **312/335-3663.** Reservations not accepted. Most items $4.50–$8. AE, DC, DISC, MC, V. Juice, espresso, and corner bakery Sun–Thurs 7:30am–9pm, Fri–Sat 7:30am–10pm. All other kiosks Sun–Thurs 11am–9pm, Fri–Sat 11am–10pm. Subway/El: Red Line to Chicago/State. ECLECTIC.

From Lettuce Entertain You's Rich Melman, the man who brought Chicago the world-class cuisine of Ambria and the family-style Maggiano's, comes foodlife, a food court with a healthy twist. Located on the mezzanine of Water Tower Place, just outside the entrance of the Mity Nice Grill, foodlife consists of a dozen or so kiosks offering both ordinary and exotic specialties. Four hundred seats are spread out cafe-style in a very pleasant environment under realistic boughs of artificial trees festooned with strings of lights in the shapes of grapes and other fruits.

The beauty of a food court, of course, is that it tries to offer something for everybody. At foodlife, the burger and pizza crowd will be satisfied, but so will vegetarians and diners looking for, say, a low-fat fresh Caesar salad. Diners here can also choose south-of-the-border dishes, an assortment of Asian fare, and veggie-oriented, low-fat fare.

Special treats include the Miracle Juice Bar's fresh orange juice and raspberry fruit smoothie, as well as a host of healthy and/or gooey desserts, and at a booth called Sacred Grounds, various espresso-based beverages. A lunch or a snack at foodlife is basically inexpensive, but the payment method (each diner receives an electronic card that records each purchase for a total payment upon exit) makes it easy to build up a big tab while holding a personal taste-testing session at each kiosk.

☉ Gino's East. 160 E. Superior St. (directly east of Michigan Ave.). ☎ **312/943-1124.** Pizza $6.95–$17.40. AE, CB, DC, DISC, MC, V. Mon–Thurs 11am–11pm, Fri–Sat 11am–midnight, Sun noon–10pm. Subway/El: Red Line to Chicago/State. PIZZA.

Gino's East is perhaps the only Chicago restaurant where patrons wait outside nightly—even in the dead of winter—for pizza. Considering that Gino's can seat about 500 patrons, the steady line is even more astounding. Then again, Gino's East upholds Chicago's proud pizza tradition year after year.

From the outside Gino's looks like a condemned building. Inside is even worse. But the pre-renovation look is purposeful, a studied part of Gino's "ambiance." Diners sit in dark-stained booths, surrounded by paneled walls covered with graffiti. Each of these effects is craftily fashioned as a form of construction art, so well done in some cases that you don't realize they are all around you unless you look closely. As for the graffiti, you are allowed to indulge, but "if it isn't clean," the earnest young manager confided, "we don't allow it."

As for the pizza, it's elaborate and tasty, "a banquet served on a lush, amber bed of dough," or so one critic described it in a burst of rhapsodic prose. A small cheese pizza is enough for two. A better bet for a satisfactory dinner is the small supreme, with layers of cheese, sausage, onions, green pepper, and mushrooms; or the vegetarian, with cheese, onions, peppers, asparagus, summer squash, zucchini, and eggplant. Next to the restaurant is Gino's carry-out, with its own telephone number (☎ 312/988-4200); pizzas take 30 to 40 minutes' cooking time. If you want to take one home on the plane, call a day in advance and Gino's will pack a special frozen pizza for the trip.

Thai Borrahn. 16 E. Huron St. (at State St.). ☎ **312/440-6003.** Reservations accepted. Main courses $8.95–$18. AE, DC, MC, V. Tues–Thurs 11am–10pm, Fri 11am–10:30pm, Sat 4–10:30pm, Sun 4–10pm. Subway/El: Red Line to Chicago/State. THAI.

Terrific, authentic Thai fare is served in a lovely tranquil setting. Start with the classic tom yum soup, a spicy broth that comes brimming with real lemongrass, straw mushrooms, crushed chile peppers, cilantro, lime, and huge tender prawns. The classic pad is a wonderful combination of flavors and textures. The $5.95 lunch special is a deal: soup, egg roll, and an entree of the day with rice.

Tucci Benucch. 900 N. Michigan Ave., 5th floor. ☎ **312/266-2500.** Reservations recommended. Pizza $8.50–$9.50; pasta $8.50–$10.95; main courses $11.95–$14.95. AE, DC, DISC, MC, V. Mon–Thurs 11:30am–9:30pm, Fri–Sat 11:30am–10:30pm, Sun noon–9pm. Subway/El: Red Line to Chicago/State. ITALIAN.

In the vertical mall that houses Bloomingdale's, Tucci Benucch was created by the Rich Melman gang to resemble an Italian country villa. Each dining area is a replica of a typical room—kitchen, living room, sunroom, and so forth—complete with all the domestic details, including garden plants and clothes on the line. The decor tries so hard to appear country Italian that it almost winds up resembling a movie set, and the effect is a little jarring in this sleek, upscale mall.

The inexpensive fare showcases different regions of Italy, and portions are generous. For about $20 total, a couple can dine on any variety of thin-crust pizzas, delicately sauced pastas, or garlic-roasted chicken, and that includes a glass of Chianti with the meal.

7 River North

River North, the area north of the Loop and west of Michigan Avenue, has become home in the last several years to the city's most prominent cluster of art galleries, as well as to some of its most fashionable restaurants. The clientele is sophisticated; the food (for the most part), Italian.

EXPENSIVE

✪ **Centro.** 710 N. Wells St. (between Huron and Superior sts.). ☎ **312/988-7775.** Reservations recommended. Main courses $11.95–$29.95. AE, DC, DISC, MC, V. Mon–Thurs 11am–11pm, Fri 11am–11:30pm, Sat noon–11:30pm, Sun 4–10pm. Subway/El: Brown Line to Chicago. NORTHERN ITALIAN.

From the folks who brought Chicago the Rosebud restaurants on Taylor and Rush streets comes Centro, a slicker interpretation of dining in the nineties. Centro is where you're more likely to see suits attached to cell phones, a fact that, combined with the acoustics and the lively crowd both inside and on the sidewalk cafe, makes for a rather loud experience.

But it's also a tasty one. For starters, you might try the *insalata di fagioli,* a salad of cannellini beans, tomatoes, and red onions in a garlic vinaigrette, or you could opt for focaccia or stuffed artichoke. The healthy portions of pasta range from baked cavatelli with marinara sauce and ricotta and mozzarella cheeses to linguine with clams, mussels, or calamari. The meat dishes are excellent as well, and a signature dish is the garlic-drenched chicken Vesuvio. If you can, save room for the tiramisu. A live three-piece jazz combo performs on Thursday nights.

☼ Coco Pazzo. 300 W. Hubbard St. (at Franklin St.). **☎ 312/836-0900.** Reservations recommended. Main courses $10–$22 at lunch, $11–$30 at dinner. AE, DC, MC, V. Daily 11:30am–2:30pm, Mon–Thurs 5:15–10:30pm, Fri–Sat 5:15–11pm, Sun 5–10pm; open on Fri–Sat an additional half hour with a limited salad and pizza menu. NORTHERN ITALIAN.

From Milan to Chicago by way of New York, the Coco Pazzo reputation has traveled well. At its best, the food of northern Italy is simple and allows the ingredients to shine through. So a lot depends on the deft touch of the cook staff and the quality of their ingredients. Coco Pazzo wins high marks on both accounts, as it does for its open, light, and airy atmosphere.

Coco Pazzo's menu, naturally, undergoes periodic changes, but there is always a tempting risotto del giorno, and at lunchtime, a focaccia, a thin-crust pizza filled with delectables, in addition to a tempting list of pastas, pizzas, seafood, veal, and chicken dishes. To begin, both the fresh vegetable antipasto and grilled portobello mushrooms are excellent. The selection of tasty breads on the table is accompanied by top-quality virgin olive oil for dipping.

The *focaccia alla gene,* a thin-crust white pizza filled with prosciutto, fontina cheese, and fresh tomatoes, is one of lunch's high points, and the daily risotto is also quite recommendable. Desserts might include a tart filled with fresh raspberries and topped with a dreamy, champagne-spiked zabaglione, or, if you're really lucky, the *cioccolato fondente,* a flourless chocolate cake with a warm mousse center, chocolate sauce, and cappuccino ice cream. Coco Pazzo has a sister restaurant, **Coco Pazzo Cafe,** at 636 N. St. Clair St. (**☎ 312/664-2777**).

☻ Crofton on Wells. 535 N. Wells St. (between Grand and Ohio sts.). **☎ 312/755-1790.** Reservations recommended. Main courses $14–$21. AE, DC, JCB, MC, V. Mon–Thurs 11:30am–2:30pm and 5:30–10pm, Fri 11:30am–2:30pm and 5:30–11pm, Sat 5:30–11pm. Subway/El: Brown Line to Merchandise Mart. AMERICAN.

It's always a special pleasure to dine at a place where a chef-owner has invested so much of her personality and craft, from the design of the menu to the design of the room itself. That's the case at the 70-seat storefront restaurant opened last year by Suzy Crofton, one of the city's rising young chefs (and one of the only female owner-operators in Chicago). The restaurant has quickly earned a loyal following thanks to Crofton's sophisticated, original dishes anchored in her classical training at Le Francais and experience as a head chef at a couple of other restaurants.

The restaurant's atmosphere, subdued and spare with light gray walls, provides a place for a casual, yet special dinner. There are wooden floors, a well-chosen piece of contemporary artwork, a whimsically shaped gilt mirror, and an antique piece doing duty as the host stand.

The menu is prepared seasonally, but you can expect appetizers like crab cake with sweet red peppers and Creole mustard sauce and a shot of farm-raised oyster with papaya and grilled scallions. Each night, Crofton offers eight seasonal main courses, including a completely vegan meal. Look for several fish and seafood selections, as well as meat, such as grilled venison medaillons on a potato and celery root cake and barbecue-glazed smoked pork loin on sweet and Yukon gold mashed potatoes with smoked apple chutney. Lunch items are equally appealing and a winning value with most items under $10.

Earth. 738 N. Wells St. (between Chicago Ave. and Superior St.). **☎ 312/335-5475.** Main courses $13.95–$17.95. Reservations for parties of 6 or more. AE, DC, DISC, MC, V. Mon

11:30am–2:30pm, Tues–Thurs 11:30am–2:30pm and 5:30–9pm, Fri–Sat 11:30am–2:30pm and 5:30–10pm. Subway/El: Brown Line to Chicago. ORGANIC/ECLECTIC.

Earth opened in 1996 with the goal of introducing diners to ecologically conscious, organically grown food prepared with all of the flavor they'd find at traditional restaurants. About 75 percent of what Earth serves is organic, all of the meats (lamb, pork, and bison) are free-range and chemical-free, and the produce is pesticide-free. Even the interior of the restaurant—a fresh aesthetic of clean white walls, a natural hickory floor, and glass-block vases stocked with seasonal flowers and plants—was designed using natural materials and nontoxic substances. The young chef has blended French, Mexican, and Asian influences and has come up with a host of interesting salads and appetizers, including a lentil salad with carrots, leeks, turnips, and mustard dressing, and spaghetti vegetables and mixed greens with grilled marinated portobello mushroom in balsamic-soy vinaigrette. There are also two appealing soups each day, usually vegetarian. Moving on to the main course, look for a vegetable stew of exotic mushrooms, apples, walnuts, and baby vegetables with golden squash puree and brown rice; grilled mahimahi with mashed potatoes and ginger-mustard sauce; roast loin of lamb with japonica wild rice, chorizo, fig and apricot confit; and an assortment of homemade pastas. Vegan dishes are indicated on the menu. For dessert, consider the homemade apple pie and the raspberry charlotte. Earth also features fresh vegetable juices, fruit smoothies, and a nice list of organic wines and beers.

✪ **Frontera Grill & Topolobampo.** 445 N. Clark St. (between Illinois and Hubbard sts.). ☎ **312/661-1434.** Reservations accepted at Frontera Grill only for parties of 5 or more; accepted at Topolobampo. Main courses $8.95–$21. AE, CB, DC, DISC, MC, V. Tues–Thurs 11:30am–2:30pm and 5:30–10pm, Fri 11:30am–2:30pm and 5–11pm, Sat 10:30am–2:30pm and 5–11pm. Subway/El: Red Line to Grand/State. MEXICAN/MESOAMERICAN.

Owners Rick and Deann Groen Bayless, authors of the seminal *Authenic Mexican: Regional Cooking from the Heart of Mexico,* have brought authentic Mexican cooking to the United States at a pair of restaurants that critics have heaped with praise as the best Mexican restaurants in the country. So don't come here looking for tacos or burritos. Instead, you'll find such fare as soufflé-battered stuffed poblano peppers with roasted tomato-chile sauce, black beans and rice, charcoaled lamb simmered with dark-and-spicy pasilla chiles, and a generous portion of grilled beef, pork, duck, or catfish, which diners fold into hot homemade corn tortillas. On the lighter side are the Mexico City–style quesadillas, corn turnovers filled with melted cheese and accompanied by fried black beans (a southern Mexican specialty), and guacamole.

To reinforce the fact that Mexican food is not all Chi-Chi's, the Baylesses opened Topolobampo, a more formal and more expensive establishment, under the same roof. Topolobampo has an intimate atmosphere and a menu all its own. For starters, there are small dishes like classic Yucatecan "enchiladas" of homemade tortillas with savory, smooth pumpkinseed sauce rolled around a hard-boiled egg, topped with roasted tomatoes and pickled red onion. For the main course you may choose from a number of intriguing dishes, including roasted black Malay chicken with classic inky Oaxacan black mole, garlicky bread pudding, and smoky green beans or pan-seared sea scallops and rock shrimp with chipotles, homemade sour cream, and fresh thyme between layers of wood-grilled cactus paddles. Or, if you just can't decide, try the chef's five-course tasting dinner for $48.

Gene & Georgetti. 500 N. Franklin St. (at Illinois St.). ☎ **312/527-3718.** Reservations recommended. Main courses $13.50–$34.50. AE, CB, DC, MC, V. Mon–Sat 11am–midnight (open Sun during major conventions). Subway/El: Brown Line to Merchandise Mart. STEAK/ITALIAN.

Another vestige of old Chicago, Gene & Georgetti is a family-run steak house that's been serving up steak and Italian fare in a wood-frame house in the shadow of the El for more than 50 years. The restaurant is dark and clubby, and the (exclusively male) waiters seem to have worked here for decades. Gene & Georgetti has a popular following, so expect to wait in the bar area. Tables are packed tightly, so close in fact that our neighbors leaned over to bet that my dining companion couldn't finish the prime rib—enormous like all of the other entrees—laid out before her. (They lost; she did.) Although the place is best known for steaks, pasta and Italian specialities are also an essential part of the menu.

Gordon. 500 N. Clark St. (at Illinois St.). ☎ **312/467-9780.** Reservations recommended. Main courses $24–$32; 5-course tasting menu $59. AE, DC, DISC, JCB, MC, V. Tues–Fri noon–2pm, Sun–Thurs 5:30–9:30pm, Fri–Sat 5:30–11:30pm. Subway/El: Red Line to Grand/ State or Brown Line to Merchandise Mart. AMERICAN/INTERNATIONAL.

Gordon's "Americanized international cuisine" epitomizes a blending of continental flare and sophistication with the quality control and freshness of the American kitchen. The roast loin of lamb with orange couscous, for example, hints of Spain, but the accompanying onion marmalade and asparagus bring the platter back to the heartland. Presentations of the meals at Gordon, moreover, are as artful as the food is delicious.

You can drop a bundle for dinner here, the quintessential Gordon experience, or sample the same fare under more mundane conditions at lunch for roughly half the price. I enjoyed the restaurant's signature appetizer—the superb artichoke fritters— went on to a very palatable sirloin plate, and ended with a trio of crème brûlées. Diners can come to dance Saturday nights from 7:30pm to midnight, and you can always opt to sit in the bar and enjoy a light meal. Another Gordon trademark is the nightly wine tasting: three 5-ounce samples of selected wines ($10 to $13).

Hudson Club. 504 N. Wells St. (between Grand Ave. and Illinois St.). ☎ **312/467-1947.** Reservations recommended. Main courses $13.95–$21.95. AE, DC, DISC, MC, V. Mon–Wed 5:30–10pm, Thurs–Sat 5:30–11pm, Sun 5:30–9pm. Subway/El: Brown Line to Merchandise Mart. AMERICAN.

A head-turner of a restaurant, the Hudson Club evokes the glamour and high style of the 1940s with fantastic curving lines and brushed aluminum fixtures. Since the Hudson Club opened in 1996 it's attracted a fashionable, good-looking crowd of singles who often show up for liquid dinners at the overflowing bar. It's easy to get distracted by all the beautiful surfaces here, but the food deserves serious attention, too. An eclectic menu of American cuisine with influences from Asia to the Mediterranean begins with hot and cold appetizers such as home-smoked salmon layered with flatbread, crème frâiche and caviar, eggplant and saganake terrine; and soft-potato ravioli with black truffle, leeks, and garlic-herb broth. Appealing main courses range from coriander-crusted seared ahi tuna, jerk-marinated pork tenderloin with mashed yams and plantain chips, and black pepper-crusted ostrich with mascarpone and wild mushroom tortellini and asparagus. The desserts are all tempting, from cappuccino crème brûlée to a strawberry rhubarb crisp. There are 100 wines by the glass and two dozen 'flights' of wine, each of which comes with sampler size glasses of four wines grouped by grape, region, or style. There's also a cigar lounge, and again, the bar has a serious life of its own.

Mango. 712 N. Clark St. (between Huron and Superior sts.). ☎ **312/337-5440.** Reservations recommended. Main courses $18–$22. AE, DC, MC, V. Mon–Fri 11:30am–2pm, Mon–Thurs 5–11pm, Fri–Sat 5pm–midnight, Sun 4–9pm. Subway/El: Red Line to Chicago/ State. BISTRO.

In case you want to be welcomed there.

We're here to see that you're always welcomed at establishments everywhere. That's why millions of people carry the American Express® Card – for peace of mind, confidence, and security, around the world or just around the corner.

do more

Cards

In case you're running low.

We're here to help with more than 118,000 Express Cash

locations around the world. In order to enroll, just call

American Express before you start your vacation.

do more

Express Cash

And just in case.

We're here with American Express® Travelers Cheques
and Cheques *for Two.*® They're the safest way to carry
money on your vacation and the surest way to get a
refund, practically anywhere, anytime.
Another way we help you...

do more

**Travelers
Cheques**

Steven Chiappetti has been one of Chicago's chefs to watch—a fact confirmed when he was awarded the prestigious James Beard Rising Chef of the Year award in 1997— and Mango is the first of three restaurants where he quickly made his mark (Grapes and Rhapsody are the others). The American bistro Mango, which opened in 1995, is a compact 75-seat restaurant decorated with bright paintings of European pastoral scenes and custom glass sconces in the form of the restaurant's namesake. The local buzz has brought in big crowds, yet the hosts are welcoming and the wait staff knowledgeable and friendly.

Chiappetti was schooled in both Italian and French cuisine in two of the city's top restaurants and has blended European and American culinary traditions at Mango. Start with the duck prosciutto or the chicken and walnut tart, a pastry-topped pot served with a salad of baby frisee lettuce, jicama, crisp bacon, and old-fashioned vinaigrette. Not surprisingly, given that Chiappetti's family runs a lamb-packing business, the menu is heavy on meats, from the lamb shank, glazed with molasses, country vegetables, and lentils to a roasted pork chop with northern white beans and carmelized onion with mustard sauce and Colorado beef tenderloin with potato puree, red onion relish, and red wine sauce. Non–meat eaters can choose from items such as a spicy Mediterranean fish soup with fennel, leeks, and a saffron broth or slow-roasted salmon. Presentation is a source of pride (sometimes a bit too precious), from the way the food has been set on the plate to the eclectic dishware itself.

✪ **Spago.** 520 N. Dearborn St. (at Grand Ave.). ☎ **312/527-3700.** Reservations recommended. Grill, main courses $10.50–$14; dining room, pasta $16; main courses $19.50–$26.50. AE, CB, DC, DISC, MC, V. Grill Tues–Fri 11:30am–2pm, Sun–Thurs 5–10:30pm, Fri–Sat 5pm–midnight. Dining room Mon–Thurs 11:30am–1pm and 5–9:30pm, Fri 11:30am–1pm and 5–10:30pm, Sat 5–10:30pm, Sun 5–9:30pm. Subway/El: Red Line to Grand/State. CALIFORNIAN/ECLECTIC.

One of the big stories of the last couple of years was the arrival of Wolfgang Puck's Spago. The celebrity chef pioneered the Californian–Asian style of cooking and brought it here with a few menu adaptations for the city's cold-weather climate. The interior design evokes California, stylish and simple with curving lines, blond wood, and contemporary artwork. Spago definitely feels like a place where you're making an entrance, escorted into the buzzing scene by one of the modelish hosts, young women straight out of Melrose Place. Even with the high-decibel scene, the servers, dressed in starched Tommy Hilfiger button-downs and ties, are friendly and efficient. Spago embraces both a semiformal dining room and a more casual and affordable grill, both of which share a similar menu. We opted to dine at the grill, and for starters we felt obliged to order one of Puck's signature thin-crust pizzas—once a revelation and now something copied everywhere—and feasted on the smoked salmon pizza with a dill cream and chives and topped with a cluster of golden caviar (the duck sausage is the other standout). The grill menu is a fairly manageable list of half a dozen pizzas from the wood-burning oven; appetizers; pastas; and fewer than 10 entrees, from pistachio-and-herb–crusted grouper to the Spago meat loaf with pancetta, roasted garlic potato puree, and port wine sauce. For dessert tempting options include an apple tart with caramel sauce and a peanut butter brownie sundae with vanilla ice cream.

✪ **Zinfandel.** 59 W. Grand Ave. (between Dearborn and Clark sts.). ☎ **312/527-1818.** www.zinfandelrestaurant.com. Main courses $16–$21. AE, CB, DC, MC, V. Tues–Thurs 11:30am–2:30pm and 5:30–10pm, Fri 11:30am–2:30pm and 5:30–11pm, Sat 10:30am–2:30pm and 5:30–11pm. Subway/El: Red Line to Grand/State. AMERICAN.

While Prairie and the Blackhawk Lodge (see above) celebrate the Midwest, Zinfandel studies the entire nation, drawing inspiration from the Carolinas to Oklahoma. Each month, the kitchen devises a special menu based on ethnic specialties, such as Arizona–Native American fare.

And yes, the name accurately implies you'll find an extensive and interesting wine list at Zinfandel, a joint venture between the Baylesses of Frontera Grill/Topolobampo fame (see above) and Susan and Drew Goss (she's the chef, he's the wine buyer).

Zinfandel's food is at once totally familiar and unique. Using many of her grand-mother's "basic" recipes as a starting point, Ms. Goss crafts such comfort-food standbys as buttermilk biscuits, but these are far from prosaic, and each batch is cooked to order in a hot iron skillet. The menu changes monthly, but if you're lucky it will include the cheese sampler with marinated salads and grilled farmhouse bread or the 'wilted' field greens with strips of Smithfield ham, Stewart pecans, sweet red onions, and a warm maple dressing. The crispy hazelnut corn cakes are grainy and delicious, served with a tangy relish of woodland mushrooms, dried cherries, and maple sugar. Other highlights include the braised pot roast, the pecan-crusted mahimahi, and the Oklahoma-style smoked barbecue spareribs. And on and on go the variations on Zinfandel's inspired menu. Another plus—vegetarian items are noted on the menu. The room is decorated appropriately with American folk art.

MODERATE

✪ **Brasserie Jo.** 59 W. Hubbard St. (between Dearborn and Clark sts.). ☎ **312/595-0800.** Main courses $8.95–$16.95. AE, DC, DISC, MC, V. Mon–Thurs 11:30am–4pm and 5–10pm, Fri 11:30am–4pm and 5–11pm, Sat 5–11pm, Sun 5–10pm. Subway/El: Red Line to Grand/State or Brown Line to Merchandise Mart. ALSATIAN/FRENCH.

The latest creation of four-star Everest chef Jean Joho and Lettuce Entertain You Enterprises, Brasserie Jo has quickly garnered critical praise and appreciative crowds. The restaurant's classic 1940s look, a dramatically designed space with potted palms, tile floors, and soaring ceilings inviting a flood of light, is reinforced by the waiters outfitted smartly in white shirts with black vests and ties and shirtsleeve clips. Brasserie Jo offers the classic Alsatian French fare of Joho's native region, including authentic custom-brewed Alsatian beer, as well as other areas of France. You might start your meal with a cup of onion soup or smoked salmon with crispy potatoes. For the main course, the menu offers everything from such traditional dishes as *choucroute à l'Alsacienne* (smoked meats and sauces cooked in a crock and served with marinated cabbage) to Joho's signature shrimp bag, a crisp phyllo bag encasing shrimp, wild mushrooms, and leeks served with a lobster cream sauce. Or you can try the roasted chicken with pomme puree, bouillabaisse, or roasted leg of lamb, but be sure to save room for Brasserie Jo's delicious desserts.

✪ **Carson's.** 612 N. Wells St. (at Ontario St.). ☎ **312/280-9200.** Reservations not accepted. Main courses $8.95–$29.95. AE, CB, DC, DISC, MC, V. Mon–Thurs 11am–11pm, Fri 11am–12:30am, Sat noon–12:30am, Sun noon–11pm. Closed Thanks-giving. Subway/El: Red Line to Grand/State. AMERICAN/BARBECUE.

A true Chicago institution, Carson's calls itself "The Place for Ribs," and boy, is it ever. The barbecue sauce is sweet and tangy, and the ribs are meaty. Included in the $15.95 price for a full slab of baby-backs are coleslaw and one of four types of potatoes (the most decadent are the au gratin), plus right-out-of-the-oven rolls. Carson's also barbe-cues chicken and pork chops.

For dinner, there's often a wait, but don't despair. In the bar area you'll find a heaping mound of some of the best chopped liver around and plenty of cocktail rye to go with it. When you're seated at your table in the darkly lit dining room with the large booths and white tablecloths, tie on your plastic bib—and indulge.

In case you don't eat ribs, Carson's steaks also have an excellent reputation, although I must confess that in the almost 2 decades that I've been eating here, I have never been able to tear myself away from the ribs. If by some remarkable feat you have room left after dinner, the candy bar sundaes are a scrumptious finale to the meal. Carson's popularity has led to something of a factory mentality among management, which evidently feels the need to herd 'em in and out, but the wait staff is responsive to requests not to be hurried through the meal.

○ **Cyrano's Bistrot & Wine Bar.** 546 N. Wells St. (between Ohio St. and Grand Ave.). ☎ **312/467-0546.** Main courses $8.95–$21.95. AE, DC, DISC, MC, V. Mon–Thurs 11:30am–2:30pm and 5:30–10pm, Fri 11:30am–2:30pm and 5–10:30pm, Sat 5–11pm. Subway/El: Brown Line to Merchandise Mart. FRENCH BISTRO.

Chef Didier Durand and his wife, Jamie, have fashioned an authentic French bistro in the heart of River North, and named it for his hometown of Bergerac. With cafe chairs and pale yellow walls adorned with gilt mirrors and French posters, Cyrano's is warm and romantic, and the chef, a veteran of several other French restaurants in the area and obviously very proud of his own place, often makes the rounds in the dining room. The menu embraces all of the usual bistro fare. The rotisserie is the house specialty: Choose duck, chicken, or lamb; two vegetables (roasted potatoes, pommes frites, stewed ratatouille, wilted spinach with garlic, tagliatelle au gratin, or the vegetable of the day); and one sauce (anything from white wine and herb jus to grained mustard sauce). Additional offerings include a fish of the day served with a timbale of rice, several other seafood items, roasted rabbit, and pan-seared beef tenderloin Wellington. Desserts are beautifully presented, such as a wonderful lemon-orange tart, served on a cream with red hearts iced into it. Or you might find an apple tart with rosemary ice cream, an interesting contrast, although one scoop of the ice cream was plenty. In temperate months, a sidewalk cafe is open all day, and the "grand lunch express"—a four-course meal—is a deal at $10.97. The wait staff is gracious and helpful; it's only slightly jarring to hear the Midwestern staff answering the phone "Bonjour."

Harry Caray's. 33 W. Kinzie St. (at Dearborn St.). ☎ **312/828-0966.** Main courses $7.95–$29.95. AE, CB, DC, DISC, MC, V. Mon–Thurs 11:30am–3pm and 5–10:30pm, Fri 11:30am–3pm and 5–11pm, Sat 11:30am–4pm (sandwich menu/bar only) and 5–11pm, Sun noon–4pm (sandwich menu/bar only) and 4–10pm. Subway/El: Brown Line to Merchandise Mart or Red Line to Grand/State. AMERICAN/ITALIAN.

Harry, of course, was the dean of baseball's play-by-play announcers. The restaurant is a proper shrine to the beloved sportscaster, who died last year. The landmark Dutch Renaissance building near the Chicago River is a repository for the staggering collection of baseball memorabilia that Harry amassed, and it covers almost every square inch of the place. But you don't have to be a baseball lover to appreciate Harry's.

The dining rooms have an old Chicago feel that is comfortable and familiar, with high tin ceilings, exposed brick walls, and red-check tablecloths. It'd be easy to lump Harry's with other celebrity restaurants, but as one reviewer pointed out, the food is better than it has to be. The portions are enormous; you'll have enough left over to eat for days. We practically got our fill grazing on a platter of lightly coated fried calamari. Main course offerings run from traditional items such as pastas with red sauce to chicken Vesuvio, veal, and a variety of seafood choices. Harry's is also a good place to order big plates of meat: dry-aged steaks, lamb, veal, and pork chops. And from the list of side dishes, be sure to order a dish of the signature Vesuvio potatoes. The desserts are rich and decadent.

If you don't want a full-service meal, the bar is a lively place for watching a game and grabbing some munchies—and, incidentally, the bar is 60 feet, 6 inches long—the same distance from the pitcher's mound to home plate. But you knew that.

Maggiano's Little Italy. 516 N. Clark St. (at Grand Ave.). ☎ **312/644-7700.** Reservations recommended. Main courses $7.50–$13.95 at lunch, $8.50–$26.95 at dinner. AE, DC, DISC, MC, V. Mon–Thurs 11:30am–2pm and 5–10pm, Fri 11:30am–2pm and 5–11pm, Sat 11:30am–11pm, Sun noon–10pm. Subway/El: Red Line to Grand/State. CLASSIC ITALIAN.

The benchmark at Maggiano's is large portions, served family style. The other novelty is tradition; many Chicago diners are turning away from the skimpy, lighter fare of northern Italy to the classic food many Italian families still get at Mama's Sunday dinner. The key to Maggiano's success, of course, is that its kitchen also manages to maintain Mama's high standards of preparation and taste.

For starters, consider the baked shrimp oreganata served with sliced tomato, mozzarella, and peppers or the calamari fritte. The pasta dishes and some main courses on the dinner menu come in two sizes, the larger of which usually satisfies at least two people. Even the salads are big enough for two. Favorites among the pastas are the rigatoni with chicken marsala sauce, the fettuccine Alfredo with broccoli, and the garlic shrimp with shells. The whole roast chicken with rosemary and garlic will certainly go around the table several times, while the smothered New York steak, cooked Maggiano style, is a house specialty. There's also an Italian brunch on weekends until 3pm.

Mambo Grill. 412 N. Clark St. (between Hubbard and Kinzie sts.). ☎ **312/467-9797.** Reservations accepted for parties of 6 or more. Main courses $6.95–$14.95. AE, DC, DISC, MC, V. Mon–Thurs 11am–10pm, Fri 11am–11pm, Sat noon–11pm, Sun 5–9pm. Subway/El: Brown Line to Merchandise Mart. LATIN AMERICAN.

If you want to see how the other half eats (other half of the Western Hemisphere, that is), check out this bright, colorful River North storefront restaurant with its pan-Latino menu. What are listed as appetizers might better be viewed as tapas, perfect for small-platter midnight grazing. You can make a meal of these treats without ever getting near the list of the more substantial entradas.

You could go Cubano and Brasileiro with mojitos and mambos to quench your thirsty demons and *tiritas* (potato-crusted calamari with dipping sauces) and *mariquitas* (plantain chips with black bean dip) to tease the palate. Move over to Mexico for some *tamal Mexicano* (tamales stuffed with pork in a spicy tomato with jalapeño cheese pesto), then sample some cornmeal-crusted catfish fingers with sweet corn salsa and mambo tartar. Dessert at the Mambo Grill can only mean the orange caramel flan.

The Mashed Potato Club. 316 W. Erie St. (at Franklin St.). ☎ **312/255-8579.** Main courses $10.95–$21.95. AE, DC, DISC, MC, V. Daily Sun–Thurs 11am–10:30pm, Fri–Sat 11am–1am. Subway/El: Brown Line to Chicago. AMERICAN.

The Mashed Potato Club answers the question, where do you go for dinner when you want to be serenaded with large-screen videos by Cher and the Spice Girls? High camp siliness is the house specialty of this bright yellow two-story-warehouse space ebulliently decorated inside with flashing holiday lights, silver garland, inflatable pink flamingos, disco balls, and debaucherous murals of nude men and women in all sorts of pairings. (The latter is no doubt why parents are forewarned at the restaurant entrance.) The waiters are cute and flirty ("Some of us are, some of us aren't" is what the menu has to say about who's straight or gay), and every dessert is garnished with a sparkler. All of this stimuli may be a bit too much for some people, but the food is actually quite good, too. Potatoes (red, sweet, and oven-roasted) are obviously the star attraction here, but be prepared to sort through a list of 100 toppings, divided into categories of peppers, veggies, meats and seafood, sauces, cheese, nuts, and even candy. (We were pleased with our selection of spinach, tomatoes, and goat cheese, and grilled chicken, peas, and sliced button mushrooms.) Other comfort foods fill out the list of signature main courses (all served with mashed potatoes), including "Aunt Helen's Pot Roast," pan-seared and served with onions, carrots, red rose potatoes, celery, and fresh herbs; southern-style pork chops; meat loaf; and a delicious herb-marinated chicken breast in home-style chicken gravy. The Mashed Potato Club also has a beer garden and sidewalk seating.

Papagus Greek Taverna. On the ground floor of the Embassy Suites Hotel, 620 N. State St. (at Ontario St.). ☎ **312/642-8450.** Reservations recommended for dinner. Main courses $7.95–$27. AE, DC, DISC, MC, V. Mon–Thurs 11:30am–10pm, Fri 11:30am–midnight, Sat noon–midnight, Sun noon–10pm. Subway/El: Red Line to Grand/State. GREEK.

Papagus is a sprawling and attractive restaurant decorated with the colorful artifacts typical of a Greek taverna. And as with most authentic Greek tavernas, you don't have to go near the main courses at Papagus to sample a wide range of dishes and flavors and come away satisfied. You can make a meal—especially lunch—from a combination of delicious hot and cold appetizers.

Every table is equipped with a stack of small plates, which you use to sample each of the items you have selected. From the list of cold appetizers, you might enjoy the whipped feta cheese or the roasted eggplant, both of which can be spread on the excellent, crusty house bread. Among the entrees are a tasty moussaka (ground beef and lamb layered with eggplant, squash, and potato) and an exceptional pastitsio (baked macaroni with ground meat wrapped in phyllo pastry). The spinach pie is a must, and the spicy lamb-and-beef meatballs possess a uniquely Greek flavoring. Finish off the meal with a shot of ouzo, a cup of espresso or thick Greek coffee, and a slice of Papagus's divine baklava.

Scoozi. 410 W. Huron St. (at Orleans St.). ☎ **312/943-5900.** Reservations recommended. Pasta $7.50–$10.95 at lunch and dinner; main courses $8.95–$14.95 at lunch, $9.95–$24.95 at dinner. AE, DC, DISC, MC, V. Mon–Thurs 11:30am–2pm and 5–9:30pm, Fri 11:30am–2pm and 5–10:30pm, Sat 5–10:30pm, Sun 4–9pm. Subway/El: Red Line to Chicago. REGIONAL ITALIAN.

Scoozi has been one of the most popular eateries in the city since opening in December 1986. You can opt for a relatively calm luncheon at Scoozi or the madcap people scene at night (when the management, thankfully, distributes pizza and beverages among the waiting masses). With its lively strains of classical music buzzing in the background, Scoozi has its own élan, every bit as important a factor in making it a Chicago mainstay as the very good food.

For an appetizer, you might begin with a pizza smothered with garlic spinach, oven-roasted tomatoes, and goat cheese. Or select from the antipasti bar. Next you might try *calamari due modo* (deep-fried calamari with basil aioli and arrabbiata sauce) and then *portobello alla griglia* (grilled portobello mushrooms with pancetta and warm balsamic vinaigrette). Main courses include *petto di pollo* (grilled chicken breast with baby artichokes, red potatoes, and warm coriander seed vinaigrette); ravioli baked in a wood oven (smoked chicken, taleggio cheese with smoked bacon, or artichoke); and *gnocchi con salsa rossa* (homemade potato dumplings in a tomato-basil cream). Finish your meal with tiramisu, a bing cherry tart, or the granita (chipped ice flavored with cantaloupe).

Tucci Milan. 6 W. Hubbard St. (at State St.). ☎ **312/222-0044.** Reservations recommended. Main courses $7.95–$24.95. AE, CB, DC, DISC, MC, V. Mon–Thurs 11:30am–10pm, Fri 11:30am–11pm, Sat noon–11pm, Sun 5–9pm. Subway/El: Red Line to Grand/State. NORTHERN ITALIAN.

You might say that Tucci Milan is the city cousin of its country kin, Tucci Benucch (see above), but this place is a good deal more sophisticated. Hundreds of tiny white lights hang above the tables and banquettes, which are laid out to resemble a traditional Italian trattoria.

You Gotta Have a Theme

No more is dining just about the food. In fact, the food often seems beside the point. Theme restaurants offer a myriad of distractions, plus T-shirts and other memorabilia to certify that you were there. In Chicago, many of these establishments have plopped down their gigantic guitars and tropical mushrooms in a kind of loosely organized street carnival along River North's Ontario Street, which not coincidentally is a kind of extended entrance ramp to the freeway (and the suburbs beyond). Unless otherwise noted, reservations are not accepted.

Ed Debevic's. 640 N. Wells St. (at Ontario St.). ☎ **312/664-1707.** Menu items under $7.35. Sun–Thurs 11am–10pm, Fri–Sat 11am–midnight. Subway/El: Red Line to Grand/State. DINER.

The concept restaurant that pioneered the Ontario corridor, Ed Debevic's is a temple to America's hometown lunch-counter culture. Wherever you sit you are surrounded by fifties nostalgia, while tunes such as "Duke of Earl" or other vintage oldies fill the air. The whole idea behind Ed's is to put you on. The waitresses play the parts of gum-chewing toughies with hearts of gold who could hail from Anywhere, USA. It's all a performance—but it works.

Hard Rock Cafe. 63 W. Ontario St. (at Clark St.). ☎ **312/943-2252.** Main courses $6–$16. Mon–Thurs 11am–11:30pm, Fri 11am–midnight, Sat 10:30am–midnight, Sun 11:30am–10pm. Subway/El: Red Line to Grand/State. AMERICAN.

Around the corner from Ed Debevic's stands another establishment replicated by franchises in various cities here and abroad. This version of the Temple of Rock looks more like a branch of the public library, except for the trademark globe twirling over the portico. It offers shakes, burgers, and fries to all who might dig the memorabilia and the loud rock soundtrack that typifies the Hard Rock style, regardless of location. If you don't binge, you can get away with $10 to $15 per person.

House of Blues. 329 N. Dearborn St. (at Kinzie St.). ☎ **312/923-2007** for reservations. Main courses $7–$23. Daily 11:30am–midnight. Subway/El: Brown Line to Merchandise Mart or Red Line to Grand/State. SOUTHERN.

The blues-and-everything-else concert venue in Marina City operates a full-service restaurant dishing up a Southern-style lunch and dinner in a setting adorned with bas-relief portraits of blues legends and a dizzying array of folk art. If you don't make it back here for a concert, you can catch one of the hometown blues acts performing during meals. The House of Blues also holds a roof-raising gospel brunch ($29 to $35 for adults, $15 for children 6 to 12 years old) each Sunday in the concert hall; all three brunches often sell out, so call the above phone number to purchase tickets in advance. The House of Blues also has added a river walk cafe called Voodoo Gardens, on the south bank of the Chicago River, which also features live music and is open in the summer Monday through Saturday 11am to 7pm.

For a light snack, try one of Tucci Milan's thin-crust pizzas grilled over oak and cherry wood and covered with fresh toppings of the day. For dessert, try the espresso tiramisu; the torta bianca, a white chocolate mascarpone cheesecake with white chocolate shavings, raspberry sauce, and fresh raspberries; or the fondente, a dense chocolate pudding cake with toasted almond sauce. The lunch and dinner menus

✪ Michael Jordan's. 500 N. LaSalle St. (at Illinois St.). ☎ **312/644-DUNK.** Main course $7–$14 at lunch, $9–$36 at dinner. Sun–Thurs 11:30am–10:30pm, Fri–Sat 11:30am–midnight. Subway/El: Brown Line to Merchandise Mart. AMERICAN.

Such is the Jordan aura that young people lunching here—mostly in the company of adults, but representing some three-quarters of the clientele—sit, eat, and act respectfully, perhaps, on the long-shot chance that Mike himself might suddenly make an appearance. That's not to imply, however, that Michael Jordan's doesn't appeal to a more mature crowd, which gathers primarily at night. The food is surprisingly good and very affordable at lunchtime (the kids' menu ranges from $1.50 to $4.95). Try a side dish of macaroni and cheese, followed by a grilled chicken sausage sandwich on jalapeño focaccia with melted provolone.

Planet Hollywood. 633 N. Wells St. (at Ontario St.). ☎ **312/266-7827.** Main courses $6.50–$17.95. Mon–Thurs 11am–11pm, Fri 11am–12:30am, Sat 10:30am–1am, Sun 11am–11:30pm. Subway/El: Red Line to Grand/State. AMERICAN.

The Planet Hollywood restaurant chain is packing them in, albeit with the same gimmicky fireworks that sell movie tickets. Some of the highlights of the Chicago outlet are suits and sunglasses worn by John Belushi and Dan Akyroyd in the *Blues Brothers*, a couple of dresses worn by Kate Winslett in *Titanic*, an Arnold robot from *The Terminator*, a Marilyn Monroe dress from *How to Marry a Millionaire*, and Batman and Robin costumes from the TV show. Kids will love the Ninja Turtle and Power Ranger outfits. The menu is broad; the most popular items seem to be the pizza and pasta. But if you go, do it for the show, not the meal.

Rainforest Cafe. 605 N. Clark St. (at Ohio St.). ☎ **312/787-1501.** Main courses $3.50–$17. Mon–Thurs and Sun 11am–11pm, Fri–Sat 11:30am–midnight. Subway/El: Red Line to Grand/State. AMERICAN.

The newest kid on the block is the Rainforest Cafe, a Minnesota-based chain that bills itself as "a wild place to shop and eat." The restaurant strives to create the feel of a rain forest with the sounds of waterfalls, thunder and lightning, and wild animals echoing throughout the place. The menu features salads, sandwiches, and a range of entrees that will please a family of picky eaters. The restaurant also sponsors educational programs designed to bring awareness to the planet's dwindling rain forests.

Rock-N-Roll McDonald's. 600 N. Clark St. (at Ohio St.). ☎ **312/664-7940.** Sun–Thurs 6am–3am, Fri–Sat 6am–5am; 24-hour drive-thru. Subway/El: Red Line to Grand/State. BURGERS.

You know the menu, but the decor at what's said to be the chain's most profitable franchise is what distinguishes this Mickey Dee's: a mix of fifties and sixties kitsch and memorabilia (including life-size figures of the Beatles). This is all worth knowing if the wait (and you should expect one) at the other kid-friendly restaurants in the neighborhood is more than your patience can bear.

at Tucci Milan are the same and offer the usual selection of antipasti, salads, and pastas.

INEXPENSIVE

Big Bowl Café. 159 W. Erie St. (between Wells and LaSalle sts.). ☎ **312/787-8297.** Reservations accepted at dinner. Main courses $7.95–$9.95. AE, DC, DISC, MC, V. Mon–Thurs

11:30am–10pm, Fri 11:30am–11pm, Sat noon–11pm, Sun 4–9pm. Subway/El: Brown Line to Chicago. CALIFORNIAN/ASIAN.

The Big Bowl Café, attached to another Lettuce Entertain You restaurant called Wildfire, but a completely separate entity, is the ideal place for a light lunch or an aftershow snack or supper. It's set up like a long, narrow dining car along the sidewalk, with two large windows that stretch to the ceiling, creating an open-air atmosphere when the weather permits. All dishes are served in bowls and may be eaten with chopsticks if desired. There are more than 15 different noodle entrees, including the Shanghai Noodle, a hand-rolled wheat noodle accompanied by Japanese eggplant, bamboo shoots, and pepper; and nine stir-fry dishes, including the Eight-Vegetable dish—one of the many vegetarian offerings on the menu—composed of baby bok choy, mushrooms, bamboo, tofu, and four other veggies. Wash it all down with a delicious glass of homemade ginger ale. The Big Bowl also has a Gold Coast location at 6 E. Cedar St., at Rush and State streets (☎ 312/640-8888).

✪ **Cafe Iberico.** 739 N. LaSalle St. (between Chicago Ave. and Superior St.). ☎ 312/573-1510. Reservations accepted during the week for parties of 6 or more. Tapas $3.50–$4.95; main courses $7.95–$12.95. DC, DISC, MC, V. Mon–Thurs 11am–11pm, Fri 11am–1:30am, Sat noon–1:30am, Sun noon–11pm. Subway/El: Red Line to Chicago/State or Brown Line to Chicago. SPANISH/TAPAS.

Whether you're extending your evening or just revving up, Cafe Iberico obliges with a festive atmosphere. Crowds begin pouring into this wildly popular tapas restaurant, which is spread over two levels with beautiful tile work and wine bottles forming a canopy overhead, at the end of the workday, so expect a wait. After you've ordered a pitcher of fruit-filled sangría to slake your thirst (do this first thing in the bar while waiting for your table), put a dent in your appetite with a plate of *queso de cabra* (baked goat cheese with fresh tomato-basil sauce). When your waiter returns with the first dish, put in a second order for a round of both hot and cold tapas. Then continue to order as your hunger demands. The waiters, most of them Spanish, are pleasant yet can get a little harried, so it sometimes takes some effort to flag them down. A few standout dishes are the vegetarian Spanish omelet, *patatas bravas* (spicy potatoes with tomato sauce), *pincho de pollo* (chicken brochette with caramelized onions and rice), *pulpo à la plancha* (grilled octopus with potatoes and olive oil), and *salmon à la pimienta* (fresh grilled salmon with green peppercorn sauce). There is a handful of entrees on the menu, and a few desserts if you're still not sated. The caramel flan and the *plantano al caramelo* (sautéed banana with caramel sauce served with vanilla ice cream) are both excellent. There's also a gift shop and gourmet food shop.

Green Door Tavern. 678 N. Orleans St. (at Huron St.). ☎ 312/664-5496. Main courses $6.95–$12. MC, V. Mon–Sat 11:30am–midnight. Subway/El: Brown Line to Chicago. BURGERS.

Green Door Tavern looks for all the world like an old off-campus hangout. The old wood-frame building was put up temporarily after the 1871 fire, presumably just before the city ordinance that banned such construction inside the newly designated "fire zone," and the Green Door has been there since 1921. Apparently the original framing crew went light on the bracing timbers in a few places because the whole building leans to the right. Typical of the items on the sandwich menu are the hickory burger, the triple-decker grilled cheese, and the Texas chili. There's even a veggie burger and a turkey burger, and the menu includes some Cajun fare and pasta. Specials, including the Wednesday meat loaf offering, are posted daily.

Mr. Beef. 666 N. Orleans St. (between Huron and Erie sts.). ☎ 312/337-8500. Sandwiches from $3. No credit cards. Mon–Fri 7am–4:45pm, Sat 10:30am–2pm. Subway/El: Brown Line to Chicago. ITALIAN BEEF SUBS.

Something the Midwest (or maybe it's only Chicago?) can boast of that is lacking on either coast is Italian beef sandwiches. Italian beef is thinly shredded slices of roast beef marinated in a tasty brine and distributed to both food stands and the public in 2-gallon jars. "Want good Italian beef? Go to Mr. Beef" is the common wisdom. What could be better than a juicy sandwich for $4? You can now also get deli offerings and submarine sandwiches.

Pizzeria Uno. 29 E. Ohio St. (at Wabash Ave.). ☎ **312/321-1000.** Lunch reservations accepted Mon–Fri. Pizza $4.29–$17.99. AE, CB, DC, DISC, MC, V. Mon–Fri 11:30am–1am, Sat 11:30am–2am, Sun 11:30am–11pm. Subway/El: Red Line to Grand. PIZZA.

Pizzeria Uno invented Chicago-style pizza, and many deep-dish aficionados still refuse to accept any imitations. You may eat in the restaurant itself on the basement level, or, weather permitting, on the outdoor patio right off the sidewalk. An individual express pizza is featured daily at lunch, with any topping you choose, and salads, sandwiches, and a house minestrone are also available.

Uno was so successful, but lacking in room for expansion, that the owners opened **Pizzeria Due** in a lovely, gray-brick Victorian town house nearby at 619 N. Wabash Ave. at Ontario Street (☎ **312/943-2400**).

One popular feature at both places is the express lunch: a choice of soup or salad, and a personal-size pizza, all for $4.99.

Reza's. 432 W. Ontario St. (between Kingsbury and Orleans sts.). ☎ **312/664-4500.** Main courses $6.95–$14.95. AE, DC, DISC, MC, V. Daily 11am–midnight. Subway/El: Brown Line to Chicago. PERSIAN/VEGETARIAN.

Reza's has brought Persian cuisine to an audience of satisfied customers far beyond the Iranian families who gather at the restaurant's two bustling locations. It's easy to see why. The menu accommodates an array of diners, particularly people looking for a filling vegetarian meal, and the portions, which come with pita bread, feta cheese, Persian rice, and lentil soup, are large.

Appetizers include skewers of grilled mushrooms, hummus, baba ghannouj, tabbouli, and stuffed grape leaves; among the entrees are lamb chops, koubideh, charbroiled ground beef, and an assortment of kebabs (lamb, beef, chicken, seafood, and combinations). While the River North restaurant, located in a former brew pub, is more convenient to downtown and the Magnificent Mile, the original Andersonville location, 5255 N. Clark St. (☎ **773/561-1898**), is more atmospheric, shares the same hours as the downtown location, and is one of a string of Mediterranean and Middle Eastern restaurants in the neighborhood.

8 Lincoln Park

Lincoln Park, the neighborhood roughly defined by North Avenue on the south, Diversey on the north, the park on the east, and Clybourn Avenue on the west, is inhabited by singles and upwardly mobile young families. No surprise then that the neighborhood has spawned a dense concentration of some of the city's best restaurants.

VERY EXPENSIVE

✪ **Ambria.** 2300 Lincoln Park West (at Belden Ave.). ☎ **773/472-0076.** Reservations recommended. Main courses $22–$35; fixed-price meals $48–$64. AE, CB, DC, DISC, MC, V. Mon–Thurs 6–9:30pm, Fri–Sat 6–10:30pm. Bus: 151. FRENCH.

Near the Lincoln Park Conservatory and housed in the impressive former Belden-Stratford Hotel, Ambria is ensconced in several large rooms off the old lobby. It is, quite simply, one of Chicago's finest restaurants. The dimly lit, wood-paneled interior is refined and intimate, almost clublike, and eminently civilized. On one national survey after another honoring the nation's finest restaurants, the name Ambria appears. There is not much room at the top, but Ambria maintains its position with grace and consistency.

The menu changes frequently, of course, so the dishes described here are simply examples of the style of the preparations you will encounter while dining at Ambria. On one recent occasion, my companion and I began our meal with a flaky, mouth-watering napoleon of lobster, bacalhao, and crispy potato, and a pastry stuffed with escargot and summer vegetables that was equally successful. This was followed by an imaginative salad comprised of tender squab with red cabbage, endive, and bacon. For our main courses, we chose a roasted rack of lamb with stuffed baby eggplant, cous-cous, and artichoke chips, served in the lamb's herb-scented natural juices; and the roasted medaillons of New Zealand venison with wild rice pancakes, caramelized rhubarb, and root vegetables, accompanied by a blackberry sauce. Both dishes were superb.

✪ **Charlie Trotter's.** 816 W. Armitage Ave. (at Halsted St.). ☎ 773/248-6228. Reservations required. Fixed-price dinners $85 and $100. AE, CB, DC, DISC, MC, V. Tues–Sat from 5:30pm. Jackets and ties requested for men. Subway/El: Brown Line to Armitage. NOUVELLE.

The mere mention of the name Charlie Trotter is enough to elicit a respectful nod from foodies familiar with the culinary inventions that usher forth from his Lincoln Park kitchen. The grand menu degustation, which changes daily, is the perfect introduction to the innovative creations of the owner/chef who has given his name to this critically acclaimed palace of a cuisine not easily classified. It clearly has roots in the French style, but Trotter, a native of nearby Wilmette, feels no constraints.

The evening I dined here, the meal began with smoked salmon and yellowfin tuna with daikon, jicama, blended horseradish, and a spicy herb sauce. Next followed baby skate wing with eggplant puree and curry emulsion, and then California pigeon breast with crispy polenta, braised Swiss chard, honji menji mushrooms, and cumin-infused broth. The final presentation was South Texas wild boar with salsify, braised legumes, yuca puree, and meat juices. A series of three desserts arrived at our table, including vanilla-yogurt, pineapple–winter melon, and tangerine sorbets, and an assortment of petits fours, accompanied by coffee freshly brewed at tableside. Along the way the waiter may bring a few off-menu surprises that "Charlie wanted you to have." A vegetable and grain degustation menu ($85) is also available and represents a similar lush parade of highly stylized items (a strictly veggie menu is possible on request).

You're in good hands choosing a suitable wine from the encyclopedic list, too, with an experienced sommelier ready to offer guidance.

The ambiance of the renovated 1908 brownstone is pleasant but takes a back seat to the food. The real show is best seen from the table for four in the kitchen. Some people may be turned off by the fussiness of the presentation and the seriousness of the staff (the backwaiter who delivered the dessert was the only one to crack a smile), but dining at Charlie Trotter's is definitely an experience. The restaurant is nonsmoking.

EXPENSIVE

✪ **Geja's Cafe.** 340 W. Armitage Ave. (between Lincoln Ave. and Clark St.). ☎ 773/281-9101. Reservations accepted every day except late Fri–Sat. Main courses $18.95–$32.95. AE, DC, DISC, MC, V. Mon–Thurs 5–10:30pm, Fri 5pm–midnight, Sat 5pm–12:30am, Sun 4:30–10pm. Subway/El: Brown Line to Armitage. Bus: 22. FONDUE.

Geja's (pronounced *Gay*-haz) was the first wine bar in Chicago, opened in 1965, and the restaurant doesn't look like it's changed much over the years. For some diners, the dark rathskeller decor will be a welcome change from the slick, commercial trattorias and bistros common all over the city, and seems a suitably romantic atmosphere for taking up the house specialty, fondue, a culinary anachronism that was quite fashionable a quarter century ago. Fortunately, the owner, John Davis, has single-handedly preserved the fondue experience in Chicago, providing a fun and welcome break from the ordinary mode of dining.

If there are at least two in your party (all main courses are served for two or more), choose the connoisseur fondue dinner, the best Geja's has to offer. The meal begins with a cheese fondue appetizer, into which you dip apple wedges and chunks of dark bread; flavorful Gruyère is the key to the tastiness of this delicious dish. Next, a huge platter arrives, brimming with squares of beef tenderloin, lobster tails, and jumbo shrimp—all raw—and a caldron of boiling oil to cook them in. These delicacies are accompanied by a variety of raw vegetables, such as green pepper, mushroom, broccoli, and small potatoes, which are also softened in the oil, and eight different dipping sauces.

When the flaming chocolate fondue arrives for dessert, with fresh fruit and pound cake for dipping and marshmallows for roasting, you want to beg for mercy. As an added incentive, Geja's usually has a flamenco or classical Spanish guitarist to provide the background music.

Mon Ami Gabi. 2300 N. Lincoln Park West (1 block south of Fullerton, 2 blocks east of Clark St.). ☎ **773/348-8886.** Main courses $15–$23. AE, CB, DC, DISC, JCB, MC, V. Mon–Thurs 6–10pm, Fri–Sat 6–11pm, Sun 5–9pm. Bus: 151. FRENCH BISTRO.

Located in the Belden-Stratford Hotel across the lobby from the upscale Ambria (see above), Mon Ami Gabi, formerly Un Grand Café, is a more casual option. The restaurant, which has begun emphasizing steaks, feels like a French bistro that's been here forever, and there's a comfortable, convivial spirit about the place. The menu is country French with such traditional dishes as steak frites, roasted chicken, and grilled fish, of which there are half a dozen options. For appetizers, definitely go for la pasta, a dish of rock shrimp, toasted garlic, pine nuts, olive oil, and brebis cheese.

✪ North Pond Cafe. 2610 N. Cannon Dr. (south of Diversey). ☎ **773/477-5845.** Reservations recommended. Main courses $14–$23. AE, DC, MC, V. Tues–Sun 11am–2:30pm and 5–9:30pm, Sun 11am–4pm. Bus: 151. AMERICAN.

The North Pond Cafe debuted last year with the goal of living up to its sublime setting in Lincoln Park, across from the duck pond, with the John Hancock building rising in the background. Housed in an old warming hut on the banks of the pond, the 80-seat restaurant takes inspiration from the Arts and Crafts movement, from the pretty hand-painted mural around the ceiling to the handsome tableware to the food preparation itself. Chef Mary Ellen Diaz, who spent time at the Ritz-Carlton's Dining Room, has crafted an imaginative, flavorful menu that celebrates American, specifically Midwestern, flavors and tastes. She uses bountiful amounts of organic produce, much of it grown on Illinois and Wisconsin farms. The menu, which changes seasonally, offers all kinds of appealing selections, with appetizers such as cream of asparagus soup with spring lobster salad and grilled calamari pizza with spicy orange-tomato jam and arugula. Main courses might include sassafras grilled duck breast with Smithfield ham and oyster gumbo, an excellent grilled tenderloin chop with truffled potato terrine and balsamic vinaigrette, and a very pleasing grilled halibut served over corn risotto with sweet peas and lobster sauce. Pies are it for dessert, but what pies! Choose from about 10 intriguing offerings, notably the boiled-cider custard, pear marsala with

Dining in Lincoln Park & Wrigleyville

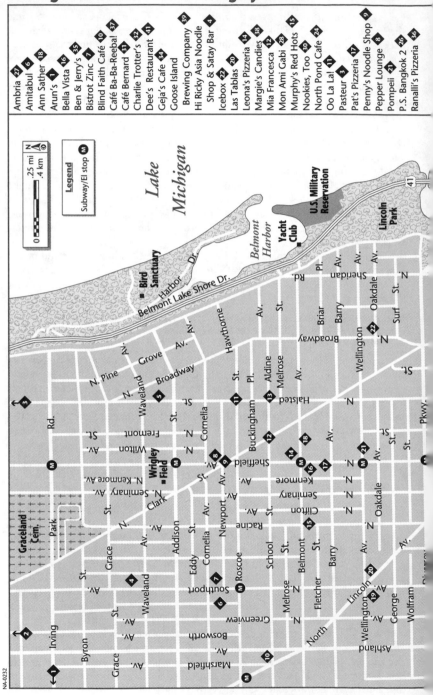

Ambria 27
Amitabul 6
Ann Sather 18
Arun's 1
Bella Vista 16
Ben & Jerry's 35
Bistrot Zinc 7
Blind Faith Café 40
Café Ba-Ba-Reebal 37
Café Bernard 31
Charlie Trotter's 32
Dee's Restaurant 41
Geja's Cafe 34
Goose Island
Brewing Company 39
Hi Ricky Asia Noodle
Shop & Satay Bar 4
Icebox 22
Las Tablas 20
Leona's Pizzeria 14
Margie's Candies 38
Mia Francesca 12
Mon Ami Gabi 28
Murphy's Red Hots 15
Nookies, Too 30
North Pond Cafe 24
Oo La La! 11
Pasteur 3
Pat's Pizzeria 17
Penny's Noodle Shop 9
Pepper Lounge 8
Pompeii 21
P.S. Bangkok 2 25
Ranalli's Pizzeria 36

NA-0232

130

Rhumba	**5**
RoseAngelis	**25**
Tiffin	**2**
Toast	**29**
Twin Anchors	**10**
Wieners Circle	**23**
The Yoshi's Cafe	**13**
Zum Deutschen Eck	**19**

chocolate crumble topping and chocolate sauce, and polka-dot pistachio. A wine list of 75 bottles is strong on California and Oregon vintages (unfortunately diners aren't permitted to drink alcohol outside, where you have the best view).

The restaurant's designer has made the most of the small brick building, and the results are charming and intimate, with my only complaint being that clatter from the open kitchen occasionally intrudes on the peace of the place.

MODERATE

Café Ba-Ba-Reeba! 2024 N. Halsted St. (at Armitage Ave.). ☎ **773/935-5000.** Limited number of reservations accepted. Tapas $1.95–$7.50; main courses $8.95–$11.95. AE, CB, DC, DISC, MC, V. Mon–Thurs 11:30am–10:30pm, Fri and Sat 11:30am–midnight, Sun noon–10pm. Subway/El: Red or Brown Line to Fullerton or Brown Line to Armitage. SPANISH/TAPAS.

Located at the southern end of Halsted Street's restaurant row, near Armitage, Café Ba-Ba-Reeba!, marked by a neon sign announcing tapas, is frequented by a young Lincoln Park crowd. Some 65 hot and cold tapas of the restaurant's own creation are on tap here.

Inside, the cafe includes a patio, two bars, and several dining rooms. The bright acrylic and oil paintings, mostly pop portraiture and other representations, are some of the most delightful you will see gathered in one room anywhere in Chicago.

The plato de la casa is a plate of very satisfactory traditional meats and cheeses. Among the hot tapas, the *pincho de pollo y chorizo*, chicken and chorizo sausage brochettes with a dip of garlic-cumin mayonnaise, was economical and very tasty. For dessert you might try the *profiteroles de chocolate*.

Café Bernard. 2100 N. Halsted St. (at Dickens Ave.). ☎ **773/871-2100.** Reservations recommended. Main courses $10–$19. AE, CB, DC, DISC, MC, V. Sun–Thurs 5–10:30pm, Fri–Sat 5–11:30pm. Subway/El: Brown Line to Armitage. FRENCH.

The Café Bernard features French country fare at moderate prices—many dishes are in the $12 to $14 range. This little French restaurant on the corner, incidentally, has the authentic look and feel of a Parisian backstreet bistro, with low lighting and a casually dressed clientele. Its main courses range from steak au poivre to stuffed breast of pheasant and other game.

Dee's Restaurant. 1114 W. Armitage Ave. (between Racine and Sheffield aves.). ☎ **773/477-1500.** Reservations recommended on weekends. Main courses $9–$13. AE, DC, DISC, JCB, MC, V. Mon–Thurs 5–10:30pm, Fri–Sat 5–11:30pm, Sun 4:30–10:30pm. Subway/El: Brown Line to Armitage. CHINESE.

A solid, reliable Chinese restaurant in the Lincoln Park neighborhood, Dee's offers a typical menu that includes all the old standbys—moo shu, Peking duck, and mandarin beef.

INEXPENSIVE

Goose Island Brewing Company. 1800 N. Clybourn Ave. (at Sheffield Ave.). ☎ **312/915-0071.** www.gooseisland.com. Reservations recommended on weekends. Sandwiches $5.95–$8.95; main courses $9.95–$11.95. AE, CB, DC, DISC, MC, V. Mon–Fri 11:30am–1am, Sat 11am–2am, Sun 11am–midnight; kitchen closes 2 hours before the bar. Subway/El: Red Line to North/Clybourn. AMERICAN.

Some of the best beer in Chicago is manufactured at this modest microbrewery in the Clybourn corridor. Don't take my word for it. An impressive cast of professional beer critics have arrived at the same conclusion. In the course of a year, Goose Island brewmeister Greg Hall (whose dad, John, is the pub/brewery's owner) mixes up some 2,500 barrels a year of about 50 different varieties of lagers, ales, stouts, pilsners, and porters that change with the seasons. Normally a pint costs $3.50, but a 6-ounce sampler glass is only $1.50, making a tasting session a fun evening's entertainment. For a behind-the-scenes look, there's a free tour of the brewing facility every Sunday at 3pm.

The menu is mostly burgers and sandwiches, brats, pizza, and a pretty good jalapeño chicken soup, but you may want to sample the beer and then dine at another of the neighborhood's more accomplished restaurants. To stave off the hunger, though, munch on the homemade potato chips. Goose Island goes through 3,000 pounds of spuds a week; after all, what goes better with beer? What else goes great with a brewsky? A game of pool, and Goose Island has five tables.

Las Tablas. 2965 N. Lincoln Ave. (at Southport Ave.). ☎ **773/871-2414.** Reservations accepted for large groups. Main courses $9.95–$21.90 (combo for 2). AE, DC, MC, V. Mon–Thurs noon–10pm, Fri–Sat noon–11pm. Subway/El: Brown Line to Diversey. COLOMBIAN.

Located on a rapidly gentrifying strip in Lincoln Park, Las Tablas is a little gem of a restaurant. You'll feel as if you're sitting outside at a plaza in a South American village. Las Tablas is casual, and there's plenty of room for big groups to gather around picnic-style tables. The cuisine is devoted to the owner-chef's native Colombia. Start with an order of empañadas, corn puffs filled with ground meat, potatoes, rice, and egg. The house specialty is churrasco, juicy char-grilled New York strip accompanied with plantain, fried yuca, a baked potato, and chimichurri sauce. Or you can go with a combination of steak and chicken breast with all the same sides. The portions, served on wooden planks, are enormous. The paella also looks good: Chicken, octopus, calamari, sausage, shrimp, clams, and fresh chopped vegetables all get thrown into the pot. The lunch special is a hearty deal: soup and your choice of chicken, steak, or vegetables with a side of plantain and potatoes, all for $4.95. For dessert, go for the coconut flan.

Nookies, Too. 2114 N. Halsted St. (between Fullerton and Armitage aves.). ☎ **773/327-1400.** Reservations not accepted. Menu items $3.25–$7.95. MC, V. Mon–Thurs 6:30am–10pm, Fri–Sat 24 hours, Sun 6:30am–6pm. Subway/El: Red Line to Fullerton or Brown Line to Armitage. DINER.

Nookies, Too is open for breakfast, lunch, and dinner, serving hash and eggs, eggs Benedict, omelets (more than a dozen varieties), pancakes, burgers, sandwiches, and blue-plate specials. Cheery, well lit, and with a big counter, it's an appealing place for a good, solid, everyday meal. Nookies also has branches in Old Town at 1746 N. Wells St. (☎ 312/337-2454) and in Lakeview at 3334 N. Halsted St. (☎ 773/248-9888).

P.S. Bangkok 2. 2521 N. Halsted St. (between Fullerton and Wrightwood aves.). ☎ **773/348-0072.** Reservations accepted on Fri and Sat only. Main courses $3.50–$12.95. AE, DISC, MC, V. Mon–Thurs 11:30am–10pm, Fri–Sat 11:30am–11:30pm, Sun 4:30–10pm. THAI.

This Thai joint offers oodles of dishes, mostly in the $5 to $8 range. With a menu of 20 appetizers, 10 soups, and more than 25 main courses, you ought to be able to find something to tempt your palate—though for many of us, practically any Thai platter is a tasty treat. The restaurant doesn't have a liquor license, so be sure to bring your own beer or wine if you're so incined.

Ranalli's Pizzeria, Libations & Collectibles. 1925 N. Lincoln Ave. (at Armitage Ave.). ☎ **312/642-4700.** Reservations not accepted. Main courses $6.75–$15.95. AE, CB, DC, DISC, MC, V. Sun–Fri 11am–2am, Sat 11am–3am. Subway/El: Brown Line to Armitage. Bus: 22 or 36. PIZZA/ITALIAN.

Yards from the farm in the Lincoln Park Zoo is Ranalli's and its three-score tables spread out on an open-air patio. Acres of memorabilia (the "collectibles") line the walls of the adjoining indoor restaurant and bar, though in the proper weather the festive potential of the outside setting far outshines the cavelike atmosphere inside (unless you're a sports fan glued to the big game). Thin-crust (as opposed to "Chicago" deep-dish) pizza is the specialty, along with Philadelphia-style hoagie sandwiches, salads, pasta, ribs, and steak. The main attraction, though, is the seemingly endless roster of beers.

RoseAngelis. 1314 W. Wrightwood Ave. (at Lakewood Ave.). ☎ **773/296-0081.** Reservations accepted for parties of 8 or more. Main courses $8.95–$12.95. DISC, MC, V. Tues–Thurs 5–10pm, Fri–Sat 5–11pm, Sun 4:30–9pm. Subway/El: Red Line to Fullerton. ITALIAN.

Two former lawyers traded in their law books for pots and pans, opening RoseAngelis in 1992. Ensconced in an old house in a residential section of Lincoln Park, the restaurant charms with its series of small dining rooms and garden patio. Then it delights with its exceptional and affordable Italian food. Try the outstanding, garlicky chicken Vesuvio (not offered on Friday and Saturday nights because of preparation time), browned to perfection, or the substantial lasagna. The specials also tend to be worth sampling, as is the tiramisu.

Twin Anchors. 1655 N. Sedgwick St. (1 block north of North Ave.). ☎ **312/266-1616.** Reservations accepted for parties of 6 or more. Main courses $7.50–$16.95; sandwiches $3.50–$6.95. AE, DC, DISC, MC, V. Mon–Thurs 5–11:30pm, Fri 5pm–12:30am, Sat noon–12:30am, Sun noon–10:30pm. Subway/El: Brown Line to Sedgwick. BARBECUE.

A landmark in Old Town since the end of Prohibition, Twin Anchors manages to maintain the flavor of old Chicago. It's a friendly, family-owned pub with Frank Sinatra on the jukebox and on the walls (he apparently hung out here on swings through town in the sixties). It's a totally unpretentious place with a long mahogany bar up front and a modest dining room in back with red Formica-topped tables crowded close. Of course, you don't need anything fancy when the ribs—the fall-off-the-bone variety—come this good. Even nonmeat eaters may be swayed if they allow themselves one bite of the enormous slabs of tender baby-back pork ribs. (Go for the zesty sauce.) All of this means that you should prepare for a long wait on weekends. Ribs and other entrees come with coleslaw, dark rye bread, plus your choice of baked potato, tasty fries, and the even better crisp onion rings. For dessert, there's a daily cheesecake selection.

9 Wrigleyville & the North Side

The area surrounding Wrigley Field has a long history of being a neighborhood of working-class families, but Wrigleyville has quickly gentrified as developers have built new town houses and apartments, and with that affluence has come a group of new, very popular restaurants spanning a range of culinary offerings and price ranges. Both here and throughout the North Side you'll find a wealth of ethnic restaurants from simple storefronts to upscale establishments that allow diners to embark on further gastronomic globe-trotting.

EXPENSIVE

✪ **Arun's.** 4156 N. Kedzie (at Irving Park Rd.). ☎ **773/539-1909.** Reservations recommended. Main courses $15.95–$30.95. AE, CB, DC, DISC, MC, V. Tues–Sat 5–10pm, Sun 5–9:30pm. Subway/El and Bus: Blue Line to Irving Park, then transfer to eastbound no. 80 bus; or Brown Line to Irving Park, then transfer to westbound no. 80 bus. THAI.

It's been called the best Thai restaurant in the city—possibly the country. Chef/owner Arun Sampanthavivat prepares a refined traditional cuisine that's authentic and flavorful without being taste-bud-burning. Try the hot-and-sour shrimp soup, the three-flavored red snapper, the garlic prawns, and, of course, the pad thai. House specialties also include *khao kriab* (steamed rice dumplings filled with crabmeat, shrimp, chicken, peanuts, and garlic with a tangy vinaigrette) and golden baskets (flower-shaped bite-size pastries filled with shrimp, chicken, sweet corn, and shiitake mushrooms). Or if you want to sample it all, try one of the degustations prepared upon request ($75). The decor is beautiful, with Thai artwork—paintings, artifacts, and antiques—as the backdrop. The restaurant is also smoke-free.

Zum Deutschen Eck. 2924 N. Southport Ave. (at Lincoln and Wellington aves.). ☎ **773/525-8389.** www.2derest.com. Reservations recommended. Main courses $15.95–$19.95. AE, CB, DC, DISC, MC, V. Mon–Thurs 11:30am–10:30pm, Fri 11:30am–midnight, Sat noon–midnight, Sun noon–10pm. Subway/El: Brown Line to Wellington, walk 4 blocks west. GERMAN.

Zum Deutschen Eck (which translates as The German Corner) is housed in a large Bavarian-style chalet with a menu that features the best of German and continental cooking.

After munching on the fresh rolls and breadsticks served at the beginning of each meal, try the liver-dumpling consommé, accompanied by a crisp cucumber salad. Owner Al Wirth, Jr., whose father opened Zum Deutschen Eck in the late fifties, suggests the Ochsenmaul, which literally means calves' cheeks, and tastes something like a sweeter, more tender version of prosciutto. Or you may want to try the German Schlact Platte, a selection of German wursts and smoked pork loin, served with parsley potatoes and sauerkraut. You'll have a hard time finding a more delicious knockwurst or Thueringer bratwurst, which it turns out are procured from local butchers and contain no filler, but only pure meat. Dinners here include soup, appetizer, and salad. You can drink draft Dortmunder lager during your meal, and for dessert there's a small but scrumptious Black Forest devil's food cake with fresh whipped cream. I don't know why anyone on a diet would go to a German restaurant, but just in case, the place has added a group of heart-healthy selections.

The music—sing-along and schmaltzy, of course—never stops, as a duo of accordion and drums bang out one familiar beer-drinking song after another, alternating between German and English.

MODERATE

Bella Vista. 1001 W. Belmont Ave. (at Sheffield Ave.). ☎ **773/404-0111.** Reservations recommended for dinner on weekends. Main courses $12–$19. AE, DC, DISC, MC, V. Mon–Thurs 11:30am–2:30pm and 5–10pm, Fri 11:30am–2:30pm and 5–11pm, Sat 5–11pm, Sun 5–9pm. Subway/El: Red Line to Belmont. ITALIAN.

Bella Vista was installed in an old bank building, and the former financial institution's glorious and ornate interior decor of columns, painted plaster, and marble—not to mention a skylight covering virtually the entire ceiling of one room—has been totally preserved. As the name implies, it is indeed a beautiful view.

The food at Bella Vista is classic Italian, with a slightly nouvelle accent. Among the appealing selections are the *antipasti di giorno,* with eight different items daily; the *vodka di capellini* with rock shrimp, scallops, sugar snap peas, tomatoes, and goat cheese; the *bistecca griglia,* grilled beef tenderloin with black pepper gorgonzola mashed potatoes and broccoli; and, of course, all of the gourmet pizzas cooked up in the wood-burning oven. If you want more casual surroundings, you can order off the menu in the funky bar area as well.

✪ Bistrot Zinc. 3443 N. Southport Ave. (between Belmont Ave. and Addison St.). ☎ **773/281-3443.** Reservations recommended. Main courses, cafe $6.95–$12.05, bistrot $9.95–$16.95. AE, DC, MC, V. Cafe Tues–Thurs 5–10pm, Fri 5–11pm, Sat

11am–11pm, Sun 11am–9pm. Bistrot Tues–Thurs 5:30–10pm, Fri–Sat 5:30–11pm, Sun 5–9pm. Subway/El: Brown Line to Southport. FRENCH BISTRO.

Southport Avenue has emerged in the last few years as one of the city's bright new restaurant rows, and Bistrot Zinc is one of its glamorous stars. In keeping with the bistro concept, diners have two dining options. Up front, the casual 50-seat cafe is furnished with self-service food stations, rattan chairs and a sidewalk cafe, and a handsome 22-foot-long zinc bar, which was imported from France. Here you can choose from a menu of French-style "fast food": salads, sandwiches, soups, crepes, and desserts. In back, there's an elegant sit-down restaurant with ochre walls in the main room and a more private dining "salon" with red leather banquettes. The menu leans toward the region of Alsace-Lorraine but covers the classics of bistro fare from all regions of France. Tempting main courses include roasted chicken with bacon, mushrooms, pearl onions, potatoes, thyme, and garlic jus; and sage-roasted pork loin with mashed, soufflé, and julienne potatoes in apple brandy sauce. There are also several daily specials. For dessert, try the tarte Tatin (upside-down warm apple tart) or the *crème au caramel de miel* (vanilla custard with honey).

✪ **Mia Francesca.** 3311 N. Clark St. (1½ blocks north of Belmont Ave.). ☎ 773/281-3310. Reservations not accepted. Main courses $8.95–$22.95. AE, DC, MC, V. Sun–Thurs 5–10:30pm, Fri–Sat 5–11pm. Subway/El: Red Line to Belmont. ITALIAN.

From the time it opened about 7 years ago, Mia Francesca has been one of the hardest tables to get in Chicago. Unless you plan on arriving as the doors open, be prepared to wait. By 7pm, that wait often exceeds an hour (people have been known to wait for 3 hours). The addition last year of a second-floor dining room has eased things a bit, but "Mia" remains an exceedingly fashionable place. They come for the scene—the decor is simple, the crowd attractive and noisy. But it's the food—unpretentious but never dull—that keeps locals coming back. The menu changes weekly, but you can count on thin-crust individual pizzas, and chicken, veal, and fish dishes nightly. The pastas are out of this world. For the same menu and a less frenzied atmosphere, the owners have opened an alternative in Little Italy, **Francesca's on Taylor,** 1400 W. Taylor St. (☎ 312/829-2828).

Oo La La! 3335 N. Halsted St. (between Belmont Ave. and Addison St.). ☎ 773/935-7708. Reservations recommended. Main courses $8.95–$18. AE, MC, V. Sun–Sat 5:30–11pm, Sun brunch 10am–3pm. Subway/El: Red Line to Belmont. FRENCH/ITALIAN.

This dark and romantic little storefront restaurant squeezes 60 lucky patrons—many of them gay residents of the neighborhood—into its swank and chummy confines on a given night. Oo La La! calls itself a border bistro for the binational inspiration of chef Jill Rosenthall's dishes, which may be traced to the typical workaday Parisian bistro or Roman trattoria, but which have been modified and pampered to satisfy the more demanding palates of those who dine out frequently. So, at Oo La La!, you may have your grilled chicken or roasted lamb shank, and eat it too, so to speak, not only with gusto but with pleasure. The pasta dishes, on the other hand, have evolved somewhat farther from the homeland trattorias. But pasta is like that, because nine-tenths of the challenge is in the sauce, and Chef Rosenthall's alchemy in this medium is on a par with the best Chicago has to offer. Her emphasis is on simplicity and preparation, rather than novelty for its own sake. Oo La La! is just north of Belmont, about an $8 cab ride from downtown. In warm weather, there's a nice outdoor patio.

✪ **Pasteur.** 5525 N. Broadway (between Bryn Mawr and Foster aves.). ☎ 773/878-1061. Reservations recommended. Main courses $10–$16. AE, DC, DISC, MC, V. Mon–Tues 5–10pm, Wed–Thurs and Sun noon–10pm, Fri–Sat noon–11pm. Subway/El: Red Line to Bryn Mawr. Bus: 36. VIETNAMESE.

Like a phoenix, Pasteur has literally risen from the ashes of a fire that had wiped out the city's most lauded Vietnamese restaurant. Owner Kim Nguyen took the time off to reinvent the restaurant and has surpassed the previous restaurant in style and substance. What had been a simple storefront operation has been reborn as a lovely room furnished with rattan cafe chairs and large potted palms, ceiling fans whirling overhead, and murals of Vietnamese life. The menu is freighted with a nice selection of seafood, and everything looks delicious, from the *ga kho gung* (chicken slow-cooked in a clay pot with ginger root and lemongrass) to *ca nuong la chuoi* (grilled fish marinated in lemongrass and wrapped in banana leaves and served with a dill-tomato sauce). We started with an order of delicious spring rolls accompanied by plum sauce for dipping. After we spied an appealing dish on a neighboring table, we inquired with our waiter. It was the lotus stem salad, which we promptly ordered. What arrived was an attractive plate of shredded lotus stem mixed with shrimp, chicken, thinly sliced apple, herbs, and a fish sauce dressing, plus a serving of prawn chips. The staff, outfitted in stylish French-Vietnamese colonial costuming, is friendly and helpful.

The menu's only weakness is a paucity of vegetarian dishes. Except for the sidewalk cafe and small lounge, the restaurant is smoke-free.

Pepper Lounge. 3441 N. Sheffield Ave. (at Clark St.). ☎ **773/665-7377.** Reservations recommended. Main courses $11–$22. AE, DC, MC, V. Tues–Sat 6pm–2am, Sun 6pm–1am. Subway/El: Red Line to Addison. ECLECTIC.

A successful melding of restaurant and nightclub, the intimate, dimly lit Pepper Lounge was slightly ahead of the retro curve a few years ago when it opened not far from Wrigley Field. The kitchen stays open late, making it a dependable place to go for the night or a stopover after a visit to the theater or a concert. For starters, go for the portobello mushrooms, prepared differently each night but delicious. The menu is evenly divided between pasta—the ravioli is the house specialty, a mix of crab and ricotta-filled red-pepper pasta topped with shrimp and peppers in a tomato cream—and entrees, which include such flavorful dishes as jerk-marinated lamb chops with coconut mashed sweet potatoes, and espresso bean–blackened catfish with potato-and-prosciutto hash drizzled with red currant butter. A couple of other amenities add to the Pepper Lounge's late-night appeal: an outdoor patio and a small bar that serves—what else?—the requisite martini (chocolate is the big seller).

✪ **Rhumba.** 3631 N. Halsted St. (1 block north of Addison St.). ☎ **773/975-2345.** Reservations recommended. Main courses $7.75–$18.75. AE, DC, MC, V. Daily 5:30–10pm. Subway/El: Red Line to Addison. BRAZILIAN.

Since Rhumba opened in 1996, the city's only Brazilian restaurant has concocted an exotic mixture of food, music, and theatrics that's as kicky as a cocktail of caipirinha, the Brazilian national drink. The carnival atmosphere kicks off when you step into the swirl of the restaurant's front bar, a loud and busy room with a full roster of Latin specialty cocktails, Brazilian soap operas on the TV monitors, and the infectious beat of lively South American music. The good times continue into the supper-club-style dining room, a colorful, high-ceilinged space with a second-story perch where a Carmen Miranda wanna-be appears for lively song-and-dance numbers.

You'll find a lot of big groups dining at Rhumba, and once the flavorful food arrives you can see why. Ask for a sampler plate of the appetizers, or a taste of items like *coxinha* (roasted chicken, thyme, and tomatoes encased in a potato shell with toasted cumin sauce); a jicama, mango, and avocado salad in a spicy carrot juice vinaigrette; and grilled pork ribs marinated in orange juice and cumin and paired with mashed sweet potatoes. For dinner, you can choose among such specialties as coconut shrimp and peppers over brown rice and quinoa, sautéed salmon with mango salsa and grilled chayote, and various "churrasco" meats (chicken, pork, steak, seafood, and lamb) and veggies skewered and served with sides of rice, beans, and plantains. Desserts are not to be overlooked: Consider the chocolate chenille cake or a Brasilnut cookie topped with fresh fruits and sorbets.

Still not ready to call the night quits? On weekends, the dining room does a costume change of its own, transforming into a late-night gay dance club called Fusion.

✪ **Yoshi's Cafe.** 3257 N. Halsted St. (at Aldine St.). ☎ **773/248-6160.** Reservations recommended. Main courses $8–$19. AE, DC, MC, V. Tues–Thurs 5–10:30pm, Fri–Sat 5–11pm, Sun 5–9:30pm. Subway/El: Red Line to Belmont. NOUVELLE/FRENCH BISTRO.

Same name, different concept. Yoshi Katsumura has been a familiar name on the Chicago restaurant scene thanks to the intimate, refined restaurant he operated for years. But when he found the demand for special-occasion dining falling off, Yoshi shifted gears and reinvented his restaurant as a casual bistro. The result has proven a hit with the neighborhood; it can even get somewhat chaotically busy here on weekends. The new Yoshi's is comfortable and casual (even if the pastel decor does kind of remind some of a hotel coffee shop) and the menu offers a number of options in the $8 to $10 range (including a number of health-conscious selections, which are noted on the menu).

The dishes reflect both Yoshi's native Japan and his French training. Look for pastas like homemade buckwheat soba with oriental vegetables and pappardelle with tomato, shrimp, squid, and scallops. For dinner, choose among a variety of fish and seafood offerings, such as sautéed grouper on a bed of pasta and oriental vegetables in a soy-sesame sauce or vegetable and shrimp tempura. There's also sautéed beef tenderloin or rotisserie chicken with tarragon. Streetscape enhancements along Halsted Street have enabled Yoshi's to add an outdoor cafe.

INEXPENSIVE

Amitabul. 3418 N. Southport Ave. (between Addison St. and Belmont Ave.). ☎ **773/ 472-4060.** Main courses $5.95–$7.95. AE, DC, MC, V. Mon–Sat 11am–9:30pm. Subway/ El: Brown Line to Southport. ASIAN/VEGETARIAN.

How about some Buddhist/Korean/vegetarian chow tonight? Amitabul (pronounced A-*mee*-ta-bul) adds to the diverse crop of restaurants and bistros on Southport Avenue with a menu of good-for-you dishes with such intriguing names as Heavenly Nirvana, Wolfman's Dreamed Treats, and Buddha Bop. Some of the entrees even suggest medicinal remedies: Dr. Linda Kinsky's Cure, a spicy noodle soup with tofu, seaweed, and vegetables, is said to be good for the flu, colds, and headaches (even hangovers). Dishes arrive piled high with steaming veggies and noodles or hearty brown rice. Fans of kimchi will be in nirvana here with the spicy pickled cabbage making an appearance on several dishes. Also on the menu are 10 types of soups, vegan pancakes, and tofu specials, as well as a variety of special juices and teas. For dessert, there's even a vegan ice cream, "Green Heaven."

Decorated with a back-lit paper ceiling and a variety of Eastern statues and landscapes, Amitabul is the second restaurant in the area for Dave and Sue Choi, who had developed such a loyal following at **Jim's Grill,** serving a similar menu in a former diner at 1429 W. Irving Park Rd. (☎ 773/525-4050).

Ann Sather. 929 W. Belmont Ave. (between Clark St. and Sheffield Ave.). ☎ **773/ 348-2378.** Reservations accepted for parties of 6 or more. Main courses $7–$11.95. AE, DC, MC, V. Sun–Thurs 7am–10pm, Fri–Sat 7am–11pm. Subway/El: Red Line to Belmont. Free parking with validation. SWEDISH/AMERICAN/BREAKFAST.

A sign hanging by Ann Sather's door bears the following inscription: "Once one of many neighborhood Swedish restaurants, Ann Sather's is the only one that remains."

It's a real Chicago institution, where you can enjoy Swedish meatballs with buttered noodles and brown gravy, or the Swedish sampler of duck breast with lingonberry glaze, meatball, potato-sausage dumpling, sauerkraut, and brown beans. All meals are full dinners, including appetizer, main course, vegetable, potato, and dessert. It's the sticky cinnamon rolls, though, that make addicts out of diners.

There are several other branches that serve only breakfast and lunch: a restaurant in Andersonville at 5207 N. Clark St. (☎ 773/271-6677) and smaller cafes, in Lincoln Park at 2665 N. Clark St. (☎ 773/327-9522) and Lakeview, at 3416 N. Southport Ave. (☎ 773/404-4475).

Blind Faith Café. 3300 N. Lincoln Ave. (1 block north of Belmont Ave.). ☎ 773/871-3820. Reservations accepted for parties of 6 or more. Main courses $7–$12. AE, MC, V. Mon–Thurs 11am–10pm, Fri 11am–11pm, Sat 9am—11pm, Sun 9am–10pm (weekend brunch until 3pm). Subway/El: Brown Line to Paulina. VEGETARIAN.

For my very first college journalism assignment more than a decade ago, I trekked in the snow from my dormitory in Evanston to the original Blind Faith, then located in a small diner on Dempster Street, to record my observations and write a short descriptive article. Soon after, the owners cast off their hippie trappings for a more polished appearance, and over the years the restaurant has become something of an institution in Evanston. Now Blind Faith has come to the city, smartly opening across the street from the Whole Foods grocery store in the Lakeview neighborhood. The roomy new restaurant is comfortable and filled with light, and the menu is slightly bigger and more sophisticated than the Evanston original, but features many of the staples of a full-service vegetarian restaurant, including sandwiches, various stir-fry dishes, seitan fajitas, a tasty veggie burger, half a dozen salads, and a bunch of fruit smoothies and fresh juices and blends. The original Blind Faith is located in Evanston at 525 Dempster St. (☎ 847/328-6875).

Hi Ricky Asia Noodle Shop & Satay Bar. 3730 N. Southport Ave. (between Irving Park Rd. and Addison St.). ☎ 773/388-0000. Reservations not accepted. Main courses $4.95–$6.95. AE, MC, V. Mon–Thurs 11:30am–10pm, Fri–Sat 11:30am–11pm, Sun noon–10pm. Subway/El: Brown Line to Southport. ASIAN/THAI.

Hi Ricky has a continent-hopping menu that spans the cuisine of Thailand, Japan, Indonesia, China, and Vietnam. The dishes feature fresh ingredients, generous portions, and reasonable prices. This big airy restaurant, installed in a former auto shop, has an industrial-hip look with downturned woks inventively employed as light fixtures along the open grill. Given the restaurant's name, you'll want to begin with an order or two of satay: You've got seven to choose from, or you can go for a sampler and try all of them (chicken, lamb, shrimp, tofu, and more). Main courses include spicy drunken noodles (broad noodles stir-fried with basil, greens, tomato, sprouts, and hot pepper—and a choice of tofu or a variety of meats), and the Malaysian Hokkien noodles (spicy curry fried egg and rice noodles with a choice of meats). The owners made a savvy move in opening their second location (the first is at 1852 W. North Ave. in Wicker Park) across the street from the Music Box Theatre, which shows foreign and offbeat flicks (see chapter 10). A third location is near downtown, at 941 W. Randolph St. (☎ 312/491-9100). Hi Ricky also has added full bars at all locations.

✪ Penny's Noodle Shop. 3400 N. Sheffield Ave. (at Roscoe and Clark sts.). ☎ 773/281-8222. Reservations not accepted. Main courses $3.85–$5.75. No credit cards. Tues–Thurs 11am–10pm, Fri–Sat 11am–10:30pm. Subway/El: Red Line to Belmont. ASIAN/THAI.

Predating many of Chicago's pan-Asian noodle shops, Penny's has kept its loyal following even as others have joined the fray. Some of its success is in the unique location tucked beneath the El tracks: a tiny, pie-shaped space brightened with sunny yellow walls. With room for only a dozen tables and stools wrapping around the grill, Penny's is packed nightly with scrub-faced young people from the neighborhood. But the overall cuteness of the place doesn't detract from what happens in the open kitchen. Penny Chiamopoulous, a Thai native, has assembled a concise menu of delectable dishes, all of them fresh and made to order. Of course, noodles unite everything on the menu, so your main decision is choosing between noodles (crispy wide rice, rice vermicelli, Japanese udon, and so on) in a heaping bowl of soup or spread out on a plate. There are several barbecued pork and beef entrees, and plenty of options for vegetarians. There's often a long wait, so you may want to try the second, larger location directly south on Sheffield at 960 W. Diversey Pkwy. (☎ 773/281-8448). Both locations are BYOB, with liquor stores nearby.

Tiffin. 2536 W. Devon Ave. (between Western Ave. and Rockwell St.). ☎ **773/338-2143.** Reservations recommended. Main courses $7.50–$13.50. AE, DC, DISC, MC, V. Daily 11:30am–3:30pm (buffet); Sun–Thurs 5:30–10pm, Fri–Sat 5:30–10:30pm. Subway/El and Bus: Red Line to Loyola and transfer to westbound bus no. 155. INDIAN.

Devon Street is one of the most diverse stretches in the city, home to a polyglot of cultures, predominant among them immigrants and first-born generations of Indians. The area is a short cab ride from the Loyola or Granville El stop on the Red Line. Here you'll find a host of fine Indian restaurants, among them **India House** (☎ 773/338-2929), **Gandhi** (☎ 773/761-8714), and **Moti Mahal** (☎ 773/262-2080). One of the best, however, is Tiffin, a new restaurant from the owner of **Udupi Palace** (☎ 773/338-2152), a vegetarian restaurant across the street. Tiffin has a pleasant upscale feel to it, and the menu has a range of dishes certain to satisfy. You'll want to start with an order of Indian breads, say, a mix of naan and shaahi paratha, a multi-layered bread stuffed with cheese, chopped onions, spinach, coriander, and bell pepper. Appetizers include samosa (a flaky golden pastry stuffed with spiced vegetables), ragara patties (potato patties stuffed with a blend of fresh herbs and spices), and kathi kabab (spiced shredded chicken cooked in a tandoor and wrapped in a crepe).

Notable main courses are the dozen or so items prepared in the restaurant's clay oven and an equal number of vegetarian entrees, including the special *rawa masala dosai* (a South Indian delight of thin wheat and lentil crepes with onion and potato masala filling served with sambar and coconut chutney) and *chole peshawari* (a dish from the Afghani border that's a mix of chick peas and diced potatoes that goes well with poori, a puffed wheat bread). House specials include *chicken kheema mattar* (ground chicken simmered with green peas and Indian seasoning) and *nargisi kolta curry* (lamb meatballs stuffed with boiled egg coated with a mix of spice paste and simmered in gravy).

10 Wicker Park/Bucktown

Now that the yuppies have conquered Lincoln Park and are making definite inroads in Wrigleyville, the Wicker Park/Bucktown area has become the neighborhood of contention. Artists, photographers, musicians, and the like began moving in years ago, drawn by the light-drenched studios, the cheap rents, and the "real people" feel of the place. It didn't take long for wanna-bes to follow. The armies have splintered into factions, with artists fighting artists—some apparently think it's a crime to sell a painting—and entrepreneurs battling developers. But from the muck has risen a happening scene, which includes some of the city's hippest restaurants.

A great evening out is to have dinner and then catch some music at a neighboring club. You'll probably feel safer if you don't venture too far from the nexus of activity at the intersection of North, Damen, and Milwaukee avenues, where you won't have to walk more than a couple of blocks in any direction to find a hot spot. Cab fare's not too bad from downtown, or you can take the El's Blue Line to Damen.

EXPENSIVE

Cafe Absinthe. 1954 W. North Ave. (at Damen and Milwaukee aves.). ☎ **773/278-4488.** Reservations recommended. Main courses $14.50–$22. AE, DC, DISC, MC, V. Mon–Thurs 5:30–10pm, Fri–Sat 5:30–11pm, Sun 5:30–9pm. Subway/El: Blue Line to Damen. ECLECTIC.

For most Chicagoans, alleys function as a place to store garbage until the sanitation crews come along, keeping the sidewalks clear. Cafe Absinthe uses its alley as the restaurant entrance. Looks can be deceiving, for Absinthe is no dive. On the contrary, it has become one of Chicago's hippest eateries, both because its out-of-the-way location is attracting trendy types and because the dining experience is interesting and elegant.

The darkly lit interior sets the mood. Along one wall, draperies divide the tables. The menu changes daily; on a typical evening Absinthe will offer such appetizers as grilled ostrich fillet with confit onion, fresh figs, and mandarin oranges, or napoleon of artichokes, roasted red peppers, and feta cheese mousse. Main courses include wasabi-seared tuna with oriental vegetable roll and macadamia-crusted beef tenderloin with grilled red onions, potatoes, and balsamic red wine bordelaise. The dessert menu is every bit as tempting, from the passion fruit tart with baked meringue and berry coulis to the black cherry, prickly pear, and coconut sorbets.

✪ **Restaurant Okno.** 1332 N. Milwaukee Ave. (between Division St. and North Ave.). ☎ **773/395-1313.** Reservations recommended. Main courses $13–$21. AE, DC, MC, V. Sun–Thurs 5:30–11:30pm, Fri–Sat 5:30pm–12:30am. Subway/El: Blue Line to Division. ECLECTIC.

The brains behind some of the city's hottest restaurants—Mia Francesca and Soul Kitchen—joined forces to open Okno. The trendy new restaurant is named for the Russian slang for window, lifted from Anthony Burgess's *A Clockwork Orange*. Appropriately, Okno has a sleek, two-story glassy face on a working-class strip of Milwaukee Avenue. Inside is a brightly colored, high-tech space. Plexiglas orbs hang from the soaring ceiling, servers are outfitted in tight-fitting jerseys, and a deejay spins jungle, techno, and other club music from a second-level perch. The unusual menu draws upon a mix of multiethnic influences. Appetizers include smoked trout tamale with avocado and chipotle crema and tandoori chicken with Israeli couscous, goat cheese, and green curry yogurt sauce. The entrees are often such eccentricities as sweet potato–crusted yellowfin tuna with ginger-soy vinaigrette and double-cut pork chop with spring succotash and rhubarb BBQ. There's also a daily vegetarian entree on the menu. For dessert, try the lime tart with berry compote or the dark chocolate gelato with chocolate phyllo and espresso chocolate sauce. An outdoor patio was added last year.

Soul Kitchen. 1576 N. Milwaukee Ave. (at Damen and North aves.). ☎ **773/342-9742.** Reservations not accepted. Main courses $12–$21. AE, MC, V. Sun–Thurs 5–10:30pm, Fri–Sat 5–11:30pm, Sun brunch 10am–2pm. Subway/El: Blue Line to Damen. CARIBBEAN/SOUTHERN/LATIN AMERICAN/CAJUN.

Soul Kitchen epitomizes the hipness that has descended upon Wicker Park. The restaurant, specializing in the cuisine of the American South, the Caribbean, and Latin America, gained its initial following in a more obscure neighborhood storefront, but when this unbeatable location at the corner of North, Damen, and Milwaukee avenues opened up, the owners relocated and gave their already popular establishment a sleek makeover of vivid tangerines, faux cheetah skin tablecloths, and windows that give passersby a peek at the sleek whirl of diners within. You should expect a long wait, but the restaurateurs have prepared for that inevitability with both a raw bar and a long undulating bar for posing and sipping cocktails. Soul Kitchen boasts "loud food, spicy music": the sixties and seventies soul and funk tunes spun here may be too loud for some diners, but those with adventurous taste buds should be at home here. Chef Monique King dabbles with a variety of unusual, ethnic ingredients. For starters, try the crab potstickers with Thai red curry, sesame seaweed salad, and smoked shiitakes or the jerk-chicken skewers with cucumber-cilantro yogurt. The many appealing entrees include grilled T-bone lamb chops with triple garlic mashed potatoes and black cherry veal sauce; garlic linguine "Jambalaya style" with okra, mussels, shrimp, andouille sausage, tomatoes, and Parmesan; and pecan-coated catfish with black-eyed peas, greens, and lemon-mustard sauce. For dessert, you can't go wrong with the toasted coconut.

MODERATE

Club Lucky. 1824 W. Wabansia Ave. (1 block north of North Ave., between Damen and Ashland aves.). ☎ **773/227-2300.** Reservations accepted for parties of 6 or more, and for any size party before Bulls and Blackhawk games. Main courses $5.95–$18.95. AE, DC, DISC, MC, V. Mon–Thurs 11:30am–11pm, Fri 11:30am–midnight, Sat 5pm–midnight, Sun 4–10pm; cocktail lounge open later. Subway/El: Blue Line to Damen. TRADITIONAL ITALIAN.

Club Lucky has endured as one of the most popular spots in Chicago. The scene here is youngish and very dress-up; expect to wait for a seat (but that just gives you time to order one of their signature martinis). Club Lucky seems to have been carved from a local fifties-era corner tavern with a catering business in the back room. In fact, the place was designed to look like that, with plenty of Naugahyde banquettes, a Formica-topped bar and tables, and Captain Video ceiling fixtures.

You may or may not take to the scene, but the food does not disappoint. Prices overall are moderate, and the family-style portions are generous. The large calamari appetizer—"for two," the menu says—will almost certainly keep you in leftover land for a day or two. The menu offers real Italian home-style cooking, such as *pasta e fagioli* (thick macaroni-and-bean soup—really a kind of stew). Or try the rigatoni with veal meatballs, served with steamed escarole and melted slabs of mozzarella; or the spicy grilled boneless pork chops served with peppers and roasted potatoes.

The lunch menu includes about a dozen Italian sandwiches for about $6.50 each, such as scrambled eggs and pesto, meatball, and Italian sausage.

✪ **Hacienda Tecalitlan.** 820 N. Ashland Ave. (½ block north of Chicago Ave.). ☎ **312/243-1166.** Reservations for parties of 6 or more. Main courses $11.50–19.95. AE, DC, MC, V. Daily 11am–11:30pm. Bus: 66, or a short cab ride from the Loop. MEXICAN.

Stepping off a gritty stretch of Ashland Avenue into Hacienda Tecalitlan is like leaving Chicago and taking a trip to a Mexican village. The dining area is centered around a striking two-story courtyard, and a band of mariachis serenade diners after 7pm nightly. The restaurant is an elaborate step-up for the owners, who started with the simpler Tecalitlan not far away at 1814 W. Chicago Ave. (☎ 773/384-4285). With Dudley Nieto, chef of the critically praised but commercially defunct Mexican restaurant Chapulin, taking over the kitchen, the menu should prove even more interesting to explore. The menu carries the usual assortment of traditional Mexican dinners. You might begin with *ceviche de camaron* (chopped shrimp with tomatoes, hot peppers, onions, lemon, and coriander) or the house special, a bowl of *sopa de tortilla* (a julienne of corn tortilla, avocado, fresh cheese, cream, dry pepper, and tomato). Equally tasty are the *empañadas de espinacas,* three Mexican corn pies filled with spinach and accompanied by rice and salad. The menu is rounded out by more elaborate entrees such as grilled chicken and quail, several seafood dishes, and fajita dinners.

Wicker Park/Bucktown

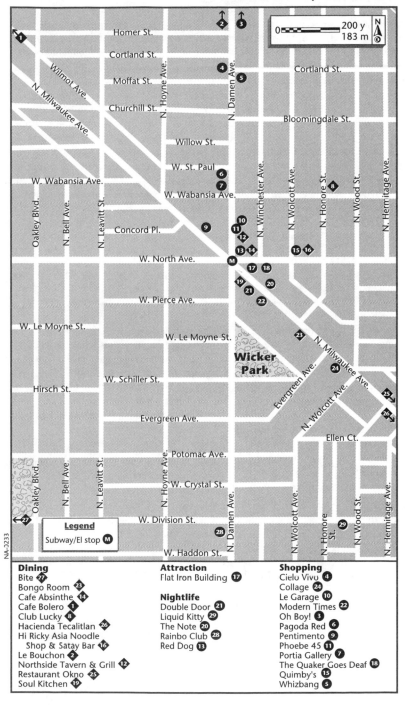

Legend
Subway/El stop Ⓜ

Dining
Bite ㉗
Bongo Room ㉓
Cafe Absinthe ⑭
Cafe Bolero ①
Club Lucky ⑧
Hacienda Tecalitlan ㉖
Hi Ricky Asia Noodle
 Shop & Satay Bar ⑯
Le Bouchon ②
Northside Tavern & Grill ⑫
Restaurant Okno ㉕
Soul Kitchen ⑲

Attraction
Flat Iron Building ⑰

Nightlife
Double Door ㉑
Liquid Kitty ㉙
The Note ⑳
Rainbo Club ㉘
Red Dog ⑬

Shopping
Cielu Vivo ④
Collage ㉔
Le Garage ⑩
Modern Times ㉒
Oh Boy! ③
Pagoda Red ⑥
Pentimento ⑨
Phoebe 45 ⑪
Portia Gallery ⑦
The Quaker Goes Deaf ⑱
Quimby's ⑮
Whizbang ⑤

NA-2233

143

⊙ **Le Bouchon.** 1958 N. Damen Ave. (at Armitage Ave.). ☎ **773/862-6600.** Reservations recommended. Main courses $11.50–$14.75. AE, DC, DISC, MC, V. Mon–Thurs 5:30–11pm, Fri–Sat 5pm–midnight. Subway/El and Bus: Blue Line to Damen and transfer to bus no. 50. FRENCH BISTRO.

One of the many storefront restaurants that has sprung up in Wicker Park in the last few years, Le Bouchon immediately became a favorite. Appropriating the charm of a French bistro, the tin-ceilinged room is cozy, romantic, and intimate. Better yet, the food is delicious and a good value. There's a small bar where you can wait—something you may expect at this popular spot even if you called ahead for a reservation. The menu, which changes seasonally, has all of the typical bistro fare: appetizers such as steamed mussels with white wine and herbs and a house pate, and main dishes such as grilled steak with house butter and homemade fries and duck breast with Chinese cabbage and wild rice. The daily specials usually include two or three seafood items, a lamb or pork dish, and a steak. A house specialty (not on the menu) is the roast duck for two ($14.25 per person) bathed in a Grand Marnier and orange marmalade sauce. Choose from half a dozen different desserts each night.

INEXPENSIVE

Bite. 1039 N. Western Ave. (between Division St. and Augusta Blvd.). ☎ **773/395-2483.** Reservations accepted for parties of 6 or more. Main courses $5.25–$9. MC, V. Mon–Fri 11am–11:30pm, Sat–Sun 10am–4pm (brunch) and 6–11:30pm. Subway/El: Blue Line to Western and transfer to bus no. 49. ECLECTIC.

Don't be deceived by the casualness of this slacker diner. Even though you may see someone wheeling their bike through or a dog ambling about, chef-owner Donna Knezek has prepared a tasty menu at a fair price. It's a good spot to go for dinner and then perhaps catch a rock show or an experimental jazz set next door at the alternative club Empty Bottle. On the menu you'll find veggie and chicken burritos, sandwiches and burgers, pasta dishes, salads, and half a dozen specials each day, which might include French onion soup, grilled lamb with pomegranate sauce and bulgar pilaf, mango chicken with rice, or morel risotto. Dessert offerings may include mango sorbet or a big piece of chocolate cake spiced with ginger and cayenne.

Cafe Bolero. 2252 N. Western Ave. (just south of Fullerton Ave.). ☎ **773/227-9000.** Main courses $4.95–$11.95. AE, DC, DISC, MC, V. Daily 11am–10pm. Subway/El and Bus: Blue Line to Western and transfer to bus no. 49. CUBAN.

This is perhaps a bit farther west than most visitors will want to travel. But the more adventurous among you will be rewarded if you do. Cafe Bolero is the combined enterprise of a multicultural husband-and-wife team; he's Cuban, she's Serbian. Most of the dishes lean toward the Caribbean; this is certainly one of the few restaurants west of the Appalachians where you can get a genuine Cuban sandwich (grilled pork and cheese on French-style bread). The paella is another house specialty. They also have tostones (fried plantains), but these are very special, cupped on top and filled with ground beef picadillo. One Slavic-style dish is the homemade grilled sausage, with feta cheese and marinated roasted peppers ($6.95 for one, $11.95 for two). Espresso and cafe con leche are also available, and there's outdoor seating in good weather.

Northside Tavern & Grill. 1635 N. Damen Ave. (at North and Milwaukee aves.). ☎ **773/384-3555.** Reservations not accepted. Menu items $3.95–$10.95. AE, DC, DISC, MC, V. Sun–Fri 11:30am–2am, Sat 11am–3am. Subway/El: Blue Line to Damen. AMERICAN/ BURGERS.

One of the best cheap eats in the city, Northside cooks up great burgers and sandwiches, all for around $5 or $6. The back dining room looks like a rec room circa

1973, complete with fireplace, pinball machines, and a pool table. In nice weather, Northside opens up its large patio for dining, and a skylit cover keeps it in use during the winter. You're always sure to find entertainment in the form of people-watching: Northside attracts all sorts. During the week it's more of a neighborhood hangout, while on weekends a touristy crowd from Lincoln Park and the suburbs piles in. A limited late-night menu is available from 10pm to 1am.

11 Only in Chicago

PIZZA

Now here's a topic about which Chicagoans are passionate. To the uninitiated: Chicago-style pizza, also known as "deep-dish," is thick-crusted and often demands a knife and fork. The thin-crust variety favored in New York is also widely available; a third type, called "stuffed," is similar to a pie, with a crust both on top and bottom. Many pizzerias serve both thick and thin, and some make all three kinds.

Two of Chicago's gourmet deep-dish restaurants, **Pizzeria Uno,** at 29 E. Ohio St., at the corner of Wabash Avenue (☎ 312/321-1000), and **Pizzeria Due,** 619 N. Wabash Ave., at the corner of Ontario Street (☎ 312/943-2400), are listed earlier in this chapter in section 7. **Gino's East,** 160 E. Superior St. (☎ 312/943-1124), is mentioned in section 6.

In River North, **Lou Malnati's Pizzeria** at 439 N. Wells St. (☎ 312/828-9800) bakes both deep-dish and thin-crust pizza and even has a low-fat cheese option. **Edwardo's** is a local pizza chain that serves all three varieties. It has several Chicago locations, including one in the Gold Coast at 1212 N. Dearborn St. at Division Street, (☎ 312/337-4490), one in Printers Row in the South Loop, at 521 S. Dearborn St. (☎ 312/939-3366), and one in Lincoln Park, at 2662 N. Halsted St. (☎ 773/871-3400). Reviewed in section 8 is **Ranalli's Pizzeria, Libations & Collectibles,** 1925 N. Lincoln Ave. (☎ 312/642-4700).

In Wrigleyville, just off Belmont Avenue, are **Leona's Pizzeria,** 3215 N. Sheffield Ave. (☎ 773/327-8861), and **Pat's Pizzeria,** 3114 N. Sheffield Ave. (☎ 773/248-0168), both of which serve all three kinds of pizza. Leona's also has a location in Little Italy at 1419 W. Taylor St. (☎ 312/850-2222), and Pat's has one downtown in the Athletic Club Illinois Center at 211 N. Stetson (☎ 312/946-0220). A new addition to the Wrigleyville neighborhood is **Pompeii,** 2955 N. Sheffield Ave. (☎ 773/325-1900), which originated in 1909 as a bakery in Little Italy and now serves cafeteria-style (don't let that deter you; the food is fresh and the service friendly) pasta and pizza offerings, including big square slices (tomato and basil is a big seller) and its signature pizza "strudels." The original location, in Little Italy, is at 1455 W. Taylor St. (☎ 312/421-5179).

HOT DOGS

Chicagoans take as much pride in their hot dogs as they do in their pizza. The facades of Chicago's hot-dog stands, as if by some unwritten convention, are all very colorful, with bright signs of red and yellow, exaggerated lettering, and comic illustrations of the wieners and fries.

Naturally, Chicago is home to a few stand-out hot-dog shops, such as **Gold Coast Dogs,** 418 N. State St., at Hubbard Street (☎ 312/527-1222). Two blocks off North Michigan Avenue, just across the river from the Loop, Gold Coast Dogs is a place where you can grab your food and run, or join the crowd at the stools around the counter. Be prepared to kibbitz with the outgoing counterstaff, who will ask you to choose your frank with hot peppers, celery salt, green relish, or veggies. Hot dogs start at $1.90 and burgers (beef, turkey and veggie) at $3.10. You can also have melted cheddar cheese on your french fries and homemade brownies for dessert. It's open Monday through Friday from 7am to 10pm and Saturday and Sunday from 11am to 8pm.

A couple of other local institutions are **The Wieners Circle,** 2622 N. Clark St. (☎ 773/477-7444), as much for the hot dogs as for the picnic tables out front, the perfect vantage point for surveying the late-night Lincoln Park scene (open until 4am weeknights, even later weekends); and **Murphy's Red Hots,** 1211 W. Belmont Ave. (☎ 773/935-2882), a neighborhoody spot not too far from Wrigley Field. Besides hot dogs, Murphy's serves charbroiled Polish sausages, burgers, and tasty hand-cut fries. A Japanese conglomerate even deemed Murphy's sufficiently authentic to select it as a model for a chain of hot-dog stands in Japan.

12 Breakfast, Brunch & Afternoon Tea

BREAKFAST & BRUNCH

You can get a good (and upscale) breakfast at one of the hotels near the Loop or the Magnificent Mile. On the seventh floor of the **Four Seasons Hotel,** 120 E. Delaware Place (☎ 312/280-8800), breakfast is served daily in the Seasons Dining Room from 6:30 to 9:30am, or beginning at 8:30am in the Seasons Cafe, where late risers can order a morning meal until midnight. Enjoy à la carte entrees from home-smoked salmon to French toast or complete meals that range from classic Midwestern fare to a Japanese breakfast. Prices range from $11 to $16.

At **The Drake,** 140 E. Walton Place at Michigan Avenue (☎ 312/787-2200), the Oak Terrace on the lobby level offers traditional morning meals from 6:30 to 11:30am Monday through Saturday and Sunday from 6:30 to 11am. Prices range from $10 to $17.95. Reservations are only necessary for parties of eight or more.

The Great Street Restaurant and Bar on the second floor of the **Renaissance Chicago Hotel,** 1 W. Wacker Dr. (☎ 312/372-7200), presents a breakfast buffet from 6 to 10:30am Monday through Saturday and until noon on Sunday. For $13.50 per person, you can help yourself to sausage, bacon, eggs, French toast, cereal, danish, and more. No reservations are required.

A more informal choice in the Loop, just across from Marshall Field's, is **Heaven on Seven,** 111 N. Wabash, 7th Floor (☎ 312/263-6443), where the Cajun and Creole specialties supplement an enormous diner-style menu that has anything you could possibly desire. It's open weekdays from 7am and Saturday from 10am; it's closed on Sunday. See section 3 for a complete listing.

For a Southern-style breakfast of spicy red eggs, cheese grits, or biscuits and gravy, head over to **Wishbone,** 1001 W. Washington St. (☎ 312/850-2663), a homespun dining hall in a warehouse district west of the Loop (see a complete listing in section 4).

For brunch with some soul, head to **House of Blues,** 329 N. Dearborn St., at Kinzie Street (☎ 312/527-2583), for its popular Sunday gospel brunch (see a complete listing in the "You Gotta Have a Theme" box earlier in this chapter). To guarantee seating, it's a good idea to book a spot two weeks in advance.

A perfect breakfast or brunch spot if you're heading up to Wrigleyville for a Cubs game or for a day of antiquing on Belmont Avenue is **Ann Sather,** at 929 W. Belmont Ave. (☎ 773/348-2378), famous for their homemade cinnamon rolls; it's open daily from 7am. See section 9 for other locations.

The **Nookies** restaurants are also Chicago favorites for all the standard morning fare. The Lincoln Park location is at 2114 N. Halsted St. (☎ 773/327-1400).

Satisfying Your Sweet Tooth

While many Chicago restaurants have top-notch dessert menus, Chicago is severely underserved by ice-cream shops. You might as well head straight to the area's only **Ben & Jerry's,** located at 338 W. Armitage Ave., between Clark Street and Lincoln Avenue (☎ 773/281-5152), in Lincoln Park for a couple of scoops of chocolate chip cookie dough. Another decadent option, just off North Michigan Avenue, is **Ghirardelli Chocolate Shop & Soda Fountain,** 830 N. Michigan Ave. (entrance on Pearson Street) (☎ 312/337-9330), where you can get a sundae topped with a flood of the San Francisco company's famed export. For a hometown twist, **Mrs. Levy's** in the Sears Tower, 233 S. Wacker Dr. (☎ 312/993-0530), offers a full fountain of sweet delights, or make the hike over to **Margie's Candies,** 1960 N. Western Ave., at Armitage Avenue (☎ 773/384-1035), an old-fashioned ice-cream shop that's been scooping ice cream for more than 75 years. Well-mannered, bow-tied soda jerks serve more than 50 old-fashioned sundaes in giant clamshell dishes.

You're probably on vacation, so why worry about fat content, but if you insist, here are a couple of low-fat alternatives: **Mario's Italian Lemonade,** a little shack at 1070 W. Taylor St. (no phone) in Little Italy, where you can get a cup of frozen lemonade in a rainbow of flavors (blue raspberry, lemon, peach, etc.), and **Icebox,** 2943 N. Broadway (☎ 773/935-9800), a successful imitator in Lakeview with a similar range of "icy fruit" treats. Both are open only in warm-weather months.

Nookies also has branches in Old Town at 1748 N. Wells St. (☎ 312/337-2454) and Lakeview at 3334 N. Halsted St. (☎ 773/248-9888).

Another North Side best bet is **Oo La La!,** 3335 N. Halsted St. (☎ 773/935-7708), which weighs in with a trendy Sunday brunch of its own from 10am to 3pm. That walk up Halsted, from say, Armitage, would really get Sunday off to a pleasant start. See section 9 for a complete listing.

Here are some other favorite breakfast joints:

✪ **Bongo Room.** 1470 N. Milwaukee Ave. (between North Ave. and Division St.). ☎ 773/489-0690. Most items $5.95–$10. AE, MC, V. Mon–Fri 8am–2:30pm, Sat–Sun 9:30am–2:30pm. Subway/El: Blue Line to Damen. AMERICAN/BREAKFAST.

The brightly colored Bongo Room is a neighborhood gathering place for the hipsters of Wicker Park/Bucktown, but the restaurant's tasty, creative breakfasts have drawn partisans from all over the city who feel right at home stretching out the morning with a late breakfast. Get your day started the right way with pineapple brioche French toast, raspberry cheesecake hotcakes, or blueberry ricotta flapjacks. Don't miss out on the tasty hash browns—you should order them as a side if they don't come with your order. On weekends there's a special brunch menu—and a long wait if you don't arrive when the doors open.

Corner Bakery. 516 N. Clark St. (at Grand Ave.). ☎ 312/644-8100. Breakfast $2.50–$6; sandwiches $5–$6.50. AE, DC, DISC, MC, V. Mon–Fri 6:30am–9pm, Sat–Sun 7am–9pm. Subway/El: Red Line to Grand/State. BREAKFAST/SANDWICHES.

Sunday morning is a nice time to visit the River North neighborhood, especially if the weather is agreeable; you could begin your day with a fine continental breakfast at the Corner Bakery, the honest-to-goodness bakery attached to Maggiano's Italian restaurant. The baked goods are exceptional. Many local office workers also come to the Corner Bakery during the week for the sandwiches, most of which are gone by 2pm. And, of course, all of Chicago—restaurants included—comes to the Corner Bakery for the fabulous bread. The concept has proven popular; there are now about a dozen Corner Bakery branches, including a location a couple of blocks east of Michigan Avenue at 676 N. St. Clair St., at Erie Street (☎ 312/266-2570); one on the Gold Coast at 1121 N. State St., at Cedar Street (☎ 312/787-1969); and another not far from the Art Institute at 224 S. Michigan Ave. (☎ 312/431-7600).

Elaine & Ina's. 448 E. Ontario St. (just west of Lake Shore Dr.). ☎ **312/337-6700.** Breakfast/lunch $3.75–$12.75, dinner $11–$24.95. AE, DC, DISC, MC, V. Mon–Fri 7am–3pm and 4:30–9pm, Sat 8am–3pm and 4:30–9pm, Sun 8am–2pm. Bus: 146, 151. AMERICAN/ BREAKFAST.

What began as a popular breakfast and lunch spot in Lincoln Park when it was known as Ina's Kitchen recently moved to this larger Streeterville location and adopted the name of its omnipresent owners, chef Elaine Farrell and pastry chef, Ina Pinkney. It's only a block from Lake Shore Drive and four blocks east of Michigan Avenue, making it an especially good way to start the day if you're headed to Navy Pier or the Ohio Street beach. (If you dine at night, you can even see Navy Pier's fireworks from the restaurant's sidewalk cafe.) The airy atrium space is a pleasant spot to soak up the morning sun and savor the good coffee, delivered by the pitcher to your table. The place has a homey feel to it, from the kitschy-cute salt and pepper shakers on each table to the basket of breakfast breads and sweets that you really should order to get things started. Among the breakfast favorites are the French toast with lemon zest and fresh fruit, scrapple (fried cornmeal, black beans, corn, and cheese), sour cream pancakes with fruit compote, and a peppery frittata with potatoes. Breakfast is served all day, but there's a tempting lunch menu, too, with sandwiches, salads, and specialty items, including several pastas, baked meat loaf, and oven-roasted salmon. In this new incarnation, the owners have also added a dinner menu, with everything from lamb chops to New York strip steak.

✪ Lou Mitchell's. 565 W. Jackson Blvd. (at Jefferson St.). ☎ **312/939-3111.** Reservations accepted for groups of 8 or more. Breakfast items $1.95–$6.95. No credit cards. Mon–Sat 5:30am–3pm, Sun 7am–3pm. Subway/El: Blue Line to Clinton. AMERICAN/ BREAKFAST/DINER.

A favorite for breakfast among Chicagoans since 1923 is Lou Mitchell's, across the south branch of the Chicago River from the Loop, a block farther west than Union Station. A French food critic passing through Chicago rated Lou Mitchell's the number one breakfast spot in America, home of the "five-star breakfast." You're greeted at the door with a basket of doughnut holes (milk duds for the ladies—don't ask), so you can nibble while waiting for a table. The wait is short, since turnover is continuous and service efficiently attentive. Here you may have the best bowl of oatmeal you've ever eaten—deliciously creamy. An order of two double-yolk fried eggs with toasted homemade Greek bread, homemade orange marmalade, and hash browns is served at your table in the same skillet it was all cooked in. There are 16 different omelets, including one made with apples and cheddar cheese. Orange juice and grapefruit juice are freshly squeezed. Of course, breakfast is served all day.

Toast. 746 W. Webster St. (at Halsted St.). ☎ **773/935-5600.** Reservations not accepted. Breakfast $3.95–$7.95. AE, CB, DC, DISC, MC, V. Tues–Fri 7am–3pm, Sat–Sun 8am–4pm. Subway/El: Red Line to Fullerton. AMERICAN/BREAKFAST.

The people who brought Chicago a few of the fabbest nocturnal spots in the city (Iggy's, Liquid Kitty) have turned their attention to a place for the daylight hours (and the morning after). Located in neighborhoody Lincoln Park, Toast is homey yet slightly funky—note the shelf of vintage toasters. Kids are welcome here: The crayons and butcher-block table coverings will keep them busy. Breakfast is served all day and includes a twist on the usual diner fare. Pancakes come in all sorts of tempting varieties, from lemon/poppy seed drizzled with honey to the "pancake orgy" of a strawberry, mango, and banana-pecan pancake topped with granola, yogurt, and honey. If pancakes equal dessert for you, try one of the omelets or the breakfast burrito. On the side, you can order grilled chicken sausage, applewood smoked bacon, or, of course, a stack of toast. There's also fresh-squeezed orange juice and grapefruit juice. The lunch menu includes a range of creative sandwiches, salads, and wraps.

A SPOT OF TEA

If you're shopping on the Magnificent Mile and feel like having an elegant afternoon tea, complete with finger sandwiches, scones, and pastry, go to the **Palm Court at The Drake,** 140 E. Walton Place (☎ **312/787-2200**). A fine afternoon tea is also served at the **Ritz-Carlton,** 160 E. Pearson St. (☎ **312/266-1000**), in the 12th-floor lobby. The Ritz-Carlton is conveniently located at Water Tower Place.

7

Seeing the Sights in Chicago

Chicago may be the city that works, but it's also the city that plays. The parks are oversize, and many of the museums have gone interactive. Navy Pier is the latest facility, boasting everything from the Chicago Children's Museum to an open-air concert stage, boat cruises, and a 15-story Ferris wheel. Most of the city's major sights are downtown, or close to it, making them within easy walking distance of (or a short cab ride from) the city's principal hotels.

SUGGESTED ITINERARIES

If You Have 1 Day

If you have only a day in Chicago, get a taste of a few things special to the city. Assuming you'll be visiting during the nicer weather, start the day in the Loop, either on a self-guided tour or on an organized one by the Chicago Architecture Foundation (the early skyscraper tour is a good primer). Thanks to the Great Fire of 1871 and the determination to rebuild, Chicago has been a world leader in architecture for more than a century. Then, in the afternoon, take the El uptown (along with a whole lot of business types taking a "long lunch") to the sublime Wrigley Field for a Cubs game. To top off the day, catch an evening show at Second City, the comedy club that gave John Belushi and Bill Murray their starts.

If You Have 2 Days

Spend the first day in the downtown area. Walk around the Loop (as mentioned above) to see buildings and the city's extensive sculpture collection. Perhaps go to the top of the Sears Tower for a view above it all. Or, if it's a Saturday, get free tickets at the Chicago Cultural Center for the Loop Tour Train, which offers a guided overview of the city from the century-old Elevated. Next, visit one or two of the city's premier museums, such as the Art Institute, the Field Museum of Natural History, the Shedd Aquarium, the Adler Planetarium, or a smaller institution of interest to you. Finish off the day either with a shopping trip up the Magnificent Mile or a gallery-hopping expedition in River North. Both areas have plenty of excellent restaurants for dinner. If you've still got the energy, take an evening stroll along Navy Pier and a spin on the Ferris wheel. Then, pick a boat along the dock for a nighttime cruise and view the shimmering skyline from the lake.

On the second day, head for a neighborhood on the North Side, such as the Gold Coast, Lincoln Park, or Wicker Park, and explore. In the afternoon, you won't be far from Wrigley Field, where you can see the Cubs play. In the evening, dine at one of the many ethnic restaurants along Clark Street. Spend the rest of the evening at Second City in Old Town or perhaps at an offbeat theater not far from Wrigley.

If You Have 3 Days

Begin the third day with a trip to Hyde Park, where you can see the University of Chicago and Frank Lloyd Wright's Robie House, among other sights. Then spend a few hours at the fascinating Museum of Science and Industry. If you have time left, you could head back north and visit another museum. If it's a nice day, however, I recommend walking up North Michigan Avenue or crossing over to Oak Street Beach for a stroll (or roll, with a rented bike or blades) along the lake up to Fullerton Avenue, where you can wander around the zoo and the conservatory. Choose one of the neighborhood's many good restaurants for dinner and then one of its jazz or blues clubs for a finale.

1 In & Around the Loop: The Art Institute, the Sears Tower & Grant Park

The Loop's major museums form a cluster in Grant Park and along South Michigan Avenue, where visitors can reach several of them through a new landscaped Museum Campus that brings them all together for the first time. (The northbound lanes of Lake Shore Drive were relocated to allow the change.) The interior streets of downtown have a good deal to offer as well, primarily in the form of innovative architecture, such as the Rookery and the Sears Tower, and grand public sculpture by Picasso, Miró, and others. The heart of the Loop is also where you'll find such oddities as the Chicago Board of Trade, the world's largest commodities, futures, and options exchange. After dark the Loop is virtually empty, except on the perimeter, where you can spend an evening at Orchestra Hall, the Auditorium Theatre, or the Civic Opera House, to name a few of the city's world-class performing arts centers.

THE TOP ATTRACTIONS IN THE LOOP

✪ **Art Institute of Chicago.** 111 S. Michigan Ave. (at Adams St.). ☎ **312/ 443-3600.** Suggested admission $7 adults, $3.50 seniors, children, and students with ID. Additional cost for special exhibitions. Free admission on Tues. Mon and Wed–Fri 10:30am–4:30pm, Tues 10:30am–8pm, Sat 10am–5pm, Sun and holidays noon–5pm. Closed Thanksgiving and Dec 25. Bus: 3, 4, 60, 145, 147, or 151. Subway/El: Green, Brown, Purple, or Orange Lines to Adams, or Red Line to Monroe or Jackson.

You can't (and shouldn't) miss the Art Institute: The signature pair of bronze lions that flank the museum's main entrance are perfect rendezvous points, and there is always a throng of people sitting on the steps on nice days. Finding the museum is easy—it's choosing which collections to view that is hard. Chicago's temple of art houses one of the world's major collections. You choose the medium and the century and the Art Institute has the works in its collection to captivate you: Japanese *ukiyo-e* prints, early-19th-century British photography, masterpieces by most of the greatest names in 20th-century sculpture, or modern American textiles. Although many of the museum's galleries are dedicated to particular periods, the pieces chosen for display are constantly rotated so that no matter how many times you visit, there are always new works to be seen.

Many visitors head straight to the museum's renowned collection of Impressionist art (which includes one of the largest collections of Monet paintings in the world), which of course makes it one of the more highly trafficked areas of the museum. Among the other treasures of the Art Institute are Seurat's pointillist masterpiece *A Sunday on La Grande Jatte—1884* and Marc Chagall's wonderful stained-glass windows. Visitors are sometimes surprised when they discover many of the icons that hang here. ("Is that the real thing?" I once heard someone saying who stood face-to-face with Grant Wood's *American Gothic*.) If you want to steer clear of the crowds, there's plenty of room to explore. Everyone finds his favorite works or special places, whether it's the quiet corridor of Indian and East Asian statuaries, the stairway displaying Georgia O'Keeffe's serene *Sky Above Clouds* (the museum's largest painting), or one of the modern galleries with photographs by Arthur Stieglitz and paintings by Arthur Dove, Georgia O'Keeffe, and Marsden Hartley. In 1997 the Art Institute opened new galleries spacious enough to contain works from its contemporary art collection, and here you'll find 85 paintings and sculptures by American and European artists from 1945 to 1980.

Don't overlook the lower level of the museum, either. The photography galleries always display visiting exhibitions with interesting and stimulating imagery. The Kraft Education Center features exhibits for children, and the Thorne Miniature Rooms are filled with tiny reproductions of furnished interiors. Another popular attraction is the original Trading Room of the old Chicago Stock Exchange, salvaged when the Adler and Sullivan Stock Exchange building was demolished in 1972.

Like many other institutions of comparable size and prestige, every year or so the Art Institute packs its galleries with visitors for big blockbuster retrospectives, typically focused on such crowd-pleasing Impressionists as Monet and Renoir. You may want to schedule your trip to Chicago around one of these shows, but plan ahead in securing tickets because weekend dates can sell out in advance. Upcoming shows in 1999 include works from the Belgian Royal Museum for Central Africa, a major exhibition marking the 100th anniversary of the death of French Symbolist painter Gustave Moreau, and early drawings by abstract artist Ellsworth Kelly.

The museum, which is really three buildings connected over the Metra tracks, also has a cafeteria and a full-service restaurant, a picturesque courtyard cafe with a jazz quintet on Tuesday evenings in the summer, and a large museum shop. There is a busy schedule of lectures, films, and other special presentations, as well as guided tours, to enhance your viewing of the art. The museum also has a research library, and the School of the Art Institute offers exhibits and a film center.

Sears Tower Skydeck. 233 S. Wacker Dr. (enter on Jackson Blvd.). ☎ **312/875-9696.** Admission $8 adults, $6 seniors, $5 children 5–12, free for children under 4 and military with active duty ID, $20 family (2 adults and up to 3 children in same household). Mar–Sept daily 9am–11pm; Oct–Feb daily 9am–10pm (last ticket sold half an hour before closing). Bus: 1, 7, 126, 146, 151, or 156. Subway/El: Brown, Purple, or Orange Line to Quincy, or Red or Blue Line to Jackson; then walk a few blocks west.

The view from the world's second tallest skyscraper is everything you'd expect it to be, a momentary suspension between earth and sky. From the Skydeck 103 floors up, the city is spread before you, both intimate and colossal. You get your bearings first with an 8-minute film on the history of Chicago and an architecture exhibition by the Chicago Architecture Foundation. The twin towers that surpassed the Sears Tower in height, in case you were wondering, are the Petronas Towers in Kuala Lumpur. Chicagoans will point out (and a diagram in the Skydeck lobby illustrates) that the Malaysian buildings won out only because of their spires.

Insider Tips for Touring the Art Institute

If you want to enjoy your favorite masterpieces in something resembling peace and quiet, put some thought into the timing of your visit to the Art Institute, a museum so popular it draws as much traffic as the Kennedy Expressway.

Here are some tips for avoiding the rush hour: Many people don't realize the museum is open on Mondays, so keep this secret to yourself, and visit when the galleries are relatively subdued. Wednesdays are a close second. Tuesdays tend to draw the masses because the Art Institute is free and open late (until 8pm). Try to arrive when the doors open in the morning or else during the lunchtime lull. Another tip: If the Michigan Avenue entrance is crowded, head around to the entrance on the Columbus Drive side, which is usually less congested and is more convenient to the Grant Park underground parking garage. There's a small gift shop near the Columbus Drive entrance, too, if the main shop is too bustling.

Here are some suggestions for hitting the highlights if you only have a few hours to explore the museum or if you want to cover as much ground as possible before museum-fatigue sets in (of course, if there is a special exhibit on display, you'll no doubt spend the bulk of your time there):

If it weren't for the bathrooms on the lower level, many visitors would no doubt overlook the museum's Photography galleries—don't make that mistake. Follow the stairway just beyond the Michigan Avenue entrance for a quick perusal of the museum's vast photography collection. You might also want to view the fascinating Thorne Miniature Rooms, also downstairs. Next, return to the first floor and climb the grand staircase to the second floor to explore the renowned European galleries. Here you'll find a sampling of many of the museum's big names: Monet, Renoir, Manet, Degas, and many other Impressionists and Post-Impressionists. There will no doubt be a crowd gathered in front of Georges Seurat's pointillist masterpiece *A Sunday on La Grande Jatte—1884.*

As you loop around the second floor, you'll go back in time passing works by Renaissance painters and the Dutch masters. Don't miss Rembrandt's *Old Man with a Gold Chain,* or El Greco's *The Assumption of the Virgin,* considered his greatest work outside Spain.

In the Modern galleries, you'll find yourself face-to-face with many familiar works, including Picasso's *The Old Guitarist,* Grant Wood's *American Gothic,* and Edward Hopper's *Nighthawks.* Georgia O'Keeffe is well represented also, including her evocative *Black Cross, New Mexico;* as you descend the stairway from the Modern galleries' southern wing (1935–1955) be sure to look up to see her sprawling *Sky Above Clouds.* Another museum treasure awaits you at the bottom of the stairs: a series of stained-glass windows by Marc Chagall.

Next, you can take a peaceful stroll among the jades, bronzes, screens, and textiles of the Chinese, Japanese, and Korean collections (the Japanese wood prints are considered among the finest in the world). Note the clever placement of pop artist Andy Warhol's epic-size *Mao,* which serves as a visual bridge between these galleries and the Contemporary galleries. In the Contemporary galleries you'll find some of the museum's most challenging works—large-scale paintings and sculpture from masters of the latter half of the 20th century, including Jackson Pollock, David Hockney, and Frank Stella.

Central Chicago Attractions

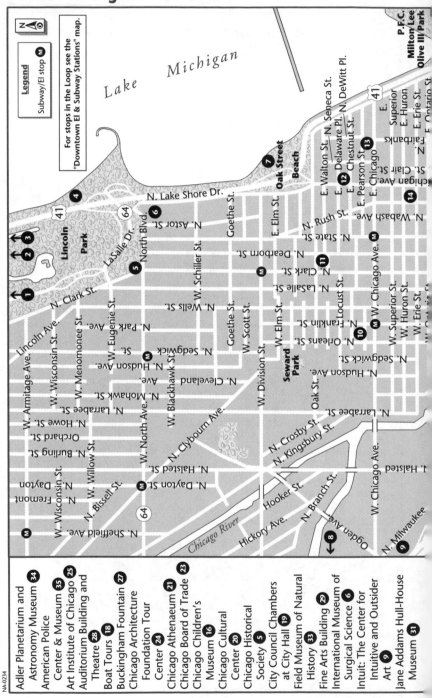

Adler Planetarium and Astronomy Museum **34**

American Police Center & Museum **35**

Art Institute of Chicago **25**

Auditorium Building and Theatre **28**

Boat Tours **18**

Buckingham Fountain **27**

Chicago Architecture Foundation Tour Center **24**

Chicago Athenaeum **21**

Chicago Board of Trade **23**

Chicago Children's Museum **16**

Chicago Cultural Center **20**

Chicago Historical Society **5**

City Council Chambers at City Hall **19**

Field Museum of Natural History **33**

Fine Arts Building **29**

International Museum of Surgical Science **6**

Intuit: The Center for Intuitive and Outsider Art **9**

Jane Addams Hull-House Museum **31**

NA-0234

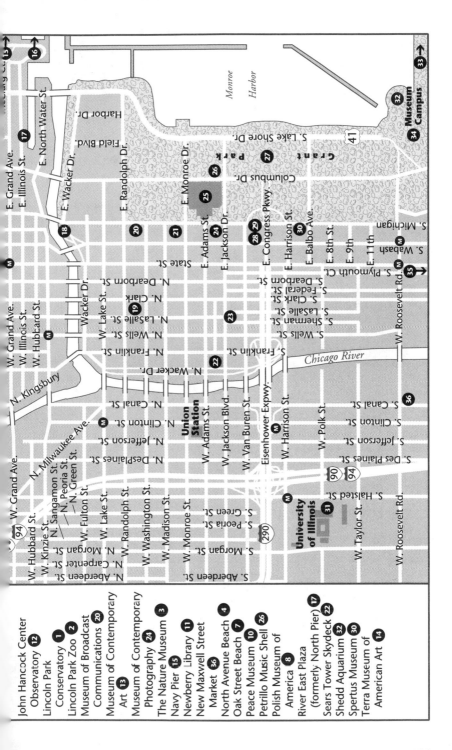

John Hancock Center
Observatory **12**

Lincoln Park
Conservatory **1**

Lincoln Park Zoo **2**

Museum of Broadcast
Communications **20**

Museum of Contemporary
Art **13**

Museum of Contemporary
Photography **24**

The Nature Museum **3**

Navy Pier **15**

Newberry Library **11**

New Maxwell Street
Market **36**

North Avenue Beach **4**

Oak Street Beach **7**

Peace Museum **10**

Petrillo Music Shell **26**

Polish Museum of
America **8**

River East Plaza
(formerly North Pier) **17**

Sears Tower Skydeck **22**

Shedd Aquarium **32**

Spertus Museum **30**

Terra Museum of
American Art **14**

⚪ **Chicago Board of Trade.** 141 W. Jackson Blvd. (at LaSalle St.). ☎ **312/435-3590.** Free admission. Visitor center, Mon–Fri 8am–2pm. For groups of 10 or more, call for reservations. Bus: 1, 7, 60, 126, 151, or 156. Subway/El: Brown, Orange, or Purple Line to LaSalle, or Blue or Red Line to Jackson.

The best live, improvisational acting in the city isn't necessarily at the theater. The Trading Pit at the Chicago Board of Trade, a massive citadel that stands at the foot of LaSalle Street, and the City Council Chambers at City Hall (see below) can—on a given day—provide the best entertainment in town. Watched over by a statue of Ceres, goddess of grain, the men (and a few women) inside the Board of Trade frantically deal in commodities and financial futures and options. From a vantage point in the fifth-floor visitor center, you can watch the traders make their deals (*watch* is the operative word—just try to figure out their hand signals). The action peaks in a shouting frenzy at the closing hour, after which these individual gamblers in pinstripes will count up their chips and learn if they've come out winners or losers for the day. Visitors are welcome beginning at 8am, but the first presentation isn't held until 9:15am, a quarter hour before the grain market opens. The visitor center can provide audiotapes in 14 languages.

City Council Chambers at City Hall. Washington, LaSalle, Randolph, and Clark sts. ☎ **312/744-4000.** Free admission. Open when City Council is in session. Bus: 20, 56, 131, 156, or 157. Subway/El: Brown, Green, Orange, or Purple Line to Clark, or Red or Blue Line to Washington.

Not far from the Board of Trade, power of a slightly different sort is brokered during the public meetings of the equally volatile Chicago City Council, which meets in the square block of the combined City Hall and the County Building. Although politics aren't nearly as colorful under Mayor Richard M. Daley as they were under his dad, when the right issue is being debated factions can still get down and dirty, and the political posturing of the 50 aldermen (the name given to the city council members) can make for the best kind of theatrics. Call ahead to find out when the council is in session (☎ **312/744-3081**). City Hall tours can also be arranged; make requests in writing, specifying your travel dates to the city, to Director of the Mayor's Office of Inquiry and Information, City Hall, 121 W. LaSalle St., Room 1111, Chicago, IL 60602.

⚪ THE LOOP SCULPTURE TOUR

Among all major American cities, Chicago has led the way with its program of public art. Examples of public art—in the form of traditional monuments, murals, and monumental contemporary sculpture—are located widely throughout the city, but their concentration within the Loop and nearby Grant Park has gradually transformed downtown Chicago into a "museum without walls." The best-known of these works are by 20th-century artists, including Picasso, Chagall, Miró, Calder, Moore, and Oldenburg.

With the help of a very comprehensive booklet, "Loop Sculpture Guide," you can steer yourself through Grant Park and much of the Loop to view some 100 examples of Chicago's monumental public art. It provides detailed descriptions of 37 major works, including photographs, plus about 60 other sites located nearby, and identifies them on a foldout map of the Loop. "Loop Sculpture Guide" is sold for $3.95 at the gift shop in the Chicago Cultural Center, 78 E. Washington.

You can also conduct a self-guided tour of the city's public sculpture by following our "Loop Sculpture Tour" map.

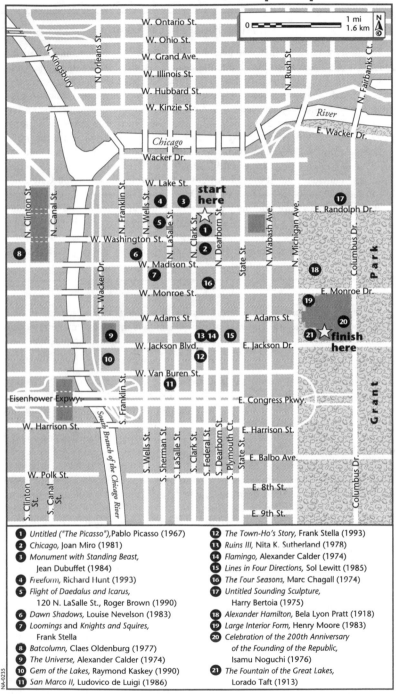

The Loop Sculpture Tour

W. Ontario St.
W. Ohio St.
W. Grand Ave.
W. Illinois St.
W. Hubbard St.
W. Kinzie St.

Chicago

Wacker Dr.

River

E. Wacker Dr.

start here

finish here

N. Kingsbury
N. Orleans St.
N. Clinton St.
N. Canal St.
N. Franklin St.
N. Wells St.
N. LaSalle St.
N. Clark St.
N. Dearborn St.
State St.
N. Wabash Ave.
N. Michigan Ave.
N. Rush St.
N. Fairbanks Ct.
Columbus Dr.

W. Lake St.
E. Randolph Dr.
W. Washington St.
W. Madison St.
W. Monroe St.
W. Adams St.   E. Adams St.
W. Jackson Blvd.   E. Jackson Dr.
W. Van Buren St.
Eisenhower Expwy.   E. Congress Pkwy.
W. Harrison St.   E. Harrison St.
W. Polk St.   E. Balbo Ave.
                   E. 8th St.
                   E. 9th St.

E. Monroe Dr.

N. Wacker Dr.
S. Franklin St.
South Branch of the Chicago River
S. Clinton St.
S. Canal St.
S. Wells St.
S. Sherman St.
S. LaSalle St.
S. Clark St.
S. Federal St.
S. Dearborn St.
S. Plymouth Ct.
State St.

Park

Grant

0 1 mi
   1.6 km
N

1 Untitled ("The Picasso"), Pablo Picasso (1967)
2 Chicago, Joan Miro (1981)
3 Monument with Standing Beast, Jean Dubuffet (1984)
4 Freeform, Richard Hunt (1993)
5 Flight of Daedalus and Icarus, 120 N. LaSalle St., Roger Brown (1990)
6 Dawn Shadows, Louise Nevelson (1983)
7 Loomings and Knights and Squires, Frank Stella
8 Batcolumn, Claes Oldenburg (1977)
9 The Universe, Alexander Calder (1974)
10 Gem of the Lakes, Raymond Kaskey (1990)
11 San Marco II, Ludovico de Luigi (1986)

12 The Town-Ho's Story, Frank Stella (1993)
13 Ruins III, Nita K. Sutherland (1978)
14 Flamingo, Alexander Calder (1974)
15 Lines in Four Directions, Sol Lewitt (1985)
16 The Four Seasons, Marc Chagall (1974)
17 Untitled Sounding Sculpture, Harry Bertoia (1975)
18 Alexander Hamilton, Bela Lyon Pratt (1918)
19 Large Interior Form, Henry Moore (1983)
20 Celebration of the 200th Anniversary of the Founding of the Republic, Isamu Noguchi (1976)
21 The Fountain of the Great Lakes, Lorado Taft (1913)

NA-0235

157

Thursday Nights in the Loop

For all its attractions, the Loop pretty much clears out in the evenings after the legions of office workers punch out and head for home. Lois Weisberg, the commissioner of the city's Department of Cultural Affairs, has been trying to change that. Weisberg has organized a variety of special concerts, plays, restaurant discounts, and other special events scheduled from 5 to 8pm on Thursdays to try to get people to stay downtown. The after-work activities take place along Michigan Avenue from the river to Roosevelt Road. Several museums offer extended hours. Open until 9pm on Thursdays, the Chicago Cultural Center, 77 E. Randolph (☎ 312/744-6630), holds a series of musical cabaret tributes called "Thursday Something" from 6:30 to 8:30pm in the Randolph Cafe. You can pick up a booklet on the seasonal Downtown Thursday Night programs at any of the city's Visitor Information Centers, at the Chicago Cultural Center; the Historic Water Tower, 806 N. Michigan Ave.; or Navy Pier, 700 E. Grand Ave.; or check on-line at www.ci.chi.il.us.Tourism/ThursdayNight. The booklet contains an application to receive a VIP card that guarantees special rates at restaurants, hotels, and shops on Thursdays.

The single most famous sculpture is **Pablo Picasso's** *Untitled,* located in Daley Plaza. Today, "The Picasso" enjoys semi-official status as the logo of modern Chicago. It is by far the city's most popular photo opportunity among visiting tourists.

GRANT PARK

Grant Park is really a patchwork of giant lawns pieced together by major roadways and a network of railroad tracks. Covering the greens are a variety of public recreational and cultural facilities. The immense **Buckingham Fountain,** accessible along Congress Parkway, is the baroque centerpiece of the park, patterned after—but twice the size of—the Latona Fountain at Versailles, with adjoining esplanades beautified by rose gardens in season. Throughout the late spring and summer, the fountain spurts columns of water up to 165 feet in the air (higher than ever, thanks to some recent rehab work), illuminated after dark by a whirl of colored lights, and building toward a grand finale before it shuts down for the night at 11pm. New concession areas and bathrooms have also opened on the plaza.

Popular outdoor concerts are staged at the **Petrillo Music Shell,** at Jackson Boulevard and Columbus Drive, over a 10-week summer period every Wednesday through Sunday evenings. Other favorite annual events are the free outdoor blues festival (in June) and the jazz festival (Labor Day). The Taste of Chicago, purportedly the largest food festival in the world, takes place every summer for 10 days around the July 4 holiday. Local restaurants serve up more ribs, pizza, hot dogs, and beer than you'd ever want to see, let alone eat. For program information, call ☎ 312/744-3315. (See chapter 2 for a comprehensive listing of summer events in Grant Park.)

At the north end of the park is an outdoor sports plaza with a dozen lighted tennis courts, a rink for ice-skating in the winter and blading or roller-skating in the summer, and a field house. Scattered about the park are a number of sculptures and monuments, including a heroic sculpture of two Native Americans on horseback entitled *The Spearman and the Bowman* (at Congress Parkway and Michigan Avenue), which has become the park's trademark since it was installed in 1928, as well as likenesses of Copernicus, Columbus, and Lincoln, the latter by the American genius Augustus

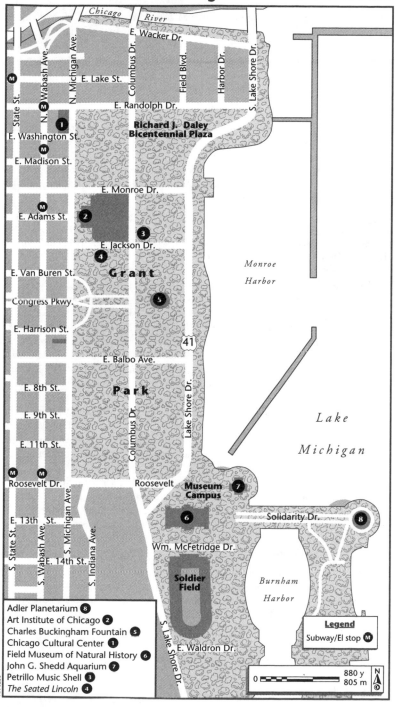

South Michigan Avenue/Grant Park

Chicago River

E. Wacker Dr.

E. Lake St.

E. Randolph Dr.

N. Wabash Ave.

N. Michigan Ave.

Columbus Dr.

Field Blvd

Harbor Dr.

S. Lake Shore Dr.

State St.

E. Washington St.

E. Madison St.

Richard J. Daley Bicentennial Plaza

E. Monroe Dr.

E. Adams St.

E. Jackson Dr.

E. Van Buren St.

Congress Pkwy.

E. Harrison St.

E. Balbo Ave.

Grant

Monroe

Harbor

E. 8th St.

E. 9th St.

E. 11th St.

Park

41

Roosevelt Dr.

Roosevelt

Lake Shore Dr.

Columbus Dr.

Lake

Michigan

E. 13th St.

S. State St.

S. Wabash Ave.

S. Michigan Ave.

S. Indiana Ave.

E. 14th St.

Museum Campus

Solidarity Dr.

Wm. McFetridge Dr.

Soldier Field

Burnham Harbor

S. Lake Shore Dr.

E. Waldron Dr.

Legend

Subway/El stop Ⓜ

Adler Planetarium ❽
Art Institute of Chicago ❷
Charles Buckingham Fountain ❺
Chicago Cultural Center ❶
Field Museum of Natural History ❻
John G. Shedd Aquarium ❼
Petrillo Music Shell ❸
The Seated Lincoln ❹

0 880 y 805 m

N

NA-0236

159

Saint-Gaudens, located on Congress between Michigan Avenue and Columbus Drive. On the western edge of the park, at Adams Street, is the **Art Institute** (see above), and at the southern tip in the newly redesigned Museum Campus are the Field Museum of Natural History, the Adler Planetarium, and the Shedd Aquarium (see below). To get to the park, take bus no. 3, 4, 6, 60, 146, or 151. If you want to take the subway or the El, get off at any stop in the Loop along State or Wabash.

MORE ATTRACTIONS IN THE LOOP

Fashion and glamour may have moved north to the Magnificent Mile, but Chicago's grandest stretch of boulevard is still Michigan Avenue south of the river. From a little north of the Michigan Avenue Bridge all the way down to the Field Museum, South Michigan Avenue runs parallel to Grant Park on one side and the Loop on the other. A stroll along this boulevard in any season offers both visual and cultural treats. The attractions are listed from north to south.

Chicago Cultural Center. 78 E. Washington St. ☎ **312/744-6630,** or 312/FINE-ART for weekly events. Free admission. Mon–Wed 10am–7pm, Thurs 10am–8pm, Fri 10am–6pm, Sat 10am–5pm, Sun noon–5pm. Closed holidays. Bus: 3, 4, 20, 56, 60, 127, 131, 145, 146, 147, 151, or 157. Subway/El: Brown, Green, Orange, or Purple Line to Randolph, or Red Line to Washington/State.

The block-long Chicago Cultural Center bills itself as "an architectural showplace for the lively and visual arts." Known as the "People's Palace" when it was built as the first permanent home for the Chicago Public Library, today it continues to offer a lively mix of art exhibitions, concerts, films, lectures, and other special events, many of them free; you may want to call to check if anything's scheduled that might appeal to you. A long-standing tradition is the 12:15pm concert every Wednesday in the Preston Bradley Hall. Other ongoing programs are a monthly cultural festival—which highlights a different city or country over a weekend with art, theater, and film—and a new magazine-format variety show on Sundays at noon.

   One of the Chicago Office of Tourism's Visitor Centers is now located here, as is the Museum of Broadcast Communications (see listing under "More Museums" below). In the corridor leading to the broadcast museum is another permanent exhibition, "Landmark Chicago Gallery," with photographs and artifacts from some of the city's architectural treasures. Don't overlook the building itself, a hodgepodge of Roman, Greek, and Italian Renaissance styles completed in 1897 by the architects of the Art Institute of Chicago. The interior is embellished with marble, elaborate mosaics, and what's said to be the world's largest Tiffany dome (overhead in the Preston Bradley Hall). Guided architectural tours are offered Tuesday through Saturday at 1:45pm. For information, call ☎ **312/744-8032.** The ground floor on the Randolph Street side of the Cultural Center houses a bakery cafe with seating inside and out.

Fine Arts Building. 410 S. Michigan Ave. ☎ **312/427-7602.** Free admission. Daily 7am–10pm. Bus: 3, 4, 60, 145, 147, or 151. Subway/El: Brown, Green, Purple, or Orange Line to Adams, or Red Line to Jackson.

Built as a showroom for Studebaker carriages in 1885, the landmark Fine Arts Building was converted at the turn of the century into a concert hall. Its upper stories sheltered a number of well-known publications (*Saturday Evening Post, Dial*) and provided offices for such luminaries as Frank Lloyd Wright, sculptor Lorado Taft, and L. Frank Baum, author of *The Wizard of Oz*. Harriet Monroe published her magazine, *Poetry*, here and first introduced American readers to Carl Sandburg, T. S. Eliot, and Ezra Pound. Movie buffs should take note that the two original ground-floor theaters have been converted into an art cinema with four separate screening rooms. Located

Museum Free Days

Plan your time in Chicago carefully, and you can save yourself admission fees to all of the city's major museums. Admission to special exhibitions and films are often extra on free days.

Monday
Chicago Historical Society

Tuesday
Adler Planetarium
Art Institute of Chicago
Museum of Contemporary Art (first Tuesday of the month only)
Terra Museum of American Art

Wednesday
Field Museum of Natural History

Thursday
DuSable Museum of African-American History
Museum of Science and Industry
John G. Shedd Aquarium (Oceanarium admission extra)
Chicago Children's Museum (5 to 8pm only)

Friday
Spertus Museum

Always Free
Chicago Cultural Center
International Museum of Surgical Science
Jane Addams Hull-House Museum
Garfield Park/Lincoln Park Conservatory
Lincoln Park Zoo
Martin D'Arcy Gallery of Art, Loyola University
Mexican Fine Arts Center Museum
Museum of Broadcast Communications
Museum of Contemporary Photography
Newberry Library
Oriental Institute Museum
David and Alfred Smart Museum of Art

throughout the building are a number of interesting studios and musical instrument shops. Take at least a quick walk through the marble-and-wood lobby, which suggests something monastic and cloisterlike, or visit the top floor (10th) to see the spectacular murals.

Auditorium Building and Theatre. 50 E. Congress Pkwy. ☎ **312/922-4046.** For ticket reservations or box office information, call Ticketmaster at ☎ 312/902-1500. Call ☎ 312/431-2354 to arrange a 1-hour theater tour. Admission $4 adults, $3 seniors and students. Bus: 145, 147, or 151. Subway/El: Brown, Green, Orange, or Purple Line to Library/Van Buren, or Red Line to Jackson.

The Auditorium Building and Theatre, on the corner of Congress Parkway and Michigan Avenue, is a national landmark that was designed and built in 1889 by Louis Sullivan and Dankmar Adler. Considered Sullivan's masterpiece, the theater's interior is a glittering display of mirrors and stained glass and is equally renowned for its excellent acoustics and sight ines. The Auditorium Building, formerly a hotel, was the first building to be wired for electric light in Chicago, and the theater was the first in the country to install air-conditioning. In the days when the Auditorium was the leading theater of Chicago, the hydraulically operated stage could be lowered from view, creating a ballroom capable of accommodating 8,000 guests. Today the Auditorium attracts major Broadway musicals, such as *Showboat* and *Les Misérables*. The building offers tours of the front public areas, but backstage is off-limits.

Museum of Contemporary Photography. 600 S. Michigan Ave. ☎ **312/663-5554.** Free admission. Mon–Wed and Fri 10am–5pm, Thurs 10am–8pm, Sat noon–5pm. Bus: 6, 146, or 151. Subway/El: Red Line to Harrison.

The Museum of Contemporary Photography occupies the first floor of Columbia College, near the corner of Harrison Street. The museum exhibits, collects, and promotes contemporary photography. Related lectures and special programs are scheduled during the year.

Spertus Museum. 618 S. Michigan Ave. ☎ **312/922-9012.** Admission $5 adults; $3 seniors, students, and children; $10 maximum family rate. Free admission on Fri. Sun–Wed 10am–5pm, Thurs 10am–8pm, Fri 10am–3pm. Bus: 3, 4, 6, 145, 147, or 151. Subway/El: Red Line to Jackson, or Brown, Purple, Orange, or Green Line to Adams.

The Spertus Museum, an extension of the Spertus Institute of Jewish Studies, houses intricately crafted and historic Jewish ceremonial objects, textiles, coins, paintings, and sculpture, tracing 5,000 years of Jewish heritage. The museum houses the Artifact Center, a simulated Middle Eastern archaeological site in which children can use authentic tools to dig for pottery and other pieces of the past. The Bariff Shop for Judaica carries a large selection of books, music, and contemporary and traditional Jewish ceremonial gifts.

2 The Earth, the Sky & the Sea: The Big Three in the Grant Park Museum Campus

The great trio of museums at the southern end of Grant Park have long been like neighbors separated by fences, yet in their case the division was traffic on Lake Shore Drive, which cut off the Field Museum from the other two institutions. Thanks to an ambitious construction project that was the dream of city leaders for a decade, the northbound lanes of Lake Shore Drive have been relocated to the west side of the area, and the three museums now sit in a landscaped 57-acre greensward called the **Museum Campus.** With terraced gardens and broad walkways, the reclaimed parkland makes it easier for pedestrians to visit the museums and has provided new space for picnicking, theater, and museum education activities. Transportation improvements call for a trolley from parking lots and the Roosevelt Road El and Metra stops, as well as bike and in-line skate valets.

To get to the Museum Campus from the Loop, you can head east across Grant Park from Balbo Street and South Michigan Avenue, trekking along the lakeshore route to the Field Museum, the aquarium, and the planetarium. Or you can make your approach on the path that begins at 11th Street and Michigan Avenue. Follow it to the walkway that spans the Metra tracks. Cross Columbus Drive and then pick up the path that will take you under Lake Shore Drive and into the Museum Campus. The

Impressions

SATAN (impatiently) to NEW-COMER: The trouble with you Chicago people is, that you think you are the best people down here; whereas you are merely the most numerous.

—Mark Twain, "Pudd'nhead Wilson's New Calendar," in *More Tramps Abroad* (1897)

CTA no. 146 bus will take you to all three of these attractions. Call ☎ **836-7000** (any city or suburban area code) for the stop locations and schedule.

☉ Field Museum of Natural History. Roosevelt Rd. and Lake Shore Dr. ☎ **312/ 922-9410.** www.fmnh.org. Admission $7 adults; $4 seniors, children 3–17, and students with ID; free for teachers, armed forces personnel in uniform, and children 2 and under. Free admission on Wed. Daily 9am–5pm. Closed Thanksgiving, Dec 25, and Jan 1. Bus: 6, 10, 12, 130, or 146. Recommended visiting time: 3 hours.

For those who find the foundations of science—anthropology, botany, zoology, and geology—more intriguing than technology, the Field Museum of Natural History will be more compelling than the Museum of Science and Industry. Indeed, the Field Museum—endowed by the formidable Chicago prince of dry goods, Marshall Field I—was initially mounted in the old Palace of Fine Arts following the World's Columbian Exposition of 1893, the very same complex in Hyde Park that now houses the Museum of Science and Industry. The current home of the Field Museum, a tour de force of classicism in marble (designed by Daniel Burnham after the Erechtheum in Athens, but completed by others long after his death), was opened to the public in 1921. Spread over the museum's acres of floor space are the scores of permanent and temporary exhibitions—some interactive, but most requiring the old-fashioned skills of observation and imagination, notably those grand presentations in taxidermy and sculpture of the flora, fauna, and early peoples of the natural world.

The museum has collected an impressive new specimen that will surely raise the museum's stature when it is unveiled next year: The museum successfully bid $8.4 million (with help from a couple of corporate sponsors) to acquire "Sue" (named for the paleontologist who found the dinosaur in 1990 in South Dakota), the biggest, most complete Tyrannosaurus Rex fossil ever unearthed. The museum's new masterpiece is already drawing crowds: The museum set up a glass-enclosed laboratory on the second floor (near the other dinosaur exhibits) where visitors can watch preparators remove rock from Sue's bones. Scientists hope to learn much from the skeleton of the biggest carnivore that ever lived. The jury is still out on whether the T. Rex was a big baddie or simply a scavenger. Museum curators plan to unveil the completed skeleton in 2000. The beast's one-ton skull is so heavy that a lighter copy will have to be mounted on the skeleton; the real one will be displayed nearby.

Another ambitious exhibit, opening in March 1999, is "Life Underground," an interactive journey beneath Illinois prairies. Visitors will shrink Alice in Wonderland–style to the size of a beetle to come face-to-face with animatronic ants, wolf spiders, and other underground creatures. One anthropological coup at the Field is a permanent exhibit entitled "Inside Ancient Egypt." In 1908 researchers in Saqqâra, Egypt, excavated two of the original chambers from the tomb of Unis-ankh, son of the Fifth Dynasty ruler Pharaoh Unis, and transported them to the museum in Chicago. This *mastaba* (tomb) of Unis-ankh now forms the core of a spellbinding exhibit that realistically depicts scenes from Egyptian funeral, religious, and other social practices.

Visitors can explore aspects of the day-to-day world of ancient Egypt, viewing 23 actual mummies and realistic burial scenes, a living marsh environment and canal works, the ancient royal barge, a religious shrine, and a reproduction of a typical marketplace of the period. Many of the exhibits allow hands-on interaction, and there are special activities for kids, such as making parchment from living papyrus plants.

Other permanent exhibits include the new "Living Together" exhibit on creating cultural understanding, "Traveling the Pacific" (employing hundreds of artifacts from the museum's oceanic collection to re-create scenes of island life in the South Pacific), dazzling gemstones, a Pawnee earth lodge for storytelling on Native American life and lore, and those appealing dioramas that depict the ways and customs of ancient peoples.

A welcome change here—instead of the traditional cafeteria found in most museums, there's a McDonald's.

Adler Planetarium and Astronomy Museum. 1300 S. Lake Shore Dr. ☎ **312/ 322-0304,** or 312/922-STAR for a recorded message. http://astro.uchicago.edu/adler. Admission $3 adults, $2 seniors and children 4–17, free for children under 4. Free admission on Tues. Sky shows are an additional $3 per person. Mon–Thurs 9am–5pm, Fri 9am–9pm, Sat–Sun 9am–6pm; summer hours: Sat–Wed 9am–6pm, Thurs–Fri 9am–9pm. Sky shows at numerous times throughout the day; call ☎ 312/922-STAR for current times. Bus: 6, 10, 12, 130, or 146. Recommended visiting time: 2 hours.

A causeway across one end of Burnham Park Harbor links the mainland here to Northerly Island, which is occupied by two tenants, Meigs Field, the landing strip for small, private aircraft, and the Adler Planetarium. The zodiacal 12-sided structure sits on a promontory at the end of ornamental Solidarity Drive, just up the road from the aquarium. The planetarium's founder, Sears, Roebuck executive Max Adler, imported a Zeiss projector, invented in Germany in 1923, to Chicago in 1930. He wanted to bring the sky closer to people, hoping the novelty of the artificial sky would redirect attention to the real experience of watching a night sky. Today the Adler Planetarium offers a range of programs for both children and adults. Multimedia sky shows re-create the nighttime skies and current topics in space exploration. In addition, the Adler has exhibits on navigation, space exploration, and "The Universe in Your Hands," which incorporates the planetarium's History of Astronomy Collection. Expect a little dust when you visit: A $40 million expansion and renovation will double the planetarium's exhibit space when it's completed in 1999, with a new two-level exhibit hall ringing the eastern half of the building. Visitors will be able to explore space themselves in a whole new way in Star Rider, the planetarium's new theater, which will utilize the latest virtual reality imaging. A closed-circuit monitor connected to the planetarium's Doane Observatory telescope, which also is getting a facelift, allows visitors to view dramatic close-ups of the moon, the planets, and distant galaxies (only on Friday after the 8pm sky show). To find out what to look for in this month's sky, call the Nightwatch 24-Hour Hot Line (☎ **312/922-STAR**), or check in on the Internet at http://astro.uchicago.edu/adler.

✪ John G. Shedd Aquarium. 1200 S. Lake Shore Dr. ☎ **312/939-2438.** www.shedd.org. Admission to both Aquarium and Oceanarium, $10 adults, $8 seniors and children 3–11, free for children under 3. Admission to original Aquarium galleries only, $4 adults, $3 seniors and children 3–11. Free admission on Thurs, when Oceanarium admission is $6 adults, $5 children 3–11 and seniors. Oceanarium tickets available on a limited, first-come, first-served basis, so it's recommended you purchase tickets in advance at any Ticketmaster outlet, or call ☎ 312/559-0200. Summer daily 9am–6pm (Thurs until 9pm); fall–spring Mon–Fri 9am–5pm, Sat–Sun 9am–6pm. Last entry into Oceanarium 4:45pm (5:45pm in summer). Bus: 6, 10, 12, 130, or 146. Recommended visiting time: 3 hours.

Chicago's Museums by Night

Many of the city's cultural heavy hitters have started opening up their galleries for after-hours events. Big surprise: The emphasis isn't really on the art or the exhibits as much as it is on people-watching. For the young singles who turn out, these events are a nice alternative to the bar scene. The museums are self-interested, too: They make a little extra money, but they're really banking that the events nurture a new generation of donors and patrons.

The **Art Institute of Chicago** holds the biggest and most popular of the museum soirees, a monthly event known as "After Hours." Well-dressed 20- and 30-something singles crowd around the museum's Grand Staircase and nosh on hors d'oeuvres and line up at the cash bars. It's an especially good time to see the art, because the social set that attends only occasionally wanders into the galleries. If you're so inclined, there are also guided tours. After Hours is usually held the third Thursday of the month from 5:30 to 8pm. Tickets are $10 for nonmembers, $5 for members and guests. The event is popular, so it's a good idea to reserve tickets in advance. Call ☎ **630/268-1111**.

The crowd is faster and funkier at the "First Friday" events held at the **Museum of Contemporary Art.** The gallery and sculpture garden are open (weather permitting) at this monthly gathering, which offers the usual passed trays, cash bar, and entertainment such as hip live music, films, and performance art. The event is held the first Friday of every month from 6 to 10pm and costs $12 for nonmembers, $6 for MCA members. Guests must be 21 years or older. Call ☎ **312/280-2660** or the box office at 312/397-4010.

The **Newberry Library** sponsors a monthly cocktail hour called the "Wednesday Club." Held the first Wednesday of the month, the event draws a crowd of young professionals for beer and wine and lectures, discussion, and music on such topics as "The Silver Screen and Jane Austen" and "Popular Culture and Advertising: Targeting Trends." Admission is $10, $5 for associates. For information, call ☎ **312/255-3510**.

The **Shedd Aquarium** holds a social event called "Jazzin' at the Shedd" featuring live jazz and cocktails around the coral reef exhibit. The party is held every Thursday from 5 to 9pm during the summer. Admission is free (there's an extra charge for tickets to the Oceanarium). For information, call ☎ **312/939-2438.**

The third point of this museum triangle is the Shedd Aquarium, a marble octagon whose Doric exterior is decorated with a motif of marine symbols and whose interior galleries are populated by thousands of denizens of river, lake, and sea. The aquarium's most popular entertainment is the feeding of the sharks and other creatures of the reefs, from the hands of divers who swim among them in a 90,000-gallon tank. It's also fun to watch the frolicking of the river otters in their naturalistic habitat, landscaped with plant life native to the Illinois prairie. But the true revelation comes from studying the collection of sea anemones, those odd flowerlike animals of the deep.

Already the world's largest indoor aquarium, the Shedd doubled its size with the opening of the 3-million-gallon saltwater **Oceanarium,** a marine mammal pavilion that re-creates a Pacific Northwest coastal environment. With its wall of windows revealing the lake outside, the Oceanarium gives the appearance of one uninterrupted expanse of sea. As you follow a winding nature trail, you encounter beluga whales, dolphins, sea otters, and harbor seals. A colony of penguins in a separate exhibit area inhabits a naturalistic environment meant to resemble the Mariana Islands in the southern sea off Argentina. You can observe all these sea mammals at play through large underwater viewing windows. On a fixed performance schedule in a large pool surrounded by an amphitheater, the whales and dolphins are put through their paces of leaps and dives by a crew of friendly trainers. However, after the death of the first set of belugas, their presence in captivity became somewhat controversial, and on weekends there was often a line of protesters.

If you want a good sit-down meal in a restaurant with a spectacular view overlooking Lake Michigan, check out Soundings, right there inside the aquarium, or the Bubble Net food court. And for a few souvenirs, visit the aquarium's spacious new gift shop, Go Overboard!

3 North of the Loop: The Magnificent Mile & Beyond

North of the Chicago River are a number of attractions you should not overlook, including several museums and buildings, the city's greatest park, a zoo, and one of the world's most impressive research libraries. Most of these sites are either on the Magnificent Mile (North Michigan Avenue) and its surrounding blocks or not too far from there, on the Near North Side.

John Hancock Center Observatory. 94th floor of the John Hancock Center, 875 N. Michigan (enter on Delaware St.). ☎ **888/875-VIEW** or 312/751-3681. Admission $8 adults, $6 seniors and children 6–17, free for children under 5 and military personnel in uniform or with active duty cards. Daily 9am–midnight. Bus: 125, 145, 146, 147, or 151. Subway/El: Red Line to Chicago/State.

The Hancock Observatory delivers an excellent panorama of the city and an intimate view over nearby Lake Michigan and the various shoreline residential areas. The view alone is enough, but a $2.5 million renovation in 1997 of the 94th floor has added a bunch of new bells and whistles to the experience, including "talking telescopes" with sound effects and narration in four languages, history walls illustrating the growth of the city, and a "screened porch" that allows visitors to feel the rush of the wind at 1,000 feet. On a clear day you can see portions of the three states surrounding this corner of Illinois (Michigan, Indiana, and Wisconsin), for a radius of 80 miles. The view up the North Side is particularly dramatic, stretching from the nearby Oak and North Street beaches, along the green strip of Lincoln Park, to the line of high-rises that you can trace up the shoreline until they suddenly halt just below the boundary of the northern suburbs. The lake itself seems like a vast sea without any boundaries at all. The view is also spectacular at night. A high-speed elevator carries passengers to the observatory in 40 seconds, and the entrance and observatory are accessible for people with disabilities. If you prefer, you could stop in at the Signature Lounge, two floors up, and (for about the same cost) take in your views with a drink.

Museum of Contemporary Art. 220 E. Chicago Ave. (1 block east of Michigan Ave.). ☎ 312/280-2660. www.mcachicago.org. Suggested admission $6.50 adults, $4 seniors and students with ID, free for children under 12. Free admission on the first Tues of the month. Tues and Thurs–Fri 11am–6pm, Wed 11am–8pm, Sat–Sun 10am–6pm. Bus: 3, 10, 11, 66, 125, 145, 146, or 151. Subway/El: Red Line to Chicago/State.

In a city with the architectural pedigree of Chicago, the new $46 million museum housing the Museum of Contemporary Art, designed by Berlin's Josef Paul Kleihues (his first project in the United States), naturally has received intense scrutiny since it opened. The MCA is the largest contemporary art museum in the country, emphasizing experimentation in a variety of media—painting, photography, video, dance, music, and performance. While it's hard to be too much of an ingrate about a building that's seven times larger than the museum's old digs, the MCA's new home is far from the dazzler some might have expected from a contemporary art museum. Sitting on a front-row piece of property between the lake and the historic Water Tower, the classically styled building, clad in aluminum panels, is a subdued, almost somber presence, and the steep rise of stairs leading to the entrance is monumental yet a bit daunting. The interior spaces are more vibrant with a sun-drenched two-story central corridor, elliptical staircases, and three floors of exhibition space, including several handsome barrel-vaulted galleries on the top floor where for the first time curators have dedicated space to display pieces from the museum's permanent collection.

Although it's a rather new museum—the MCA was founded in 1967—it has collected more than 7,000 objects, highlighting the work of the Chicago school of artists, but gathered from all over the nation and the world as well, with in-depth holdings of works by Alexander Calder, Sol LeWitt, Donald Judd, and Bruce Nauman, among others. The museum also hosts major touring retrospectives of working artists such as Cindy Sherman and Chuck Close.

For visitors who'd like a little guidance making sense of the rather challenging works found at a contemporary art museum, there is a free daily tour as well as an audio tour for rent, narrated by, of all people, Siskel and Ebert. In addition to a range of special activities and educational programming, including films, performances, and a lecture series in a 366-seat theater, the MCA features the M Cafe with seating that overlooks a 1-acre terraced sculpture garden and a store with one-of-a-kind gift items that's worth a stop even if you don't make it into the museum.

Navy Pier. 600 E. Grand Ave. (at Lake Michigan). ☎ **800/595-PIER** (outside 312 area code) or 312/595-PIER. www.navypier.com. Free admission. Summer Sun–Thurs 10am–10pm, Fri–Sat 10am–midnight; fall–spring Mon–Sat 10am–10pm, Sun 10am–7pm. Bus: 29, 56, 65, 66, 120, or 121. Subway/El: Red Line to Grand/State; transfer to city bus or board a free pier trolley bus. Parking: Rates start at $5.50 for the first hour and go up to $13.50 for up to 6 hours. However, the lots fill quickly. Valet parking is $7 with a restaurant validation. There are also surface lots west of the pier, and free trolley buses make stops on Grand and Illinois sts. from State St.

Built during World War I, Navy Pier has been a ballroom, a training center for Navy pilots during World War II, and a satellite campus of the University of Illinois. In 1995 it underwent yet one more long-anticipated transformation, one that has returned it—at least in spirit—to its original intended purpose, a place for Chicagoans to come to relax and to be entertained. Sheer numbers alone show that the renovation has been a huge success: The pier has leaped to the top of Chicago's attractions, with more than five million visitors each year.

Developers have resurrected the Grand Ballroom and have installed Crystal Gardens, with 70 full-size palm trees, dancing fountains, and other flora in a glass-enclosed atrium; a white-canopied open-air Skyline Stage that hosts concerts, dance

New Water Taxi Service

In the summer months, water taxis operated by **Shoreline Sightseeing** (☎ 312/222-9328) speed between Navy Pier and other Chicago sights. The **River Taxi** cruises between Navy Pier and downtown near the Sears Tower, and the **Harbor Taxi** cruises between Navy Pier and the Shedd Aquarium and the Field Museum. The boats run frequently daily from 10am to 6pm. One-way fare is $6 for adults, $5 for seniors, and $3 for children under 12; round-trip is $10 for adults, $8 for seniors, and $5 for children. An all-day pass is $14 for adults and seniors and $7 for children.

Navy Pier

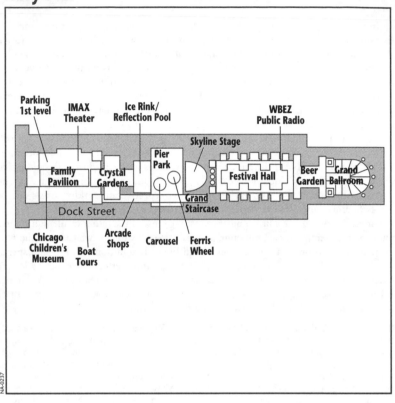

performances, and film screenings; a carousel; and a 15-story Ferris wheel that's a replica of the original that debuted at Chicago's 1893 world's fair. The 50 acres of pier and lakefront property, bedecked with lights and displaying summer fireworks, also are home to the **Chicago Children's Museum** (see "Kid Stuff," below), a 3-D Imax theater (☎ 312/595-0090), and a small ice rink. Naturally, there are a handful of rather bland shops and push-cart vendors (excepting Barbara's Bookstore), and several restaurants, from a "high-tech" McDonald's to the white-tablecloth seafood restaurant Riva. There's also a beer garden with live music and the new Joe's Be-Bop Cafe & Jazz Emporium, a Southern-style BBQ restaurant with live music nightly (run by the father-son proprietors of one of the city's jazz institutions, Jazz Showcase).

Navy Pier has a large exposition space that hosts a variety of conventions and trade shows, including an international art exposition, pro tennis exhibitions, and a flower and garden show. There's definitely something for everyone, but the commercialism of the place may be too much for some people. If that's the case for you, take the half-mile stroll to the end of the pier, east of the ballroom, where you may find a little respite and enjoy the wind, the waves, and the city view, which is the real delight of a place like this.

Moored along the south dock, you'll find more than half a dozen different sailing vessels, including a couple of dinner cruise ships, the pristine white-masted sailboat *Windy*, and, the latest additions, the "rocket" speedboats *Seadog I* and *II*. For more specifics on sightseeing and dinner cruises, see "Lake & River Cruises," later in this chapter.

Newberry Library. 60 W. Walton St. (at Dearborn Pkwy.). ☎ **312/943-9090** or 312/ 255-3700 for programs. www.newberry.org. Reading room, Tues–Thurs 10am–6pm, Fri–Sat 9am–5pm. Gallery, Mon and Fri–Sat 8:15am–5:30pm, Tues–Thurs 8:15am–7:30pm. Free 1-hour tours Thurs at 3pm and Sat at 10:30am. Bus: 22, 36, 125, 145, 146, 147, or 151. Subway/El: Red Line to Chicago/State.

The Newberry Library is a bibliophile's dream. Established in 1887 at the bequest of the Chicago merchant and financier Walter Loomis Newberry, the noncirculating research library today contains many rare books and manuscripts (such as Shakespeare's first folio and Jefferson's copy of *The Federalist Papers*) and a vast depository of published resources for those who are seriously delving into American and European history and literature, as well as other aspects of the humanities from the late Middle Ages onward. The library is also a major destination for genealogists digging at their roots, and its holdings are open for the use of the public for free (over the age of 16 with a photo ID). The collections, many items of which are on display, include more than 1.5 million volumes and 75,000 maps, housed in a comely five-story granite building, designed in the Spanish-Romanesque style by Henry Ives Cobb and built for the library in 1893. Beyond being a sanctuary in which to conduct research, the Newberry has staked out a little piece of civilization, sponsoring a series of concerts (including those by its resident early music ensemble, the Newberry Consort), lectures, and children's story hours throughout the year. The library also operates a fine bookstore. Validated parking for library visitors is available at Clark and Chestnut streets for $5 for 6 hours.

Terra Museum of American Art. 666 N. Michigan Ave. (near Erie St.). ☎ **312/ 664-3939.** Admission $5 adults, $2.50 seniors, $1 students with ID, free for children under 14. Free admission on Tues. Tues noon–8pm, Wed–Sat 10am–5pm, Sun noon–5pm. Bus: 3, 11, 125, 145, 146, 147, or 151. Subway/El: Red Line to Grand/State or Chicago/State.

Housing the formerly private collection of industrialist Daniel J. Terra, the Terra Museum of American Art has assembled some 400 pieces of 18th-, 19th-, and 20th-century American art.

4 Lincoln Park Attractions

Lincoln Park is the city's largest, and certainly one of the longest, parks. Straight and narrow, Lincoln Park begins at North Avenue and follows the shoreline of Lake Michigan northward as far as Ardmore Avenue (not far from the "new" Chinatown and Andersonville). Within its elongated 1,200 acres are a first-class zoo, a half-dozen bathing beaches, a botanical conservatory, two excellent museums, a golf course, and the usual meadows, formal gardens, sporting fields, and tennis courts typical of urban parks. To get to the park, take bus no. 22, 145, 146, 147, 151, or 156.

The **statue of the standing Abraham Lincoln** in the park that bears his name is one of two in Chicago by Augustus Saint-Gaudens (Saint-Gaudens's seated Lincoln is in Grant Park). Saint-Gaudens also did the Bates Fountain near the conservatory.

Chicago Historical Society. 1601 N. Clark St. (at North Ave.). ☎ **312/642-4600.** www.chicagohistory.org. Admission $5 adults, $3 seniors and students, $1 children 6–12; free for children under 6. Free admission on Mon. Mon–Sat 9:30am–4:30pm, Sun noon–5pm. Research center, Tues–Sat 10am–4:30pm. Bus: 11, 22, 36, 72, 151, or 156.

At the southwestern tip of Lincoln Park stands one of Chicago's most interesting exhibition halls. Despite its name, this place is not only for scholarly types. In the society's permanent second-floor exhibition, called "We the People," among the objects on display are an original copy of the Ephrata Cloister Hymnal, a memento of a little-known early communal religious group in colonial Pennsylvania, and the Boweles' New Pocket Map (1784), which depicts Mount Desert Island and Penobscot Bay along the coast of Maine in reverse order. Various other articles and documents reveal how the nation's mercantile interests prolonged the practice of importing slaves from Africa. Also rare—as both a document and the tale it refers to—is the copy of Herman Mann's 1866 biography of Deborah Sampson, the "female soldier in the war of Revolution." I had a hard time leaving because each time I started to go my eye would catch something else, such as the touching painting of Washington's farewell to his staff at New York's Fraunces Tavern, which shows many of the officers openly and unashamedly weeping as they take leave of their commander-in-chief. "A House Divided," perhaps the most exciting, emotionally charged exhibit on the Civil War you will ever see, opened at the Historical Society in February 1990 and is scheduled to close in the year 2000. The exhibition is divided into eight sections and draws on the society's antebellum Lincoln and Civil War holdings. Through a display of more than 600 artifacts, it examines the major political and social forces of mid-19th-century America, with a strong emphasis on Abraham Lincoln. Some of the major artifacts include the "Railsplitter" painting of Lincoln, the Emancipation Proclamation table, the Appomattox table, Lincoln's deathbed, John Brown's Bible, and a diorama of the Lincoln–Douglas debates.

On the ground floor of the museum, past the gift shop, is the attractive Big Shoulders Café, entered through a terra-cotta arch. Its facade is adorned with animals and historical figures in relief and was removed intact from the old Stockyard Bank and reassembled here. The food is light, delicious, and imaginative.

Lincoln Park Zoo. 2200 N. Cannon Dr. (at Fullerton Pkwy.). ☎ **312/742-2000.** www.lpzoo.com. Free admission. Summer Mon–Fri 10am–5pm, Sat–Sun 10am–7pm; fall–spring daily 10am–5pm; grounds open at 8am year-round. Bus: 151 or 156.

The Lincoln Park Zoo is spread over 35 acres, is open 365 days a year, and is always free. The zoo is imaginatively designed, with the animals occupying separate habitats appropriate to their species. Over the last several years, the zoo has been modernizing many of its facilities, and in 1997 it debuted the new Small Mammal–Reptile House with 200 species of mammals, amphibians, reptiles, and birds that are endangered in the wild. The zoo has a population of more than 1,000 animals, birds, and reptiles. Just the names of the large mammals are enough to excite interest: gorillas, rhinos, wolves, bears, camels, gazelles, big cats, zebras, elephants, and hippos. For the adjoining children's zoo, see "Kid Stuff" later in this chapter. The zoo has opened a new food court called Park Place Café, located in the original aquarium and later reptile house, that offers seven food stations and terrace seating.

Lincoln Park Conservatory. Fullerton Dr. (at Stockton Dr.). ☎ **312/742-7736.** Free admission. Daily 9am–5pm. Bus: 73, 151, or 156.

Inside are four great halls filled with thousands of plants, the closest thing (other than several smaller conservatories scattered in a few neighborhood parks) that Chicago has to a botanical garden within the city limits. The Palm House features giant palms and rubber trees, the Fernery nurtures plants that grow close to the forest floor, and the Tropical House is a symphony of shiny greenery. The fourth environment is the Show House, where seasonal flower shows are held.

The Nature Museum of the Chicago Academy of Sciences. Fullerton Pkwy. and Cannon Dr. ☎ 773/871-2668. www.chias.org. Bus: 151. Subway/El: Red Line to Fullerton.

These swell new digs for the Chicago Academy of Sciences' Nature Museum are expected to open in spring 1999. The museum's temporary home at North Pier closed in December 1997. The new site promises to be "a state-of-the-art environmental museum for the 21st century." The museum will feature plenty of indoor and outdoor interactive exhibits on nature and the environment, including a butterfly haven, a wilderness walk, and a children's gallery. Admission prices and open hours were unavailable when this book went to press.

Café Brauer. 2021 Stockton Dr. ☎ **312/742-2480.** Daily 10am–5pm. Bus: 151 or 156.

A onetime Chicago institution near the zoo, Café Brauer has reopened its doors to the public following a massive restoration costing more than $4 million. Operating a cafe and ice cream parlor on the ground floor, and a ballroom called the Great Hall on the second floor, the return of the Brauer restores some of the elegant atmosphere that characterized the park around the turn of the century, when this landmark building was erected. There are also paddleboats for rent here at the edge of the South Pond with nice views of the John Hancock Center beyond the treetops of Lincoln Park ($9 per half hour, $15 per hour).

5 Exploring Hyde Park: The Museum of Science and Industry & More

Birthplace of atomic fission, home to the University of Chicago and to one of the Midwest's most popular tourist attractions, the Museum of Science and Industry, Hyde Park, is also one of Chicago's most successfully integrated middle-class neighborhoods. You could easily set aside a full day to explore this southeast corner of Chicago.

SOME HYDE PARK HISTORY   When Hyde Park was settled in 1850, it became Chicago's first suburb. A hundred years later, in the 1950s, Hyde Park added another first to its impressive resume, one that the current neighborhood is not particularly proud of: an urban-renewal plan. At the time, a certain amount of old commercial and housing stock was demolished rather than rehabilitated—just those kinds of buildings that would be much prized today—and replaced by projects and small shopping malls that actually make some corners of Hyde Park look more suburban, in the modern sense, than they really are.

What Hyde Park does have to be proud of is that, in racially balkanized Chicago, this neighborhood has found an alternative vision. As Southern blacks began to migrate to Chicago's South Side during World War I, many whites fled. But most whites here, especially those who wanted to stay near the university, chose integration as the only realistic strategy to preserve their neighborhood. The 1990 census numbered 14,400 whites and 10,700 blacks in the neighborhood's population. Hyde Park is decidedly middle class, with pockets of true affluence in Kenwood that reflect the days when the well-to-do moved here in the beginning of the century to escape the decline of Prairie Avenue. Among those old Chicago families who once occupied the estates in Kenwood were meat packer Gustavus Swift; lumber merchant Martin Ryerson; Sears, Roebuck executive Julius Rosenwald (who endowed the Museum of Science and Industry); John Shedd (the president of Marshall Field's who gave the city the aquarium that bears his name); and William Goodman (who sponsored the Art Institute and the theater to which his name is affixed). Among Hyde Park–Kenwood's well-known black residents in recent years were the late Elijah Muhammad, Muhammad Ali, and, currently, Louis Farrakhan, along with numerous other Nation of Islam families who continue to worship in a mosque, formerly a Greek Orthodox cathedral, that is one of the neighborhood's architectural landmarks. The late Mayor

Harold Washington also lived here. Surrounding this unusual enclave, however, are many marginal blocks where poverty and slum housing abound. For all its nobility, Hyde Park's achievement in integration merely emphasizes that even more unwieldy than racial differences are socioeconomic ones.

Through its fight for self-preservation, Hyde Park has gained a reputation as an activist community. A certain vitality springs from acts of coping with the world as you find it, and it is this element that distinguishes Hyde Park from other middle-class neighborhoods in Chicago. Hyde Park, in a word, is cosmopolitan.

The University of Chicago is widely hailed as one of the more intellectually exciting institutions of higher learning in the country and has been home to some 68 Nobel laureates. The year the university opened its doors, 1892, was a big one for Hyde Park, but 1893 was even bigger. In that year, Chicago, chosen over other cities in a competitive international field, hosted the World's Columbian Exposition, commemorating the 400th anniversary of Columbus's arrival in America.

To create a fairground, the landscape architect Frederick Law Olmsted was enlisted to fill in the marshlands along Hyde Park's lakefront and link what was to become Jackson Park to existing Washington Park on the neighborhood's western boundary with a narrow concourse called the Midway Plaisance. On the resulting 650 acres—at a cost of $30 million—12 exhibit palaces, 57 buildings devoted to U.S. states and foreign governments, and dozens of smaller structures were constructed under the supervision of architect Daniel Burnham. Most of the building followed Burnham's preference for the Classical Revival style and exterior surfaces finished in white stucco. With the innovation of outdoor electric lighting, the sparkling result was the "White City," which attracted 27 million visitors in a single season, running from May 1 to October 31, 1893. The exposition sponsors, in that brief time, had remarkably recovered their investment, but within a few short years of its closing most of the fair's buildings were destroyed by vandalism and fire. Only the Palace of Fine Arts, occupying the eastern tip of the midway, survives to this day, and now houses the Museum of Science and Industry.

GETTING THERE   From the Loop, the ride to Hyde Park on the **no. 6 Jeffrey Express bus** takes about 30 minutes. The bus originates on Wacker Drive, travels south along State Street, and ultimately follows Lake Shore Drive to Hyde Park. Weekdays the bus runs from around 5:30am to 10:30pm, and on weekends and holidays from around 7:30am to 7pm. The southbound express bus adds a surcharge of 25¢ to the normal fare of $1.50 (there's no surcharge if you use a CTA transit card). The **no. 1 local bus** originates at Union Station on Jackson Boulevard and Canal Street.

The **Metra Electric train** follows the old Illinois Central Line (often still referred to as the IC), arriving in Hyde Park in about 15 minutes from downtown. Trains run every hour (more frequently during rush hour) Monday through Saturday from 5:15am to 12:50am, and from every half hour to 90 minutes on Sunday and holidays from 5am to 12:55am. Downtown stations are at Randolph and Michigan, Van Buren and Michigan, and Roosevelt Road and Michigan (near the Museum Campus in Grant Park). Printed schedules are available at the stations. The fare is approximately $1.95 each way.

For CTA bus and Metra train information, call ☎ 836-7000 (any city or suburban area code).

For taxis, dial ☎ 312/TAXI-CAB (☎ 312/829-4222) for Yellow Cab or ☎ 312/ CHECKER (☎ 312/243-2537) for Checker. The one-way fare from downtown is around $12.

A SUGGESTED ITINERARY   A long 1-day itinerary for Hyde Park should include the following: a selected tour of the U of C campus with a walk along the

Hyde Park

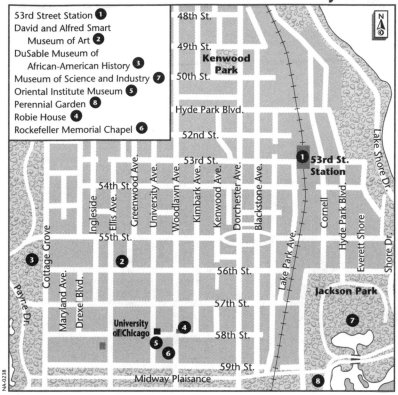

53rd Street Station **1**
David and Alfred Smart
    Museum of Art **2**
DuSable Museum of
    African-American History **3**
Museum of Science and Industry **7**
Oriental Institute Museum **5**
Perennial Garden **8**
Robie House **4**
Rockefeller Memorial Chapel **6**

Midway Plaisance, a visit to several museums and cultural institutions, a tour of the Kenwood mansions (preferably by car), and a walk through the area's commercial center. (See chapter 8 for a self-guided walking tour of the neighborhood.)

THE TOP ATTRACTIONS

✪ **Museum of Science and Industry.** 57th St. and Lake Shore Dr. ☎ **800/ 468-6674** outside the Chicago area, 773/684-1414, or TTY 773/684-3323. www. msichicago.org. Admission to museum only, $7 adults, $6 seniors, $3.50 children 3–11, free for children under 3. Free admission on Thurs. Combination museum and Omnimax Theater, $11 adults, $9 seniors, $6.50 children 3–11, free for children under 3 if seated on an adult's lap. Omnimax Theater only, evening shows $10 adults, $8 seniors, $6 children, free for children under 3 if on adult's lap; Thurs $7 adults, $6 seniors, $5 children 3–11. Memorial Day–Labor Day, daily 9:30am–5:30pm; rest of the year, Mon–Fri 9:30am–4pm, Sat–Sun and holidays 9:30am–5:30pm. Closed Christmas. Bus: 6, 10, 55, 151, or 156. Recommended visiting time: 3 hours.

Hyde Park is probably already on your must-do itinerary of Chicago, in the form of a visit to this world-famous museum, the granddaddy of every interactive museum. In statistical terms alone, the museum's collection is awesome: some 2,000 exhibits spread over 14 acres in 75 exhibition halls. Visitors arriving by car get their first glimpse of the museum's newest exhibit, "All Aboard the Silver Streak," practically before they exit their vehicle: After a major refurbishing, the museum's Burlington Pioneer Zephyr, the world's first streamlined, diesel-electric, articulated train, has been moved indoors and installed in the museum's new three-story underground parking garage. The Zephyr gained fame in 1934 when it set a land speed record by hauling

The Museum of Science and Industry

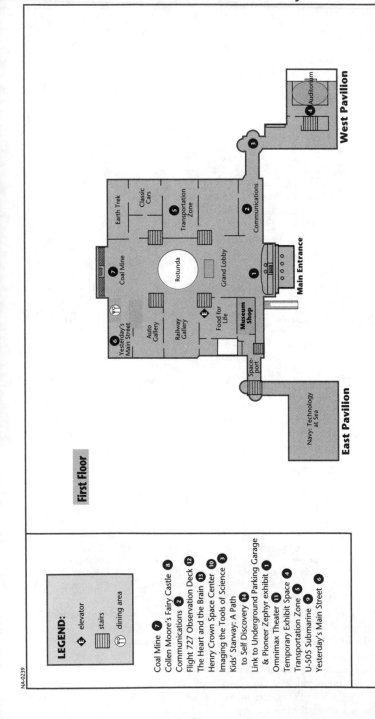

First Floor

LEGEND:
- ◆ elevator
- ▦ stairs
- 🍴 dining area

Coal Mine **7**
Collen Moore's Fairy Castle **8**
Communications **2**
Flight 727 Observation Deck **12**
The Heart and the Brain **13**
Henry Crown Space Center **10**
Imaging the Tools of Science **3**
Kids' Starway: A Path
  to Self Discovery **14**
Link to Underground Parking Garage
  & Pioneer Zephyr exhibit **1**
Omnimax Theater **11**
Temporary Exhibit Space **4**
Transportation Zone **5**
U-505 Submarine **9**
Yesterday's Main Street **6**

NA-0239

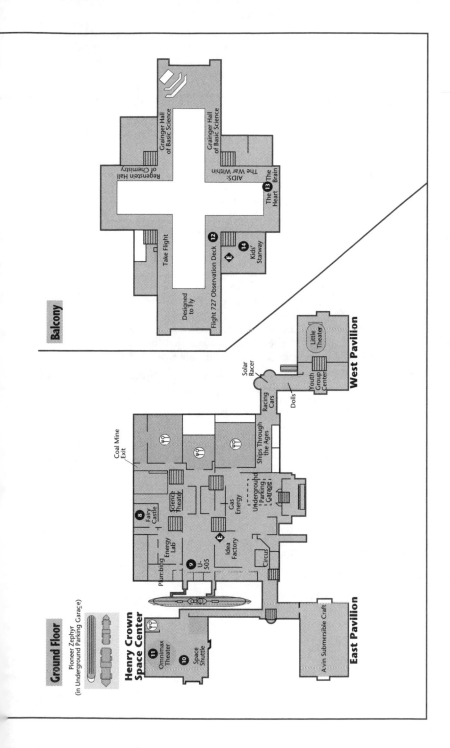

non-stop from Denver to Chicago in slightly more than 13 hours. A simulated train station has been installed along the 197-foot-long Zephyr, and visitors can explore the train and its new on-board interactive exhibits.

Old hat now, but a favorite of any child who grew up in Chicago, is the descent into a full-scale replica of a southern Illinois coal mine, which dates to 1934. The mine reopened in 1997 after a renovation that preserved all of the much-loved aspects of the experience but incorporated 1990s mining techniques into the exhibit. The museum's latest permanent exhibit, "Idea Factory," which debuted in 1997, is a "learning through play" environment that allows children up to 10 years old to explore scientific principles themselves. Another innovation was "AIDS: The War Within," which when it opened a few years ago became the first permanent exhibit on the immune system and HIV, the virus that causes AIDS.

A major attraction at the museum is the Henry Crown Space Center, where the story of space exploration, still in its infancy, is documented in copious detail, highlighted by a simulated space shuttle experience through sight and sound at the center's five-story Omnimax Theater.

But whatever your particular technofetish—from submarines to space capsules, from special effects to the mysteries of the human organism—you will find the object of your curiosity somewhere in this amazing museum. There's even a 133-foot United Airlines 727 attached to the balcony.

The Omnimax Theater offers double features on the weekends; call for show times. When you've worked up an appetite, the museum has five restaurants, including a Pizza Hut and an ice cream parlor, and there are also two gift shops.

DuSable Museum of African-American History. 740 E. 56th Place. ☎ **773/947-0600,** TDD 773/947-7203. www.dusable.org. Admission $3 adults, $2 students and seniors, $1 children 6–12, free for children under 6. Free admission on Thurs. Mon–Sat 10am–5pm, Sun noon–5pm. Closed Easter, Thanksgiving, Dec 25, and Jan 1. Bus: 3, 4, or 55. Subway/El: Red Line to 55th or 63rd in Washington Park.

The DuSable Museum is a repository of the history, art, and artifacts pertaining to the African-American experience and culture. The exhibits the museum offers are very worthwhile, but unfortunately the bulk of the collection dates only from the WPA period in the late thirties and the black arts movement of the sixties, with only sketchy exhibits tracing the earlier stages of the African-American experience in this country. The museum, located on the eastern edge of Washington Park, also has a gift shop, a research library, and an extensive program of community-related events, such as a jazz and blues music series, poetry readings, film screenings, and other cultural events, all of which are presented in a 466-seat auditorium.

The University of Chicago

The University of Chicago offers a free weekly campus architecture tour organized by the university's **Office of Special Events** (☎ 773/702-8374). The 1-hour tour begins at 10am on Saturday from Ida Noyes Hall, 1212 E. 59th St. (Paid tours can be arranged for alternate times.) You can pick up free campus maps and copies of "The Chronicle," a calendar of events (also accessible through the university Web site at www.uchicago.edu) put out by the university's information service, at several locations on campus, including the Reynolds Club student center. You can also inquire about campus goings-on (concerts, performances, lectures, and the like) by calling the **Reynolds Club** information desk (☎ 773/702-8787) or the university ticket office (☎ 773/702-7300).

Just walking around the Gothic spires of the University of Chicago campus is bound to conjure up images of the cloistered academic life. Wander on the stone paths

More Frank Lloyd Wright Homes

In addition to Robie House, several of Wright's earlier works, still privately owned, dot the streets of Hyde Park, such as the **Heller House,** 5132 S. Woodlawn (1897); the **Blossom House,** 1332 E. 49th St. (1882); and the **McArthur House,** 4852 S. Kenwood Ave. (1892).

---

among the quads or just choose a nice patch of grass and vegetate. Some stops to consider are the **Henry Moore statue,** *Nuclear Energy,* on South Ellis Avenue between 56th and 57th streets. It's next to the Regenstein Library, which marks the site of the old Stagg Field, where on December 2, 1942, the world's first sustained nuclear reaction was achieved. The **Seminary Co-op Bookstore,** 5757 S. University Ave. (☎ 773/752-4381), has just about everything you might want, including the full collection of Penguin paperbacks. It's open Monday through Friday from 8:30am to 9pm, Saturday from 10am to 6pm, and Sunday from noon to 6pm. (See chapter 8 for a self-guided walking tour that highlights additional campus landmarks.)

Robie House. 5757 S. Woodlawn Ave. (at 58th St.). ☎ **708/848-1976.** Admission $8 adults, $6 seniors and children 7–18. Weekday tours at 11am, 1pm, and 3pm; weekends continuously 11am–3:30pm. Bus: 55.

One of Frank Lloyd Wright's finest works, the Robie House is considered among the five masterpieces of 20th-century American architecture. The open layout and craftsmanship are typical of a Wright design. Its institutional-looking exterior, though, may make Robie House less satisfying for some observers than some of the homes he designed in Oak Park. Docents from Oak Park's Frank Lloyd Wright Home and Studio Foundation, which recently took over management from the University of Chicago and has embarked on a 10-year, $4 million restoration, now give visitors access to areas of the house once occupied by university offices, adding views of the first-level playroom and billiard room to the long-standing tours of the second-level living/dining room. The foundation has announced a decade-long restoration of the house, built in 1909. Another new addition is a Wright specialty bookshop in the building's former three-car garage.

Rockefeller Memorial Chapel. 5850 S. Woodlawn Ave. ☎ **773/702-2100.** Free admission. Daily 8am–4pm (except during religious services). Bus: 6 or 55.

The Rockefeller Memorial Chapel is just across from Robie House. Did someone say chapel? This is false modesty, even for a Rockefeller. When the university first opened its doors, the students sang the following ditty:

> *John D. Rockefeller, wonderful man is he*
> *Gives all his spare change to the U of C.*

John D. was a generous patron, indeed. He founded the university (in cooperation with the American Baptist Society), built the magnificent minicathedral that now bears his name, and shelled out an additional $35 million in donations to the institution over the course of his lifetime.

The Memorial Chapel's outstanding features are the circular stained-glass window high above the main altar and the world's second-largest carillon. Choir concerts, carillon performances, and other musical programs are presented throughout the year, usually for a small donation. The building is open to the public, but more in-depth tours can be arranged through the university's Office of Special Events at ☎ 773/702-9202. Tours of the carillon are done during the academic year at 5:30pm weekdays and at noon on Sunday following services.

Oriental Institute Museum. 1155 E. 58th St. (at University Ave.). ☎ **773/702-9521** for information, 773/702-9507 for special tours. www.oi.uchicago.edu. Free admission. Tues and Thurs–Sat 10am–4pm, Wed 10am–8:30pm, Sun noon–4pm. Bus: 6.

Near the midpoint of the campus, just north of the Memorial Chapel, is the Oriental Institute, housing one of the world's major collections of Near Eastern art, dating from 9000 B.C. to the 10th century A.D. These ancient objects are extraordinarily beautiful to the eye, subtle in form, texture, and hue. After more than a year of extensive renovation and expansion that closed the museum to the public, the galleries are slowly reopening, with the Egyptian Gallery debuting in December 1998. The new space is now one of the most up-to-date exhibitions of Egyptian artifacts in the country, offering information about how Egyptians actually lived with examples of their clothing, furniture, tools, toys and games, and musical instruments in exhibits on the history of Egypt, mummies and mummification, religious practices, kingship, and women and family. The Assyrian and Mesopotamian Gallery is scheduled to reopen later in 1999, and galleries devoted to ancient Turkey, Syria, Israel, Palestine, and Iran will open over the next 2 years.

The gift shop at the Oriental Institute, called the Suq, is renowned in its own right as a shopper's treasure trove. Deck yourself with the jewelry of the Fertile Crescent . . . and walk like an Egyptian. The gift shop remains open during construction. Hours are Tuesday, Thursday, and Saturday from 10am to 4pm, Wednesday from 10am to 7pm, and Sunday from noon to 4pm. Call the above number for more information.

David and Alfred Smart Museum of Art. 5550 S. Greenwood Ave. (at E. 55th St.). ☎ **773/702-0200.** http://csmaclab-www.uchicago.edu/SmartMuseum. Free admission; donations welcome. Tues–Wed and Fri 10am–4pm, Thurs 10am–9pm, Sat–Sun noon–6pm. Closed holidays. Bus: 6 or 55.

The David and Alfred Smart Museum of Art is named for two of the founders of *Esquire* magazine, whose family foundation created the University of Chicago's fine arts museum. The Smart Museum houses a permanent collection of more than 7,000 works ranging from classical antiquity to the contemporary. In keeping with its university setting, the Smart also hosts an intriguing variety of temporary exhibitions. Recent exhibits included "From Blast to Pop: Aspects of Modern British Art 1915–1965" and "The Sublime and the Fantastic: African Art from the Faletti Family Collection."

ENJOYING THE OUTDOORS IN HYDE PARK

Hyde Park is not only a haven for book lovers and culture aficionados—the community also has its open-air attractions. A number of worthy outdoor environments are located near Lake Michigan, including **Lake Shore Drive** itself, where many stately apartment houses follow the contour of the shoreline. A very suitable locale for a quiet stroll during the day is **Promontory Point**, at 55th Street and Lake Michigan, a bulb of land that juts into the lake and offers a good view of Chicago to the north, and the seasonally active 57th Street beach to the south.

Farther south, just below the Museum of Science and Industry, is **Wooded Island** in Jackson Park, the site of the Japanese Pavilion during the Columbian Exposition and today a lovely garden of meandering paths. The **Perennial Garden** in Jackson Park is at 59th Street and Stony Island Avenue, where more than 180 varieties of flowering plants display a palette of colors that changes with the seasons.

6 More Museums

Chicago has a horde of smaller museums devoted to all manner of subjects. Many of their collections preserve the stories and heritage of a particular immigrant group that has become inseparable from the history of the city as a whole.

American Police Center and Museum. 1717 S. State St. (at 17th St.). ☎ **312/ 431-0005.** Admission $4 adults, $3 seniors, $2.50 children 3–11; free for children under 3. Tours require reservations and a minimum of 20 people. Mon–Fri 9:30am–4:30pm. Bus: 29, 44, 62, or 164.

Carrying a mandate to help prevent crime by fostering better civilian understanding of law enforcement, the museum displays police equipment and memorabilia. It must have been where Nelson Algren brought Simone de Beauvoir to show her the electric chair, an event Algren refers to in an interview for the *Paris Review*. The museum has added a new exhibit on the history of women in law enforcement.

Balzekas Museum of Lithuanian Culture. 6500 S. Pulaski Rd. (at 65th St.). ☎ **773/ 582-6500.** Admission $4 adults, $3 students and seniors, $1 children. Daily 10am–4pm. Subway/El: Orange Line to Pulaski, transfer to bus no. 53A south.

The Balzekas Museum of Lithuanian Culture gives insight into the history and ancient culture of the tiny Baltic state that was absorbed into the former Soviet Union and achieved independence in August 1991. The museum is located on the Far Southwest Side, home to the largest Lithuanian community outside of Lithuania. The collection contains a range of objects, including books, artworks, arms and armor, maps, and decorative ornaments.

Chicago Athenaeum: Museum of Architecture and Design. 6 N. Michigan Ave. (at Madison St.). ☎ **312/251-0175.** www.chi-athenaeum.org. Suggested donation $3 adults, $2 seniors and students. Tues–Sat 11am–6pm, Sun 11am–5pm. Bus: 3, 4, 20, 56, 60, 127, 131, 145, 146, 147, 151, or 157. Subway/El: Brown, Orange, Green, or Purple Line to Madison, or Red Line to Washington/State.

The collection at the Chicago Athenaeum reaches across several fields of design, including architectural, industrial, and graphic, all with a special emphasis on Chicago, including a permanent exhibit on the history of the city's architecture from 1880 to the present. Only a small portion of the collection is on public view at once, but serious researchers can see more by appointment. The gift shop, Good Design, sells books and decorative items.

Martin D'Arcy Gallery of Art. Loyola University, 6525 N. Sheridan Rd. ☎ **773/ 508-2679.** Free admission. Mon–Fri noon–4pm. Closed May–Aug. Bus: 151. Subway/El: Red Line to Loyola.

A treasure trove of medieval, Renaissance, and Baroque art, the Martin D'Arcy Gallery of Art covers the years A.D. 1100 to 1700. All the rich symbolism of Catholicism through the Baroque era is embodied in such works as a gem-encrusted silver and ebony sculpture of Christ's scourging, a head of John the Baptist on a silver platter, golden chalices, rosary beads carved with biblical scenes, and many other highly ornamented ritual objects.

Jane Addams Hull-House Museum. University of Illinois at Chicago, 800 S. Halsted St. (at Polk St.). ☎ **312/413-5353.** www.uic.edu/jaddams/hull/hull-house. Free admission. Mon–Fri 10am–4pm, Sun noon–5pm. Bus: 8. Subway/El: Blue Line to Halsted/University of Illinois.

Three years after the Haymarket Riot, a young woman named Jane Addams bought an old mansion on Halsted Street that had been built in 1856 as a "country home" but was now surrounded by the shanties of the immigrant poor. Here Addams and her coworker, Ellen Gates Starr, launched the American settlement-house movement with the establishment of Hull House, an institution that endured on this site in Chicago until 1963. (It continues today as a decentralized social-service agency known as Hull House Association.) In that year all but two of the settlement's 13 buildings, along with the entire residential neighborhood in its immediate vicinity, were demolished to make room for the new University of Illinois at Chicago campus, which now owns the museum buildings. The story of the opposition to this project is eloquently told in the words of the participants themselves, who appear among the scores of others interviewed by Studs Terkel for his book *Division Street: America*. Of the original settlement, what remains today is the Hull-House Museum, the mansion itself, and the residents' dining hall, snuggled among the ultramodern, poured-concrete buildings of the university campus. Inside are the original furnishings, Jane Addams's office, and numerous settlement maps and photographs. Rotating exhibits re-create the history of the settlement and the work of its residents, showing how Addams was able to help transform the dismal streets around her into stable inner-city environments worth fighting over.

International Museum of Surgical Science. 1524 N. Lake Shore Dr. (at North Blvd.). ☎ 312/642-6502. www.imss.org. E-mail: imss@interaccess.com. Free admission; $3 suggested donation. Tues–Sat 10am–4pm. Bus: 151.

Housed in a 1917 Gold Coast mansion, the museum has a collection of surgical instruments, paintings, and sculpture depicting the history of surgery. A turn-of-the-century apothecary shop and dentist's office are re-created in a historic street exhibit.

Mexican Fine Arts Center Museum. 1852 W. 19th St. (a few blocks west of Ashland Ave.). ☎ 312/738-1503. www.mfacmchicago.org. Free admission. Tues–Sun 10am–5pm. Bus: 9. Subway/El: Blue Line to 18th St.

Located in the heart of the city's Mexican community of Pilsen, southwest of the Loop, the Mexican Fine Arts Center Museum, the largest of its kind in the country, features the work of Mexican and Mexican-American artists. The museum draws upon its own collection of 1,200 works and features temporary exhibitions, from pre-Colombian art to avant-garde installations, and organizes one of the most ambitious Day of the Dead celebrations in the country, running for about 8 weeks beginning in September. The museum regularly sponsors concerts and performances on its own stage, operates its own radio station (WRTE, 90.5 FM), and has a nice gift shop. For more details on what to see and do in Pilsen, see chapter 8, "Chicago Strolls."

Museum of Broadcast Communications. 78 E. Washington St. (at Michigan Ave.). ☎ 312/629-6000. www.neog.com/mbc. Free admission. Mon–Sat 10am–4:30pm, Sun noon–5pm. Bus: 3, 4, 60, 145, 147, or 151. Subway/El: Red Line to Washington/State or Brown, Green, Orange, or Purple Line to Randolph.

Housed in the Chicago Cultural Center, the Museum of Broadcast Communications includes both the Radio Hall of Fame and the Kraft TeleCenter. Pay a visit if you'd like to listen to or watch the classic programs of yore, or if you've always dreamed of anchoring your own newscast.

Intuit: The Center for Intuitive and Outsider Art. 756 N. Milwaukee Ave. (at Chicago and Odgen aves.). ☎ 773/929-7122. http://outsider.art.org. Free admission. Wed–Sat noon–5pm. Subway/El: Blue Line to Chicago.

Note: At press time, Intuit had plans to move to a new as-of-yet-unannounced site by the end of 1998; call for details. Chicago is home to an active community of collectors of so-called "outsider" art, a term attached to a group of unknown, unconventional artists who do their own artwork without any formal training or connection to the mainstream art world. Often called folk or self-taught artists, their work is highly personal and idiosyncratic, and they work in a range of media, from bottle caps to immense canvases. Intuit was founded in 1991 to bring attention to these artists through exhibitions and educational lectures. The move to this new space, previously occupied by the now-defunct Randolph Street Gallery, is certain to give Intuit a higher profile on the city's art scene and may spur an expanded program of lectures and films and the creation of a permanent collection.

National Vietnam Veterans Art Museum. 1801 S. Indiana Ave. (at 18th St.). ☎ **312/326-0270.** E-mail: nvvam@aol.com. Admission $4 adults, $3 students with ID and children under 16. Tues–Fri 11am–6pm, Sat 10am–5pm, Sun 11am–5pm. Closed major holidays. Bus: 3 or 4.

One of the newest museums in the city, the National Vietnam Veterans Art Museum opened in 1996 in the Historic Prairie Avenue District in an abandoned brick warehouse donated by the city. It houses one of the most stirring art collections anywhere, telling the story of the men who fought in Vietnam. Since the war, many of the veterans made art as personal therapy, never expecting to show it to anyone, but in 1981 a small group of them began showing their works together in Chicago and in touring exhibitions. The collection has grown to more than 600 paintings, drawings, photographs, and sculpture from all over the country and other countries, including Vietnam. Titles such as *We Regret to Inform You, Blood Spots on a Rice Paddy,* and *The Wound* should give you an idea of the power of the images in this unique legacy to the war. The complex also houses a small theater, a cafe open for breakfast and lunch, a gift shop, and an outdoor plaza with a flagpole that has deliberately been left leaning because that's how veterans saw them in combat.

Peace Museum. 314 W. Institute Place. (at Orleans St.). ☎ **312/440-1860.** Admission $3.50 adults, $2 seniors, students, and children. Tues–Wed and Fri–Sat 11am–5pm, Thurs noon–5pm. Bus: 11, 22, or 65. Subway/El: Brown Line to Chicago.

Perhaps you might want to visit here after spending a couple of hours at the National Vietnam Veterans Art Museum. The museum presents four exhibits a year and keeps on permanent display such items as manuscripts by Joan Baez, Civil Rights–era photos, and a John Lennon guitar. Here's a little trivia for you: The rock group U2 named one of its albums, *The Unforgettable Fire,* for an exhibition of drawings by survivors of Hiroshima and Nagasaki that Bono and the boys viewed at this museum. (A couple of those pieces are usually kept on permanent display.)

Polish Museum of America. 984 N. Milwaukee Ave. (at Augusta Blvd.). ☎ **773/384-3352.** E-mail: PGSAmerican@aol.com. Suggested donation $2 adults, $1 children. Daily 11am–4pm. Subway/El: Blue Line to Division.

Located in the heart of the first Polish neighborhood in Chicago, this museum has one of the most important collections of Polish art and historical materials outside Poland. It is also the largest museum in the country devoted exclusively to an ethnic group. The museum's programs include rotating exhibitions, films, lectures, and concerts, and a new permanent exhibit about Pope John Paul II.

Swedish-American Museum Center. 5211 N. Clark St. (near Foster Ave.). ☎ **773/728-8111.** Suggested donation $4 adults, $2 seniors and students, $1 children. Tues–Fri 10am–4pm, Sat–Sun 10am–3pm. Bus: 22. Subway/El: Red Line to Bryn Mawr; then walk several blocks west to Clark.

This storefront exhibit chronicles the Swedish immigrant contribution to American life and is a hub of activity with cultural lectures, concerts, and classes geared to

Swedish-Americans, some of whom still live in the surrounding Andersonville neighborhood. There's also a gift shop for typical items of Scandinavian manufacture.

Ukrainian National Museum. 721 N. Oakley Blvd. (near Chicago Ave.). ☎ **312/421-8020.** Suggested donation $2 adults, $1 students. Mon–Wed by appointment, Thurs–Sun 11am–4pm. Bus: 66.

The Ukrainian National Museum possesses an unmistakable old-world atmosphere; few cultures seem to have changed as little over the ages as that of the Ukrainians. Throughout the museum you will find decorative Easter eggs, fine embroidery, wood carvings, artwork, crafts, and folk costumes, all of which reflect an incredible continuity in technique over the years. The museum is ideally located for a walk around the neighborhood known as Ukrainian Village, where there are also a couple of beautiful churches and a small retail strip of ethnic businesses.

7 Exploring the 'Burbs

With all that the city proper has to offer, if you're in town for several days, or if you're staying with friends and relatives in the suburbs, you may want to venture beyond the city limits and check out some of the sights in the surrounding areas. For a map of the greater Chicagoland area, see chapter 1.

OAK PARK

Architecture and literary buffs alike make pilgrimages to Oak Park, a near suburb on the western border of the city that is easily accessible by car or train. The reason fans of both disciplines flock to this same small town is that Ernest Hemingway was born and grew up here and Frank Lloyd Wright spent a great deal of his career designing the homes that line the well-maintained streets.

GETTING THERE   By Car   Oak Park is 10 miles due west of downtown Chicago. By car, take the Eisenhower Expressway west (I-290) to Harlem Avenue (Ill. 43) and exit north. Continue on Harlem north to Lake Street. Take a right on Lake and continue to Forest Avenue. Turn left here and immediately on your right you'll see the **Oak Park Visitor Center,** 158 Forest Ave. (☎ **708/848-1500**), open daily from 10am to 5pm. Stop here for orientation, maps, and guidebooks. There's a city-operated parking lot next door. From here it's only a few blocks to the heart of the historic district and the Frank Lloyd Wright Home and Studio.

By Public Transportation   Take the Green Line west to the Harlem stop, roughly a 25-minute ride from downtown. Exit the station onto Harlem Avenue, and proceed north to Lake Street. Take a right on Lake to Forest Avenue, then turn left.

THE (FRANK LLOYD) WRIGHT STUFF

Oak Park has the highest concentration of houses or buildings anywhere designed and built by Wright. People come here to marvel at the work of a man who saw his life as a twofold mission: to wage a single-handed battle against the ornamental excesses of architecture, Victorian in particular, and to create in its place a new form that would be at the same time functional, appropriate to its natural setting, and stimulating to the imagination.

Not everyone who comes to Oak Park shares Wright's architectural philosophy. But scholars and enthusiasts admire Wright for being consistently true to his own vision, out of which emerged a unique and genuinely American architectural statement. The reason for Wright's success may stem from the fact that he himself was a living exemplar of a quintessential American type. In a deep sense, he embodied the ideal of the

Oak Park

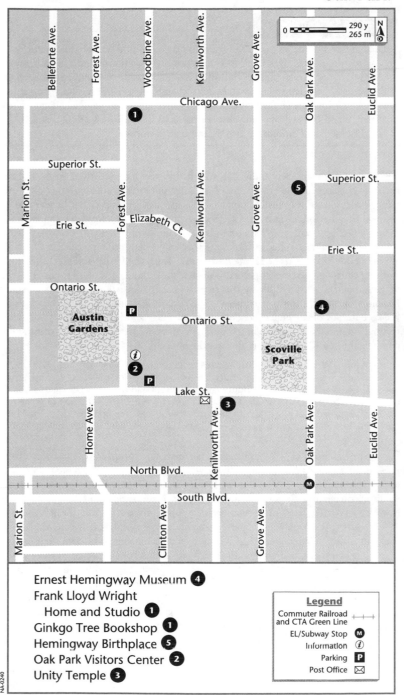

Ernest Hemingway Museum ④
Frank Lloyd Wright
    Home and Studio ①
Ginkgo Tree Bookshop ①
Hemingway Birthplace ⑤
Oak Park Visitors Center ②
Unity Temple ③

Legend

Commuter Railroad
and CTA Green Line   +–+–+
EL/Subway Stop   Ⓜ
Information   ⓘ
Parking   🅿
Post Office   ✉

NA-0240

The Wright Plus Tour

Die-hard fans of the architect will want to plan to be in town the third Saturday in May for the annual Wright Plus Tour, during which the public can tour several Lloyd-designed homes and several other notable Oak Park buildings, in both the Prairie and Victorian styles, in addition to Frank Lloyd Wright's home and studio and the Unity Temple. The tour includes 10 buildings in all. Tickets go on sale March 1 and can sell out within 6 weeks. Call ☎ **708/848-1976** (Frank Lloyd Wright Home and Studio) for details and ticket information.

self-made and self-sufficient individual who had survived, even thrived, in the frontier society—qualities that he expressed in his almost puritanical insistence that each spatial or structural form in his buildings serve some useful purpose. But he was also an aesthete in Emersonian fashion, deriving his idea of beauty from natural environments, where apparent simplicity often belies a subtle complexity.

The three principal ingredients of a tour of Wright-designed structures in Oak Park are the **Frank Lloyd Wright Home and Studio Tour, the Unity Temple Tour,** and a **walking tour**—guided or self-guided—to view the exteriors of homes throughout the neighborhood that were built by the architect. Oak Park has, in all, 25 homes and buildings by Wright, constructed between the years 1892 and 1913, which constitute the core output of his Prairie School period. Visiting another 50 dwellings of architectural interest by Wright's contemporaries, scattered throughout this community and neighboring River Forest, is also worthwhile.

Frank Lloyd Wright Home and Studio. 951 Chicago Ave. ☎ **708/848-1976.** www.wrightplus.org. Admission $8 adults, $6 seniors and children 7–18; free for children under 7. Combined admission for Home and Studio tour and guided or self-guided historic district tour (see below) $14 adults, $10 seniors and children 7–18. Admission to home and studio is by guided tour only; tours depart from the Ginkgo Tree Bookshop Mon–Fri 11am, 1pm, and 3pm; Sat–Sun every 15 minutes 11am–3:30pm. Facilities for people with disabilities are limited; please call in advance.

For the first 20 years of Wright's career, this remarkable complex served first and foremost as the sanctuary from which Wright was to design and execute more than 130 of an extraordinary output of 430 completed buildings. The home began as a simple shingled cottage that Wright built for his bride in 1889 at the age of 22, but it became a work in progress, as Wright remodeled it constantly until 1911 (he left there in 1909). During this highly fertile period, the house was Wright's showcase and laboratory, but it also embraces many idiosyncratic features molded to his own needs, rather than those of a client. With many add-ons—including a barrel-vaulted children's playroom and a studio with an octagonal balcony suspended by chains—the place has a certain whimsy that others may have found less livable. This, however, was not an architect's masterpiece, but the master's home, and every room in it can be savored for the view it reflects of the workings of a remarkable mind. The Home and Studio Foundation has restored the residence and studio to its 1909 vintage.

HISTORIC DISTRICT WALKING TOURS An extensive tour of the neighborhood surrounding the Home and Studio leaves the **Ginkgo Tree Bookshop,** 951 Chicago Ave., on weekends from 10:30am to 4pm. This tour lasts 1 hour and costs $8 for adults, $6 for seniors and children 7 to 18, and is free for children under 7. If you can't make it to Oak Park on the weekend, you can follow a self-guided map and audiocassette tour of the historic district (recorded in English, French, Spanish, German, Japanese, and Italian). Available at the Ginkgo Tree Bookshop from 10am to

3:30pm, the self-guided tour costs $8 for adults and $6 for seniors and children. In addition to Wright's work, you will see that of several of his disciples, as well as some very charming examples of the Victorian styling that he so disdained. A more detailed map sold for $3 at the bookshop, "Architectural Guide Map of Oak Park and River Forest," includes text and photos of all 80 sites of interest in Oak Park and neighboring River Forest.

Unity Temple. 875 Lake St. ☎ **708/383-8873.** Self-guided tours $4 adults; $3 seniors, children, and students with ID. 45-minute guided tours $6 adults; $4 seniors, children, and students with ID. Guided tours Sat–Sun on the hour 1–3pm. General hours: summer daily 10am–5pm; fall–spring Mon–Fri noon–4pm, Sat–Sun 10am–5pm. Church events can alter the schedule; call in advance.

Closest to the Visitor Center is Unity Temple. In 1871 a community of Unitarian/Universalists settled near here and built a Wren-style church, a timber-framed house of worship typical of their native New England. Fire destroyed the church around the turn of the century. The congregation asked Wright, who was a member, to design an affordable replacement. Using poured concrete with metal reinforcements—a necessity owing to the small budget of $40,000 allocated for the project—Wright created a building that on the outside seems as forbidding as a mausoleum, but that inside contains in its detailing the entire architectural alphabet of the Prairie School that has since made Wright's name immortal. Following the example of H. H. Richardson (Glessner House), Wright placed the building's main entrance on the side, behind an enclosure—a feature often employed in his houses as well—to create a sense of privacy and intimacy. Front entrances were too anonymous for these two architects. And Wright complained, furthermore, that other architectural conventions of the church idiom, such as the nave in the Gothic-style cathedral across from the future site of Unity Temple, were overpowering. Of that particular church, he commented that he didn't feel a part of it.

Yet his own vision in this regard was somewhat confused and contradictory. He wanted Unity Temple to be "democratic." But perhaps Wright was unable to subdue his own personal hubris and hauteur in the creative process, for the ultimate effect of his chapel, and much of the building's interior, is very grand and imperial. Unity Temple is no simple meetinghouse in the tradition of Calvinist iconoclasm. Rather, its principal chapel looks like the chamber of the Roman Senate. Even so, the interior, with its unpredictable geometric arrangements and its decor reminiscent of Native American art, is no less beautiful.

Wright used color sparingly within Unity Temple, but the pale, natural effects he achieved are owed in part to his decision to add pigment to the plaster rather than use paint. Wright's use of wood for trim and other decorative touches is still exciting to behold; his sensitivity to grain and tone and placement was akin to that of an exceptionally gifted woodworker. Wright was a true hands-on, can-do person; he knew the materials he chose to use as intimately as the artisans who carried out his plans. And his stunning, almost minimalist use of form is what still sets him apart as a relevant and brilliant artist. Other details to which the docent guide will call your attention, as

Oak Park Bus Tours

The **Chicago Architecture Foundation** offers a 3½-hour bus tour of Wright sights in Oak Park once a month on Saturday from May to October. The tour leaves from the John Hancock Center, 875 N. Michigan Ave., and costs $25. Reservations are required; call ☎ **312/922-3432**, ext. 240.

you complete a circuit of the temple, are the great fireplace, the pulpit, the skylights, and the clerestory (gallery) windows. Suffice it to say, Unity Temple—only one of Wright's masterpieces—is counted among the 10 greatest American architectural achievements.

ON THE TRAIL OF HEMINGWAY

Frank Lloyd Wright may be Oak Park's favorite son, but the town's most famous native son is Ernest Hemingway. Maybe because Hemingway left when he had the chance and didn't write much about the town of his boyhood, Oak Park only recently has begun to rally around the memory of the Nobel and Pulitzer Prize–winning writer with the opening of a **Hemingway Museum,** 200 N. Oak Park Ave. (☎ **708/ 848-2222**). A portion of the ground floor of this former church, now the Oak Park Arts Center, is given over to a small but interesting display of Hemingway memorabilia. A 6-minute video presentation sheds considerable light on Hemingway's time in Oak Park, where he spent the first 18 years of his life, and is particularly good on his high school experiences. The museum is open Thursday and Friday from 1 to 5pm, Saturday 10am to 5pm, and Sunday 1 to 5pm. Admission is $6 for adults and $4.50 for seniors and children (children under 5 are free).

To see where Hemingway was born, on July 21, 1899, continue up the block to 339 N. Oak Park Ave, the home of his maternal grandparents. A local foundation recently purchased the home to serve as a museum and has restored it to reflect its appearance during Hemingway's boyhood in time for the centenary of his birth in 1999. Hemingway's actual boyhood home, still privately owned, is located several blocks from here, not far from the Wright Home and Studio, at 600 N. Kenilworth Ave. The hours at the Hemingway Birthplace museum are the same as the Hemingway Museum above. A special $6 admission price for adults and $4.50 for seniors and children (children under 5 are free) covers both museums.

THE NORTHERN SUBURBS

Between Chicago and the state border of Wisconsin to the north is the affluent section of suburbia known as the North Shore. Following are some of the most popular attractions here.

EXPLORING EVANSTON

Despite being Chicago's nearest neighbor to the north—and a place much frequented by Chicagoans themselves—Evanston retains an identity all its own. **Northwestern University** makes its home here on a beautiful lakefront campus. Evanston was also the home of Frances Willard, founder of the Women's Christian Temperance Union. **Willard House,** 1730 Chicago Ave. (☎ **847/864-1397**), is open to visitors; call ahead to arrange a tour. Nine of the 17 rooms in this old Victorian "Rest Cottage" (as Willard called it) have been converted into a museum of period furnishings and temperance memorabilia. Among her personal effects is the bicycle she affectionately called "Gladys," and upon which she learned to ride late in life, in the process spurring women across the country to do the same. The headquarters of the WCTU is still located on the site.

Neither cultural nor recreational facilities are lacking in Evanston. The unusual and informative **Mitchell Museum of the American Indian** is located in a new, larger gallery at 2600 Central Park Ave. (☎ **847/475-1030**), with a collection ranging from pre-contact stoneware tools and weapons to the work of contemporary Native American artists. The museum is open Tuesday through Friday from 10am to 6pm and Saturday and Sunday from 11am to 4pm. It's closed on holidays and during the month of August. Admission is $4 for adults, $3 for seniors, and free for children. Call in advance to arrange a volunteer-led tour.

For an ecological experience, visit the **Ladd Arboretum,** 2024 McCormick Blvd. (☎ 847/864-5181), a public park where you will also find the Evanston Ecology Center, which houses nature exhibits.

OTHER ATTRACTIONS IN THE NORTHERN SUBURBS

Baha'i House of Worship. 100 Linden Ave. (at Sheridan Rd.), Wilmette. ☎ 847/ 853-2300. Free admission. Visitor center, daily May–Sept 10am–10pm and Oct–Apr 10am–5pm. Temple, daily from 7am. Devotional services are held Mon–Sat at 12:15pm and Sun at 1:15pm (with choral accompaniment). To get there from Chicago, take the Red Line of the El north to Howard Street. Change trains for the Evanston train and go to the end of the Line, Linden Ave. (Or take the Purple/Evanston Express and stay on the same train all the way.) Turn right on Linden and walk 2 blocks east. If you're driving, take the Outer Dr. (Lake Shore Dr.) north, which feeds into Sheridan Rd.

Up the road in Wilmette is the most visited of all the sights in the northern suburbs, the Baha'i House of Worship, at a very non–Prairie-style temple surrounded by formal gardens. With a lacelike facade and a 135-foot dome, designed by the French Canadian Louis Bourgeois, the temple strongly reveals the Eastern influence of the Baha'i faith's native Iran and is one of seven Baha'i temples in the world.

✪ Chicago Botanic Garden. 1000 Lake Cook Rd. (just east of Edens Expressway/I-94), Glencoe. ☎ 847/835-5440. www.chicago-botanic-org. Parking $5 weekdays, $6 weekends, which includes admission to the grounds. Daily (except Christmas) 8am–sunset. Tram tours offered Apr–Nov. To get there from Chicago, take Sheridan Rd. north along Lake Michigan or the Edens Expressway (I-94) to Lake Cook Rd.

Despite its name, the Chicago Botanic Garden is located 25 miles north of the city in the suburb of Glencoe. Experience intimately the variations of nature over four seasons in this 385-acre living preserve, with its variety of distinct botanical environments, from the Illinois prairie to an English walled garden and a three-island Japanese garden. Also on the grounds are the newly renovated fruit and vegetable garden (the largest in the Midwest), a cafe, a library, a garden shop, and a designated bike path.

✪ Ravinia Festival. Green Bay and Lake Cook rds., Highland Park. ☎ 847/266-5100 or 312/RAVINIA. www.ravinia.org. Tickets: pavilion $15–$40; lawn $8–$10. Most concerts are held in the evening. Catch the Ravinia bus at the following locations: Marshall Field's (State and Randolph sts.); the Palmer House Hilton (Monroe St. entrance); Westin River North, 320 N. Dearborn St. (the Clark St. side); The Drake hotel (Walton St. and Michigan Ave.); Harbor House (3200 N. Lake Shore Dr.); Sheridan and Hollywood; Sheridan and Devon; or at the Davis St. Station in Evanston. Round-trip tickets are $12. Many of the major hotels also charter buses during the season. You can also catch the 5:50pm commuter train, which leaves from the North Western Station near the Loop at Madison and Canal sts. The train stops in Highland Park directly at the festival; the "Ravinia Special" round-trip fare is $4.

Ravinia is the summer home of the highly regarded Chicago Symphony, which has an 11-week season here. It's also a bucolic setting for chamber music, world music, jazz and pop concerts, dance, and music study. Christoph Eschenbach is music director of the festival, which takes place in suburban Highland Park. The series runs from mid-June through Labor Day. Tickets are sold to both the covered pavilion, where you get a reserved seat and a view of the stage, and the lawn, which is the real joy of Ravinia: sitting on the grass listening to music and indulging in an elaborate picnic.

Dining options available at the park range from the fine-dining restaurant **Mirabelle** (☎ 847/432-7550 for reservations) to prepacked picnic spreads from the **Gatehouse,** featuring gourmet items to go. Lawn catering is also available for parties of 20 or more. But what most cognoscenti do is pack a picnic of delectables and eat on the great lawn; some go all out with candles, flowers, the whole bit (bringing along a citronella candle or some bug spray is a good idea, too). For $8, you can rent a pair of lawn chairs and a table. In case you're wondering about the weather conditions at concert time, dial Ravinia's weather Line (☎ 847/433-5010).

Six Flags Great America. 1-94 at Rte. 132 East., Gurnee. ☎ **847/249-4636.** www.sixflags.com. Admission (including unlimited rides, shows, and attractions) $34 adults, $17 seniors, $29 children 4–10, free for children under 4. Open seasonally, Apr–Oct (call or check Internet for exact hours). Parking $7. Take I-94 or I-294 West to Rte. 132 (Grand Ave.). Approximate driving time from Chicago city limits is 45 min.

One of the Midwest's biggest theme/amusement parks is located midway between Chicago and Milwaukee on I-94 in Gurnee, Illinois. The park has more than 100 rides and attractions, including the new Giant Drop, a 227-foot tower from which riders fall back to the ground at 60 miles per hour, and Shock Wave, said to be one of the world's fastest and tallest steel-loop roller coasters. Six Flags also has shows, restaurants, and theme areas.

THE WESTERN SUBURBS

So many corporations have taken to locating their offices beyond the city limits that today more people work in the suburbs than commute into Chicago. At the hub of this development is O'Hare International, and all around the airport are the kinds of shops, restaurants, and bistros that once only the city could boast. Those people visiting the Chicago area who are quartered in and around O'Hare also have easy access to a variety of very special museums and nature-oriented facilities.

Brookfield Zoo. First Ave. and 31st St., Brookfield. ☎ **708/485-0263.** www.brook-fieldzoo.mus.il.us. Regular admission $6 adults, $3 seniors and children 3–11, free for children under 3. Tues and Thurs Apr–Sept, $4 adults, $1.50 seniors and children 3–11. Free admission Tues and Thurs Oct–Mar. Summer daily 9:30am–5:30pm; fall–spring daily 10am–4:30pm. Parking $4. Take the Stevenson (I-55) and Eisenhower (I-290) expressways 14 miles west of the Loop. Bus: 304 or 311.

Brookfield is the Chicago area's largest zoo. In contrast to the rather efficient Lincoln Park Zoo, Brookfield is spacious and spreads out over 216 acres with 2,200 animal residents—camels, dolphins, giraffes, baboons, wolves, tigers, green sea turtles, Siberian tigers, snow leopards, and more—living in naturalistic environments that put them side-by-side with other inhabitants of their regions. One of the newest exhibits, "The Living Coast," explores of the western coast of Chile and Peru and includes everything from a tank of plate-size moon jellies to a rocky shore where Humboldt penguins swim and nest as Inca terns and gray gulls fly freely overhead. Another interesting new exhibit is "The Swamp," which re-creates the bioregions of a southern cypress swamp and an Illinois river scene and discusses what people can do to protect wetlands. The "Quest to Save the Earth" exhibit doesn't have any animals, but rather employs a series of interactive stations that put the focus on humans and what they can do to create a sustainable planet.

Lizzadro Museum of Lapidary Art. 220 Cottage Hill, Elmhurst. ☎ **630/833-1616.** Admission $2.50 adults, $1.50 seniors, $1 students and youths 13–18, free for children under 13. Free admission on Friday. Tues–Sat 10am–5pm and Sun 1–5pm. Closed major holidays.

Not far from the zoo, off I-90 in nearby Elmhurst, you will find the Lizzadro Museum. The museum's jade collection is internationally renowned, a fact that is punctuated by the presence of a chunk of jade weighing over half a ton that greets you at the entrance. The word lapidary, of course, refers to the art of stone cutting, and

For the Architecture Buff: A Side Trip to the Farnsworth House

Architecture fans will want to make a pilgrimage to the small town of Plano, about 60 miles southwest of the city. Here along the serene banks of the Fox River is the Farnsworth House, the first house designed by Ludwig Mies van der Rohe in the United States. The glass and steel house was commissioned in the mid-1940s by Dr. Edith Farnsworth, a Chicago physician, and was completed in 1951, but not without all kinds of high drama between the architect and his patron. The simple one-story horizontal structure, which appears to float above the ground, supported by eight steel columns, is immediately recognizable as a Mies building. The floors both inside and on the terrace are made of travertine marble, and the steel is painted white, giving the house the appearance of a modern-day Greek temple.

The building was purchased in 1972 by Lord Peter Palumbo, a member of the British Parliament and a former chairman of the Arts Council of Great Britain. Lord Palumbo, who also owns homes designed by Frank Lloyd Wright and Le Corbusier, opened the Farnsworth House to the public for the first time in 1997. He has furnished the home with Mies original and reproduction furniture and planted the bucolic grounds (designed by landscape architect Lanning Roper) with a collection of two dozen modern sculptures (even a chunk of the Berlin Wall) by such artists as Henry Moore, Andy Goldsworthy, Wendy Taylor, Claes Oldenburg, Harry Bertoia, and Ellsworth Kelly.

The entire visit to the house and grounds takes a little more than an hour; it's a good idea to wear comfortable walking shoes and dress for the weather for the 1-mile tour. Special arrangements can be made for people with physical disabilities. Depending on the weather, tours are given everyday, except Wednesday, from 10am to 4pm, and admission is $15. For $30, visitors can take an in-depth tour that examines some of the house's inner workings. Reservations (☎ **630/ 662-8622**) are required for all tours, and visitors must be 12 years or older. The Visitor Center also has a cafe and gift shop, and the staff can recommend several restaurants in Plano.

GETTING THERE   From the Chicago Loop, travel west on I-290 to I-88, then take the Route 47 Sugar Grove exit. Call the Visitor Center for specific directions.

this repository of that art displays hard-stone carvings, gemstones, mineral specimens, and such oddities as an ivory carving of the Last Supper.

Morton Arboretum. Rte. 53, just north of the East–West Tollway (I-88), Lisle. ☎ **630/ 968-0074.** Admission $7 per car ($3 per car on Wed). Early Apr to late Oct daily 7am–7pm; late Oct to early Apr daily 7am–5pm.

South and west of the Brookfield Zoo, in Lisle, is this 1,700-acre arboretum. Not only is this park, which celebrated its 75th anniversary in 1997, a nature showcase of flora from around the world, organized into both formal and natural settings, but it is also a wildlife refuge for many forest critters, such as foxes, beavers, and, of course, birds. There are 30,000 different tree specimens, classified into 3,600 species. Eleven miles of paved roadways allow you to drive through the grounds, but a walk along the more than 25 miles of pathways, including 12 miles of hiking paths through prairie, dense woods, and waterways, will give you a more satisfying and intimate view of the plant and woods life. A 1-hour tram ride offers an overview of the entire grounds; the tour is operated twice daily, April through October, and costs $2. When you want to take a break, there's a restaurant, cafe, and gift shop.

Lynfred Winery. 15 S. Roselle Rd. (off I-90), Roselle. ☎ **630/529-9463.** Free admission. Wine tasting $2. Daily 10am–7pm.

Off I-90, past O'Hare airport, is the Lynfred Winery in Roselle. This suburban winery purchases grapes from around the country and ferments them here in oak casks. You may sample up to seven of the company's fruit and grape wines for $2. The operation is planning to open a new tasting room. Tours are offered Saturday and Sunday at 2 and 4pm.

Fermi National Accelerator Laboratory (Fermilab). Kirk Rd. and Pine St., Batavia. ☎ **630/840-3351.** Free admission. Daily 8:30am–5pm. Fermilab is located about an hour from the city. The main entrance is on Kirk Rd., a north–south highway that exits from the East–West Tollway (I-88), opposite Pine St., between Butterfield Rd. and Wilson St.

Named for the Nobel Prize–winning physicist Enrico Fermi, Fermilab houses the world's highest energy particle accelerator, the Tevatron. Here scientists probe the fundamental structure of the universe. Free guided tours are available by appointment for groups of 10 or more Monday through Friday from 9am to 3:30pm. The tours consist of an orientation talk and slide presentation, a visit to various laboratory environments, and an opportunity to take in a panoramic view of the accelerator from the 15th floor of the lab's main building. The tour lasts about 2 hours. Self-guided tours are also available. After the tour, visitors may want to take the kids to the Leon Lederman Science Education Center, a one-story building located just west of the visitor center, where they can explore a variety of creative, hands-on exhibits demonstrating some of the principles of physics. The education center is open Monday through Friday from 8:30am to 5pm and the first and third Saturday of the month from 9am to 3pm; call ☎ **630/840-8258** for information.

After all that science, you may be in the mood for getting back to nature: Visitors are welcome to drive around the 6,800-acre site, to look at the distinctive architecture of the Fermilab buildings, and to see the thousand acres of restored tall-grass prairie and buffalo and waterfowl that also occupy these lands. Paths on the grounds are open for walking and biking.

8 Kid Stuff

Chicago has plenty of places to take the kids—places, in fact, that make every effort to turn a bored child into a stimulated one. All of the city's museums are leaders in the "please touch me" school of interactive exhibitions, with buttons and lights and levers and sounds and bright colors, and activities for kids at special exhibitions.

✪ **Chicago Children's Museum.** Navy Pier, 700 E. Grand Ave. ☎ **312/527-1000.** www.chichildrensmuseum.org. Admission $6 adults and children, $5 seniors. Free admission Thurs 5–8pm. Summer daily 10am–5pm (Tues and Thurs until 8pm); fall–spring Tues–Sun 10am–5pm (Thurs until 8pm). Bus: 29, 56, 65, or 66. Subway/El: Red Line to Grand/State; transfer to city bus or Navy Pier's free trolley bus.

Since the Chicago Children's Museum moved to a new $14.5 million home in a prominent location at the refurbished Navy Pier entertainment center in 1996, it has become one of the most popular cultural attractions in the city. The museum has areas especially for preschoolers as well as for older children, and several permanent exhibits allow kids a maximum of hands-on fun. One of the newest exhibits, "Seuss" (running through October 1999), allows visitors to walk through the *Cat in the Hat*'s house and other 3D worlds from the mind of everyone's favorite children's author and illustrator. WaterWays allows visitors to learn about the uses and benefits of water resources by constructing dams to direct the flow of water, constructing fountains, and teaming up with others to blast a stream of water 50 feet in the air. "Face to Face: Dealing with Prejudice and Discrimination" is a multimedia display that helps kids identify prejudice and find ways to deal with it. There's also a three-level schooner that children can board for a little climbing, from the crow's nest to the gang plank; Play-Maze, a toddler-scale cityscape with everything from a gas station to a city bus that children under 5 can touch and explore; and an arts-and-crafts area where visitors can create original artwork to take home.

Lincoln Park Pritzker Children's Zoo. 2200 N. Cannon Dr. ☎ **312/742-2000.** Free admission. Daily 9am–5pm. Bus: 151 or 156.

The Children's Zoo is a delight for children and adults alike. Kids have the opportunity to touch many of the animals, which are handled by zookeepers. Chicks, snakes, and rabbits are common residents, and if you're lucky, you might find a baby chimp or some unusual species.

At the **Farm-in-the-Zoo,** kids will discover a working reproduction of a Midwestern farm, complete with a white-picket-fenced barnyard, chicken coops, and stalls filled with livestock, including cows, sheep, and pigs. Even the aroma is authentic.

MORE ATTRACTIONS

I have already described most of the following attractions listed in this section, but I'm grouping them together for the sake of convenience.

The **Art Institute of Chicago,** 111 S. Michigan Ave. (at Adams Street) (☎ **312/443-3600**), has designated several galleries on the lower level as a "junior museum," known as the Kraft Education Center, where children can engage in art projects of their own. "Telling Images: Stories in Art," an engaging new exhibit on display through 1999 designed by Chicago architect Stanley Tigerman and a team of children, uses six works from the museum collection as a springboard for exploring storytelling traditions in folklore, mythology, history, and fantasy. (See section 1, "In & Around the Loop," in this chapter for details.)

The **DuSable Museum of African-American History,** 740 E. 56th Place, in Hyde Park (☎ **773/947-0600**), has a summer program offering cultural and educational activities for children, including one Saturday each month of dance, music, and other performances in the Kraft Children's Theater. (See section 5, "Exploring Hyde Park," in this chapter for details.)

The **Field Museum of Natural History,** Roosevelt Road and Lake Shore Drive (☎ **312/922-9410**), has a "place for wonder" with many curiosities that children can touch. Most kids also go nuts over the dinosaurs and the mummies. (See section 2, "The Earth, the Sky & the Sea," in this chapter for details.)

The **Museum of Science and Industry,** 57th Street and Lake Shore Drive (☎ **773/684-1414**), has high-tech, push-button exhibits for children, and kids are particularly awed by the large-screen Omnimax Theater. (See section 5, "Exploring Hyde Park," in this chapter for a more detailed listing.)

The **Newberry Library,** 60 W. Walton St. (☎ **312/943-9090**), has children's literature story hours many Saturday mornings in the fall and spring. (See section 3, "North of the Loop," in this chapter for details.)

At the **Shedd Aquarium,** 1200 S. Lake Shore Dr. (☎ **312/939-2438**), divers hand-feed sharks while swimming in the same tank and explaining everything via an underwater intercom. (See section 2, "The Earth, the Sky & the Sea," in this chapter for details.)

The **Spertus Museum,** 618 S. Michigan Ave. (☎ 312/322-1769), operated by the Spertus Institute of Jewish Studies, has an exhibit called the Artifact Center with a hands-on simulated archaeological dig with authentic tools. (See section 1, "In & Around the Loop," in this chapter for details.)

The **Harold Washington Library Center,** 400 S. State St. (☎ 312/747-4200), has a busy roster of free events in its spacious second-floor children's library, including story hours, weekly puppet shows (for which reservations are required), and other special programs.

Finally, every kid should also get to go at least once to a Cubs baseball game at **Wrigley Field.** (See section 11, "In the Grandstand," in this chapter for details).

9 Sightseeing Tours

If you want someone else to organize your sightseeing, by bus or by boat, Chicago has a number of experienced companies that provide just about any kind of itinerary you can imagine.

ORIENTATION TOURS

American Sightseeing. 17 E. Monroe St. (in the arcade of the Palmer House Hilton). ☎ **312/251-3100.** Tickets $16–$32.

This outfit offers a variety of narrated city tours. The tours range from 2 to 5 hours and cover daytime sights and nightlife.

Chicago Trolley Company. ☎ **312/663-0260.** All-day hop-on, hop-off pass $15 adults, $12 seniors, $8 children. Summer, weekdays 9am–5pm; hours vary the rest of the year and depend upon the weather (when the vehicles are enclosed and heated).

Chicago Trolley Company offers guided tours on a fleet of rubber-wheeled "San Francisco–style" trolleys that stop at a number of popular spots around the city, including Navy Pier, the Grant Park museums, the Museum of Science and Industry, Lincoln Park Zoo, and the cluster of theme restaurants in River North (Hard Rock Cafe, Planet Hollywood, etc.).

Chicago Motor Coach Company. ☎ **888/DDBUSES** or 312/666-1000. All-day hop-on, hop-off pass $12 adults, $10 seniors, $8 for children under 11 and military personnel in uniform. Apr–Oct daily 9:30am–5pm. Usually closed Nov–Mar.

This company offers 1½ -hour narrated double-decker bus tours of the Loop, Michigan Avenue, and the lakefront. Board the buses, which stop every 15 to 25 minutes, at several stops around the city, including the Sears Tower, Navy Pier, and the Water Tower, and buy your ticket from the driver, who will then give you a brochure describing the day's stops. You can get off at any number of attractions along the way and reboard throughout the day.

Gray Line. ☎ **312/251-3107.**

And then there's the company whose name is synonymous with bus tours. Gray Line offers a variety of tours in Chicago; call the number above for more information.

✪ CHICAGO ARCHITECTURE FOUNDATION TOURS

Chicago is the first city of architecture, and the **Chicago Architecture Foundation (CAF),** 224 S. Michigan Ave. (☎ 312/922-3432, or 312/922-TOUR for recorded information; www.architecture.org), offers first-rate guided programs, led by nearly 400 trained and enthusiastic docents. The foundation offers walking, bike, boat, and bus tours to more than 60 different architectural sites and environments in and

---

Fun on the Fly

Ticketed passengers with time to kill at O'Hare airport can visit the Chicago Children's Museum's free satellite exhibit, "Kids on the Fly." Little ones get to perform simulated airport tasks, such as unloading a cargo plane and guiding planes to safe landings from an air traffic control tower. The exhibit is located in Terminal 2.

---

around Chicago. The foundation also has another tour center in the John Hancock Center, 875 N. Michigan Ave. Below is a sampling of the tours the foundation offers.

BY BOAT

Perhaps the CAF's most popular tour is its 1½-hour **"Architecture River Cruise,"** which glides along both the north and south branches of the Chicago River. Although you can see the same 50 or so buildings the cruise covers on your own by foot, traveling by water lets you enjoy the buildings from a unique perspective. The excellent docents also provide interesting historical details as well as some fun facts (David Letterman once called the busts of the nation's retailing legends that face the Merchandise Mart the "Pez Hall of Fame"). Since the cruise opens on the main branch of the river, right at the Michigan Avenue bridge, my docent took the opportunity to explain how the opening of the bridge, a part of Daniel Burnham's Plan of Chicago—nicknamed Paris on the Prairie—transformed the street from one of grand mansions to a major commercial thoroughfare. The cruise points out both landmark buildings, such as the Gothic 1925 Tribune Tower, designed by a New York architect who won a contest, and contemporary ones, including the late eighties NBC Tower, constructed in wedding-cake style in homage to the city's old zoning codes mandating that sunlight reach down to the street.

The docents generally do a good job of making the cruise enjoyable for visitors with all levels of architectural knowledge. Mine, for example, gave a thumbnail sketch of the difference between the modern, function-as-form school of Mies van der Rohe's IBM Building and the postmodern look of 333 Wacker, which addresses its environment with its curved line that follows the river. In addition to pointing out famous buildings—Marina City, the Civic Opera House, the Sears Tower, to name a few—the docents approach the sites thematically, explaining, for example, how Chicagoans' use of, and attitudes toward, the river have changed in the last 2 centuries.

Tickets are $18 per person. Tours are operated several times a day from May through October. The trips are extremely popular, so purchase tickets in advance through **Ticketmaster** at ☎ **312/902-1500** (www.ticketmaster.com), or avoid the service charge and buy your tickets at one of the foundation's tour centers: 224 S. Michigan Ave. or the John Hancock Center, or from the CAF/Mercury boat launch on the southwest corner of the Michigan Avenue bridge. The cruises leave from the southwest side of the Michigan Avenue bridge, on the river level.

By Bus

Reservations are required for all bus tours, although walk-ins are welcome if there's space.

The **"Chicago Architecture Highlights by Bus"** is a 3½-hour tour offered Saturdays at 9:30am that covers the Loop, Hyde Park, and the Gold Coast, plus several other historic districts. The tour includes a visit to the interior of Frank Lloyd Wright's Robie House. Tickets are $25 per person; tours depart from the CAF tour center on 224 S. Michigan Ave.

The **"Loop and Near North by Bus"** is a 2-hour tour that concentrates on downtown and the ritzy residential neighborhoods north of the Loop. It offers dramatic views of the skyline and includes the site where the Great Chicago Fire started. Tickets are $15 per person; tours depart from the CAF tour center in the John Hancock Center from May through October.

On select Saturdays at 10am, the CAF offers a 3½-hour **"Frank Lloyd Wright by Bus"** excursion to Oak Park. The tour includes a visit to the interior of Wright's Home and Studio. Tickets are $25 per person; tours depart from the CAF tour center in the John Hancock Center.

BY TRAIN

The architecture foundation's **"Loop Tour Train"** offers a guided way to see and feel the city aboard the CTA's Elevated. Of course, you can always take your own tour with bunches of regular Chicago folks (the Ravenswood Brown Line offers impressive vistas heading south toward downtown), but the weekly (Saturday only) 40-minute, docent-led tour details the history of the century-old Elevated and the downtown area, visible as the train circles the "loop" of tracks that give the central business district its name. The train departs from the Randolph and Wabash station every 40 minutes from 12:15 to 2:15pm Saturdays from mid-June through mid-October. Tickets are free, but they must be obtained in advance from the Visitor Information Center on the first floor of the **Chicago Cultural Center,** 77 E. Randolph St. (a block east of the CTA station).

ON FOOT

If you prefer exploring on your own two feet, the CAF offers a variety of guided walking tours. Two popular walking tours in the Loop are **"Early Skyscrapers,"** which covers buildings built between 1880 and 1940, including the Rookery and the Chicago Board of Trade, and **"Modern and Beyond,"** which includes modern masterpieces by Mies van der Rohe and postmodern works by contemporary architects. The 2-hour tours cost $10 each ($15 for both) for adults and $7 each ($10 for both) for seniors and students. The tours are offered daily and depart from the CAF tour center at 224 S. Michigan Ave. Call ☎ 312/922-TOUR for exact tour times.

The CAF also offers more than 50 **neighborhood tours,** including the Gold Coast, River North, Grant Park, Old Town, the Jackson Boulevard Historic District, and even the Lincoln Park Zoo. Most cost $5 to $10 and last a couple of hours. Call ☎ 312/922-TOUR for details.

MORE ARCHITECTURE TOURS

For do-it-yourselfers, **audio walking tours** are offered by the **Chicago Department of Cultural Affairs.** The 90-minute tape, narrated by local broadcast journalist Bill Kurtis, provides visitors with an overview of downtown's skyscrapers, public spaces, and sculptures. The tour package costs $5 (with a $50 returnable deposit, cash or credit card) and includes rental of a tape player and a map and booklet of the downtown area. For more information, call the **Chicago Office of Tourism** at ☎ 312/744-2400.

Architecture junkies also may want to inquire about house tours of the **Charnley-Persky House** (☎ 312/915-0105 or 312/573-1365), designed by Frank Lloyd Wright and Louis Sullivan in 1891. The house is located in the Gold Coast at 1365 N. Astor St. and would make a nice highlight to an informal walking tour of the area.

LAKE & RIVER CRUISES

Tired of just looking out at the deep blue water from the top of the Hancock, the Shedd Aquarium, Oak Street Beach, and a host of other spots? Reverse your perspective. Take a sightseeing cruise and check out Chicago's incredible skyline from an offshore vantage point.

Mercury Chicago's Skyline Cruiseline. Departing from Michigan Ave. and Wacker Dr. (on the south side of the river). ☎ **312/332-1353.** Tickets $11–$15 adults, $5.50–$7.50 children under 12. Daily May 1–Oct 1.

Wendella Sightseeing Boats. Departing from Michigan Ave. and Wacker Dr. (on the north side of the river at the Wrigley Building). ☎ **312/337-1446.** www.wendellaboats.com. Tickets $11–$15 adults, $10–$14 seniors, $5.50–$7.50 children under 12. Daily Apr–Oct.

Both of these outfits operate similar 1- to 2-hour water tours between late April and early October. Both lines take in a stretch of the Chicago River and the area of the lake off the downtown district. In the summer, Mercury operates a 2-hour sunset cruise that departs nightly at 7:30pm and makes a stop at 9pm to admire the lights of Buckingham Fountain. Scheduling for these cruises depends on the season and the weather, so call ahead for the current hours. One of the most dramatic events during the boat tours is passing through the locks that the separate river from lake. Sunset is a good time to go.

Another Mercury Line offering is a daylong cruise along the National Heritage Corridor, the river route that links Chicago with the Mississippi River, taking in everything from the cityscape to the prairie lands. The cruise, narrated by a geography expert, runs weekends in September only; call for details (☎ **312/332-1353**). The price is $57.50 per person, including coffee.

Shoreline Sightseeing. Departing from Navy Pier, Shedd Aquarium, Buckingham Fountain in Grant Park. ☎ **312/222-9328.** Tickets $9 adults, $8 seniors, and $4 children under 12. Daily Memorial Day to Labor Day.

Shoreline schedules 30-minute lake cruises every half hour from its three different dock locations: the Shedd Aquarium, Navy Pier, and Buckingham Fountain in Grant Park. Shoreline also recently added a water taxi that runs every half hour from Navy Pier to both the Sears Tower and Shedd Aquarium. One-way tickets for the water taxi are $6 for adults, $5 for seniors, and $3 for children under 12; round-trip tickets cost $10 for adults, $8 for seniors, and $5 for children; all-day passes cost $14 for adults and $7 for children.

Chicago from the Lake Ltd. Departing from Ogden Slip adjacent to River East Plaza (formerly North Pier) at the end of E. Illinois St. ☎ **312/527-2002.** Tickets $18.50 adults, $16.50 seniors, $12 children 7–17, free for children under 7. Daily May–Oct.

This company runs 90-minute architectural river cruises and lake and river historical cruises. Complimentary coffee (Starbucks, no less), lemonade, cookies, and muffins are served. For tickets, call the above number or stop by the company's ticket office, located on the lower level on the east end of River East Plaza.

The Spirit of Chicago. Departing from Navy Pier. ☎ **312/836-7899.** www.spiritcruises. com. Lunch cruises $31.70–37.35, Sun brunch $37.35, dinner (seated) $56.70–$73, dinner buffet (Jan–Mar only) $34.60, cocktails $28.85–$35.20; moonlight cruises $24.55–$26.65. Ask about children's rates. Daily year-round.

This luxury yacht offers a variety of wining and dining harbor cruises, from the Big Band Lunch Buffet to the Midnight Moonlight Dance Party. Spirit Cruises operates similar ships in eight other cities, including Boston, New York, Seattle, and Washington, D.C.

Odyssey II. Departing from Navy Pier. ☎ **630/990-0800.** www.odyssey-cruises.com. Lunch cruise $32–$36, Sun brunch $42, dinner $73–$86, moonlight cruise $28. Rates for children

3–11 are ½ the adult rates; free for children under 3. Cruises run year-round with certain restrictions.

Another luxury passenger yacht with offerings similar to *The Spirit of Chicago.*

uglyduck Cruises. Departing from Navy Pier. ☎ **888/289-8833** or 312/396-9007. www.uglyduckcruises.com. Lunch cruises $21.95, dinner $34.95–$39.95, midday cruise $15.95, moonlight cruise $14.95. Cruises run year-round.

It's hard to overlook the newest boat at Navy Pier. This big, yellow 550-passenger cruiser operates daily lunch and dinner excursions on the lake, as well as midnight weekend voyages. Meals are served buffet-style and tend toward comfort foods like chicken pot pie, honey glazed ham, and macaroni and cheese.

Windy. Departing from Navy Pier. ☎ **312/595-5555.** Tickets $25 adults, $15 seniors and children under 12. Tickets go on sale 1 hour before the first sail of the day at the boat's ticket office, on the dock at Navy Pier. Reservations (except for groups) and credit cards are not accepted. Call for sailing times and more information.

One of the more breathtaking scenes on the lake is watching this tall ship approach the docks at Navy Pier. The 148-foot-long, four-masted schooner sets sail for 90-minute cruises two to five times a day both day and evening. Of course, the boat is at the whims of the wind, so every cruise charts a different course. Passengers are welcome to help raise and trim the sails and occasionally take turns at the ship's helm (with the captain standing close by). The boat is not accessible for people with disabilities.

CARRIAGE & PEDICAB RIDES

Noble Horse (☎ 312/266-7878) maintains the largest fleet of antique horse carriages, stationed around the old Water Tower Square, at the northwest corner of Chicago and Michigan avenues. Each of the drivers, outfitted in black tie and top hat, has his or her own variation on the basic Magnificent Mile itinerary (and can also do tours of the lakefront, river, Lincoln Park, and Buckingham Fountain). The charge is $30 for each half hour. The coaches run year-round, with convertible coaches in the warm months and enclosed carriages furnished with wool blankets on bone-chilling nights. There are several other carriage operators, all of which pick up riders in the vicinity.

If you want to explore the city by bike but want to leave the pedaling to somebody else, flag down one of the half-dozen guys who operate colorful tricycle **pedicabs,** the self-powered rickshaws so ubiquitous in many Asian capitals. You'll find these guys congregating around Wrigley Field on game days, where they ferry lazy Cubs fans to their cars, at many of the summer festivals, and often along Southport and Lincoln avenues in Lincoln Park and Lakeview. Rides generally cost about $10 per mile for two passengers. Remember to wave to the crowd!

SPECIAL-INTEREST TOURS

NEIGHBORHOOD TOURS   It's a bit of a cliché to say that Chicago is a city of neighborhoods, but if you want to see what really makes Chicago special that's where you have to go. **Chicago Neighborhood Tours** are half-day, narrated bus excursions to about a dozen diverse communities throughout the city. Embarking from the Chicago Cultural Center, 78 E. Washington St., every Saturday, the tours visit different neighborhoods, from Chinatown and historic Bronzeville on the South Side to the ethnic enclaves of Devon Avenue and Uptown on the North Side. Neighborhood representatives serve as guides and greeters along the way as tour participants visit area landmarks, murals, museums, and shopping districts. The tours, organized by the

Chicago Office of Tourism, have sparked some neighborhood organizations to develop gift shops aimed at capitalizing on the arrival of visitors. Tickets (including a light snack) are $28 for adults and $25 for seniors, students, and children 8 to 18. For reservations and more information, call ☎ **312/742-1190.**

Groups can arrange tours of Chicago's **"Black Metropolis,"** the name given to a South Side area of Bronzeville where African Americans created a flourishing business and artistic community after World War II. Contact **Tour Black Chicago** (☎ 312/ 332-2323) for more information.

GANGSTER TOURS   **Untouchable Tours,** or so-called "gangster tours," P.O. Box 43185, Chicago, IL 60643 (☎ **773/881-1195**), is the only bus tour that takes you to all of the city's old hoodlum hangouts from the Prohibition era. The focus is definitely more on entertainment (the guides appear in costume and role-play their way through the tour) than a seriously historic take on the era, but the bus trip gives you a pretty thorough overview of the city, in addition to the gangster hot spots. You'll see the site of O'Bannion's flower shop, the site of the St. Valentine's Day massacre, plus much more. (The old Lexington Hotel, Capone's South Side headquarters, was recently demolished and has been cut from the tour.) The cost is $20 for adults, $15 for children. Tours, which depart from the **Rock-N-Roll McDonald's** at Clark and Ohio streets (the east side of the restaurant), run Monday to Wednesday at 10am; Thursday at 10am and 1pm; Friday at 10am, 1pm, and 7:30pm; Saturday at 10am, 1pm, and 5pm; and Sunday at 11am and 2pm. The same company also offers Sunday tours of the historic Beverly Hills/Morgan Park neighborhood of stately old homes; call ☎ **773/881-1831** for details.

GHOST TOURS   Another offbeat way to experience the real "spirit" of Chicago is to take a narrated **supernatural bus tour** of cemeteries, murder sites, Indian burial grounds, haunted pubs, and other spooky places. Richard Crowe, who bills himself as a "professional ghost hunter," spins out ghost stories, legends, and lore on the 5-hour trip, held both day and night (afraid of the dark?). Tickets are $28 per person, and the tour begins at **Goose Island Restaurant,** 1800 N. Clybourn Ave. (a short walk from the North/Clybourn El station on the Red Line). Two-hour **supernatural boat excursions** are available for $18 per person in July and August, and board at 10:30pm from the Mercury boat dock, at Michigan Avenue and Wacker Drive. Reservations are required for each tour; call ☎ **708/499-0300.**

CEMETERY TOURS   Don't wait until it's too late to take a cemetery tour. Cemeteries are fascinating places, whether in New Orleans, where the dearly departed aren't really buried at all but are enclosed in aboveground sarcophagi, or in Boston, where Revolutionary War heroes are crowded together, or here in Chicago, where some of the cemeteries are as pretty as parks.

One of the best area cemeteries is **Graceland,** which stretches along Clark Street in the Swedish neighborhood of Andersonville. The land between Irving Park Road and Montrose Avenue, running for about a mile along Clark, is occupied exclusively by cemeteries—primarily Graceland. Here you can view the tombs and monuments of many Chicago notables. When Graceland was laid out in 1860, public parks as such did not exist. The elaborate burial grounds that were constructed in many large American cities around this same time had the dual purpose of relieving the congestion of the municipal cemeteries closer to town and of providing pastoral recreational settings for the Sunday outings of the living. Indeed, cemeteries like Graceland (and Green-Wood in Brooklyn) were the precursors of such great municipal green spaces as Lincoln Park in Chicago and Central Park in New York. Much of Lincoln Park, in fact, had been a public cemetery since Chicago's earliest times. Many who once rested there

You're on TV: How to Get Tickets to Oprah, Jenny & Jerry

She's definitely the most famous female Chicagoan, and next to Michael Jordan, she's probably the most famous local resident of either gender. Oprah Winfrey has built her media empire in Chicago, and though she seems to have her hand in everything these days, her top-rated talk show is still Oprah's bread and butter. She's one of the original audience stackers (preinterviewing would-be audience members to ensure a rambunctious discussion), but some tickets are available for average, run-of-the-mill folks who want to see a TV show taping. *Oprah* tapes from September through May at **Harpo Studios,** 1058 W. Washington St. (☎ **312/591-9222**). If you'd like tickets, call (don't write) 1 to 2 months in advance. If you don't get reservations, don't bother showing up; no standby tickets are available.

A couple of other well-known shows tape at NBC Tower, 454 N. Columbus Dr. The *Jenny Jones Show* tapes August through May and takes audience reservations 2 months ahead of time. Jenny Jones usually tapes 3 days a week, at 9:45am and 1:30pm, and you should plan on 3 hours. All guests must be 18 or older, and you'll need to provide a Chicago-area phone number where you can be reached when you're visiting the city. For ticket reservations call ☎ **312/ 836-9485,** Monday through Friday 9am to 6pm.

To make reservations to appear in the audience at the *Jerry Springer Show,* call the ticket line (☎ **312/321-5365**) Tuesday through Thursday 10am to 3pm.

were reinterred in Graceland when the plans for building Lincoln Park went forward.

The **Chicago Architecture Foundation** (☎ **312/922-3432**) offers walking tours of Graceland on selected Sundays during August, September, and October. The tour costs $5 per person and lasts about 2 hours. Among the points of interest you will discover as you meander the paths of these 121 beautifully landscaped acres are the Ryerson and Getty tombs, famous architectural monuments designed by Louis Sullivan. Sullivan himself rests here in the company of several of his most distinguished colleagues: Daniel Burnham, Ludwig Mies van der Rohe, and Howard Van Doren Shaw, an establishment architect whose summer home in Lake Forest, called Ragdale, now operates as a writers' and artists' colony. Some of Chicago's giants of industry and commerce are also buried at Graceland, including Potter Palmer, Marshall Field, and George Pullman. An ambiguous reference in the *WPA Guide to Illinois* (Pantheon Books, 1983), reprinted without revisions, records that Graceland also contains the grave of Chicago's first white civilian settler, John Kinzie. The racial adjective is a reminder that Chicago's very first settler was a black man named Jean Baptiste Point du Sable.

The Chicago Architecture Foundation offers tours of some other cemeteries, as well, including the Oak Woods Cemetery, Rosehill Cemetery, and the suburban Lake Forest Cemetery. Call for details.

FRIENDS OF THE CHICAGO RIVER TOURS A nonprofit organization with a mission to foster the vitality of the river both for people and the ecosystems that depend on it, the **Friends of the Chicago River,** 407 S. Dearborn St., Ste. 1580, Chicago, IL 60605 (☎ **312/939-0490;** www.chicagoriver.org), each summer sponsors walking tours, canoe trips, bicycling excursions, and boat tours. The organization also publishes and sells five excellent canoe trail maps for self-guided walking tours along the north and south branches and the downtown section of the river.

Docent-guided canoe trips and walks along half a dozen sections of the river, both bucolic and industrial, are scheduled on many Saturdays from May through October. Tours meet at varying locations depending on the specific tour, and last approximately 2 hours, although some tours last half a day or longer. Costs are $10 to $15 per person for walking tours, $15 to $40 for canoe and boat trips.

10 Staying Active

Perhaps because Chicago's winters can be so brutal, Chicagoans take their summers very seriously. In the warmer months, with the wide blue lake and the ample green parks, it's easy to think the city is one big grown-up playground. Whether your fancy is water sports or land-based ones, you'll probably be able to find it here. The park district can be reached at ☎ **312/742-PLAY;** for questions about the 29 miles of beaches and parks along Lake Michigan, call the park district's lakefront region office at ☎ **312/747-2474.**

BEACHES Public beaches line Lake Michigan all the way up north into the suburbs and Wisconsin and southeast through Indiana and into Michigan. A few of the most popular in Chicago are **Oak Street Beach,** the location of which at the northern tip of the Magnificent Mile creates some interesting sights as sun worshippers in swimsuits and carting coolers make their way down Michigan Avenue; **North Avenue Beach,** about 6 blocks farther north, which has developed into a volleyball hot spot and has added an outdoor street hockey rink and a Venice Beach–style gym; and **Hollywood Beach** (officially Kathy Osterman Beach), at the northern end of Lake Shore Drive, where gays have colonized (moving up the lakefront from the Belmont Rocks, a longtime hangout). If you've brought the pooch along, you may want to take him or her for a dip at the **doggie beach** south of Addison Street, at about Hawthorne and Lake Shore Drive. Beaches are officially open with a full retinue of lifeguards on duty beginning about June 20, but swimmers can wade into the chilly water from Memorial Day to Labor Day. Only the bravest souls venture into the water before July, when the temperature creeps up enough to make swimming an attractive proposition. Please take note that the entire lakefront is not beach, and don't go doing anything stupid such as diving off the rocks.

BEACH VOLLEYBALL You'd never know the "surf" actually freezes over from the California-like scene at **North Avenue Beach** in the summer, when volleyball leagues and pick-up games occupy practically every square foot of sand. On busy weekends, you need to reserve court space ($10 for 2 hours). Equipment—net, ball, and court markers—is available for $5 for the day. Equipment is also rented at **Montrose Beach.** Beach volleyball is also popular at **Oak Street Beach** and the gay stretch of **Hollywood Beach.** For more information or to reserve a court (no more than 6 days in advance), call the park district's North Beach volleyball office at ☎ **312/74-BEACH.**

BIKING Biking is a great way to see the city, particularly the lakefront, along which there's a bike path that extends for more than 18 miles. To rent bikes, try **Bike Chicago** (☎ **800/915-BIKE**), with four locations: Oak Street Beach, Buckingham Fountain in Grant Park, Navy Pier, and at Cannon Drive and Fullerton in Lincoln Park. Open from May through October (weather permitting), Bike Chicago stocks mountain and touring bikes, as well as tandems, kids' bikes, and strollers. Rates are $8.50 an hour, $34 a day, helmets and pads included; the company offers free downtown deliveries for group day rentals. Once a day, the company leads a

1-hour bike tour from Navy Pier designed for all fitness levels. Both the park district (☎ 312/747-2474) and the **Chicagoland Bicycle Federation** (☎ 312/42-PEDAL) offer free maps that detail popular biking routes.

BOWLING   Bowling? Yes, bowling. Maybe it's not your first choice for getting a little exercise, but what if it's raining? The bowling alley closest to the major hotels is a new 26-lane facility that opened in late 1998 in the House of Blues complex in Marina Towers along the Chicago River at Dearborn and Kinzie streets.

Bowling has gone electronic everywhere these days, and that's what makes **Southport Lanes & Billiards,** 3325 N. Southport Ave. (☎ 773/472-6600), a real treasure: The vintage four-lane alley, housed in a former Schlitz tavern in Lakeview, not only forces you to do the scorekeeping yourself, but you have to wait for human "pin boys" to reset the pins by hand. Remember to tip them (or offer a bribe for a little help next time you're faced with a split): Roll up a bill and stick it in the hole of your ball. The same 30-something owners have opened a second bowling "alley," **The Lucky Strike,** a handsome bowling palace at 2747 N. Lincoln Ave. (☎ 773/549-2695) in Lincoln Park. Eight Brunswick lanes were rescued from a demolished bowling hall and installed in a space surrounded by old-time murals, handsome French advertising posters, and vintage light fixtures. Both bowling venues, at which bowling is really a diversion from food, drink, and flirting among the young patrons, serve a pretty good selection of pub food and an extensive list of microbrew beers.

GOLF   It's amazing, astounding, but Chicago really does have a golf course right downtown. **Family Golf Center** at Illinois Center, 221 N. Columbus Dr. (☎ 312/616-1234), is a nine-hole course east of Michigan Avenue. It's open 7 days a week; greens fees are $12 to $15. The lighted driving range is open year-round; a bucket of balls is $10 to $15.

The Park District also maintains a number of golf courses. The course most convenient to the majority of visitors is **Sydney R. Marovitz,** 3600 N. Lake Shore Dr. Still referred to as Waveland by many Chicagoans, it's a nine-hole course right on the lake. If you feel like just hitting a bucket of balls, the **Diversey Driving Range,** 140 W. Diversey Pkwy. (at the lake), is right in Lincoln Park. For information on all the Park District's courses' hours, greens fees, and price per bucket of balls for driving ranges, or to make same-day tee-time reservations, call ☎ 312/245-0909. For general questions, call the management office at ☎ 847/291-9666.

ICE-SKATING   A downturn in the real estate market was a blessing for Chicagoans who love to skate outside in the chilly winter air. A proposed downtown office project went unbuilt in the late eighties and left a huge gaping hole in the heart of the Loop; some creative thinking led to the creation of **Skate on State** (☎ 312/744-3315). The seasonal rink is installed in November across from Marshall Field's, along State Street between Washington and Madison streets. It operates daily until 7:30pm through March. Skating is free if you bring your own skates, $2 to $3 if you rent a pair. Concessions and a warming hut are available. It's fun, but developers are again eyeing the block, so it's impossible to know whether the rink will be back again next year.

The park district runs dozens of other skating surfaces throughout the city, both along the lakefront and in neighborhood parks. Call ☎ 312/742-PLAY for locations. A few other places to find ice are **Daley Bicentennial Plaza** (☎ 312/742-7650), located in the shadow of downtown skyscrapers at Randolph Street and Lake Shore Drive, which has fine views of the skyline and the lake; a smallish rink at **Navy Pier,** 600 E. Grand Ave. (☎ 312/595-PIER); and an indoor year-round rink at **McFetridge Sports Center,** 3843 N. California Ave. (☎ 312/742-7585).

IN-LINE SKATING   The wheeled ones have been taking over Chicago's side-walks, streets, and bike paths since the early nineties. Numerous rental places have popped up, and several sporting goods shops that sell in-line skates also rent them. The rentals generally include helmets and pads. **Bike Chicago** (☎ **800/915-BIKE**) also rents in-line skates at its four locations: Oak Street Beach, Buckingham Fountain in Grant Park (directly east of the fountain, across Lake Shore Drive), Navy Pier, and Cannon Drive and Fullerton in Lincoln Park. Bike Chicago charges $8.50 an hour or $34 a day (pick them up Saturday morning and keep them until closing on Sunday at 7pm), and offers free delivery to downtown locations for day rentals. A second spot is **Londo Mondo,** 1100 N. Dearborn St. (☎ **312/751-2794**), on the Gold Coast, renting blades for $7 an hour or $20 a day. Every Wednesday from about April through Labor Day at 6:30pm, Londo Mondo is the starting point for a free skate-through-the-city party open to all. It ends at Melvin B's, a Gold Coast cafe where the first drink is on the house. A second, beginner-oriented roll-about hits the streets on Tuesdays.

RUNNING   Despite all the bikers and skaters, runners still manage to hold their own on the pathways of Chicago's parks and lakefront. Many parks also have exercise stations with outdoor apparatus. A good spot to run downtown is the lighted quarter-mile track in Lake Shore Park, at Lake Shore Drive and Chicago Avenue, just east of the Museum of Contemporary Art. For information about running clubs and competitive marathons, call the **Chicago Area Runners Association** (☎ **312/666-9836**), which can provide you with schedules for several clubs that hold weekly runs along the lakefront and details on the Chicago Marathon (☎ **312/243-0003**), held in October.

SAILING   It seems a shame just to sit on the beach and watch all those beautiful sailboats gliding across the lake. Go on, get out there. The **Chicago Sailing Club,** in Belmont Harbor (☎ **773/871-SAIL**), rents J-22 and J-30 boats from 9am to sunset, weather permitting, May through October. A J-22 holds four or five adults. Rates range from $30 to $45 an hour ($10 extra for a skipper), depending on the time and day of the week. A J-30 accommodates up to 10 people and can sail at night. Rates are $60 to $80 per hour, plus $20 per hour for a skipper. If you want to take the boat out without a skipper, you need to demonstrate your skills first (for an additional $10 checkout fee). Reservations are recommended. Charters are also available.

SWIMMING   The park district maintains about 30 indoor pools for lap swimming and general splashing around. In addition, the lakefront is open for swimming until 9:30pm from Memorial Day to Labor Day in areas watched over by lifeguards (no swimming off the rocks, please). A good place for lake swimming is the water along the wall beginning at Ohio Street Beach, located slightly northwest of Navy Pier. The Chicago Triathlon Club marks a course here each summer with a buoy at both the quarter- and half-mile distance. It's a popular swimming route because it follows the shoreline in a straight line, and the water is fairly shallow. For more information, call the park district's beach and pool office (☎ **312/747-0832**).

TENNIS   For a listing of the hundreds of tennis courts in the city, call the park district (☎ **312/742-PLAY,** or 773/276-9454 in the summer). A couple of lighted facilities are **Daley Bicentennial Plaza,** located near the Loop at Randolph Street and Lake Shore Drive (☎ **312/742-7650**), and farther north at Waveland, Addison Street and Lake Shore Drive (☎ **312/742-7674**). Call for information about fees and reservation procedures.

11 In the Grandstand

With Michael Jordan the most recognized athlete in the world, Bears fans immortalized in *Saturday Night Live*'s "Da Bears" sketches, and Cub slugger Sammy Sosa making home-run history, I wonder sometimes if outsiders think of Chicago in any other context than that of spectator sports. Chicago fans are nothing if not loyal, and for that reason attending a home game in any sport is an uplifting experience.

BASEBALL   Baseball is imprinted in the national consciousness as part of Chicago, not because of victorious dynasties, but rather because of the opposite—the Black Sox scandal of 1919 and the perennially pennant-chasing Cubs.

Let's start with the **Chicago Cubs.** The Cubbies haven't made a World Series appearance since 1945 and haven't been World Champs since 1908, but when the team plays in so perfect a place as Wrigley Field, with its ivy-covered outfield walls, its hand-operated scoreboard, its view of the shimmering lake from the upper deck, and its "W" or "L" flag announcing the outcome of the game to the unfortunates who couldn't attend, how could anyone stay away? After all the strikes and temper tantrums and other nonsense, Wrigley has managed to hold onto something like purity. Maybe it emanates from the retired no. 14 jersey of Ernie Banks, the legendary shortstop and first baseman from the fifties and sixties, eras when the Cubs rarely climbed more than a rung or two out of the cellar in the standings. Banks once said, "It's a beautiful day, so let's play two," or words to that effect.

Enough with the romanticizing. On to the practical matters. Yes, *Chicago Tribune–* owned Wrigley finally installed lights a decade ago, but by agreement with the residential neighborhood it occupies, the Cubs still play most games in the daylight, as they should. I wholeheartedly suggest you attend a day game, the price of which, including a hot dog, a beer, and of course, a box of Crackerjacks, will run you about $20. Because Wrigley is small, just about every seat is decent.

Wrigley Field, 1060 W. Addison St. (☎ 773/404-CUBS; www.cubs.com), is easy to reach. Take the Red Line to the Addison stop, and you're there. You could also take the no. 22 bus, which runs up Clark Street. To order tickets in person, stop by the ticket windows at Wrigley Field, Monday through Friday from 9am to 6pm, Saturday from 9am to 4pm, and on game days. Or call ☎ 312/831-CUBS for tickets through **Ticketmaster** (☎ 800/347-CUBS outside Illinois).

About a dozen tours of the ballpark are led each season; tickets are $10 and are sold through the Wrigley Field ticket office or Ticketmaster. Known as Wrigleyville, the entire area around the stadium is surrounded by souvenir shops, sports bars, and restaurants. One sandwich shop, the **Friendly Confines,** is actually located within the stadium itself, just off the sidewalk. **Sluggers,** a sports bar with real batting cages, is right around the corner from Wrigley at 3540 N. Clark St. (☎ 773/248-0055).

The **Chicago White Sox** play at **Comiskey Park,** 333 W. 35th St. (☎ 312/674-1000; www.chisox.com), in the South Side neighborhood of Bridgeport. As baseball legend has it, some young fan confronted Shoeless Joe Jackson with the words

Throw It Back!

A word of warning if you attend a Cubs game: If you're sitting in the bleachers and you happen to catch a home-run ball hit by the visiting team (hey, it could happen), don't even think about keeping it. Wrigley etiquette dictates that you throw it back on the field or risk intense verbal abuse from 38,000 fans!

"Joe, say it ain't so!" hoping his idol would deny his role in the conspiracy labeled the Black Sox scandal, in which eight White Sox players allegedly sold out to the book-makers and threw the 1919 World Series—a drama emblematic of the end of the age of innocence for America after World War I.

To get Sox tickets, call **Ticketmaster** at ☎ **312/831-1769** or visit the ticket office at Comiskey, open Monday through Friday from 10am to 6pm, Saturday and Sunday from 10am to 4pm, except on game days when it opens at 9am. To get to Comiskey by subway/El, take the Red Line to Sox/35th Street.

BASKETBALL   The **Chicago Bulls,** NBA champs in 1991, 1992, 1993, 1996, 1997, and 1998, play at the **United Center,** 1901 W. Madison St. (☎ **312/455-4000**). Tickets are tough to come by, particularly late in the season. If you're not lucky enough to have an old buddy with season tickets, try your concierge or a ticket broker, such as **Gold Coast Tickets** (☎ **312/644-6446**) or **Center Stage** (☎ **773/233-8686**).

The **DePaul Blue Demons,** the local college team, play mostly at the **Rosemont Horizon,** 6920 N. Mannheim Rd., Rosemont (☎ **773/325-7526**), although some of their games are at the United Center.

BEACH VOLLEYBALL   The sand at North Avenue Beach has become the site of a string of summer professional tournaments, held nearly every weekend during the summer, featuring all the studs and babes of the professional beach volleyball circuit. Big crowds turn out to watch.

FOOTBALL   The **Chicago Bears** play at **Soldier Field,** Lake Shore Drive and 16th Street (☎ **847/615-2327**). Just in case you weren't aware, Soldier Field is not one of those modern, enclosed, air-conditioned monstrosities. The Bears play the old-fashioned way—in the open air, which is usually below freezing and quite often wet, too, otherwise known as "Bear weather."

The resurgent **Northwestern Wildcats** play Big Ten college ball at newly rehabbed and renamed **Ryan Field,** 1501 Central St., in nearby Evanston (☎ **847/491-CATS**).

GOLF   The **PGA's Western Open** takes place at **Cog Hill Golf and Country Club,** 119th Street and Archer, in Lemont (☎ **630/257-5872**), typically in early July.

HOCKEY   The **Chicago Blackhawks** have a devoted, impassioned following of fans who work themselves into a frenzy with the first note of the *Star Spangled Banner.* The Blackhawks play at the **United Center,** 1901 W. Madison St. (☎ **312/455-7000;** www.chiblackhawks.com).

HORSE RACING   There's thoroughbred racing at **Hawthorne Race Track,** 3501 S. Laramie Ave., in Stickney (☎ **708/780-3700**) and **Sportman's Park,** 3301 S. Laramie Ave., in Cicero (☎ **708/652-2812**); and harness racing at **Balmoral Park Race Track,** Illinois Highway 394 and Elms Court Lane, in Crete (☎ **708/672-7544**), and at **Maywood Park Race Track,** 8600 W. North (at Fifth Avenue), in Maywood (☎ **708/343-4800**).

TENNIS   Chicago has a few international tennis tournaments throughout the year, including the **Ameritech Cup** women's pro tournament (previously known as the Virginia Slims) and occasional exhibitions usually held at Navy Pier. Call the **United States Tennis Association's** Chicago office (☎ **847/803-2382**) for information, as well as for information about amateur competitions.

8 Chicago Strolls

Rushing around from one attraction to another can sometimes leave travelers feeling that they've seen nothing while they've seen a lot. There is something very satisfying about mastering a city, about sensing that if you were to return you'd be able to find your way back to that favorite bistro or little jazz club. That mastery comes not by taking taxis or buses but by walking. The sidewalks carry a certain rhythm that vehicles just don't. Being a city of neighborhoods—by one count 77—Chicago is an opportune place to put on a pair of comfortable shoes and explore.

In this chapter are detailed walking tours of three popular areas to visit. As Nelson Algren writes in *Chicago: City on the Make,* "It isn't hard to love a town for its greater and its lesser towers, its pleasant parks, or its flashing ballet. Or for its broad boulevards. . . . But you can never truly love it till you can love its alleys too."

For even more walking tours of the city, be sure to get a copy of *Frommer's Memorable Walks in Chicago,* which includes 10 tours of the city.

WALKING TOUR 1
The Loop

Start: Sears Tower, 233 S. Wacker Dr.
Finish: Fine Arts Building, 410 S. Michigan Ave.
Time: 2½ hours, not counting food stops or prolonged visits at individual sites, such as the Sears Tower observation deck.
Best Times: Daytime, on weekdays. During business hours you'll witness the city's business district in full swing. On weekends the Loop is very quiet, a nice time for a long walk, but it won't have the same kind of energy. And on weekends keep in mind that some restaurants and attractions will not be open.
Worst Times: Nighttime. The Loop, except for its seedier fringes, is virtually abandoned after dark and is not the safest place to be wandering. The strip of South Michigan Avenue covered in this tour, with its hotels and cultural centers, remains active in the evenings. Even so, I strongly recommend taking this stroll before the sun sets.

Begin this tour at the:
1. **Sears Tower,** the world's second tallest skyscraper, where the sky deck is open daily at 9am and the last ticket is sold at 10:30pm

1. Sears Tower
2. Wacker Drive
3. Chicago Mercantile Exchange
4. Civic Opera House
5. Merchandise Mart
6. James R. Thompson Center
7. Heald Square Monument
8. Michigan Avenue Bridge
9. 360 N. Michigan Bldg.
10. Carbide & Carbon Bldg.
11. Stone Container Building
12. Chicago Cultural Center
13. Art Institute of Chicago
14. State Street
15. Symphony Hall
16. Santa Fe Building
17. Chicago Board of Trade
18. The Rookery Building
19. Monadnock Building
20. The Fisher Building
21. The Old Colony Building
22. The Manhattan Building
23. Printer's Row
24. Dearborn Station
25. Harold Washington Library Center
26. Auditorium Building and Theatre
27. Fine Arts Building

(9:30pm from October through February). Enter on Jackson Boulevard. From the 103rd floor, you can orient yourself pretty well before embarking on the rest of your walking tour.

☕ **STARTING OUT**   To make sure you have enough energy for the long walk, you could head a few blocks to the west, across the Chicago River near Union Station, to **Lou Mitchell's,** 565 W. Jackson (☎ **312/939-3111**), one of the great all-day breakfast spots in Chicago, open Monday through Saturday from 5:30am to 3pm and Sunday from 7am to 3pm. City bus no. 151 or 157, both of which run down North Michigan Avenue and turn into the Loop, will get you close to the restaurant.

From the Sears Tower, begin walking north along:

2. **Wacker Drive,** which follows the contour of the Chicago River. While you're strolling you can observe the architectural gems that line the riverside and see many of the bridges that cross it at strategic points. The first building of note is the:

3. **Chicago Mercantile Exchange,** 30 S. Wacker. The "Merc" has been the great commodities exchange of the heartland since 1919. Visitors are welcome during trading hours.

   Just north of the Merc, you'll see the:

4. **Civic Opera House,** at Madison and Wacker, where the Lyric Opera of Chicago performs. The building is grand and imposing, just as an opera house should be. The opera season runs from late September through early March, and the box office is open Monday through Saturday from noon to 6pm (later on performance nights).

   A few blocks up, Wacker Drive curves to the east. As it does, take a glance at the enormous building across the river. It's the:

5. **Merchandise Mart,** recently sold by its longtime owners, the Kennedy family (one of Robert Kennedy's sons, Christopher, is an executive there). If you turn back and look into the green glass of 333 Wacker, you'll see a stunning reflection of the Mart and the river.

   At LaSalle Street, take a right and walk 2 blocks to Randolph Street. Occupying this entire block is:

6. **The James R. Thompson Center** (formerly the State of Illinois Center), 100 W. Randolph, built in 1985 from a design by Chicago architect Helmut Jahn and named for the long-serving governor. The orange-and-blue glass-and-steel structure with its soaring 17-story atrium is still controversial among Chicagoans. The monumental sculpture near the entrance is by Jean Dubuffet.

   Return to Wacker Drive and continue east. As you approach Wabash Avenue, note the:

7. **Heald Square Monument,** Lorado Taft's final work, dedicated on December 15, 1941, the anniversary of the ratification of the Bill of Rights. The bronze statue, a symbol of tolerance and unity, shows George Washington flanked by American Revolution heroes Robert Morris and Haym Salomon.

   The next block takes you to the:

8. **Michigan Avenue bridge,** across which you can see the Tribune Tower (to the east) and the Wrigley Building (on the west). As you approach the bridge, you may see signs for river tour boats and the double-decker tour bus that makes a circuit of this area.

   Turn to the right on Michigan Avenue and note—on the left—the:

9. **360 N. Michigan building,** an architectural landmark in Chicago since 1923. Notice the domed roof supported by columns and the building's trapezoidal shape. The building occupies the spot where Fort Dearborn stood from 1803 to 1812.

Continue south along Michigan Avenue to Water Street, where you'll see the elegant gilded facade of the:

10. **Carbide & Carbon Building,** 230 N. Michigan.

Two blocks south at the corner of Randolph is the:

11. **Stone Container Building,** 150 N. Michigan. The slanted, diamond-shaped top of this mid-1980s building is best seen from a few blocks' distance. Try looking back at it, say, from the steps of the Art Institute of Chicago.

Before you get to the museum, though, you'll come across the:

12. **Chicago Cultural Center,** 78 E. Washington, with many art exhibitions, concerts, and other programs, most of them free, and the home of the Museum of Broadcast Communications.

Three more blocks south along Michigan Avenue, at Adams Street, is the:

13. **Art Institute of Chicago,** the city's most prestigious museum. It sits on the edge of Grant Park, which accompanies this walk the entire length south along Michigan Avenue. If you don't have time now, be sure to come back to the museum to see some of its wonderful collections (admission is free on Tuesday).

☕ **TAKE A BREAK**   Turn right on Adams and walk 2½ blocks to **The Berghoff,** 17 W. Adams (☎ **312/427-3170**), a favorite Chicago watering hole and restaurant from the turn of the century. Order a "light" pick-me-up at the bar. A stein of Maibock beer and a bratwurst will cost about $6.

On the way back to Michigan Avenue from Adams Street, make a digression northward along:

14. **State Street.** One of the most famous department stores along this strip is **Carson Pirie Scott,** 1 S. State, a Chicago architectural gem designed by Louis Sullivan. Two blocks farther north is **Marshall Field's** landmark building. Across the street there's a public skating rink in the winter and a youth art program in the summer. Note the handsome new "vintage" street lights and subway entrances, elements of a streetscape improvement made in 1997 when the former bus and pedestrian "mall" was reopened to auto traffic.

Return to Michigan Avenue and continue south to:

15. **Symphony Center,** 220 S. Michigan, home of the Chicago Symphony and its great concert venue, Orchestra Hall. The latter is one of the avenue's grandest buildings, dating from 1905, and was augmented last year with additional concert halls, an education center, and an upscale restaurant, all of which was rechristened Symphony Center.

One door down from here you can stop in at the:

16. **Santa Fe Building,** 224 S. Michigan. When it was built in 1904 by Daniel Burnham, the white-glazed terra-cotta Railway Exchange Building was one of the first high-rises (it has 17 stories). Burnham liked his handiwork so much that he moved his offices here. The building has been restored, so go inside and check out the skylit lobby court, with its polished mahogany, detailed grillwork, and marble floors. Fittingly, the **Chicago Architecture Foundation (CAF)** has a gift shop and tour center here. Here you can arrange for a more intensive tour of the downtown architectural highlights. Call ☎ **312/922-TOUR** for a recorded message of available tours (see "Sightseeing Tours" in chapter 7 for more information on CAF tours). The Chicago Symphony's shop is also in the building.

A digression to the interior streets will pick up some of the outstanding architectural sights in the Loop. Walk west along Jackson to LaSalle. On the northeast corner is a plaque commemorating the adoption of standard time in the United States in 1883—before that more than 100 different local times were in use, an Excedrin headache for the railroads. On the left, you'll see the:

17. **Chicago Board of Trade,** 141 W. Jackson, facing north, looming over LaSalle. Walking north now on LaSalle, you'll approach:

18. **The Rookery Building,** 209 S. LaSalle, a Burnham and Root building. Take a peek at the gilded marble lobby, designed by Frank Lloyd Wright and restored several years ago with magnificent results.

Return east along Jackson to see the:

19. **Monadnock Building,** 53 W. Jackson, the north half of which was designed in 1891 by Burnham and Root, the south half by Holabird and Roche. For a short time the world's tallest office building, it's the tallest masonry building in Chicago.

Continue south along Dearborn Street and note some other standout relics of Chicago's revival after the Great Fire of 1871:

20. **The Fisher Building,** 343 S. Dearborn, built by Burnham in 1896, with an addition dating from 1907.

21. **The Old Colony Building,** 407 S. Dearborn, constructed in 1894 by Holabird and Roche.

22. **The Manhattan Building,** 431 S. Dearborn, erected in 1891 by William Baron Le Jenney. It's Chicago's oldest surviving steel-frame building, an innovation that, along with elevators, made skyscrapers possible.

Cross Congress Parkway to enter:

23. **Printers Row,** as this stretch of Dearborn is known, where the oldest concentration of the city's postfire buildings is found, many of them former printing warehouses. Today this neighborhood has undergone a revival, becoming a trendy alternative to living on the Gold Coast or in Lincoln Park. Several interesting shops and restaurants line the row.

☺ **TAKE A BREAK   Prairie,** at 500 S. Dearborn (☎ 312/663-1143), is an ideal place for lunch or dinner, offering gourmet dishes from heartland recipes and ingredients in a setting with stylings inspired by Frank Lloyd Wright (see complete listing in chapter 6).

Continue south along Dearborn to:

24. **Dearborn Station,** the oldest surviving train station in Chicago, but now converted into a small mall of shops and restaurants.

Head back north to Congress and go 1 block east to State Street to see the:

25. **Harold Washington Library Center,** the block-square red brick building built in 1991. Look for the playful cherubs with their lips puckered to blow, a visual pun on the city's reputation as the "Windy City."

Continue east to the corner of Congress and Michigan, where you'll find the:

26. **Auditorium Building and Theatre,** 430 S. Michigan. Dankmar Adler and Louis Sullivan designed this masterpiece and supervised its construction in 1889. Much of the building now houses Roosevelt University, but the theater (around the corner at 50 E. Congress) is still in use, and it is considered to be one of the most acoustically perfect performing spaces in the world.

Make a left on Michigan, heading north, to see the:

27. Fine Arts Building, 410 S. Michigan, which was originally constructed in 1885 to serve the needs of the Studebaker automobile company. Around the turn of the century it was converted into a beehive of art and music studios. Chicagoans also know it as the place to go for a fix of art-house movies.

From here you can cross the street into Grant Park and stroll toward Buckingham Fountain, which operates from May to October. Or, if you have any energy left, you could walk (or take a quick cab ride) to the Museum Campus, where three great museums—the Field, Shedd Aquarium, and Adler Planetarium—are connected by a new green space at the lower end of Grant Park.

WALKING TOUR 2
Hyde Park

Start: 53rd Street station of the Metra Railroad.
Finish: Museum of Science and Industry, 57th Street and Lake Shore Drive, or the DuSable Museum of African-American History, in Washington Park.
Time: 3 hours, depending on stops and digressions.
Best Times: Any day of the week before dusk.
Worst Times: After dark. This walking tour must be taken during daylight hours, since the experience is largely visual, and you may not feel entirely safe walking around here at night.

Hyde Park is described in detail under "Exploring Hyde Park: The Museum of Science and Industry & More" in chapter 7. Assuming you are staying in or near downtown Chicago, you may get to Hyde Park in a half hour or less on one of several modes of public transportation or by cab.

This tour begins at the:

1. 53rd Street station of the Metra train. The Metra train has two stops on South Michigan Avenue. Make sure you board the train that makes all stops; if you board an express train you won't be able to get off until you reach the 59th Street station, still in Hyde Park, but several long blocks from where the tour begins.

🗨 **STARTING OUT**   If you're going to make a day of it in Hyde Park, you might as well start off with a traditional breakfast at **Valois,** 1518 E. 53rd St. (☎ 773/667-0647). "See Your Food" is the slogan that greets you on the sign outside Valois, a small cafeteria-style restaurant and hangout for the whole Hyde Park community for several generations. Short-order meals are the specialty here. An alternative refueling stop near the tour's first stop is the **Starbucks** on the corner of Harper and 53rd.

After leaving the train station, or Valois, as the case may be, start heading west on 53rd Street until you come to:

2. Harper Court, a complex of interesting shops and restaurants. For a sampling of the shops, see chapter 9.

From Harper Court, continue west on 53rd Street until you reach Dorchester Avenue, where on the southeast corner directly beyond a vacant lot you will see:

3. The oldest house in Hyde Park, dating from 1859. Actually it is the rear section of a more recent structure, with a steep roof and something of the shed or outbuilding about it.

Continue west on 53rd. Just past Kenwood, you will see:

4. Nichols Park, a pretty little park where only recently an ugly lot stood. Make a left on Kimbark, heading south. At the corner of 55th Street, notice:

5. St. Thomas the Apostle School and Church. The lacy terra-cotta trim at the church entrance was completed in 1924 by an apprentice of Frank Lloyd Wright.

Hang right on 55th and cross it 1 block west at Woodlawn (cross at the light—Hyde Park drivers are notorious). Then head back east 1 block to Kimbark. Here you're entering the:

6. Golden rectangle, an area bordering the U of C campus where the neighborhood's priciest real estate is located. On the west corners, on both sides of 56th Street, is a complex of homes called:

7. Professor's Row, dating from 1904 to 1907, some of the most desirable residences in Hyde Park. Migratory parrots, which have somehow drifted here from the South American rain forests, have nested within the confines of Professor's Row, causing a heated controversy in recent years between local "Friends of the Birds" and Illinois farmers who claim the presence of the parrots is a danger to crops.

Now walk 1 block west to Woodlawn to see one of the prettiest residential streets in the neighborhood. If you're a physics fanatic, you might want to scoot back north to see:

8. No. 5537 Woodlawn, the former home of Enrico Fermi, the physicist responsible for the first sustained nuclear chain reaction.

Otherwise, at the northeast corner of Woodlawn and 56th Street is the:

9. McCormick Theological Seminary, and on the southwest corner is the Hyde Park Union Church.

Heading south on Woodlawn, at 58th Street you will reach a highlight of the tour, the:

10. Robie House, 5757 S. Woodlawn, perhaps the ultimate expression of Frank Lloyd Wright's Prairie School style. Robie House offers several tours a day (see chapter 7); the cost is $8 for adults and $6 for seniors and children 7 to 18.

On the southwest corner of this intersection is the:

11. Oriental Institute Museum, 1155 E. 58th St., an extraordinary collection of ancient art and artifacts dating from 9000 B.C. The institute is closed Monday. Note that after more than a year of extensive renovation and expansion that closed the museum to the public, the galleries are slowly reopening with the Egyptian Gallery debuting in December 1998.

Continue south on Woodlawn 1 block to the:

12. Rockefeller Memorial Chapel, at 59th and Woodlawn, a tour de force of modern Gothic architecture, housing the world's second-largest carillon. Carillon concerts may be heard Sunday at noon and Monday through Friday at 6pm. (During the summer, the bells chime only on Sunday at noon and 6pm.)

That wide stretch of green in front of you is the:

13. Midway Plaisance, which divides the main campus from the law school and other satellite buildings, many of which were designed by well-known modernist architects such as Eliel Saarinen, Edward Durell Stone, and Ludwig Mies van der Rohe.

Make a right in front of Rockefeller Chapel and head west along 59th Street. After you pass University Avenue, the University of Chicago campus will be on your right. Enter through:

14. Cobb Gate. You have two options here. Either continue on this self-guided tour, or depending on the time of day, take the official university tour, which departs

Walking Tour—Hyde Park

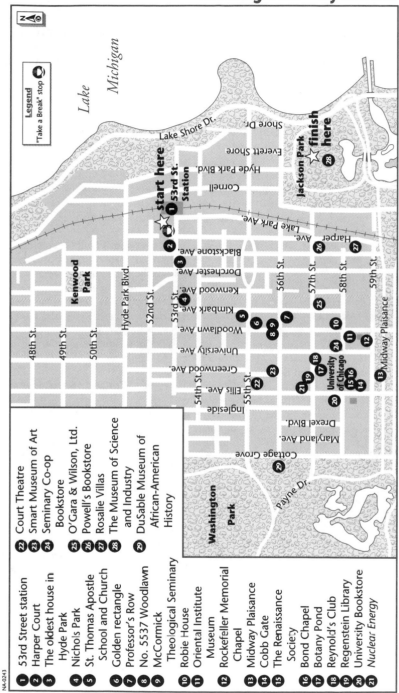

Legend
"Take a Break" stop

Lake Michigan

start here
① 53rd St. Station

finish here
㉘ Jackson Park

Lake Shore Dr.
Everett Shore
Hyde Park Blvd.
Cornell
Lake Park Ave.
Harper Ave.

Kenwood Park

Hyde Park Blvd.

Kenwood Park

Blackstone Ave.
Dorchester Ave.
Kenwood Ave.
Kimbark Ave.
Woodlawn Ave.
University Ave.
Greenwood Ave.
Ellis Ave.
Ingleside
Drexel Blvd.
Maryland Ave.
Cottage Grove

48th St.
49th St.
50th St.
52nd St.
53rd St.
54th St.
55th St.
56th St.
57th St.
58th St.
59th St.

Midway Plaisance
University of Chicago

Washington Park
Payne Dr.

- ① 53rd Street station
- ② Harper Court
- ③ The oldest house in Hyde Park
- ④ Nichols Park
- ⑤ St. Thomas Apostle School and Church
- ⑥ Golden rectangle
- ⑦ Professor's Row
- ⑧ No. 5537 Woodlawn
- ⑨ McCormick Theological Seminary
- ⑩ Robie House
- ⑪ Oriental Institute Museum
- ⑫ Rockefeller Memorial Chapel
- ⑬ Midway Plaisance
- ⑭ Cobb Gate
- ⑮ The Renaissance Society
- ⑯ Bond Chapel
- ⑰ Botany Pond
- ⑱ Reynold's Club
- ⑲ Regenstein Library
- ⑳ University Bookstore
- ㉑ *Nuclear Energy*
- ㉒ Court Theatre
- ㉓ Smart Museum of Art
- ㉔ Seminary Co-op Bookstore
- ㉕ O'Gara & Wilson, Ltd.
- ㉖ Powell's Bookstore
- ㉗ Rosalie Villas
- ㉘ The Museum of Science and Industry
- ㉙ DuSable Museum of African-American History

NA-0243

from Ida Noyes Hall, 1212 E. 59th St., Saturday at 10am (groups of 10 or more can arrange tours through the campus visitor center; ☎ 773/702-8374).

The main attractions for those continuing on the self-guided tour are listed below. Given the campus layout, you'll probably have to ask directions. At some point, I strongly recommend just lying down on the grass and soaking up some of that academia. For you movie buffs, near the center of the Quad is where Harry and Sally met for the first time, before that long drive to New York. Near where you entered the campus is:

15. The Renaissance Society, on the fourth floor of Cobb Hall, which introduced to the Midwest such artists as Klee, Miró, and Matisse and continues to exhibit vanguard artists. Between Classics and Harper quads, you must visit the:

16. Bond Chapel, with its ornate stained glass and carved wood. On the opposite side of the Quad is the peaceful:

17. Botany Pond, designed by the two sons of the great landscape architect Frederick Law Olmsted. This section of the campus houses many of the science buildings.

If you exit the Quad here (the big gate near the pond is Hull Gate, but most students don't seem to call gates by their names), a few steps to the east is the:

18. Reynolds Club, housing the student union and the University Theater.

Across the street and half a block to the west is the:

19. Regenstein Library, the main undergraduate library, a modern—some would say monstrous—facility built where Stagg Field, the university's stadium, once stood.

Take 57th Street west to Ellis Avenue. A block or so south is the:

20. University Bookstore, a good place to shop for books and U of C souvenirs—T-shirts, caps, and the like.

Reversing direction and heading north, between 57th and 56th streets, you will come to the famous bronze sculpture:

21. *Nuclear Energy* by Henry Moore. It is built over the site where in 1942 Enrico Fermi conducted the first self-sustaining, controlled nuclear chain reaction.

Continue north on Ellis and make a right on 55th Street. Here is the:

22. Court Theatre, an Equity house that specializes in staging works of Shakespeare and French literature.

Go east on 55th to the corner and make a right on Greenwood Avenue, heading south 1 block to the:

23. David and Alfred Smart Museum of Art, 5550 S. Greenwood, where the university's impressive collection of nearly 7,000 works is housed.

From here another lengthy digression is possible. If you'd like to see the elegant Kenwood neighborhood, walk north here about 5 blocks, preferably along Woodlawn (2 blocks to the east). If you choose not to digress, return south along University Avenue to 58th Street, where you can drop in at the:

24. Seminary Co-op Bookstore, 5757 S. University Ave. (☎ 773/752-4381), on the northeast corner of 58th Street, making sure to also take a peek into the lovely and diminutive **Thorndike Hilton Chapel,** in the same building.

We will now begin to head east again. Either walk down 57th Street, taking note of two interesting bookstores. First:

25. O'Gara & Wilson, Ltd., 1448 E. 57th St. (☎ 773/363-0993), Chicago's oldest book dealer, and then farther down the street:

26. Powell's Bookstore, 1501 E. 57th St. (☎ 773/955-7780), crammed with used titles in every subject from the classics to the social sciences.

Or follow 59th Street and take Harper up to 57th to see the:

27. **Rosalie Villas,** where the cottages once formed a miniature planned community constructed in the 1880s.

From here, continue on 57th Street into Jackson Park until you reach the final stops on this tour:

28. **The Museum of Science and Industry,** 57th Street and Lake Shore Drive, one of the most popular tourist attractions in Chicago.

For those of you with a different academic bent, a short cab ride away is the:

29. **DuSable Museum of African-American History,** 740 E. 56th Place (see chapter 7 for complete listing).

WALKING TOUR 3
The Gold Coast

Start: East Lake Shore Drive, across from the Oak Street Beach (behind the Drake Hotel).

Finish: Subway station at Clark and Division streets, where you can catch the Red Line back to the Magnificent Mile or the Loop.

Time: 2 hours.

Best Times: Before or after the morning rush on weekdays, when the streets are empty, or on Sunday.

Worst Times: Whenever crowds could make the walk heavy going.

In Chicago the "Gold Coast" refers not only to the bank of high-rises along the lakefront between Oak Street and North Avenue but also to the interior blocks off this strip. Although the Gold Coast has its share of restaurants and shops, it is primarily a residential neighborhood, and for this reason it makes for a peaceful walk on a weekday. Weekends are a bit busier, as the professionals who work hard all week tend to play just as hard in their off time.

To begin this tour, take the underpass beneath Michigan Avenue to reach the:

1. **Oak Street Beach.** Stroll along the sands (or on the concrete path if you prefer) and drink in the view of Lake Michigan to your right and Lake Shore Drive to your left. (But be sure to keep an eye out for speeding bicyclists and in-line skaters as you amble.) If you'd like a closer view of the high-rises and few remaining mansions lining Lake Shore Drive, cross under the Drive at the pedestrian tunnel at Division Street and turn right. If you stay on the beach, there's another pedestrian tunnel at North Avenue.

This stretch of Lake Shore Drive, as well as those streets in the immediate vicinity, first received the appellation "Gold Coast" because many of Chicago's wealthiest families built their mansions here in the years following the Chicago Fire. The fire had virtually destroyed all of the Near North Side, once a prosperous neighborhood of artisans and craftspeople, primarily German immigrants. State Street merchant Potter Palmer began the trend in 1882 with his million-dollar castle at what is now the high-rise apartment building at:

2. **1350 N. Lake Shore Dr.** Other affluent Chicagoans followed Potter's lead, but most of these shoreside estates have long been replaced by elegant apartment buildings, with the exception of several survivors like those at:

3. **1516 N. Lake Shore Dr. and 1530 N. Lake Shore Dr.,** now housing the International College of Surgeons and the Polish Consulate General, respectively.

A winding, self-guided architectural tour through the interior streets of the Gold Coast is a must to appreciate the eclectic variety of building styles that flowered in Chicago after the Great Fire of 1871. On these streets, the preservation of Chicago's oldest mansions and fine town houses has fared better than on the drive itself, though the architectural relics here are likewise sheltered beneath the shadows of modern high-rises.

Walk south to Burton Place (or backtrack to Burton, if you took the pedestrian tunnel at Division Street and have been walking north up the Drive) and then head west 1 block to Astor Street, a designated landmark along its entire length between Division Street and North Avenue, with many well-preserved houses.

On a side street off Astor, at 20 E. Burton, is the:

4. **Patterson–McCormick Mansion.** The original building, an Italianate palazzo, was designed by Stanford White as a wedding present for the daughter of the *Chicago Tribune*'s publisher and expanded in 1927 by David Adler for Cyrus McCormick II. Today the complex has been broken up into condos.

Before exploring the rest of Astor Street head north to North Boulevard and take a left. On the corner of North Boulevard and North State Parkway is the:

5. **Residence of the Roman Catholic Archbishop of Chicago,** 1555 N. State Pkwy. The Queen Anne–style red brick mansion with many chimneys was one of the first houses built in the district, erected in the 1880s on land that had previously been a cemetery.

Across the street is:

6. **1550 N. State Parkway,** where each of the 10 floors originally housed a single apartment of 9,000 square feet. The building was designed by Benjamin Marshall, the architect for the Blackstone and Drake hotels.

Next head south on State Parkway. At 4 W. Burton is the:

7. **Madlener House,** built in 1902 by the firm of Richard E. Schmidt. It's one of the city's earliest examples of the horizontal architecture that would come to characterize the Prairie School and the work of Frank Lloyd Wright. Today the building is home to the Graham Foundation for Advanced Studies in Fine Arts.

At Burton Place, turn left and return to Astor Street and turn right. In just a few short blocks along Astor you can take in a variety of architectural styles, beginning with the Tudor house at:

8. **1451 N. Astor St.,** designed by architect Howard Van Doren Shaw and built in 1910. Note the narrow, elongated windows, the split-level roofs, and the multiple chimney stacks. The magnificent house at no. 1449, built around the turn of the century, is a sturdy example of the Romanesque style.

Two other neighborhood homes of interest, facing each other across the street are:

9. **1443 and 1444 N. Astor St.** The May House, at no. 1443, is reminiscent of H. H. Richardson's Glessner House on South Prairie Avenue, while the house at no. 1444, constructed in 1929 by Holabird and Root, is distinctly art deco.

At 1406 N. Astor St. is the:

10. **Joseph T. Ryerson House,** designed by David Adler in 1922, whose design in this case was inspired by the hotels of Paris constructed during the Second Empire.

At 1365 N. Astor St., on the southeast corner of Schiller Street, is the:

11. **Charnley–Persky House,** built in 1892 by Adler and Sullivan during the period when Frank Lloyd Wright (who played a major role in the design) worked for the firm. Wright later called the house "the first modern house in America," and it is quite a departure from the other homes on the street. Today the house is the national headquarters of the Society of Architectural Historians. The house is open for tours year-round Wednesday at noon and Saturday at 10am. From

Walking Tour—The Gold Coast

1. Oak Street Beach
2. 1350 N. Lake Shore Dr.
3. 1516 N. Lake Shore Dr. and 1530 N. Lake Shore Dr.
4. Patterson–McCormick Mansion
5. Residence of the Roman Catholic Archbishop of Chicago
6. 1550 N. State Parkway
7. Madlener House
8. 1451 N. Astor St.
9. 1443 and 1444 N. Astor St.
10. Joseph T. Ryerson House
11. Charnley–Persky House
12. 1316 to 1322 N. Astor St
13. James L. Houghteling houses
14. 1301 and 1260 N. Astor St.
15. Omni Ambassador East Hotel
16. Playboy Mansion
17. The Frank Fisher Apartments

April 1 through November 30, there's an additional tour Saturday at 1pm. The tour on Wednesday lasts 1 hour and is free of charge. On Saturday, you can either take a 1-hour tour of the Charnley–Persky House ($5 adults) or a 2-hour tour that also includes a visit to the Madlener House ($9 adults). For more information, call ☎ **312/915-0105.**

A few blocks south, the standouts to look for are:

12. 1316 to 1322 N. Astor St., which also show a Romanesque influence in the manner of the Boston architect H. H. Richardson's style. (The only actual sample of Richardson's work in Chicago, however, is the South Side's Glessner House at 1800 S. Prairie Avenue in the Prairie Avenue Historical District.)

At 1308 to 1312 N. Astor St., at the corner of Astor and Goethe, look at the:

13. James L. Houghteling houses, an eclectic cluster of Chicago town houses built by Burnham and Root between 1887 and 1888. Originally there were four dwellings, but no. 1306 was torn down. John Wellborn Root, who is credited with the design of the buildings, actually lived here with his family in no. 1310. Here the brilliant architect also met his untimely end from pneumonia at the age of 40.

On opposite corners diagonally across Goethe Street are two apartment towers that represent the trend toward high-rise living within the interior streets of the Gold Coast, beginning in the 1930s:

14. 1301 and 1260 N. Astor St. Constructed by Philip B. Maher in 1932 and 1931 respectively, these two apartment buildings are classics of the sleek modernism that characterized American commercial architecture after World War I. 1300 N. Astor St., on the other hand, is a 1960s version of the high-rise apartment house, by Bertrand Goldberg, of a form that seemed so avant-garde in that period (like the fins on Detroit gas guzzlers) and today seems dated.

Now turn right on Goethe Street and walk to State Parkway, where, on the corner, stands the:

15. Omni Ambassador East Hotel and its famous Pump Room restaurant. You may want to walk into the Pump Room to scan the celebrity photos lining the walls (or maybe have a drink).

Next head north on State Parkway to 1340 N. State, better known as Hugh Hefner's:

16. Playboy Mansion. It was originally built in 1899 for an upright Calvinist named George S. Isham. After Hef moved out, the mansion later became a women's dormitory for the School of the Art Institute. It recently was turned into condominiums.

Next head south again on State Parkway. Finally, near Division Street, are:

17. The Frank Fisher Apartments, 1209 N. State, a small white-brick building with a curved glass-block facade in the art moderne tradition, built around an appealing inner courtyard.

👁 **WINDING DOWN**   For a lunch, a light snack, or just a rejuvenating cup of coffee, head to the **Third Coast,** 1260 N. Dearborn St. (☎ **312/649-0730**), a charming cafe just north of Division Street.

The tour concludes at the Clark and Division subway station. From here you can take the Red Line south to the Magnificent Mile (State and Chicago stop) or the Loop, or north to Lincoln Park (Fullerton stop), Lakeview (Belmont stop), or Wrigley Field (Addison stop). You could also either walk or take a bus north on Clark Street to the **Chicago Historical Society,** at the corner of Clark and North Avenue.

OTHER NEIGHBORHOODS TO EXPLORE

OLD TOWN

West of LaSalle Street stretches a strip of old Chicago bohemia called Old Town, separating the Gold Coast from Cabrini-Green, one of the most disastrous experiments ever in low-income housing. Old Town's main drag is **Wells Street,** covering a stretch three-quarters of a mile long between Division Street and Lincoln Avenue. During the day, it's a pleasant area to explore for its quaint shops and intimate, tree-lined residential streets. By night, Wells Street is a lively entertainment zone, offering nationally renowned comedy clubs—the most famous being Second City—a cinema, and numerous bars and restaurants.

A good place to start your walk is the corner of Wells Street and North Avenue, the commercial hub of Old Town. The nearest El stop is just a few blocks away at Sedgwick Street and North Avenue (on the Brown Line).

Old Town, like much of the Near North Side of Chicago, was once a German neighborhood, settled in the 1840s by immigrants who had begun to flee the continent in great numbers due to crop failures, famine, and the decline of cottage industry. North Avenue, with its many specialty shops and beer halls, for years was known as German Broadway. The eventual arrival of substantial industry, like the Oscar Mayer Sausage Company, plus a brewery and a piano factory, provided Old Town with a level of economic self-sufficiency. Many residents were able to duplicate a town life similar to the one they had left behind, living and working in the same community.

Old Town retained its German flavor well into the 1930s, and even now the many shells of the Germans' clubs and institutions remain as testament to the heyday of that culture. But around the beginning of the Great Depression in the early thirties, the area around Wells had begun to fray, attracting a new generation of artists and writers trying to eke out a living on the government's Works Progress Administration. Under these circumstances, Old Town became the center of Chicago's bohemian life, a status it maintained through the hippie era of the sixties and beyond. With the almost complete gentrification of Lincoln Park to the north and east, Old Town soon took its place as a prime real estate market for people of means who chose to remain near their jobs in downtown Chicago rather than commute to town from the suburbs. At present, Old Town combines these two roles: bedroom community for middle- to upper-income Chicagoans and entertainment zone for the entire city.

Today, although lined with boutiques, bars, restaurants, and nightspots, the neighborhood still emanates artsy, quasi-radical vibes, an aura enhanced each year in mid-June, when Well Street is transformed into an outdoor gallery for its annual art festival.

Just north of the corner of North Avenue and Wells Street, on the west side of Wells, is perhaps the neighborhood's most famous resident, the **Second City** comedy club, at 1616 N. Wells (☎ 312/337-3992). Alumni of the group, which has been making funny for more than 3 decades, include much of the cast from the glory days of *Saturday Night Live* (Bill Murray, Gilda Radner, et al.), and actors and comedians working today, including Dan Castallaneta, the voice of Homer Simpson.

A few interesting stores on this stretch of Wells are **Handle with Care,** at no. 1706 (☎ 312/751-2929), a largish boutique full of interesting clothes for women and baby, jewelry, and other gifts; and **The Heartworks,** at no. 1704 (☎ 312/943-1972), for cards, candles, and more gifts. **A New Leaf,** a florist plus a whole lot more, has two shops on the street, no. 1645 (☎ 312/642-1576) and no. 1818 (☎ 312/642-8553); while both locations are worth a browse whether you have a green thumb or not, the rambling emporium at no. 1818 offers everything from copper pots to candles and has a detached building out back full of folksy antiques.

If you're hungry, you can stop at **Nookies,** 1746 N. Wells St. (☎ **312/337-2454**), which serves breakfast all day as well as sandwiches and other specials; open daily 6:30am to 10pm (Sun until 9pm). If you're in the mood for something lighter, **Breadsmith,** 1710 N. Wells St. (☎ **312/642-5858**), offers a variety of fresh-baked breads, cookies, and brownies; they even sell fresh-baked "Good Dog" biscuits if you're strolling with Fido. It's open daily 7:30am to 7:30pm.

South of North Avenue on Wells are more shops and restaurants, as well as a few caffeine purveyors, including the requisite Starbucks, duking it out on the block. If you've succumbed to the cigar craze, or if you've been puffing for years, you won't want to miss the **Up Down Tobacco Shop** at 1550 N. Wells.

A few neighborhood institutions provide a real Chicago flavor. **Twin Anchors,** 1655 N. Sedgwick (☎ **312/266-1616**), a longtime Chicago restaurant at Sedgwick and Eugenie streets was a favorite with the late Frank Sinatra and likely will be with you, too, once you taste their signature ribs. Just up the street at the corner of Sedgwick and Menomonee, is **Marge's,** 1758 N. Sedgwick (☎ **312/787-3900**), a typical old-style corner bar that becomes party central during the Old Town Art Fair in June. The delightfully dingy **Old Town Ale House,** at 219 W. North Ave. (☎ **312/944-7020**), and **O'Rourke's,** 1625 N. Halsted St. (☎ **312/335-1806**), a decidedly erudite Irish Pub across the street from Steppenwolf Theatre, are a pair of venerable bars that formed two sides of a "Bermuda Triangle"—the Billy Goat Tavern formed the third—into which reporters and literary types were known to disappear.

The residential part of the neighborhood, sometimes referred to as the **Old Town Triangle,** begins roughly above North Avenue, only 2 blocks west of Lincoln Park at this point. A walk through these quiet streets is rewarded by a vision of Old Town the way it was around the turn of the century and earlier. Many of the **wood-frame houses** built just after the Great Fire of 1871, some of which are located at 217, 219, 225, and 229 W. Eugenie St., are still standing and coexist with residential creations of more recent vintage, notably the **10 luxury town houses** on Sedgwick Street between Wisconsin and Menomonee, designed by nine of Chicago's top contemporary architectural firms. On the corner of nearby Eugenie and Cleveland streets is an enormous Bavarian baroque church, **St. Michael's,** rebuilt from its standing walls after the fire. For most of the second half of the 19th century, St. Michael's was the parish center of Chicago's largest German Catholic community. Another important religious center in the neighborhood is the **Midwest Buddhist Temple,** 435 W. Menomonee St., which brings people to the neighborhood in August for Ginza Holiday, a celebration of Japanese culture. The Old Town Triangle is also home to the **Old Town Art Fair,** a juried fine arts fair centered at Wisconsin Street and Lincoln Park West that is held the same weekend as the Wells Street Art Fair, mentioned above. (See the "Calendar of Events" in chapter 2 for more information about all three events.)

WICKER PARK/BUCKTOWN

Note: See page 143 for a map of this area.

Even a decade ago, this neighborhood west of the Gold Coast was a mix of working-class housing and light industrial buildings. Today, if you're really hip—say, a photographer or a musician, or you just like renovating slightly decayed houses—this is where you live. Artists in search of good light and low rent were the first outsiders to move

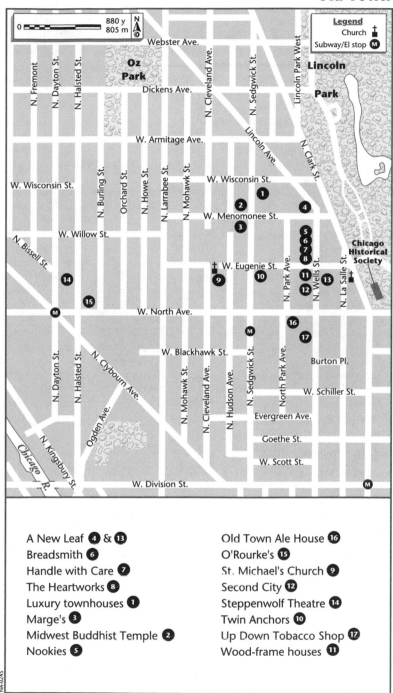

Old Town

Legend
Church †
Subway/El stop Ⓜ

A New Leaf ④ & ⑬
Breadsmith ⑥
Handle with Care ⑦
The Heartworks ⑧
Luxury townhouses ①
Marge's ③
Midwest Buddhist Temple ②
Nookies ⑤

Old Town Ale House ⑯
O'Rourke's ⑮
St. Michael's Church ⑨
Second City ⑫
Steppenwolf Theatre ⑭
Twin Anchors ⑩
Up Down Tobacco Shop ⑰
Wood-frame houses ⑪

into what had become a Hispanic neighborhood. Before that the area had been a Polish enclave, and in the late 19th century it was originally settled by well-to-do Germans, whose magnificent mansions still preside over Wicker Park, the small greensward that gives the area its name.

After the artists moved in, next came the merely artsy, followed shortly by the wanna-bes. The rent isn't quite so low anymore, and loft conversions and new construction continue at breakneck speed. Some thoroughly residential and commercial areas now resemble blocks in Lincoln Park. Not surprisingly, the original artists are appalled by their new neighbors, and the chic boutiques and hypertrendy eateries that have followed (see chapter 6 and 9 for some recommendations). Some residents even object to **Around the Coyote,** the weekend festival in early September when artists open up their studios to the public.

If you miss Around the Coyote, during which detailed maps of artists' work spaces are made available, go to the main intersection of **North, Damen, and Milwaukee avenues,** and stroll from there down the main arteries. A good starting point is the landmark **Flat Iron Building,** 1579 N. Milwaukee Ave., which houses numerous artists and galleries.

For the time being, most of the trendy shopping spots and restaurants are concentrated on Milwaukee Avenue between North Avenue and Evergreen Street (where Nelson Algren once lived), and north along Damen Avenue up to Webster Avenue (a rather long walk).

If you get the munchies while strolling, stop into **Red Hen Bread** at 1623 N. Milwaukee Ave., just north of North Avenue (☎ 773/342-6823), for a fresh loaf (the bittersweet chocolate chunk bread is a tasty steal at $3.50) wrapped in white paper and tied with red ribbon. You can enjoy your snack in the little park that has given the neighborhood its name. To get there, walk back south to North Avenue, then a few blocks south on Damen until you see mansion-lined Wicker Park on your left.

You may want to stay on for the neighborhood's cooler-by-the-minute nocturnal scene, catching an alternative rock band at one of the music clubs (see chapter 10 for details).

THE NEAR WEST SIDE

Late Sunday evening on October 8, 1871, a fire broke out somewhere near the O'Leary home. Legend has it that the fire began in the O'Learys' barn, a freak accident caused when a cow—or a neighbor named Daniel "Peg Leg" Sullivan or a group of kids playing, as recent scrutiny of the original legend has largely exonerated the O'Learys' "scapecow"—upended an oil-filled lantern. The fire raged mostly to the east and north, jumping the Chicago River in both directions, leveling all of downtown Chicago and most of the Near North Side as far as the city line along Fullerton Avenue.

Two days later, as the city lay in smoldering ash, the O'Leary home stood unscathed, marking the western limit of the fire that, owing to the direction of the wind and to pure luck, left much of the Near West Side intact. A monument shaped like a **Pillar of Fire** stands today in the courtyard of the **Chicago Fire Academy** at Jefferson and DeKoven streets, where the O'Learys lived and the fire was believed to have started.

From the 1850s on, the Near West Side, broadly defined as the area just west of the Loop, was a study in social contrasts, the town houses of wealthy merchants standing near the most wretched hovels of the immigrant families: at first, the Irish, Germans, and Bohemians; later, Jews, Greeks, and Italians; and still later, Mexicans and African Americans from the south.

PILSEN

Most of Pilsen remains an immigrant neighborhood, a narrow, rectangular box of streets stretching as far west as Damen Avenue, and shaped north and south by the old rail yards and the remaining industrial infrastructure of the 19th century. The area is named for the second-largest city in what was then Bohemia, a region of what is now the Czech Republic. English is still the second language of Pilsen, but the first is no longer Czech—it's Mexican Spanish. The Bohemians left their mark on the physical appearance of the neighborhood, however, with the colorful brick- and stonework that decorates the facades of many houses and tall commercial structures.

Every September, usually the last weekend of the month, many artists and artisans of Pilsen throw open their studio doors and invite the public to view the work they've produced over the preceding year during the **Pilsen Artists' Open House** (for more information, call ☎ **312/738-0786**).

The epicenter of the Pilsen art scene is located in the eastern corner of the neighborhood at **Halsted and 18th streets.** Most of the studios occupy spaces in what are some of the oldest and most charming houses and commercial buildings in Chicago remaining within a single, unified residential zone. Behind the block-long row of buildings along the 1800 block of Halsted (between 18th and 19th streets), a large courtyard with wonderful gardens lies hidden from public view. On summer days, artists and their patrons fill the courtyard, sipping white wine from plastic glasses.

Even if your stay in Chicago does not coincide with the Pilsen Artists' Open House, you can spend an interesting afternoon exploring this neighborhood. If you choose to wander around beyond the daylight hours, it's a good idea to stick to the area of restaurants on 18th Street; the typical visitor probably would not feel nearly as safe here in the evening as, say, in River North or Lincoln Park.

To reach Pilsen from the general vicinity of the Loop, take the Blue Line (from the Dearborn Street subway) to the 18th Street station. The station itself is an unusual sight: From the walls of the El platform to the step risers down to the street, the station has been covered with pre-Colombian murals painted by neighborhood kids and volunteers. When you leave the station, head east toward Halsted; it's about a 1-mile walk, or you can catch the no. 18 Halsted bus. From the station it's also a short walk 1 block south to the **Orozco Community Academy,** a public school at 1645 W. 18th Place that's clad in elaborate mosaic murals on the outside and a variety of painted murals inside.

As you wander among the residential side streets that encircle the intersection of Halsted and 18th, heading in a westerly direction and zigzagging the streets between 18th Street and Cermak Road, see how many of the **murals** you can find of the 30 or more that have been painted on building exteriors by artists and their friends in the community. Many draw heavily from pre-Colombian myths and customs and combine them with a vision of social realism in the manner of Diego Rivera and other great muralists of Central America.

A nice place to stop for a break is **Cafe Jumping Bean,** 1439 W. 18th St., 2 blocks east of Ashland Avenue (☎ **312/455-0019**), a coffee shop that displays local art on the walls and is a gathering place for artists in the area. One of Chicago's most experimental theaters, the **Blue Rider,** is in Pilsen, at Halsted and 18th streets (see chapter 10). The **Mexican Fine Arts Museum,** the largest museum of its kind, is also in Pilsen at 1852 W. 19th St. (☎ **312/629-6000**), between Wolcott and Wood streets, 3 blocks west of Ashland Avenue.

9 Shopping

It should come as no surprise that shopping in the Windy City is first-rate. The art of merchandising has a rich history here. From the time when the city was little more than a frontier town up until just a few years ago, few homes lacked a catalog from Sears or Montgomery Ward, both of which grew up in Chicago. East to west, or back the other way, whether it was livestock, overalls, or the newest books, just about everything passed through Chicago.

And the 19th-century merchants' legacy continues, from the imposing Merchandise Mart (recently sold by the Kennedy family), which houses showroom after showroom of fine furniture, to the chic designer boutiques lining Oak Street. The quality of the stores is top-notch, and since so many of the best are concentrated on North Michigan Avenue, the convenience is unmatched.

This chapter concentrates on the Magnificent Mile, State Street, and several trendy neighborhoods, where you'll find one-of-a-kind shops and boutiques that make shopping such an adventure. It also includes a sampling, organized by merchandise category, of specific retailers where you'll find specific goods.

SHOPPING HOURS As a general rule, shop hours are Monday through Saturday from 10am to 6 or 7pm and Sunday from noon to 5pm. Neighborhood stores tend to keep later hours, some remaining open until 8pm Monday through Saturday and until 6pm on Sunday. Many stores are open later on Thursday, and almost all have extended hours during the holiday season. Nearly all of the stores in the Loop are open for daytime shopping only, generally from 9 or 10am to no later than 6pm Monday through Saturday. (The few remaining big downtown department stores have some selected evening hours; see below.) Many Loop stores not on State Street are closed Saturday, and on Sunday the Loop—except for a few restaurants, theaters, and cultural attractions—is shut down pretty tight.

SALES TAX You may do a double take after checking the total on your purchase: At 8.75%, the state and local sales tax on nonfood items is one of the steepest in the country.

1 Shopping the Magnificent Mile

The nickname "Magnificent Mile"—hyperbole to some, an understatement to others—refers to the roughly mile-long stretch of North Michigan Avenue between Oak Street and the Chicago River.

Magnificent Mile Shopping

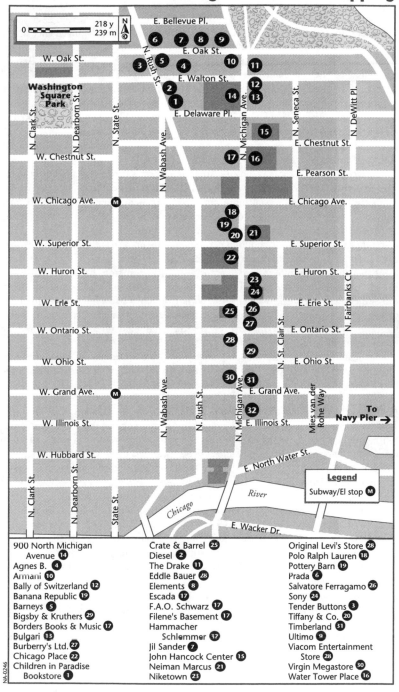

900 North Michigan Avenue **14**
Agnes B. **4**
Armani **10**
Bally of Switzerland **12**
Banana Republic **19**
Barneys **5**
Bigsby & Kruthers **29**
Borders Books & Music **17**
Bulgari **13**
Burberry's Ltd. **27**
Chicago Place **22**
Children in Paradise Bookstore **1**

Crate & Barrel **25**
Diesel **2**
The Drake **11**
Eddie Bauer **28**
Elements **8**
Escada **17**
F.A.O. Schwarz **17**
Filene's Basement **17**
Hammacher Schlemmer **17**
Jil Sander **7**
John Hancock Center **15**
Neiman Marcus **21**
Niketown **23**

Original Levi's Store **28**
Polo Ralph Lauren **18**
Pottery Barn **19**
Prada **6**
Salvatore Ferragamo **26**
Sony **24**
Tender Buttons **3**
Tiffany & Co. **20**
Timberland **31**
Ultimo **9**
Viacom Entertainment Store **28**
Virgin Megastore **30**
Water Tower Place **16**

223

The density of first-rate shopping is, quite simply, unmatched anywhere. Even jaded shoppers from other worldly capitals are delighted at the ease and convenience of the stores concentrated here. Taking into account that tony Oak Street (see below) is just around a corner, the overall area is a little like New York's Fifth Avenue and Beverly Hills' Rodeo Drive rolled into one. Whether your passion is Tiffany diamonds, Chanel suits, or Gap jeans, you'll find it on this stretch of concrete. Window-shoppers, people-watchers, and others who prefer keeping their plastic pristine also will find plenty to amuse them. This is the city's liveliest corridor: The sidewalks are packed in the summer and on weekends with hordes of shoppers strolling up and down the street and pausing to enjoy a mime, a group of Peruvian folk musicians, or one of the other performers who enliven the streetscape.

The face of one of Chicago's most prestigious addresses has been dramatically transformed over the two decades since the first mall—Water Tower Place—went up on the north end of the street. Several more malls and large-scale hotel-retail projects have followed. As the rush for square footage escalated beginning in the late 1980s, many city residents lamented the transformation of the street from a rather intimate and graceful promenade of 1920s buildings to a glitzy canyon of retail theater. Some snobs have attempted (unsuccessfully) to block middle-brow retailers such as Filene's Basement, which recently moved into the former I. Magnin store on North Michigan Avenue, from joining the party, but discounters have found a place on the street, too—often discreetly tucked around the corner or above street level. Eager to get in on the action, national and international retailers have continued to look for front-row locations to squeeze into, and have pretty much gobbled up all of the remaining vacancies on the street.

For the ultimate Mag Mile shopping adventure, start at one end of North Michigan Avenue and try to work your way to the other. In this section are listed some of the best-known shops on the avenue and on nearby side streets.

A NORTH MICHIGAN AVENUE SHOPPER'S STROLL

This shopper's stroll begins at Oak Street at the northern end of the avenue and heads south toward the river. It just hits the highlights; you're sure to find much more to tickle your fancy and tempt your wallet as you meander, from designer landmarks to well-known chain stores. North Michigan Avenue's three vertical malls—each a major shopping destination in its own right—are discussed below under "The Magnificent Malls."

The parade of designer names begins at the intersection of Michigan Avenue and Oak Street, including a couple housed in The Drake hotel, such as the legendary Danish silversmith **Georg Jensen,** 959 N. Michigan Ave. (☎ 312/642-9160), known for outstanding craftsmanship in sterling silver and gold, including earrings, brooches, watches, tie clips, and flatware; and **Chanel,** 935 N. Michigan Ave. (☎ 312/787-5500).

Continuing south, in the next block is **Bally of Switzerland,** 919 N. Michigan Ave. (☎ 312/787-8110), a place for high-quality leather goods, including shoes, attaché cases, handbags, and accessories; and the Chicago store for the famed Italian jeweler **Bulgari,** 909 N. Michigan Ave. (☎ 312/255-1313), which sells timepieces, necklaces, bracelets, rings, and silver gift items. Just across the street is **900 North Michigan,** commonly referred to as the Bloomingdale's building (see "The Magnificent Malls," below).

The plaza of the **John Hancock Center,** 875 N. Michigan Ave., one of the world's tallest buildings, got a handsome makeover a couple of years ago that added retail space to the street level. Anchoring the first floor are **Paul Stuart Clothiers,** purveyor of fine tailored men's clothing and accessories (☎ **312/640-2650**) and the **North Face** (☎ **312/337-7200**), a supplier of apparel and equipment for the outdoor enthusiast. **Bottega Veneta** (☎ **312/664-3220**), Italian purveyor of beautiful leather handbags, scarves, shoes, and jackets, recently moved here from Oak Street. On the Hancock's plaza level is the **Chicago Architecture Foundation Shop and Tour Center** (☎ **312/751-1380**), where you can find just the Wright (Frank Lloyd, that is) gift for the architecture and design buff, and **Aveda** (☎ **312/664-0417**), the skin and hair-care emporium.

Just south of the Hancock Center and across the street is another new development, **Plaza Escada,** 840 N. Michigan Ave. (☎ **312/915-0500**), an elegant four-story building between Chestnut and Pearson streets that houses the country's most comprehensive collection of apparel and accessories from Escada, the German designer firm. The fourth-floor cafe offers a small but excellent lunch and dessert menu with a terrific view over Michigan Avenue. In the same building is **F.A.O. Schwarz** (☎ **312/587-5000**), the ultimate fantasy toy store with a giant stuffed teddy bear peering down on the street. Next door at 830 N. Michigan are **Filene's Basement** (☎ **312/482-8918**) and **Border's Books & Music** (☎ **312/573-0564**).

A spiffy new retail row was completed in 1997 at Chicago and Michigan avenues with roomier digs for **Banana Republic** (☎ **312/642-0020**), a four-story location that includes a home furnishing department; **Tiffany & Co.** (☎ **312/944-7500**), with its signature clock, a spacious main floor like the New York original, and the finest jewels and tabletop accessories, as well as some sterling silver pieces for less than $100; **Pottery Barn** (☎ **312/587-9602**), the tasteful home goods store that makes everything look just so right in their catalog; and the world's largest **Polo Ralph Lauren** (☎ **312/280-1655**), a four-floor faux neoclassical manse.

Across the street on the southeast corner of the Chicago Avenue intersection there's a **Walgreens Drugstore** (☎ **312/664-8686**) for those little things that you forgot to pack. This full-line pharmacy is open 24 hours a day. Next door to Walgreens is **Neiman Marcus,** 737 N. Michigan Ave. (☎ **312/642-5900**).

A bit farther down on the avenue on the same side of the street you'll find the obligatory **Gap,** a two-level store at 679 N. Michigan Ave. (☎ **312/335-1896**), with a **Baby Gap** boutique (there's a second Gap in Water Tower Place).

A few doors down is **Niketown,** 669 N. Michigan Ave. (☎ **312/642-6363**), which rivals many of the museums as one of the most popular tourist attractions in Chicago. Well, it makes sense: Chicago is the ultimate sports town, and Niketown is a virtual shrine to Michael Jordan. (It also has memorabilia from a few other lesser superstars.) Nike has led the way in exploiting the entertainment value of shopping, and the multilevel complex is a feast for the senses.

Despite all of the mega-development on Michigan Avenue, a few innovative developers have recycled a handful of vintage buildings with sensitivity and taste, notably **Sony Gallery of Consumer Electronics,** next door to Niketown at 663 N. Michigan Ave. (☎ **312/943-3334**), where the latest in electronic gizmos are displayed in a hands-on showcase that includes a video "shooting gallery" for live camcorder demos, a 10-foot diorama of Chicago complete with working El train, and an area for portables to check out boom boxes, tape and disc players, telephones, and so forth.

At the intersection of Michigan Avenue and Erie Street is another Chicago retail institution, the appropriately barrel-shaped flagship store of **Crate & Barrel,** 646 N. Michigan Ave. (☎ **312/787-5900**). Just try walking through here without buying something. Countless varieties of glassware, dishes, cookware, and kitchen gadgets for everyday use line the shelves. Crate & Barrel is also a master at nudging you to entertain. The light, airy store is filled with all sorts of special items—fondue sets, unusual vases, serving pieces, and even furniture. The Chicago chain also has a store in the Loop at 101 N. Wabash Ave., at Washington Street (☎ **312/372-0100**) and a new location in Lincoln Park (see below).

In the past a Michigan Avenue shopping stroll might have lost steam at this point, with few stores of note south of Crate & Barrel. However, in recent years a few store openings have made the walk to the river's edge worth it. You'll no doubt see a lot of construction, but you'll have to wait until 2000 for the new **Nordstrom** to open at its long-sought-after location.

A couple of recent additions, both Italian, to this stretch of the Mag Mile share the same address, 645 N. Michigan Ave.: the first Chicago location for the shoemaker **Salvatore Ferragamo** (☎ **312/397-0464**), which also sells men's and women's clothing, and **Ermenegildo Zegna** (☎ **312/587-9660**), designer of finely tailored menswear.

Continuing south you'll find **Burberry's Ltd.,** 633 N. Michigan Ave. (☎ **312/787-2500**). Where else would you go for the classic trench with that conservative chic plaid lining? Burberry's can also furnish your wardrobe with sports coats and other casual wear, such as cashmere sweaters for men and women or even flippy little skirts in the famous plaid.

If there was any doubt that the lines between shopping and entertainment have blurred, check out the **Viacom Entertainment Store,** across the street at 600 N. Michigan Ave. (☎ **312/867-3500**), an interactive two-level extravaganza with a hodgepodge of themed merchandising areas representing the various areas of the media conglomerate, including MTV and Nickelodeon. In the same complex are a couple of giant-size clothing retailers: a woodsy, two-level **Eddie Bauer** (☎ **312/951-5888**), stocked with its traditional casual outdoor wear as well as its dressier AKA line, home furnishings, and outdoor travel accessories; and the **Original Levi's Store** (☎ **312/642-9613**) for jeans in all fades and fabrics, as well as a custom-fit jeans service for women. Also located on the block is **H2O Plus** (☎ **312/397-1243**), a Chicago-based chain stocked full of colorful, yummy-smelling gels and lotions for the bath, body, and face.

Across the street at the corner of Michigan Avenue and Ohio Street is the recently opened flagship store of **Bigsby & Kruthers,** 605 N. Michigan Ave. (☎ **312/397-0430**), the unquestioned leader in Chicago men's apparel for years. Here you can find both top men's designer fashion, sportswear, and accessories, including some of co-owner Joe Silverberg's antique cuff links. Here's something you don't find at many stores on Michigan Avenue: Complimentary parking across the street from the store for customers who get their parking vouchers validated at the store. (The chain now has a total of six locations in the Chicago area, including a branch on the seventh level of Water Tower Place; ☎ **312/944-6955.**)

The retail wing of the **Chicago Marriot,** 540 N. Michigan Ave., got a badly needed makeover recently that hopefully will please aesthetes who often complained about its ugly facade. The redevelopment brought in a few new retailers, including **Virgin Megastore,** (sorry, no telephone number when this book went to press), the big-box of CDs, videos, and all things pop culture.

Nearing the river is a final stop on a shopping stroll that's worth a look. Located in the Tribune Tower, **Hammacher Schlemmer,** 445 N. Michigan Ave. (☎ **312/527-9100**), is a fun gadget shop where you can find everything from a giant backyard chess set to a handheld massager.

THE MAGNIFICENT MALLS

WATER TOWER PLACE   Chicago's first—and still busiest—vertical mall is Water Tower Place, a block-size marble-sheathed building at 835 N. Michigan Ave. (☎ **312/**

440-3165), between East Pearson and East Chestnut streets. The mall's seven floors contain more than 100 separate stores that reportedly account for roughly half of all the retail trade transacted along the Magnificent Mile. The construction in recent years of two more vertical malls on the avenue has not seemed to affect the traffic flow at Water Tower; leases here are still among the most coveted retail real estate in the country. The mall also houses a dozen different cafes and restaurants and a cinema. If you need some guidance, there's always an immaculately dressed woman at the ground-floor information to answer your questions.

For all its fame as both a movie backdrop and retail temple, Water Tower is the most accessible of the developments on the street. You'll find a few surprises, but you'll also see many of the same stores from your mall back home. This is where packs of kids rove from floor to floor. They amuse themselves picking up Bugs Bunny, the Tazmanian Devil, and friends on all manner of merchandise at the **Warner Bros. Studio Store** (second and third floors; ☎ **312/664-9440**), or the familiar faces of Disney World without the rides at the **Disney Store** (fourth floor; ☎ **312/280-1199**).

Kids (and adults) will find distractions of a more intellectual sort at the **WTTW Store of Knowledge** (seventh floor; ☎ **312/642-6826**), named for the local PBS television station and stocked with games, videotapes of PBS documentaries, and other items designed to encourage learning. Another place to while away your day is **Rizzoli Bookstore** (third floor; ☎ **312/642-3500**), a beautiful bookstore with loads of coffee-table books and a large selection of international magazines and music.

900 NORTH MICHIGAN AVENUE   The most upscale of the Magnificent Mile's three vertical malls, 900 North Michigan (often known as the Bloomingdale's building for its most prominent tenant) avoids the tumult of Water Tower Place while still generating the vitality essential to a satisfying shopping spree. In addition to about 75 stores are a few good restaurants and a nice movie multiplex on the lower level. For mall information, call ☎ **312/915-3916.**

The Italian leather goods company **Gucci** (ground floor; ☎ **312/664-5504**) has had a resurgence of late, as its legendary loafer has found a new generation of fans. Thanks to designer Tom Ford, the clothing is about the hippest around, favored by celebrities from Madonna to Alicia Silverstone.

There are plenty of other clothing stores in 900 North to suit a variety of tastes and needs, including **Club Monaco** (sorry, no phone number when this book went to press), with casual chic clothes for men and women; **Cashmere Cashmere** (fourth floor; ☎ **312/337-6558**), featuring cashmere, cashmere, and more cashmere; the **Coach Store** (second floor; ☎ **312/440-1777**), which has some men's apparel and shoes for men and women in addition to handbags, briefcases, wallets, and gloves; **Fogal** (ground floor; ☎ **312/944-7866**), for high-priced legwear and bodysuits for the well-heeled; **J. Crew** (second floor; ☎ **312/751-2739**), the catalog-driven women's and men's clothes and shoes retailer; and **Oilily** (fifth floor; ☎ **312/ 642-1166**), a Dutch children's clothier known for bold and bright colors and patterns for women and children.

For a few gift ideas, try **Montblanc** (ground floor; ☎ **312/943-1200**), the maker of fancy pens and date books; **Glove Me Tender** (fourth floor; ☎ **312/664-4022**), selling all kinds of gloves and hats, too; and the **Museum Shop of the Art Institute of Chicago** (fifth floor; ☎ **312/482-8275**), one of several gift shops the Art Institute has opened in the Chicago area with a good selection of prints, books, tableware, postcards, and the like.

CHICAGO PLACE   Inaugurated in 1991 at 700 N. Michigan Ave., Chicago Place (☎ **312/266-7710**) is the city's newest—and least compelling—vertical shopping mall. Other than **Saks Fifth Avenue** (☎ 312/944-6500) and a three-floor **Ann Taylor** (first, mezzanine, and second floors; ☎ 312/335-0117), there isn't much to write about. One shop you won't find anywhere else is the **Real Nancy Drew** (eighth floor; ☎ 312/944-4282), a gallery named for a Michigan artist (and not the famed fictional sleuth) featuring idiosyncratic and playfully designed pillows, T-shirts, dinnerware, collage-type constructions, and other gift items.

On the eighth floor is a pretty atrium, complete with fountain, skylight, and greenery. If you don't care for the fast-food counters that surround it, you might try buying a sandwich at **Bockwinkel's** (☎ 312/482-9900), a grocery located in the mall's basement, and bringing it up.

CHIC SHOPPING ON NEARBY OAK & WALTON STREETS

If you're truly in the market for some designer duds, you'll have to venture off the Mag Mile and head over to Oak Street. Even if you're not shopping for a new Armani suit, the charming street is great for window-shopping and people-watching. Walton Street, 1 block south of Oak, is now home to some of the city's trendier designers.

OAK STREET   At the northern tip of the Magnificent Mile, where Michigan Avenue ends and Lake Shore Drive begins, is Oak Street, a posh 1-block stretch of exclusive shops. Most of the city's designer boutiques—including **Gianni Versace,** 101 E. Oak St. (☎ 312/337-1111); **Giorgio Armani,** 113 E. Oak St. (☎ 312/751-2244); and **Hermès of Paris,** 110 E. Oak St. (☎ 312/787-8175)—are along this row of converted town houses. Quaint and rarefied with its antique light posts and slate-gray sidewalks, the street is a kind of private domain for its wealthy customers, the kind who shy away from the vastness and middle-class appeal of Michigan Avenue today. It's not uncommon to see stretch limos or spit-clean four-wheel-drive vehicles double parked, couriers running between stores with special orders, and store owners greeting each other on the neighborhoody street. Most of Oak Street is closed on Sunday, except during the holiday season.

Other major designers are the German minimalist **Jil Sander,** 48 E. Oak St. (☎ 312/335-0006), who now sells her new men's line on the store's second floor; **Pratesi Linens Co.,** 67 E. Oak St. (☎ 312/943-8422), for bath and table linens priced for more than most people pay in rent; **St. John,** 51 E. Oak St. (☎ 312/943-1941), for classic women's knits; and **Chacok,** 47 E. Oak St. (☎ 312/943-9391), the first stateside store for the Paris retailer of exotic and colorful women's fashion. A very exclusive retailer of men's tailored clothing and furnishings is **Sulka,** 55 E. Oak St. (☎ 312/951-9500), a longtime presence in Chicago with a private room on the top floor where experts will custom tailor suits.

Without a doubt, the top designer shop in Chicago is **Ultimo,** 114 E. Oak St. (☎ 312/787-0906), which carries both men's and women's clothing and accessories, including such labels as Isaac Mizrahi and John Galliano. One drawback, though, is Ultimo's exclusive atmosphere, not exactly conducive to browsing—unless, of course, you're serious about buying (in which case you'll get doted on by Ultimo's skilled salespeople).

Some of the other shops without international reputations, yet no less interesting, are **Elements,** 102 E. Oak St. (☎ 312/642-6574), an emporium as beautiful as the high-design, high-end gifts, contemporary French furniture, decorative pieces, and jewelry displayed so stylishly here; **Hino & Malee Boutique,** 50 E. Oak St. (☎ 312/664-7475), a store owned by a Chicago-based design team who create women's clothes that are almost architectural in perspective, with no adornment or fuss; and **Sugar Magnolia,** 34 E. Oak St. (☎ 312/944-0885), one of the more affordable shops on the street, full of fun, youthful fashions.

Anchoring the western end of the block, **Barneys New York,** 25 E. Oak St. (☎ 312/587-1700), may have been mired in a bankruptcy battle, but the clothes are still chic in that black, understated way. The shoes are also excellent, and the home accessories are interesting. The store has tripled the size of its antique and decorative home furnishings department, Chelsea Passage (the department even has its own separate entrance at 39 E. Oak).

Across the street, the hot Italian designer **Prada** is building a store that will offer another exclamation point at the end of the block.

WALTON STREET   With precious little room on Oak Street, a handful of hip retailers, including clothing boutiques and furniture makers, have begun colonizing Walton Street, 1 block south of Oak Street.

At the corner of Rush and Walton streets, **Urban Outfitters,** 935 N. Rush St. (☎ 312/640-1919), once described as "the Gap's evil twin," was the first to arrive on the scene, with its trendy Gen X fashion, retro-kitsch home furnishings, books, and gifts gathered in a massive two-level store with a soaring industrial interior. Across the street, the fiercely hip **Diesel,** 923 N. Rush St. (☎ 312/255-0157), promoter of odd and provocative magazine advertising, has racks of body-clinging, club fashions that would make anyone feel like a rock star.

On the other end of the spectrum is the French import **Agnes B.,** 46 E. Walton St. (☎ 312/642-7483), a small gallery-sparse boutique carrying the designer's simple, stylish women's clothing and accessories.

2 More Shopping Neighborhoods

STATE STREET & THE LOOP

Before the Magnificent Mile grew into Chicago's first boulevard of fashion, State Street, "That Great Street," was the center of retailing in Chicago for more than 100 years, ever since Potter Palmer's decision to develop the street and to establish his dry goods business there in 1852. Palmer's original emporium evolved over time into **Marshall Field's,** 111 N. State St., at Randolph Street (☎ 312/781-1000). Field's and **Carson Pirie Scott & Company** (☎ 312/641-7000), the other Chicago hometown department store, which set up shop just a couple of blocks south, at 1 S. State St., at the corner of State and Madison, became rivals, building State Street into a prime shopping district in the process. Both buildings are city landmarks and attractions in themselves. Architecturally speaking, the Louis Sullivan–designed Carson's is the more celebrated of the two; Field's, with its Tiffany-domed and skylit courts, is also eminently worth touring.

By the early seventies, the Magnificent Mile had begun to supplant State Street. Many of the Loop's old department stores—Sears, Roebuck & Co., Montgomery Ward, Goldblatts, Wieboldt—closed their doors in favor of greener pastures in the suburbs. Marshall Field's and Carson Pirie Scott managed to hang on, keeping State Street alive—if barely—until the city took notice in the eighties and began to revive it.

In a controversial move, the city turned State Street into a modified pedestrian mall by closing the street to all traffic but CTA buses on the stretch between Wacker Drive and the Congress Expressway. But with a few exceptions, that only seemed to diminish the bustle of the street, and so in 1996 the city reopened the street to cars and cabs, and added vintage streetlights, planters, and subway entrances designed to restore some of the street's luster. It looks and feels great. Although State Street has not recaptured the glamour of decades past, it has managed to draw loyal customers from the Loop's office towers and from Chicagoans turned off by Michigan Avenue's snob factor.

Shopper's Tip

If the quick change from north to south in the Loop confuses you, keep in mind that in Chicago point zero for the purposes of address numbering is the intersection of State and Madison.

In recent years a number of retailers, particularly in the moderate price range, have opened on State Street, including **Toys Я Us,** 10 S. State St. (☎ **312/857-0667**); **Filene's Basement,** 1 N. State St. (☎ **312/553-1055**); and a new three-story **Old Navy** store, at Washington and State streets.

The southern end of State Street got a boost a few years ago when DePaul University recycled the old Goldblatts department store building for classrooms, offices, and a two-story retail arcade known as the **Music Mart,** State Street and Jackson Boulevard (☎ **312/362-6700**). The idea was a noble one—nearby Wabash Avenue was once a thriving "music row" inhabited by piano manufacturers and other music-related businesses—and the music-themed mall has attracted about 10 music-related businesses, including several piano showrooms, the Chicago Percussion Center, and an outlet of the sheet-music publisher Carl Fischer, one of the only music businesses remaining on Wabash. In keeping with the theme, the Music Mart offers free musical performances at noon during the week, from jazz to piano recitals. There are also several food vendors, and the Blue Note Coffee Bar.

If you're in Chicago between Thanksgiving and New Year's, a visit to Marshall Field's, fronting State Street between Randolph and Washington streets, to see the holiday windows and to have lunch under the Great Tree in the Walnut Room is in keeping with local tradition.

ELSEWHERE IN THE LOOP   In recent years, retailing in the Loop has spread out some, with shops finding homes on LaSalle Street, Chicago's main financial thoroughfare, and on a number of side streets. They tend to cater to businessmen, but some smart retailers are discovering a steady clientele of businesswomen as well.

Maternity Works, 50 E. Randolph St., located on the second floor of the Garland Building (☎ **312/332-0022**), is a maternity store that understands that some pregnant women work. Every man should walk around at one time or another in a custom-made shirt, the only product sold by **Riddle-McIntyre Inc.,** 175 N. Franklin St., between Randolph and Lake streets (☎ **312/782-3317**). You must order a minimum of four shirts at a clip. Around the corner you'll find a downtown location of **Tower Records,** 214 S. Wabash Ave. (☎ **312/663-9660**), always a lot of fun for browsing and listening to what's new.

One of the only independent bookstores in the Loop is **Brent Books & Cards,** which apparently is flourishing with the opening of a second, bigger store near the Chicago River at 316 N. Michigan Ave. The original store is located at 309 W. Washington St., at Franklin Street (☎ **312/364-0126**). The proprietor's father, Stuart Brent, was a fixture on North Michigan Avenue for decades until his old-world bookshop closed in 1996. The new Brent stores carry a broad range of titles, as well as a strong selection of psychiatric books, always a specialty of the elder Brent.

Another hometown fixture still in business all these years is **Carl Fischer of Chicago,** 312 S. Wabash Ave., at Jackson Boulevard (☎ **312/427-6652**), a publisher of every kind of sheet music imaginable.

Whether you love to write or you love the status of owning a fine writing instrument, you'll find a visit to **B. Collins Limited,** 318 S. Dearborn St., between Jackson

Boulevard and Van Buren Street (☎ 800/404-7367 outside Illinois, or 312/431-1888), located in the Monadnock Building, in order. The store specializes in old-fashioned fountain pens and is purportedly the only "full-service" pen (and pencil) store in Chicago. It also carries stationery.

For some made-in-Chicago gifts, browse the colorful paintings, jewelry, ceramics, decorated furniture, textiles, sculptures, and more at the **Gallery 37 Store,** 70 E. Randolph St., between State Street and Michigan Avenue (☎ 312/251-0371; www.gallery37.org). All of the imaginative items on display were made by Chicago young people ages 14 to 21 who are participants in Gallery 37, a not-for-profit arts training program that pairs them with experienced artists to develop skills in the arts. Proceeds from sales benefit the program.

RIVER NORTH

Along with becoming Chicago's primary art gallery district, River North—the area west of the Magnificent Mile and north of the Chicago River—has attracted many interesting shops, concentrated on Wells Street from Kinzie Street to Chicago Avenue. The neighborhood even has a mall of its own—**The Shops at the Mart** (☎ 312/527-7990)—in the Merchandise Mart, at Wells and Kinzie streets. Geared to the working population, the complex also has the usual suspects—Gap, The Limited, and a food court among them.

Not all of the furniture trade in Chicago is confined to the Merchandise Mart. In River North, you'll find **Manifesto,** 755 N. Wells St., at Chicago Avenue (☎ 312/664-0733), a serendipitous furniture store selling high-quality reproductions of architect-designed furniture by such masters as Frank Lloyd Wright and Mies van der Rohe; and **Mig & Tig,** 549 N. Wells St., at Ohio Street (☎ 312/644-8277), a charming furniture and decorative accessories shop.

Stepping into the **Golden Triangle,** 72 W. Hubbard St., at Clark Street (☎ 312/755-1266), you'll find an exotic environment of antique furniture and artifacts from Thailand, Burma, Laos, and China, ranging in price from thousands of dollars to $50 for a small Chinese glazed bowl. **Fly-by-Nite Gallery,** 714 N. Wells St., between Huron and Superior streets (☎ 312/664-8136), is a treasure house for European art deco and art nouveau objets d'art from pottery to jewelry displayed in antique cabinetry.

One of the few clothing shops in the neighborhood is **June Blaker,** 200 W. Superior St., at Wells Street (☎ 312/751-9220), where you'll find severely stylish designer fashions from Europe and Japan.

Creative types will find their imagination running wild with homemade projects at **Paper Source,** 232 W. Chicago Ave., at Franklin Street (☎ 312/337-0798), a three-level store where you won't find anyone talking about a paperless society. Artists, designers, and other paper fetishists can choose among reams of exotic and unusual paper, as well as journals, gift items, handmade wedding albums, and a roomful of fun rubber stamps.

NAVY PIER

A short walk toward the lake will take you to Navy Pier, the city's newest playground. There are a few small shops in the Family Pavilion primarily looking for tourist dollars, including the **Chicago Children's Museum Store** (☎ 312/595-0600), a branch of the local independent **Barbara's Bookstore** (☎ 312/222-0890), and the **Illinois Market Place Store** (☎ 312/832-0010), a one-stop shopping center for Illinois-flavored souvenirs, including goods from the DuSable Museum of African-American History, the Art Institute of Chicago, and both area zoos.

The Maxwell Street Market

For some shopping that offers a bona fide Chicago experience, get up early and wander around the **Maxwell Street Market** (☎ 312/922-3100), on the near South Side a few blocks west of the Field Museum, at Canal and Roosevelt Road. The open-air market, which is open Sunday year-round from 7am to 3pm, has roots stretching back to the 19th century, when it was a bustling market of Jewish merchants in what was then an immigrant gateway. Little Italy and Greektown are nearby, and Jane Addams set up Hull House near here in 1856 to serve the poor and newly arrived.

The market has evolved over the years, and eventually became known for the blues musicians who set up to play impromptu gigs. Several years ago, the market generated a lot of attention when the city and the University of Illinois at Chicago, its neighbor and landlord, decided to reclaim the land and evict the market.

In 1994, the new Maxwell Street Market reopened half a mile east, although fans of the original market say it's not the same, with fewer vendors and a cleaned-up site. For an interesting collection of historical photos and odes to the market of today and yesterday, check out this Web site: www.openair.org/maxwell/newmax.html.

You've got to be a junk lover to appreciate the wares for sale here: tires and auto parts, old TVs, Latin disco tapes, random tools, glassware, thrift-store art, T-shirts, and some fresh produce and vendors cooking tamales and churrascos. You never know what you'll find here, and that's the charm of any flea market. Shoppers tend to be Mexican and African-American families, and a few white artists in the mix looking for found objects for their artwork.

Parking is available at the Soo Terminal, Canal Street and Roosevelt Road, and River West Plaza, Roosevelt Road and Jefferson Street, as well as street parking where you can find it.

LINCOLN PARK

The North Side neighborhood of Lincoln Park has a variety of unique specialty shops that make it easy to browse your way through this leafy, picturesque community. While many of the shops on Michigan Avenue are branches of national chains and offer few surprises, the shops and boutiques in Lincoln Park tend to be locally owned and offer unique and interesting wares. Shops are located on the primary commercial arteries running through the area, including Armitage Avenue, Webster Avenue, Halsted Street, Clark Street, and Lincoln Avenue.

ARMITAGE AVENUE   Armitage Avenue has emerged as a shopping destination in its own right, with a variety of shops and boutiques selling everything from artisan-made apparel to interesting, offbeat gifts. Most of the shops are concentrated between Halsted Street and Clybourn Avenue.

Here you'll find **Urban Gardener,** 1006 W. Armitage Ave. (☎ 773/477-2070), a two-story garden shop in an old Victorian row house with lovely displays of gardening books and tools, topiaries, garden furniture, and other gifts; **Lori's Designer Shoes,** 824 W. Armitage Ave. (☎ 773/281-5655), for a great selection of shoes at great prices; **Findables,** 907 W. Armitage Ave. (☎ 773/348-0674), for exquisite gifts and decorative accessories; and **Tabula Tua,** 1015 W. Armitage Ave. (☎ 773/525-3500), with everything you need to set the perfect table.

A few blocks east of Halsted, but also worth a look is **Art Effect,** 651 W. Armitage Ave. (☎ 312/664-0997), for women's clothing and accessories and home furnishings with a creative flair.

WEBSTER AVENUE   Webster Avenue, from Halsted to Clybourn, has also emerged as a quiet street populated with a few artsy shops, notably **Krivoy,** 1145 W. Webster Ave., between Clifton and Racine streets (☎ 773/248-1466), a friendly neighborhood shop where the young owner has expanded from her beginnings as a hat maker to a designer of fanciful slippers and clothing for women (and girls) with an eclectic sensibility. The owner will design just about anything for you. One recent obsession is fashioning skirts and jackets out of old Japanese kimonos. Also for sale are a smattering of home furnishings and accessories.

One of the newer additions to the area is the **Chopping Block,** 1324 W. Webster Ave., at Wayne Street (☎ 773/472-6700), a charming little shop in an old brick house featuring all things culinary. The chef-owner has blended everything from the latest professional cookware, accessories, and cooking classes led by guest chefs ($35 to $45 a session) to a fun collection of cooking collectibles and antiques (her parents are in the antique trade).

CLYBOURN CORRIDOR   If you stroll west on either Armitage or Webster, you'll eventually hit the Clybourn Corridor, an industrial area skirting Lincoln Park that has been dramatically redeveloped. You'll find a series of suburban-style shopping centers, but there is also a number of interesting shops in some of the rehabbed buildings, including **A. Arsenault Designer Cooperative** (formerly known as Made to Fit), 2229 N. Clybourn Ave., at Webster Avenue (☎ 773/975-1914), a cooperative of about 16 independent clothing designers, as well as a few milliners, jewelry makers, and even furniture designers, who present their collections for sale or take custom orders. The shop is named for its owner, the chair of the fashion design department at the School of the Art Institute fashion design professor.

A bunch of national chains is grouped near Clybourn's congested intersection with North Avenue, including the **Gap, Best Buy, Erehwon Mountain Outfitter,** the yuppie garden store **Smith and Hawken,** and a new full-fledged **Crate & Barrel,** 850 W. North Ave. (☎ 312/573-9800), which opened last summer to become the company's largest in the city. It even has a third-floor cafe.

LAKEVIEW & OTHER NORTH SIDE NEIGHBORHOODS

Shoppers will find elements of both prosperous Lincoln Park and alternativish Wicker Park when they're wandering along Lakeview's principal commercial avenues.

BELMONT AVENUE & CLARK STREET   Radiating from the intersection of Belmont Avenue and Clark Street is a string of shops catering to punkish kids on tour from their homes in the 'burbs, side by side with some fairly upscale designer boutiques.

One constant in the ever-changing youth culture has been the **Alley,** 858 W. Belmont Ave., at Clark Street (☎ 773/525-3180), an "alternative shopping complex" selling everything from plaster gargoyles to racks of leather jackets. It has separate shops specializing in condoms, cigars, and bondage wear.

You can find all the latest men's (and some women's) fashion styles—from names like Fresh Jive, Fuct, Diesel, and Mossimo—under the same roof at the multiroom scene housing the **Aero** and **Untitled shops,** 2701 N. Clark St. (☎ 773/404-9225). Whether you're into tight, fitted fashion or the layered, droopy pants look (this store has got to have the world's largest pants), it's here.

HALSTED STREET   North of Belmont toward Addison Street, Halsted Street takes on a funky, youthful attitude and is dotted with several fun vintage and used clothing stores, as well as a few shops selling clothing and accessories geared to the largely gay residents and visitors to the neighborhood. You can find all kinds of souvenirs emblazoned with the gay pride flag, greeting cards, and other campy items at **Gay Mart,** 3457 N. Halsted St. (☎ 773/929-4272). Clubby gay men eager to show off their hard work in the gym can find the right apparel at the body-conscious clothing store **Hardwear,** 3243 N. Broadway (☎ 773/296-0801).

SOUTHPORT AVENUE   Another strip worth a stroll is the gentrifying retail row along Southport Avenue, a few blocks west of Wrigley Field. With the Music Box Theater at 3733 N. Southport, north of Addison Street, as its anchor, the area has an interesting mix of quirky and artsy merchants and restaurateurs. Two flight attendants have brought back souvenirs from their European travels to sell in their shop, **P.O.S.H.,** 3729 N. Southport Ave., between Waveland Avenue and Grace Street (☎ 773/529-7674): seconds and reproductions from continental hotels and resorts that make for fun, quirky tableware. If you love all things retro, you'll have no trouble finding something to tempt your wallet here. Next door, the **Phylis Rascht Gallery** displays an interesting theme with each new show of artwork, furniture, and collectibles.

LINCOLN SQUARE   A little farther north on Lincoln Avenue between Leland and Lawrence avenues is the old German neighborhood of Lincoln Square. Here you'll find the old-fashioned (dating to 1875) **Merz Apothecary,** 4716 N. Lincoln Ave., between Wilson and Lawrence avenues (☎ 773/989-0900), an olfactory overload with everything from soap to the latest herbal remedy.

WICKER PARK/BUCKTOWN

Note: For a map of the shops in this area, see the Wicker Park/Bucktown section in chapter 6.

The go-go gentrification of the Wicker Park/Bucktown area has been followed by not only a rash of restaurants but retailers with an artsy bent reflecting the neighborhood's bohemian spirit. Mixed in with old neighborhood businesses, such as discount furniture stores and religious icon purveyors, is a proliferation of antique furniture shops and eclectic galleries and gift emporiums.

Whizbang, 1959 W. Cortland Ave., at Damen Avenue (☎ 773/292-9602), is a theatrical store that specializes in secondhand furniture and invites customers to choose from a variety of unusual, funky fabrics for upholstered slipcovers, curtains, window coverings, and other goods. Nearby is **Oh Boy!,** 2060 N. Damen Ave., near Armitage Avenue (☎ 773/772-0101), a shop offering a visually stimulating mix of artist-made folk-art pieces mixed in with antique farm furniture and other collectibles.

The Latino layer of the evolving multicultural neighborhood is reflected in **Collage,** 1520 N. Milwaukee Ave. (☎ 773/252-2562), a Puerto Rican–owned shop with a colorful mix of masks, Day of the Dead items, and other folk-art handicrafts by both local and international artists from Central and South America, the Caribbean, and Africa.

The globe-trotting proprietor of artifact-laden **Cielo Vivo,** 1866 N. Damen Ave. (☎ 773/276-8012), has an eye for antique Asian ceramics, Middle Eastern bronzes, and old African pottery, as well as art books, rugs, and silver jewelry, while the friendly modern-day Marco Polos at **Pagoda Red,** 1714 N. Damen Ave., second floor (☎ 773/235-1188), have imported beautiful (and expensive) antique furniture and art objects, everything from Chinese wedding cabinets to hand-painted Tibetan cabinets.

A few clothing boutiques have opened, including the cool little boutique **Phoebe 45,** 1643 N. Damen Ave. (☎ 773/862-4523), specializing in women's and men's wear by young designers from Chicago, New York City, and elsewhere; **Le Garage,** 1649 N. Damen Ave. (☎ 773/278-2234), for comfortably worn "vintage" jeans and the latest from Diesel and Mossimo; and the Victorian fantasia of **Pentimento,** 1629 N. Milwaukee Ave. (☎ 773/227-0576), which offers artisan-made clothing (including a bridal shop), home furnishings, and jewelry.

And what would a neighborhood be without a bookstore and a record store? Wicker Park offers its own interpretations. The source for every kind of obscure, alternative, and possibly offensive comic, magazine, and self-published 'zine is **Quimby's,** 1854 N. Damen Ave. (☎ 773/342-0910), which recently moved to a new location closer to the action. The latest music percolating up from the subculture surfaces at **The Quaker Goes Deaf,** 1937 W. North Ave. (☎ 773/252-9334), a packed-to-the-rafters record store where you can listen to both new and used CDs for sale in categories spanning ambient to country-and-western.

HYDE PARK

Commercial Hyde Park is centered on 53rd Street close to the lakefront, although the other numbered streets also house shops and restaurants. Considering its status as home of the University of Chicago, it's no wonder that Hyde Park is chockful of well-stocked bookstores. **O'Gara & Wilson, Ltd.,** 1448 E. 57th St. (☎ 773/363-0993), is a rumpled storefront of a bookseller that might easily have migrated from a back street in London or Cardiff; it has good used and rare books and old titles by the hopperful. Here in Hyde Park you'll also find **57th Street Books,** 1301 E. 57th St. (☎ 773/684-1300), known especially for its children's books. The shop also has a small working fireplace.

Harper Court, on Harper Avenue between 52nd and 53rd streets, today is an arts-oriented mall with about 20 shops and two restaurants. At one time it housed artists, displaced when the ramshackle wood houses in which they were living (built originally as souvenir and popcorn stands for the Columbian Exposition) were torn down.

Although Hyde Park's artist colony once harbored such luminaries as Carl Sandburg, Theodore Dreiser, Sherwood Anderson, Vachel Lindsay, and Edgar Lee Masters, today only a single artist-in-residence remains. But the Harper Court Foundation is expanding its cultural programs, and the old art colony is saluted each year at the popular **57th Street Art Fair** (call ☎ 773/493-3247 for details), a weekend outdoor art show scheduled in early June.

One eye-catching shop to note is **Window to Africa,** 5210 S. Harper Ave. (☎ 773/955-7742), which sells masks, fabrics, wood carvings, baskets, drums, and other artifacts imported from Africa. The store also carries a line of contemporary urban wear and hosts occasional fashion shows featuring African designs and fabrics.

3 Shopping A to Z

As you might expect, Chicago has shops selling just about anything you could want or need, be it functional or ornamental, whimsical or exotic. The following list only scratches the surface, but it will give you an idea of the range of merchandise available. Of course, many of the categories, such as apparel and gifts, have been covered in depth earlier in the chapter.

ANTIQUES

The greatest concentration of antique businesses, from packed-to-the-rafters malls to idiosyncratic individual shops, can be found on Belmont Avenue west of Southport, or stretching north and south of Belmont along intersecting Lincoln Avenue. Here are a few others.

Chicago Riverfront Antique Mart. 2929 N. Western Ave. (between Diversey Pkwy. and Belmont Ave.). ☎ 773/252-2500.

Four floors of antiques, from a basement of collectibles to books to furniture.

Jay Robert's Antique Warehouse. 149 W. Kinzie St. (at LaSalle Dr.). ☎ 312/222-0167.

This mammoth space boasts 60,000 square feet of fine furniture, as well as fireplaces, stained glass, and an impressive selection of antique clocks.

Jazzé Junque. 3831 N. Lincoln Ave. (between Addison St. and Irving Park Rd.). ☎ 773/472-1500.

Yes, there is a store for the devoted cookie jar collector. Who knew? The proprietor also stocks assorted kitsch-en stuff.

Modern Times. 1538 N. Milwaukee Ave. (between Division St. and North Ave.). ☎ 773/772-8871.

A few antique shops have opened to furnish the wave of lofts that has washed over trendy Wicker Park. This one specializes in the major designers of home furnishings from the 1930s to the 1960s, plus some jewelry and clothing.

Salvage One. 1524 S. Sangamon St. (between Halsted St. and Racine Ave.). ☎ 312/733-0098.

Everything and the kitchen sink is for sale at this sprawling source for the home handyperson: doors, mantels, tubs, stained glass, and light fixtures.

Wrigleyville Antique Mall. 3336 N. Clark St. (between Belmont Ave. and Addison St.). ☎ 773/868-0285. www.ANTKonline.com.

Spread over two spacious floors, the collectibles and antiques with a decidedly modern edge—gathered by 65 dealers—can be on the pricey side, but they're so fun and funky you'll want them anyway. Check out the vintage Chicago case.

ART

Those in search of something artsy should stroll around River North, just wandering in and out of the horde of galleries. The Wicker Park/Bucktown neighborhood, the heart of which is at the intersection of Milwaukee, North, and Damen avenues, has become something of an artists' colony, as well. Below are some recommended galleries in those areas and others.

Carl Hammer Gallery. 200 W. Superior St. (at Wells St.). ☎ 312/266-8512. Fax 312/266-8510.

Carl Hammer is the city's leading authority on "outsider" or self-taught artists. The gallery also represents contemporary and selected historical master works.

Fabrile Gallery. 224 S. Michigan Ave. (at Jackson Blvd.). ☎ 312/427-1510.

Located across the street from the Art Institute of Chicago, this gallery specializes in decorative art glass and carries works from many major artists and studios. It also has a collection of designer jewelry.

Inside Art. 1651 W. North Ave. (between Ashland and Damen aves.). ☎ 773/772-4416.

This is a small gallery with a big mission: encouraging young art collectors with lectures and field trips to art studios and exhibiting artwork that they can afford to buy (most everything is under $1,000).

Kelmscott Gallery. 4611 N. Lincoln Ave. (between Wilson and Lawrence aves.). ☎ 773/784-2559.

The ornate glazed terra-cotta facade of the former Krause Music Store designed by Louis Sullivan is appropriately occupied today by the Kelmscott Gallery, specialists in drawings and manuscripts of Frank Lloyd Wright and the Prairie School of architecture. The gallery also trades in furniture, jewelry, photography, and English and American arts and crafts, and presents several exhibitions each year that are open to the public.

Palette & Chisel Academy of Fine Arts. 1012 N. Dearborn Pkwy. (at Oak St.). ☎ 312/642-4400.

The Palette & Chisel is a nonprofit cooperative of painters and sculptors, who beginning in 1921 pooled their funds to purchase this circa 1870s mansion, one of the first buildings erected after the Chicago Fire. About 240 professional artists now use the facilities to paint and to sculpt—and to exhibit work in their own galleries and private studio areas. Call for hours.

Portia Gallery. 1702 N. Damen Ave. (between North and Armitage aves.). ☎ 773/862-1700.

This Bucktown gallery specializes in high-end sculptural glass pieces—blown and cast sculptures, decorative vases, goblets, lamps, and centerpieces—designed by established and emerging Venetian and American artists. Glass-making demonstrations are also held from time to time.

Steve Starr Studios. 2779 N. Lincoln Ave. (at Diversey Pkwy.). ☎ 773/525-6530.

Some of the city's finest art deco items are sold at this tiny shop that marked its 30th anniversary in 1997. More than 700 art deco frames filled with Hollywood stars from Starr's personal collection line the walls.

Tobai. 320 N. Dearborn Ave., in the Westin River North Hotel. ☎ 312/661-0394.

Tobai contains an extensive collection of Japanese prints and also features classic Korean temple paintings and works by contemporary Chinese artists.

BOOKS

Abraham Lincoln Book Shop. 357 W. Chicago Ave. (between Orleans and Sedgwick sts.). ☎ 312/944-3085.

This bookstore is truly the land of Lincoln, with one of the country's most outstanding collections of Lincolniana, from rare and antique books about the 16th president to collectible signatures, letters, and other documents illuminating the lives of other U.S. presidents and historical figures. The shop carries new historical and academic works, too.

Afrocentric Bookstore. 333 S. State St. (at Jackson Blvd.). ☎ 312/939-1956.

Located in the DePaul Music Mart, this bookstore has grown rapidly from its modest start behind a beauty supply business. It now houses more than 10,000 titles focused on African and African-American life, as well as magazines, greeting cards, and other gift items. The store also hosts visits from writers, including Maya Angelou, Johnnie Cochran, and Gen. Colin Powell.

Barbara's Bookstore. 1350 N. Wells St. (between Division St. and North Ave.). ☎ **312/642-5044.**

A haven for small, independent press titles, as well as extensive selections of everything current. In addition, it has a well-stocked children's section, with sitting areas for the tots to peruse the books. If you enjoy author readings, call the store to see if your visit coincides with one of your favorite writers. Two other branches are a small tourist-targeted shop at Navy Pier, 700 E. Grand Ave. (☎ **312/222-0890**), and a shop in Oak Park at 1100 Lake St. (☎ **708/848-9140**).

Barnes & Noble Booksellers. 1130 N. State St. (at Elm St.). No telephone number assigned at press time.

Barnes & Noble opened its first downtown store in the heart of the Gold Coast in November 1998. The two-level store comes complete with a cafe, in case you get the munchies while perusing the miles of books. The store also hosts readings, book groups, and other special events. There's another store in Lincoln Park, at 659 W. Diversey Ave., 1 block west of Clark Street (☎ **773/871-9004**).

Borders Books & Music. 830 N. Michigan Ave. (at Pearson St.). ☎ **312/573-0564.**

You couldn't ask for a better location, right across from Water Tower Place. This place is like a mini-department store, with books, magazines, CDs, and computer software spread over four floors and a cafe with a view overlooking the Mag Mile. There are also author readings, book signings, and other special events. Borders has another location in Lincoln Park at 2817 N. Clark St., at Diversey Avenue (☎ **773/935-3909).**

Children in Paradise Bookstore. 909 N. Rush St. (between Delaware Place and Walton St.). ☎ **312/951-5437.**

This is Chicago's largest children's bookstore, with storytelling hours.

Powell's Bookstore. 828 S. Wabash Ave. (between 8th and 9th sts.). ☎ **312/341-0748.**

Used textbooks, dog-eared paperbacks, hardcover classics, and former best-sellers fill the shelves. There are also outlets in Lakeview at 2850 N. Lincoln Ave. (☎ **773/248-1444**) and Hyde Park at 1501 E. 57th St. (☎ **773/955-7780**).

Prairie Avenue Bookshop. 418 S. Wabash Ave. (between Congress Pkwy. and Van Buren St.). ☎ **312/922-8311.**

This South Loop store does Chicago's architectural tradition proud with the city's finest stock of architecture, design, and technical books.

The Savvy Traveller. 310 S. Michigan Ave. (between Van Buren St. and Jackson Blvd.). ☎ **312/913-9800.**

Smart travelers buy their Frommer's guides here. This Loop specialty bookstore, in fact, carries just about everything a traveler might need, from maps to rain gear to games to keep the kids occupied on long car trips.

Seminary Co-op Bookstore. 5757 S. University Ave. (between 57th and 58th sts.). ☎ **773/752-4381.**

A classic campus bookstore located near the University of Chicago, this shop has extensive philosophy and theology sections and is one of the premier academic book-stores in the country.

The Stars Our Destination. 1021 W. Belmont Ave. (between Racine Ave. and Clark St.). ☎ **773/871-2722.**

Calling all sci-fi, fantasy, and horror fanatics in search of new or used books.

Transitions Bookplace and Café. 1000 W. North Ave. (at Sheffield Ave.). ☎ **312/951-READ.**

If you're seeking, you may find it here. This New Age bookstore, appropriately located next door to Whole Foods, offers more than 30,000 titles on personal growth, including sections on Eastern and Western spirituality, alternative healing, psychology, and creativity.

Unabridged Books. 3251 N. Broadway (between Belmont Ave. and Addison St.). ☎ **773/883-9119.**

A quintessential neighborhood bookseller with strong sections in travel, film, sci-fi, and gay and lesbian literature. Yellow tags hanging from the shelves penned with smartly written reviews indicate staff favorites. The shop hosts frequent author readings.

Women & Children First. 5233 N. Clark St. (between Foster and Bryn Mawr aves.). ☎ **773/769-9299.**

This feminist and children's bookstore holds the best selection in the city of titles for, by, and about women. Co-owner Linda Bubon holds a children's storybook hour every Wednesday at 10:30am; several book groups meet regularly as well, including one for mothers and daughters. The store also hosts frequent readings by the likes of Gloria Steinem, Amy Tan, Alice Walker, and Naomi Wolf.

BUTTONS

Renaissance Buttons. 826 W. Armitage Ave. (between Sheffield Ave. and Halsted St.). ☎ **773/883-9508.**

Never given much thought to buttons? After looking at some of the thousands of buttons—both antique and contemporary hand crafted—this shop has to offer, you'll look at these functional objects in a whole new way. The shop carries specialty button jewelry made from antique and modern buttons.

Tender Buttons. 946 N. Rush St. (at Oak St.). ☎ **312/337-7033.**

Another button shop with a museumlike decor and upscale address, this shop carries men's cufflinks and studs, too.

CANDY & CHOCOLATES

FAO Schweetz. Water Tower Place, 2nd floor, 835 N. Michigan Ave. ☎ **312/787-3773.**

The toy merchant has no shame in the lengths it'll go to tempt children (and adults). Just like the toy store, this new candy shop is busy and theatrical (witness the giant licorice ball), offering every kind of candy, from PEZ to Dennis Rodman lollypops to 1-pound bricks of chocolate.

Godiva Chocolatier. Water Tower Place, 3rd floor, 835 N. Michigan Ave. ☎ **312/280-1133.**

Inhaling is free and calorie-free. The store offers the famed chocolate in individual truffles or in a variety of gift boxes and baskets. The complimentary cups of coffee are heavenly, too (crème brûlée was the flavor of the day when I stopped by).

Vivante Chocolatier. 1056 W. Webster Ave. (between Racine and Sheffield aves.). ☎ **773/549-0123.**

All of the chocolate is sculpted at this Lincoln Park shop and cafe, and the staff can custom-design a piece with just about any form, from a simple monogram to the likeness of your cat. Try a mocha shake, too.

CRAFTS

Alaska Shop. 104 E. Oak St. (between Michigan Ave. and Rush St.). ☎ **312/943-3393.**

Somewhat offbeat, given its fashion boutique neighbors, is the Alaska Shop, a showcase for Alaskan, Canadian, and Siberian Inuit arts and crafts.

Landmark of Andersonville. 5301 N. Clark St. (between Foster and Bryn Mawr aves.). ☎ **773/728-5301.**

A cooperative of shops on three floors, all individually owned businesses with a broad range of products—lamps, dollhouses, frames, paper supplies, toys, antiques, handcrafts, and women's clothes—and services, from knitting classes to photo restoration.

Lill Street Gallery. 1021 W. Lill St. ☎ **773/477-6185.**

Located in Lincoln Park just 3 blocks north of Fullerton, at Sheffield, is the Midwest's largest ceramics center, housing private and group studios, a gallery (with rotating exhibits), a retail store, and six classrooms. Among the wares for sale is a large selection of high-quality handcrafted artwork for home or office.

To Life! 224 S. Michigan Ave. (between Adams St. and Jackson Blvd.). ☎ **312/362-0255.**

A gallery of fine crafts, including marionettes and puppets, music boxes, handmade jewelry, ceramic sculptures, wood puzzles, toys, and games. Another branch is at 333 N. Michigan Ave. (☎ **312/541-1951**), and the owners have a new gallery of contemporary crafts called **Arts & Artisans** at 108 S. Michigan Ave. (☎ **312/641-0088**).

DEPARTMENT STORES

Bloomingdale's. 900 N. Michigan Ave. (at Walton St.). ☎ **312/440-4460.**

The first Midwestern branch of the famed New York department store, Bloomingdale's is on par in terms of size and selection with Marshall Field's Water Tower store. Among its special sections is the one for its souveniresque Bloomingdale's logo merchandise.

Carson Pirie Scott & Company. 1 S. State St. (at Madison St.). ☎ **312/641-7000.**

Carson's still appeals primarily to working- and middle-class shoppers. But this venerable Chicago institution that was almost wiped out by the Chicago Fire has made a recent bid to capture the corporate, if not the carriage, trade. Carson's has added a number of more upscale apparel lines, plus a trendy housewares department, to appeal to the moneyed crowd that works in the Loop.

Lord & Taylor. Water Tower Place, 835 N. Michigan Ave. ☎ **312/787-7400.**

Lord & Taylor, one of two large department stores in Water Tower Place (see Marshall Field's, below), carries about what you'd expect: women's, men's, and children's clothing, cosmetics, and accessories. Its star department is most definitely shoes; the selection is fairly broad, and something's usually on sale.

Marshall Field's. 111 N. State St. (at Randolph St.). ☎ **312/781-1000.** Water Tower Place, 835 N. Michigan Ave. (at Pearson St.). ☎ **312/335-7700.**

Although it's now owned by a Minneapolis company, Marshall Field's is still the hometown store in the minds of most Chicagoans. Spread over 73 acres of floor space, with 450 departments, Marshall Field's flagship store covering an entire block on State Street is second in size only to Macy's in New York City. Within this overwhelming space, shoppers will find areas unusual for today's homogeneous department stores, such as the Victorian antique jewelry department, an antiquarian bookshop, and a gallery of antique furniture reproductions. Store craftspeople are still on hand to fix antique clocks, repair jewelry, and restore old paintings. A basement marketplace offers gourmet goodies, including Field's renowned Frango mints, a succulent chocolate candy that comes in a rainbow of flavors. Go for the original in the green box.

Field's breadth is what makes the store impressive; shoppers can find a rainbow of turtlenecks for $12 or $15 each, a floor or so away from the 28 Shop, Field's homage to designer fashion, from the exquisite luxury of Yves Saint Laurent to the masterful artistry of Issey Miyake.

The Water Tower store—the mall's primary anchor—is a scaled-down but respectable version of the State Street store. Its eight floors are actually much more manageable than the enormous flagship, and its merchandise selection is still vast. Although this branch tends to focus on the more expensive brands, shoppers at this location still can find outfits for less than $100 or more than $2,000.

Neiman Marcus. 737 N. Michigan Ave. (between Superior St. and Chicago Ave.). ☎ **312/ 642-5900.**

Your mouth may water at the thought of the Chanels, the Karl Lagerfelds, the Donna Karans, and the Calvin Kleins, all so skillfully merchandised on Neiman Marcus's selling floors. Yes, you'll pay top dollar for such designer names here—the store does, after all, need to live up to its Needless Mark-up moniker—but Neiman's has a broader price range than many of its critics care to admit. It also has some mighty good sales. The four-story store, a beautiful environment in its own right, also sells cosmetics, shoes, furs, fine and fashion jewelry, and men's and children's wear. On the top floor is a fun gourmet food department as well as a pretty home accessories area. Neiman's has two restaurants: one relaxed, the other a little more formal.

Saks Fifth Avenue. Chicago Place, 700 N. Michigan Ave. (at Superior St.). ☎ **312/ 944-6500.**

Saks Fifth Avenue may be best known for its designer collections—Valentino, Chloe, and Giorgio Armani, to name a few—but the store also does a swell job of buying more casual and less expensive merchandise. Check out, for example, Saks's own "Real Clothes" or "The Works" women's lines. Plus the store has a very good large-size women's apparel department, as well as jewelry, accessories, and men's and children's clothes. Don't forget to make a visit to the cosmetics department, where Saks is known in particular for its varied selection of fragrances.

FASHION

The stores listed in this section are only a sampling of those not mentioned above in the main shopping districts.

CHILDREN'S

Besides such well-known chains as Benetton and Gap Kids, Chicago is well supplied with specialty shops offering children's wear.

All Our Children. 2217 N. Halsted St. (between Webster and Fullerton aves.). ☎ **773/ 327-1868.**

This small and friendly boutique carries darling accessories and clothes from newborn sizes to size 10.

Gymboree. Water Tower Place, 6th floor, 835 N. Michigan Ave. ☎ **312/649-9074.**

Adorable, cuddly clothes in charming prints for babies and toddlers.

Madison and Friends. 11 E. Oak St. (at Rush St.). ☎ **312/642-6403.**

Cute, hip clothes, all reasonably priced.

The Second Child. 954 W. Armitage Ave. (at Sheffield Ave.). ☎ **773/883-0880.**

A resale boutique offering quality clothing for a fraction of the price, this store also carries maternity clothes, furniture, equipment, and toys.

MEN'S

Alfred Dunhill. Water Tower Place, 2nd floor, 835 N. Michigan Ave. ☎ **312/467-4455.**

Pipes, humidors, and men's apparel.

Brooks Brothers. 209 S. LaSalle St. (at Adams St.). ☎ **312/263-0100.**

Businessmen of a certain set would probably go naked were it not for the existence of Brooks Brothers, where conservative never goes out of style. This branch is located in the historic Rookery Building in the thick of the financial district.

Rochester Big & Tall. 840 N. Michigan Ave. (entrance on Chestnut St.). ☎ **312/337-8877.**

The name pretty much says it all—a menswear store for big guys.

WOMEN'S

Betsey Johnson. 72 E. Oak St. (between Michigan Ave. and Rush St.). ☎ **312/664-5901.**

Youthful, exuberant clothing for funky young women.

Cynthia Rowley. 808 W. Armitage Ave. (at Halsted St.). ☎ **773/528-6160.**

The Chicago native and new star of the New York fashion world has brought home a boutique filled with her cute little dresses and other designs.

Episode. 107 E. Oak St. (between Michigan Ave. and Rush St.). ☎ **312/266-9760.**

Catering to professional women who prefer to dress with a little flair, this shop recently relocated to Oak Street.

Nicole Miller. 63 E. Oak St. (between Michigan Ave. and Rush St.). ☎ **312/664-3532.**

Women's clothes and men's ties in those wacky pop art prints, plus scores of great little dresses.

A Pea in the Pod. 46 E. Oak St. (between Michigan Ave. and Rush St.). ☎ **312/944-3080.**

Maternity clothes that won't make you feel silly when you're pregnant.

Toshiro. 3309 N. Clark St. (between Belmont Ave. and Addison St.). ☎ **773/248-1487.**

Housed in an artfully appointed boutique spread over two floors is women's clothing that's simple and sophisticated, from suits to funky stuff for the young set.

MEN'S & WOMEN'S

Alacala's Western Wear. 1733 W. Chicago Ave. (between Ashland and Damen aves.). ☎ **312/226-0152.**

One-stop shopping for boots (10,000 in stock), hats, jeans, and other cowboy regalia.

Blake. 2448 N. Lincoln Ave. (near Fullerton and Lincoln aves.). ☎ **773/477-3364.**

This DePaul area boutique maintains an exclusive (some say snobby) air, beginning with the buzzer on the door and continuing until you are admitted to peruse the spare racks of fashion-forward clothing designs for women and men, featuring such Chicago area exclusives as Dries Van Noten and Martin Margiela.

Fitigues. 939 N. Rush St. (between Oak and Walton sts.). ☎ **312/943-8676.**

These cute, comfortable clothes in waffle-knit cotton are favored by the Gold Coast's young mothers. The home-grown store also carries denim and some men's and children's things. There's another location in Lincoln Park at 2130 N. Halsted St. (☎ **773/404-9696**) and an outlet store at 1535 N. Dayton St. (☎ **312/255-0095**).

Robave. 3270 N. Clark St. (at School St.). ☎ **773/665-8600.**

The designer-owners fill their boutique with strong, fashion-forward clothing for women and men.

RESALE

Brown Elephant Resale Shop. 3651 N. Halsted St. (between Addison St. and Irving Park Rd.). ☎ **773/549-5943.**

The city's biggest resale shop, the Brown Elephant takes donations of clothes, furniture, books, records, electronics, and kitchenware, and sells them to raise money for the Howard Brown Health Center, a medical clinic specializing in the treatment of AIDS and other health concerns of gay men and lesbians.

Daisy Shop. 67 E. Oak St., 6th floor (between Michigan Ave. and Rush St.). ☎ **312/943-8880.**

Wealthy Gold Coast matrons cast off their couture and jewelry in this discreetly located shop where you can pick up last season's "gently worn" fashions with big savings.

VINTAGE

You can do some serious thrifting in a short tour around the Lakeview neighborhood, starting on Halsted Street at Addison Street and working your way south to Belmont Avenue. Then head west past the El tracks and proceed north on Clark Street. Here are a few highlights:

Beatnix. 3400 N. Halsted St. (at Roscoe St.). ☎ **773/281-6933.**

A solid vintage store with both men's and women's apparel, both day-to-day and dress-up, including a huge selection of old tuxes.

Flashy Trash. 3524 N. Halsted St. (between Belmont Ave. and Addison St.). ☎ **773/327-6900.**

One of the best vintage stores around, Flashy Trash mixes used and new clothing, from Todd Oldham jeans to used tuxes to dress-up accessories such as feather boas, wigs, and jewelry. Naturally, Halloween is a busy time here, but the clubby sales clerks are always in one costume or another.

Hollywood Mirror. 812 W. Belmont Ave. (at Clark St.). Fax **773/665-8790.**

Two floors of fun recycled stuff, including lots of blue jeans on the first floor and fifties furniture and lamps in the basement.

Ragstock. 812 W. Belmont Ave., enter in the alley (at Clark St.). ☎ **773/868-9263.**

Located above Hollywood Mirror, this branch of the Minneapolis-based thrift store chain has everything for the slacker on the go at reasonable prices, and mixes in new stuff, too.

MAPS & TRAVEL GEAR

Rand McNally Map and Travel Store. 444 N. Michigan Ave. (at Illinois St.). ☎ **312/321-1751.**

Map lovers will be satiated. The store also stocks, among its 10,000-item inventory, travel guides, videotapes, globes, and travel supplies and gift items from around the world.

MUSIC

Dr. Wax. 2523 N. Clark St. (between Fullerton and Wrightwood aves.). ☎ **773/549-3377.**

New and used LPs, tapes, and CDs, with a first-rate selection of jazz and classical music. There's a Hyde Park store in Harper Court (☎ **773/493-8696**).

Evil Clown. 3418 N. Halsted St. (between Belmont Ave. and Addison St.). ☎ **773/472-4761.**

Flip through one of the trendy magazines provided by this alternative music shop while you listen to any disk in the racks on one of the store's CD players.

Gramaphone Records. 2663 N. Clark St. (between Diversey and Wrightwood aves.). ☎ **773/472-3683.**

This is where deejays pick up the latest dance records (yes, records, as in vinyl) to spin in clubland.

Hear Music. 932 N. Rush St. (at Walton St.). ☎ **312/951-0242.**

The personality of this store (one of a small chain) is one of a hip friend who is always pointing you to a cool new singer or record. The selection is limited, but some of the pop, folk, jazz, and classical CDs are organized in categories such as the "dark side of love" and "backyard barbecue" to help shoppers find music that suits their mood.

Jazz Record Mart. 444 N. Wabash Ave. (at Grand Ave.). ☎ **312/222-1467.**

You can uncover some super finds in recycled jazz records (also big band, bebop, Latin, and so on) at the Jazz Record Mart, which also stocks a full line of new jazz and blues CDs, even 78s and singles dating to the 1920s. The store, home to the Delmark Records label, is also host to jazz performances on many Saturdays at 1pm.

PAPER & STATIONERY

In addition to the **Paper Source,** at Franklin Street and Chicago Avenue, discussed above under "River North" in "More Shopping Neighborhoods," aspiring Griffin and Sabines can head to the following:

Fly Paper. 3402 N. Southport Ave. (between Belmont Ave. and Addison St.). ☎ **773/296-4359.**

One of several cute shops to have opened in the last few years on this stretch of Southport in the Wrigleyville neighborhood, Fly Paper has one of the most offbeat and artsy selections of greeting cards in the city, as well as other novelty and gift items.

The Heartworks. 1704 N. Wells St. (between North and Lincoln aves.). ☎ **312/943-1972.**

This Old Town shop is another good source for cards, paper goods, journals, photo albums, and impulse gift items.

Write Impressions. 211 W. Huron St. (between Wells and Franklin sts.). ☎ **312/943-3306.**

One of those magical stationery stores that stocks all the desktop goodies you need, from the mundane to the whimsical, from wedding invites to gift items.

SALONS

Charles Ifergan. 106 E. Oak St. (between Michigan Ave. and Rush St.). ☎ **312/642-4484.**

One of Chicago's top hair salons. Rates, which vary according to the seniority of the stylist, are relatively high. But if you're a little daring, you can get a cut for the price of the tip. On Tuesday evenings (call the salon for a schedule) junior stylists do their thing gratis—under the watchful eye of Monsieur Ifergan. Closed Sunday and Monday. Valet parking.

Georgette Klinger. Water Tower Place, 3rd floor, 835 N. Michigan Ave. ☎ **312/ 787-4300.**

If you're looking for a day of pampering, try a deep-cleaning facial, a tension-relieving massage, or a soothing scalp treatment at this salon—and maybe top it off with a manicure or pedicure.

Truefitt & Hill. 900 N. Michigan, 6th floor. ☎ **312/337-2525.**

Women have their pick of hair and beauty salons, but men don't often come across a place like Truefitt & Hill, a British barbershop listed in the *Guinness Book of World Records* as the oldest barbershop in the world. Bow-tied barbers give haircuts ($42) while guests sit in antique chairs; other services include lather shaves ($40), manicures ($24), massages ($40), and shoe shines ($6). Up front, the apothecary sells imported English shaving implements and toiletries.

Urban Oasis. 12 W. Maple St., 3rd floor (between Dearborn and State sts.). ☎ **312/ 587-3500.**

After a long day of sightseeing, try a soothing massage in a subdued, Zen-like atmosphere. The ritual begins with a steam or rain shower in a private changing room, followed by the spa treatment you elect—various forms of massage (including a couples massage, in which you learn to do it yourself), mud or herbal body wrap, aromatherapy, and so forth. Fruit, juices, or herbal teas are offered on completion. A 1-hour massage is $70; an herbal wrap is $50. Call for exact scheduling.

SHOES

Alternatives. 942 N. Rush St. (at Oak St.). ☎ **312/266-1545.**

Black shoes and more black shoes, trendy and relatively affordable, for men and women. There's a second location in Lincoln Park at 1969 N. Halsted St. (☎ **312/ 943-1951**), which also carries a collection of fine children's shoes.

Joan & David. 670 Michigan Ave. (between Ontario and Huron sts.). ☎ **312/482-8585.**

Stylish shoes of fine leather for men and women.

Lori's Designer Shoes. 824 W. Armitage Ave. (between Sheffield Ave. and Halsted St.). ☎ **773/281-5655.**

You'll find a wide assortment of women's styles—at discount prices, no less—at this Lincoln Park store.

Sole Junkies. 3176 N. Clark St. (at Belmont Ave.). ☎ **773/348-8935.**

Sole Junkies is where discriminating club kids go to pick up their platforms and all the coolest sneaks. Dancing vibes supplied by an occasional live deejay. A second store (with a different owner) devoted to women's shoes is located around the corner on Belmont Avenue.

Stephane Kélian. 121 E. Oak St. (at Michigan Ave.). ☎ **312/951-2868.**

Pricey, high-style shoes for men and women from the French designer.

SPORTING GOODS

Active Endeavors. 935 W. Armitage Ave. (between Sheffield Ave. and Halsted St.). ☎ **773/ 281-8100.**

A good source for camping gear, running shoes, and everyday sporty apparel. For the little ones, head to nearby **Active Kids,** 1967 N. Fremont St. (☎ **773/ 281-2002**).

Sportmart. 620 N. LaSalle St. (at Ontario St.). ☎ **312/337-6151.**

The largest sporting goods store in the city, the flagship store of this chain offers seven floors of merchandise, from running apparel to camping gear. Sports fans in search of a Bulls jersey will be in heaven in the first floor team merchandise department.

Vertel's. 2001 N. Clybourn Ave. (between North and Fullerton aves.). ☎ **773/248-7400.**

A store that takes running seriously. Shoe shoppers are advised to bring in their old shoes and invest at least half an hour while the salespeople help fit you for a new pair, including letting you do a lap on the sidewalk out front. The store stocks running apparel and accessories, as well as swimwear. A weekly run takes off from the store Mondays at 6:30pm.

Windward Sports. 3317 N. Clark St. (between Belmont Ave. and Addison St.). ☎ **773/ 472-6868.**

This shop offers equipment and clothing to keep anyone in the surfer-skater-sporty lifestyle outfitted all through the seasons, from in-line skates and swimsuits to snowboards.

TOYS

Galt Toys. 900 N. Michigan Ave., 6th floor. ☎ **312/440-9550.**

Okay, F.A.O. Schwarz is just down the street, but Galt Toys carries a more rarefied selection of children's playthings.

Kite Harbor. 435 E. Illinois St. ☎ **312/321-5483.**

If you want to take advantage of that wind off the lake, stop in here first and pick up a colorful kite, either standard kid-size or one of those spectacular jumbo things. The shop stocks all sorts of flying objects, from boomerangs to whirligigs.

Saturday's Child. 2146 N. Halsted St. (south of Webster Ave.). ☎ **773/525-8697.**

The clever toys here range from rubber snakes and frogs to sidewalk chalk and kids' large-faced wristwatches.

Toyscape. 2911 N. Broadway (between Diversey Pkwy. and Belmont Ave.). ☎ **773/ 665-7400.**

The proprietors bar the door to Barbie at this cluttered Lakeview toy shop. Their tastes run to good old-fashioned wooden toys, musical instruments, and puppets, most of which don't require batteries.

WINE & LIQUOR

Fine Wine Brokers. 4621 N. Lincoln Ave. (between Wilson and Lawrence aves.). ☎ **773/ 989-8166.**

At this little shop in the German neighborhood of Lincoln Square, you'll get lots of attention from the owners, who can help you pick out an excellent bottle of wine for under $10. The shop also carries a growing number of European organic wines and ships its inventory anywhere in the country.

Sam's Wines & Spirits. 1720 N. Marcey St. (near Sheffield and Clybourn aves.). ☎ **800/ 777-9137** or 312/664-4394. www.sams-wine.com.

Believe it or not, this football field–size warehouse store (with its own Web site to boot) evolved from a modest packaged goods store. Today, the family-owned operation is the best-stocked wine and spirits merchant in the city and offers pleasant, friendly service. It also features a superb cheese selection in the on-site Epicurean shop.

Chicago After Dark

Hearing the world-class Chicago Symphony Orchestra, attending a performance of the critically acclaimed Lyric Opera of Chicago, and seeing the Tony Award–winning Steppenwolf and Goodman theater companies are a few of the best—but by no means the only—ways to spend your evenings in the city. Chicago's vibrant and innovative theaters are dispersed throughout a wide range of neighborhoods. Chicago also has a thriving music scene, with clubs devoted to everything from jazz and blues to alternative rock, country, and Latin beats. Music haunts are scattered throughout the city, but many are concentrated in several distinct quarters: Rush Street, Old Town, Lincoln Park, and Wicker Park. Many of the larger hotels provide on their premises some form of nighttime entertainment—sometimes just a cozy piano bar, but in a few cases, full-blown nightclub acts. And if you're just looking to hang out, you only have to pick a neighborhood and wander. You won't have to go far to find a tavern filled with locals and maybe a pool table or a dartboard or two.

For up-to-date entertainment listings, check the local newspapers and magazines, particularly the "Friday" and "Weekend Plus" sections of the two dailies, the *Chicago Tribune* and the *Chicago Sun-Times;* the *Chicago Reader* and *New City,* two free weekly tabloids with extensive listings; and the monthly *Chicago* magazine.

1 The Performing Arts

CLASSICAL MUSIC

For current listings of classical music concerts and opera, call the **Chicago Music Alliance** (☎ 312/987-1123).

✪ **Chicago Symphony Orchestra.** Orchestra Hall, in Symphony Center, 220 S. Michigan Ave. ☎ **312/294-3000.** Fax 312/294-3065. Tickets $10–$91, box seats $165. Call or fax for availability. Box office, Mon–Sat 10am–6pm, Sun 11am–4pm.

The Chicago Symphony Orchestra (CSO) is being led into its second century by Music Director Daniel Barenboim, and it remains among the best in the world. A CSO concert proves Chicagoans can be as passionate about their music as they are about their sports. Although they're high in demand, good seats often become available on concert day. During the last three seasons of the century, the CSO is focusing on the works of a select few great masters. The 1998–99 season is dedicated to the music of Johannes Brahms, while the 1999–2000 season will present the works of Mozart. Another focus for the CSO is a 3-year retrospective entitled "Roots and Branches," which will explore the diverse musical styles of the century through concerts as well as seminars and discussions. Among the guests last season were violinist Itzhak Perlman, cellist Yo-Yo Ma, and conductors Christoph Eschenbach and Zubin Mehta.

Summertime visitors have an opportunity to hear a CSO performance at the delightful **Ravinia Festival** (☎ 847/433-5100) in suburban Highland Park, led by well-known guest conductors. (For more information, see "Exploring the 'Burbs," in chapter 7.)

The **Civic Orchestra of Chicago,** the training orchestra of the Chicago Symphony since 1919, is also highly regarded and presents free programs at Orchestra Hall. The Chicago Symphony Chorus, which celebrated its 40th anniversary in 1998, also performs there.

ADDITIONAL OFFERINGS

The **Chicago Chamber Musicians** (☎ 312/225-5226), a 14-member ensemble drawn from performers from the CSO and Northwestern and DePaul universities, presents chamber music concerts at various locales around the city. While their season runs from October through May, you can always find the CCM performing free noontime concerts on the first Monday of the month (except September and March) at the Chicago Cultural Center. The ensemble has embarked on a 3-year 20th-century music festival, "Music at the Millennium," performing a mix of chamber classics from this century and new works written for the next. The concerts are held each May through 2000. The **Chicago String Quartet,** in residence at DePaul, is also affiliated with the group.

The **Chicago String Ensemble** (☎ 312/332-0567), which celebrated its 20th season in 1997, is one of the few professional string orchestras in the country. The 22-player group performs everything from the classics to contemporary Chicago compositions and appears at city and suburban churches for four blocks of concerts a year (September, November, March, and May).

The **Chicago Sinfonietta** (☎ 312/857-1062), with its a racially diverse 45-member orchestra and a wide-ranging repertoire, seeks to broaden the audience for classical music. In the past, the group has followed a Beethoven piano concerto with a piece featuring a steel drum. Playing about 15 times a year, at Orchestra Hall and other venues throughout the city, the orchestra often takes a multimedia approach to its multicultural mission, accompanying its performances with art slides from the Art Institute and the Mexican Fine Arts Center Museum.

Music of the Baroque (☎ 312/551-1414 for box office), a small orchestra and chorus that pulls members from both the CSO and the Lyric Opera orchestra and features professional singers from across the country, performs the music of the 16th, 17th, and 18th centuries, appropriately in Gothic church settings in Chicago neighborhoods. The group has made several recordings and has introduced works by Mozart and Monteverdi to Chicago audiences.

A great Chicago event from late June through August is the series of free outdoor classical music concerts given by the **Grant Park Symphony and Chorus,** as well as a number of visiting artists, performing in Grant Park at the **James C. Petrillo Music Shell.** Concerts are held Wednesday through Sunday. Bring a blanket if you plan to sit on the lawn; vacant seats in the music shell are offered about 15 minutes before the concert begins. Call ☎ 312/742-4763 for information.

OPERA

✪ **Lyric Opera of Chicago.** Civic Opera House, at Madison St. and Wacker Dr.
☎ **312/332-2244.** Fax 312/332-8120. www.lyricopera.org. Tickets $26–$125. Box office, Mon–Sat noon–6pm, Sun (on performance days only) 11am to first intermission.

A major American opera company, the Lyric attracts top-notch singers from all over the world. Much of its acclaim is attributed to the innovative and widely admired Ardis Krainik, the general director who died in 1997 soon after announcing her retirement. The reins of the general director have been passed to another longtime Lyric Opera devotee, William Mason. Opening night in September remains the quasi-official kickoff of the Chicago social season, but don't be scared off by the snooty factor. The Lyric offers English supertitles, and in any case, the opera is a great spectacle with outstanding musical performances and sumptuous sets. Productions taking the stage for the 1998–99 season include Verdi's *La Traviata,* Charles Gounod's *Roméo et Juliette,* and Richard Wagner's *Die Meistersiner von Nürnberg.* Once or twice a season, the company performs new and sometimes avant-garde works by contemporary American composers. The season, which runs through early March, sells out far in advance, but turn-back tickets are often available just before the performance.

The Lyric Opera performs in the handsome 3,563-seat art deco Civic Opera House, the second-largest opera house in the country, built in 1929. In 1997, the Lyric completed a $100 million renovation of the Civic Opera House, both out front and behind the scenes. The opera has an adjunct, the Lyric Opera Center for American Artists, which also gives performances.

Chicago Opera Theater. Athenaeum Theater, 2936 N. Southport Ave. (at Lincoln Ave.).
☎ **773/292-7578.** Tickets $25–$55.

The "other" opera company in town, Chicago Opera Theater, doesn't get all the big names, but it does make opera accessible to a wider audience with an emphasis on American composers and performers who sing in English. It also helps that tickets are less expensive and more plentiful than those to the Lyric Opera. The company performs three operas a year (April, June, and November), ranging from Mozart's *Don Giovanni* to a Chicago premiere of *Shining Brow,* an operatic ode to Frank Lloyd Wright.

DANCE

Chicago's dance scene is a lively one, with both resident companies and local groups often hosting performances by visiting companies such as the Kirov Ballet, the American Ballet Theatre, and the Dance Theater of Harlem. While there are plans for a dance and music theater center that will serve many of the city's groups, the dance community is still deprived of its own performance venue. The city's itinerant groups usually can be found performing at the Shubert, the Auditorium Theater, and other big downtown venues. Your best bet to see dance is from March through May, when the major companies perform during the **Spring Festival of Dance.** For complete information on what's scheduled, call the Chicago Dance Coalition's information line at ☎ **312/419-8383.**

Ballet Chicago. ☎ **312/251-8838.**

Under artistic director Daniel Duell, a former New York City Ballet dancer, the group is notable for its specialty, the ballets of Balanchine. The ballet performs one full-length story ballet a year, usually in April during the Spring Festival of Dance.

The Dance Center–Columbia College Chicago. 4730 N. Sheridan Rd. (between Lawrence and Wilson aves.). ☎ **773/989-3310.** Tickets $10–$25. Bus: 151. Subway/El: Red Line to Lawrence.

Putting up more than 50 performances a year, the city's hub for modern dance has its own resident company and hosts both touring groups and young homegrown choreographers. One special event is the annual DanceAfrica festival of dance and music, which is held in October. The intimate theater, located in the gritty neighborhood of Uptown, puts audience members close to the moves on stage. There's a paid parking lot across the street.

○ **Hubbard Street Dance Chicago.** Offices at 1147 W. Jackson Blvd. ☎ **312/663-0853.** Tickets $16–$46.

Broadway alum Lou Conte is the artistic director of this major contemporary dance company that last year celebrated its 20th anniversary season. Sometimes whimsical, sometimes romantic, the crowd-pleasing, widely touring 22-member ensemble incorporates a range of dance traditions, from Kevin O'Day to Twyla Tharp, who has choreographed pieces exclusively for Hubbard Street.

○ **Joffrey Ballet of Chicago.** ☎ **312/739-0120.** Fax 312/739-0119. Tickets $15–$50.

This major classical company, which marked its 40th anniversary in 1996, recently relocated to Chicago from New York and has quickly set to work putting down roots with 6 weeks of performances a year in its adopted hometown. Led by cofounder and artistic director Gerald Arpino, the company is committed to the classic works of the 20th century. Its repertoire extends from the ballets of Arpino, Robert Joffrey, Balanchine, and Jerome Robbins to the cutting-edge works of Alonzo King and Chicago choreographer Randy Duncan. The Joffrey continues to draw crowds to its popular rock ballet, Billboards, which is set to the music of Prince, and continues to tour internationally. When the company is in town, it divides its time between the Auditorium Theatre—performing in 1999 in March, October, and December, when it stages its rendition of the holiday favorite *The Nutcracker*—and in the summer at the open-air Ravinia Festival in north-suburban Highland Park (see "Exploring the 'Burbs," in chapter 7).

Links Hall. 3435 N. Sheffield Ave. (at Clark St.). ☎ **773/281-0824.** Tickets $5–$10.

This small second-story studio is an experimental space to watch local choreographers try out their new stuff, mostly modern. The venue presents its own performance series, as well as independent productions of dance and performance art.

Muntu Dance Theatre of Chicago. Offices at 6800 S. Wentworth Ave. ☎ **773/602-1135.** Tickets $12–$35.

The tribal costumes, drumming, and energetic moves of this widely touring group, which focuses on both traditional and contemporary African and African-American dance, is always a hit with audiences. The company performs in town several times a year, including a run during the Spring Festival of Dance.

River North Dance Company. Offices at 1016 N. Dearborn Pkwy. ☎ **312/944-2888.** Tickets $20–$25.

A young upstart to watch is this entertaining jazz-oriented troupe.

MAJOR CONCERT HALLS & AUDITORIUMS
Arie Crown Theater. McCormick Place, 23rd St. and Lake Shore Dr. ☎ **312/791-6000.** Box office, Mon–Sat 10am–6pm.

The Arie Crown Theater is a showcase for Broadway-style traveling musicals and rock and pop acts. Because of its enormous size (it holds almost 3,400 seats), it's well worth paying the extra money for seats near the stage or bringing a good pair of opera glasses.

A recent $6 million renovation improved the rather tinny acoustics and gave the theater some flexibility to tent off the hall for more intimate shows.

Auditorium Theatre. 50 E. Congress Pkwy. (between Michigan and Wabash aves.). ☎ **312/922-4046.** For tickets call ☎ 312/902-1500 (Ticketmaster). To arrange a tour call ☎ 312/431-2354.

Designed and built in 1889 by Louis Sullivan and Dankmar Adler, the Auditorium Theatre is today a national landmark. Most of the building is now occupied by Roosevelt University, but the theater—one of the premier concert halls in the country—was restored in 1967 and now hosts a season of Broadway exports as well as fine dance and musical performances, attracting such names as Twyla Tharp, Luciano Pavarotti, Alvin Ailey, and the Moscow Ballet. Tours of the theater are available with advance reservations; admission is $4 for adults and $3 for seniors and students.

Chicago Theatre. 175 N. State St. (at Lake St.). ☎ **312/443-1130.** Fax 312/263-9505. Box office, Mon–Fri 10am–6pm, Sat 10am–4pm.

The Chicago Theatre is the 1921 baroque centerpiece of the old Balaban and Katz movie-house chain. By the end of the Vietnam War, the theater had deteriorated badly. It was about to fall victim to the wrecking ball when developers' plans were foiled by a group of preservationists who restored this ornate landmark and reopened it in 1986. Today, the Chicago Theatre, managed by Disney, is the Chicago landing pad for the Broadway adaptations of its animated films. The rest of the time the theater is booked with dance performances, pop concerts, and other entertainment fare.

North Shore Center for the Performing Arts. 9501 Skokie Blvd., Skokie. ☎ **847/673-6300** (box office), or 847/679-9501 (office).

A major new musical and theatrical venue in north-suburban Skokie is home to the Northlight Theater and the Skokie Valley Symphony, and books touring vocalists.

Rosemont Theatre. 5400 N. River Rd., Rosemont. ☎ **847/671-5100** for information, or 312/902-1500 for Ticketmaster orders.

City dwellers sometimes have to trek out to this new 4,000-seat theater, located near O'Hare airport, to catch touring musicals, concerts, and dance groups. The theater is no architectural triumph, but the sound and sight lines are excellent.

Symphony Center. 220 S. Michigan Ave. (between Adams St. and Jackson Blvd.). ☎ **312/294-3000.**

Looking for Orchestra Hall, the home of the Chicago Symphony Orchestra? It hasn't gone anywhere. But the intimate concert hall, built by Daniel Burnham in 1905, has been embraced by a series of new additions in a $105 million renovation. The hall itself was treated to a successful acoustical touch-up, with a new panel installed over the stage that remarkably telegraphs the sounds of even the softest tinkling of a triangle. The stage has been expanded and terrace seating added behind it, giving concert-goers an unusual close-up look at the musicians. Other improvements for the audience are wider, more comfortable seating and access through an internal corridor and six-story skylit arcade to additional recital spaces, an education center, and a wonderful new fine-dining restaurant, the appropriately named Rhapsody. While the CSO is the main attraction, the Symphony Center hosts a series of piano recitals, classical and chamber music concerts, and the occasional jazz or pop artist.

THEATER

Chicago's theater community is a vibrant one, about as varied and interesting as regional theater gets—more interesting than the frequently bland revivals produced on Broadway these days. The Steppenwolf and Goodman companies have led the way in developing Chicago's theater reputation, but a host of other performers are creating their own special styles. With more than 300 theaters, Chicago may have as many as 150 different productions playing on any given weekend. The venues vary from a basement-level space seating 25 to an auditorium built for 4,000. If you're looking for a big, splashy musical imported from Broadway, one or two productions are usually playing in Loop theaters. And there may be more to come: There's talk of a revived theater district in the North Loop. Blueprints are rolling out for proposed renovations of several old movie palaces that city planners hope collectively will light up the dead-after-dark Loop with touring Broadway road shows and other entertainment.

If you're up for something a little more offbeat, you should be able to find it at one of dozens of theaters beyond the Loop.

The listings below represent only a fraction of the city's theater offerings, but will lead you to Chicago's most noted venues and companies. For a complete listing of current productions playing on a given evening, check the comprehensive listings in the two free weeklies, the *Reader* (which reviews just about every show in town) and *New City*, or the Friday sections of the two dailies.

GETTING TICKETS

To order tickets for many plays and events, call **Ticketmaster Arts Line** (☎ 312/ 902-1500), a centralized phone-reservation system that allows you to charge full-price tickets (with an additional service charge) for productions at more than 50 Chicago theaters. Individual box offices will also take credit-card orders by phone, and many of the smaller theaters will reserve seats for you with a simple request under your name left on their answering machine. For hard-to-get tickets, try the **Ticket Exchange** (☎ 800/666-0779 outside Chicago or 312/902-1888).

HALF-PRICE TICKETS　For half-price tickets on the day of the show (on Friday you can also purchase tickets for weekend performances), drop by one of the **Hot Tix** ticket centers (☎ 312/977-1755), located in the Loop at the corner of Washington and State streets (across the street from Marshall Field's); at the Visitor Center inside the Historic Water Tower at Chicago and Michigan avenues; in Lincoln Park at Tower Records at 2301 N. Clark St.; and in several suburban locations. Hot Tix also offers advance-purchase tickets at full price. Tickets are not sold over the phone. For a daily listing of discounted shows, as well as information about upcoming shows and a current theater guide published by the **Chicago League of Theatres,** call ☎ 900/ 225-2225 (or, if your phone is blocked, call ☎ 888/225-8844 and use a credit card); calls are $1 a minute, with average calls taking about 3 minutes.

In addition, a few theaters offer last-minute discounts on their leftover seats. Steppenwolf Theatre Company often has half-price tickets on the day of a performance; call or stop by the box office after 5pm. The "Tix by Six" program at the Goodman Theatre offers half-price, day-of-show tickets; many of them are excellent seats that have been returned by subscribers. Tickets go on sale at 6pm for evening performances, noon for matinees.

DOWNTOWN THEATERS

Goodman Theatre. 200 S. Columbus Dr. ☎ 312/443-3800. Tickets $28–$42 main stage, $18–$29 studio. Box office, daily 10am–5pm, 10am–8pm on show days.

The dean of legitimate theaters in Chicago is the Goodman. Under artistic director Robert Falls, the Goodman produces both original productions—such as Horton Foote's *The Young Man from Atlanta* before it went directly to Broadway and Pulitzer Prize–winning playwright August Wilson's *Seven Guitars*—and familiar standards, including Shakespeare, in its 683-seat house. The 1998–99 season has already brought Brian Dennehy to town to portray Willy Loman in *Death of a Salesman*. Shows to follow include a major revival of Samuel Beckett's *Waiting for Godot,* starring Harry J. Lennix; a world premiere of Regina Taylor's *Oo Bla Dee,* the post–World War II story of a black female jazz musician; and a new musical, *Floyd Collins,* named for the Kentucky farmer trapped in a Kentucky cave whose plight became a media sensation. The season also stages its perennial holiday draw, *A Christmas Carol.* The theater also supports a 135-seat auditorium for experimental stagings, called the Goodman Studio Theater.

While the Goodman recently announced plans for a $44 million new theater complex scheduled to open in 2000 in the Loop's theater district (check on its progress at Randolph and Dearborn), for now the theater occupies a wing of the Art Institute complex in Grant Park. Gourmet buffet meals are served on the premises in the Rehearsal Room, open after 6pm. Parking is available in the Monroe Street garage for less than $6.

Ford Center for the Performing Arts/Oriental Theatre. 24 W. Randolph St. ☎ **312/902-1500** for Ticketmaster orders.

The North Loop's Oriental Theatre, built in 1925, is the latest historic downtown movie palace to get a multimillion-dollar facelift. The renovation both restored much of the Oriental's "Roaring Twenties" grandeur and modernized the space, making it a state-of-the-art venue for Broadway-caliber musicals. The 2,180-seat Ford Center reopened in October 1998 with the Chicago premiere of *Ragtime,* the new musical adaptation of E. L. Doctorow's novel, which has received rave reviews on Broadway ever since it opened in January 1998.

Shubert Theatre. 22 W. Monroe St. ☎ **312/902-1500** for Ticketmaster orders.

Built in 1906, this grand Vaudevillian stage is busy with a subscription series of the latest Broadway fare, including hot new Tony winners such as *Rent* and *Bring in 'Da Noise, Bring in 'Da Funk* and perennials like *Peter Pan.*

OFF-LOOP THEATERS

Chicago's off-Loop theaters have produced a number of legendary comedic actors, including comic-turned-director Mike Nichols (*The Graduate, Working Girl*), as well as fine dramatic actors, notably John Malkovich and Gary Sinise, both of whom hail from the Steppenwolf. Sinise and Malkovich toiled at Steppenwolf back in the days when the company performed anywhere it could. Steppenwolf may have hit the big time when it moved into its new digs on North Halsted Street, but the little non-Equity house occupying a small, strange space on some remote block remains Chicago theater's energizing force.

Annoyance Theatre. 3747 N. Clark St. (at Racine Ave.). ☎ **773/929-6200.** Tickets $5–$10.

Infamous for its send-up of the *Brady Bunch* in the late 1980s, the Annoyance has its own special definition of the word irreverent: Recent productions include *Co-Ed Prison Sluts,* purportedly the longest-running comedy musical in Chicago history; *I'm Not Rappaport, I'm Captain Asshole;* and *Choked on Love.* There's also a late-night (or at 12:30am, you might call it early morning) improv show, *Screw Puppies.* Audiences can really make themselves at home here, too: It's BYOB.

Bailiwick Arts Center. 1229 W. Belmont Ave. (at Racine Ave.). ☎ **773/883-1090.** Tickets $15–$18.

Now at home in its own space, Bailiwick Repertory is one of Chicago's young and risk-taking off-Loop theaters, each year producing a main-stage series of classics, the Director's Festival of one-act plays, and gay-oriented shows during the Pride Performance series.

Blue Rider. 1822 S. Halsted St. (at 18th St.). ☎ **312/733-4668.** Tickets $10–$15.

One of Chicago's most experimental theaters, the Blue Rider is located on the artistic fringe of Pilsen, a Mexican immigrant neighborhood. The group was founded by Donna Blue Lachman, who once played the streets of San Francisco as a "loud mime" she called Blue the Clown. But the deeper inspiration for the name, she says, comes from the title of the Kandinsky painting *The Blue Rider.* Now under the direction of Tim Fiori, Blue Rider produces some of the more unconventional theater in town.

Briar Street Theatre. 3133 N. Halsted St. (at Briar St.). ☎ **773/348-4000.** Tickets $39–$46.

The Briar Street Theatre has been turned into the Blue Man theater for the past year. Since October 1997, the avant-garde New York City performance phenomenon known as Blue Man Group has transformed the 625-seat theater, beginning with the lobby, which is now a jumble of tubes and wires and things approximating computer innards. The show—which mixes percussion, performance art, mime, and rock-and-roll—looks to become a permanent fixture on the Chicago theater scene. The three strangely endearing performers, whose faces and heads are covered in latex and blue paint, know how to get the audience involved. Your first decision: Do you want the safe or the unsafe seats? (You'll have to ask.) This show is often a sell-out, so call for tickets in advance.

Court Theatre. 5535 S. Ellis Ave. (at 55th St.). ☎ **773/753-4472.** Tickets $20–$34.

This 250-seat theater, affiliated with the University of Chicago, started out heavily steeped in Molière but has branched into other classics of French literature, Shakespeare, and equally highbrow stuff. This Actors Equity house often performs two plays in rotating repertory, such as Oscar Wilde's *An Ideal Husband* and Anton Chekhov's *The Cherry Orchard.*

ETA Creative Arts Foundation. 7558 S. Chicago Ave. (at 76th St.). ☎ **773/752-3955.** Tickets $20. Subway/El: Red Line to 69th St., transfer to bus no. 30.

For more than 25 years, this theater has been staging original or seldom-seen dramatic works by African-American writers from both Chicago and beyond. The company stages six plays a year in its 200-seat theater, including works geared toward children performed on Saturday afternoons.

Lookingglass Theatre Company. Office at 2936 N. Southport Ave. ☎ **773/477-9257.** Tickets $10–$24.

A young theater now reaching its 10th anniversary, Lookingglass has a style all its own, producing original shows and unusual literary adaptations in a highly physical and visually imaginative style. The company stages several shows each year. Recent ones included a revival and national tour of its immensely pleasing *The Arabian Nights,* a show directed and adapted by the wonderfully talented director/ensemble member Mary Zimmerman, and the first show—Dostoyevsky's *The Idiot*—to feature the company's certified star among its founding ranks, *Friends* star David Schwimmer (who has reportedly pledged some of his new fortune to help his "friends" in the theater company secure a permanent home). Until it settles into a permanent theater, Lookingglass vagabonds around town in a variety of theater spaces yet still manages to guarantee a limited number of $10 tickets for each performance.

Neo-Futurists. 5153 N. Ashland Ave. (at Foster Ave., above the Nelson Funeral Home). ☎ **773/275-5255.** Tickets $5–$10.

A fixture on Chicago's late-night theater scene, the Neo-Futurists have been doing their hit *Too Much Light Makes the Baby Go Blind* for a decade—and there doesn't seem to be any stopping them. No chance they'll get bored anyway: The performers draw upon a repertoire of more than a couple thousand original plays to stage "30 plays in 60 minutes." The lively Gen X audiences show up nearly an hour in advance of the 11:30pm curtain call on weekends (there's less of a crowd at the Sunday shows, beginning at 7pm). The "plays" vary from a 3-minute comedy sketch to a poetic blink of the eye. They may even get the audience on its feet to traipse through the building. Admission is random too: Theater-goers pay $4 plus the roll of a six-sided die. The Neo-Futurists occasionally produce solo shows and full-length plays and have set up an outpost in Manhattan.

Royal George Theatre Center. 1641 N. Halsted St. (at North Ave.). ☎ **312/988-9000.** Tickets $20–$45.

This theater complex, located across the street from the Steppenwolf, has produced such long-running and entertaining hits as the musical *Forever Plaid* and a main-stage production of *The Gin Game* with Charles Durning and Julie Harris.

Shakespeare Repertory Theater. 1016 N. Dearborn St. (between Oak and Maple sts.). ☎ **312/642-2273.** Tickets $22–$34.

This well-regarded theater produces three of the Bard's plays each year—recent seasons featured *The Merchant of Venice, Henry V,* and *The Comedy of Errors*—in the intimate Ruth Page Theater. Plans call for a move in the fall of 1999 to a new theater at Navy Pier.

✪ Steppenwolf Theatre Company. 1650 N. Halsted St. (at North Ave.). ☎ **312/335-1650.** Tickets $31.50–$36.50 main stage (preview tickets begin at $24.50), $14.50–$19.50 studio. Box office, Sun–Mon 11am–5pm, Tues–Fri 11am–7pm, Sat 11am–8pm. If they're available, rush tickets for the main stage are sold at half price (studio tickets for $10) an hour before a performance (call or stop by the box office).

One of the great Chicago success stories of recent years is the brilliant repertory company Steppenwolf Theater. Steppenwolf has garnered many awards, including five Tonys—one for regional theater excellence. It has also launched the careers of several highly respected and well-known actors, including John Malkovich, Gary Sinise, and Laurie Metcalf (of *Roseanne*). Under new artistic director Martha Lavey, Steppenwolf has drawn upon its star power—bringing back its big names to perform or direct—to cope with what many locals viewed as growing pains that had left Steppenwolf looking for new direction. Last year, Sinise was largely responsible for an instant sell-out of a critically acclaimed revival of *A Streetcar Named Desire.* Other productions last year included Tina Landau's *Space* (called one of 1997's best plays by *Time* magazine), and Hart and Kaufman's *The Man Who Came to Dinner* starring ensemble member John Mahoney (of *Frasier* fame). The 1998–99 season will include Charles L. Mee's *The Berlin Circle,* a variant on the legend behind Brecht's *The Caucasian Chalk Circle;* Richard Greenberg's *Three Days of Rain;* and Sylvia Regan's *Morning Star.*

The works featured are almost always thoughtful, occasionally a bit heavy-handed, and sometimes a little too in-your-face for Chicago's original in-your-face theater. Steppenwolf's breakthrough, following the usual years of artistic struggle, now provides inspiration for other small theater companies. Many of those kindred workshops and theaters can be found in Lincoln Park and other North Side neighborhoods; they often take the stage in the Steppenwolf's upstairs studio theater. Parking in a new garage next door is $6.

Theatre Building. 1225 W. Belmont Ave. (at Racine Ave.). ☎ **773/327-5252.** Tickets $15–$30.

With four theaters of varying size, this Lakeview space is an incubator for upstart theater groups and offbeat performances. There's always something going on here, including theater fare geared to kids.

Theatre on the Lake. Fullerton Ave. and Lake Shore Dr. ☎ **312/742-7994.** Tickets $9.

What a great way to see two of the city's signature strengths: a sublime skyline view from the water's edge and an evening of off-Loop Chicago theater. The Prairie-style theater has hosted theatrical productions along the lake for nearly half a century. In a departure from the usual summer-stock fare, the park district has begun scheduling a summer series featuring a reprise of some of the more offbeat and interesting shows staged during the previous season by the city's smaller experimental companies. At intermission, you can walk out the theater's back door and look south to the city lights. If it's a cool night, it's a good idea to bring a sweater, because the screened-in theater is open to the night air (allowing the noise of traffic on Lake Shore Drive to intrude somewhat, too).

Victory Gardens Theater. 2257 N. Lincoln Ave. (at Belden St.). ☎ **773/871-3000.** Tickets $10–$30.

Victory Gardens has taken over space from its defunct upstairs neighbor, the Body Politic theater, and fills this four-stage complex with a combination of five main-stage productions of contemporary works and many more shows produced by smaller companies. Devoted to the development of the playwright, Victory Gardens frequently presents world premieres of homegrown plays and sponsors free readings of new works, which are held twice a month on Sunday.

2 Comedy & Improv

In the mid-1970s, *Saturday Night Live* brought Chicago's unique brand of comedy to national attention. But even back then, John Belushi and Bill Murray were just the latest brood to hatch from the number-one incubator of Chicago-style humor, Second City. From Mike Nichols, Robin Williams, and Robert Klein to Joan Rivers, John Candy, and David Steinberg, two generations of American comics have honed their skills in Chicago before making their fortunes as film and TV stars. Chicago continues to nurture young comics, drawn to Chicago for the chance to hone their improvisational skills at Second City, the ImprovOlympic, and numerous other comedy and improv outlets.

All Jokes Aside. 1000 S. Wabash Ave. (between 9th and 11th sts.). ☎ **312/922-0577** (box office). Tickets $5.75–$12.75 plus a 2-drink minimum.

This Near South Side comedy club spotlights the humor of African-American and Latino comic artists, both local and national in reputation, such as *Saturday Night Live* veteran Chris Rock. The club is open Wednesday, which is the open mike "Apollo" showcase, through Sunday, and tickets are sold each night after 6pm. The cover is free or reduced some nights before 7pm.

ImprovOlympic. 3541 N. Clark St. (at Addison St.). ☎ **773/880-0199.** Tickets $6–$10.

A training ground for improv actors, the ImprovOlympic offers a nightclub setting for a variety of unscripted nightly performances, from free-form shows to shows loosely based on concepts like *Star Trek* or dating. Like all improv, you're gambling here: It could be a big laugh or the amateur performers could go down in flames. Monday is an off night for most other clubs in town, and ImprovOlympic takes advantage with a show called the Armando Diaz Experience, an all-star improv night that teams up some of the best improvisers in Chicago, from Second City and elsewhere. Successful alums incude Mike Myers and the late Chris Farley. The Hollywood connection has also been formalized: In 1997 the club added a branch in Los Angeles.

✪ **Second City.** 1616 N. Wells St. (at North Ave.). ☎ **312/337-3992.** Tickets $6–$16.

Having celebrated its 35th anniversary, Second City remains the top comedy club in Chicago. Photos of its vast class of famous graduates line the lobby walls, including more recent alumni such as George Wendt and the late Chris Farley. The successful Second City sketch comedy formula had gotten stale, but in the last few seasons the club's regained top form by adopting a long-form improvisational program pioneered by some of the other improv hothouses in town. What remains the same is the fun postshow improv session; no ticket is necessary for the improv session if you skip the main show (except Friday).

Zanies Comedy Club. 1548 N. Wells St. (between North Ave. and Schiller St.). ☎ **312/337-4027.** Tickets $13 plus 2-drink minimum.

Just down the street from Second City in Old Town is Zanies, which often draws its headliners straight off *The Late Show with David Letterman* and *The Tonight Show.* Satirical skits and stand-up routines are the usual fare, played to packed, appreciative houses. Inquire about smoke-free shows. You must be 21 or older to attend a show.

3 The Music Scene

JAZZ
Born in the Storyville section of New Orleans, jazz moved upriver to Chicago some 75 years ago, and it still has a home here.

✪ **Andy's Jazz Club.** 11 E. Hubbard St. (between State St. and Wabash Ave.). ☎ **312/642-6805.** Cover $3–$10.

Casual and comfortable, Andy's, a full restaurant and bar, is popular with both the hard-core and the neophyte jazz enthusiast. It's the only place in town where you can hear jazz nearly all day long. To listen to the likes of Dr. Bop and the Headliners or clarinetist Chuck Hedges and his "swingtet," take in a set Monday through Friday from noon to 2:30pm, 5 to 8:30pm, or 9pm to 1:30am; Saturday from 6 to 9pm or 9:30pm to 1:30am; or Sunday from 6pm to 1am.

Back Room. 1007 N. Rush St. (between Oak St. and Bellevue Place). ☎ **312/751-2433.** Cover $6–$10 with a 2-drink minimum.

One of the vestiges of the celebrated old Rush Street, the Back Room still packs a well-dressed crowd into this intimate candlelit spot tucked away at the back of a long gangway like a speakeasy. The tuxedoed doorman offers patrons a seat on the main floor or in the balcony overlooking the stage. Jazz quartets and trios perform four times a night.

Cotton Club. 1710 S. Michigan Ave. (between 16th and 18th sts.). ☎ **312/341-9787.** Cover $7–$10 (free Thursday).

This is an upscale jazz room on the Near South Side, named for the legendary Harlem nightclub. There are sets 3 or 4 nights a week, including an open mike on Monday. There's an adjoining dance club.

Green Dolphin Street. 2200 N. Ashland Ave. (at Webster Ave.). ☎ **773/395-0066.** Cover $5–$10.

The newest jazz club in town hearkens back to the past. An old auto garage on the north branch of the Chicago River has been transformed Cinderella-like into a sexy retro forties-style nightclub and restaurant. The beautiful, well-appointed crowd shows up to smoke stogies from the club's humidor, lap up martinis, and make the

Lincoln Park/Wrigleyville After Dark

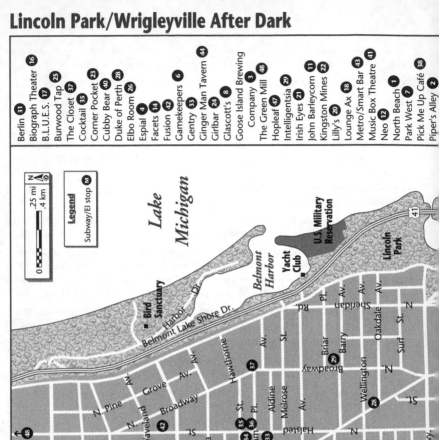

Berlin **31**
Biograph Theater **16**
B.L.U.E.S. **17**
Burwood Tap **25**
The Closet **37**
Cocktail **35**
Corner Pocket **23**
Cubby Bear **40**
Duke of Perth **28**
Elbo Room **26**
Espial **4**
Facets **14**
Fusion **42**
Gamekeepers **6**
Gentry **33**
Ginger Man Tavern **44**
Girlbar **24**
Glascott's **8**
Goose Island Brewing Company **3**
The Green Mill **48**
Hopleaf **47**
Intelligentsia **29**
Irish Eyes **21**
John Barleycorn **11**
Kingston Mines **22**
Lilly's **20**
Lounge Ax **18**
Metro/Smart Bar **43**
Music Box Theatre **41**
Neo **12**
North Beach **1**
Park West **7**
Pick Me Up Café **38**
Piper's Alley **2**

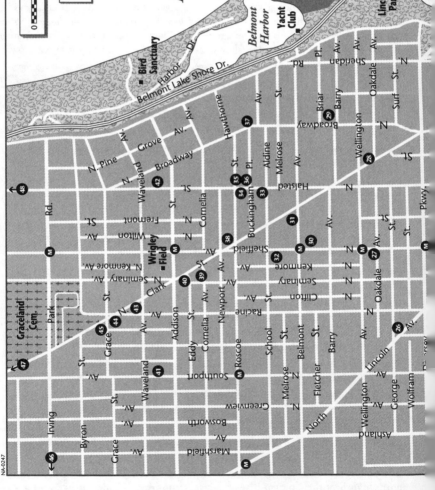

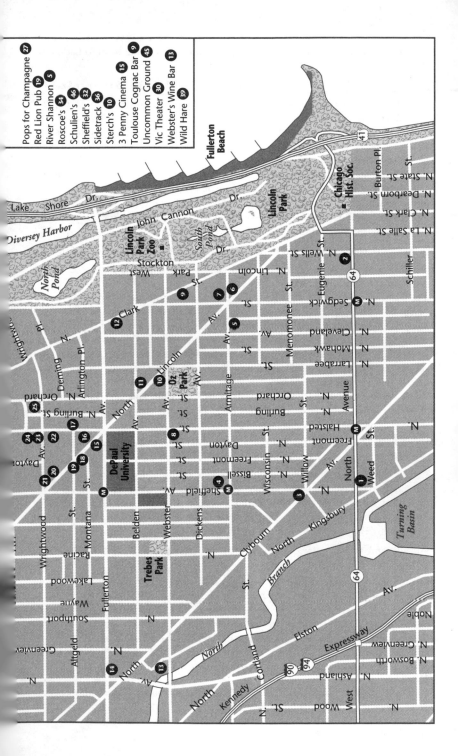

Pops for Champagne **27**
Red Lion Pub **19**
River Shannon **5**
Roscoe's **34**
Schulien's **46**
Sheffield's **32**
Sidetrack **36**
Sterch's **10**
3 Penny Cinema **15**
Toulouse Cognac Bar **9**
Uncommon Ground **45**
Vic Theater **30**
Webster's Wine Bar **13**
Wild Hare **39**

scene. Green Dolphin books jazz in all its permutations, from big band to Latin jazz. The club's main room is closed Monday and Tuesday.

○ **Green Mill.** 4802 N. Broadway (at Lawrence). ☎ **773/878-5552.** Cover $2–$7.

In the heart of Uptown, the Green Mill is "Old Chicago" to the rafters. A popular watering hole during the twenties and thirties, when Al Capone was a regular and the headliners included Sophie Tucker—the Red Hot Mama—and Al Jolson, it still retains its speakeasy atmosphere and flavor. On Sunday night, the Green Mill hosts the Uptown Poetry Slam, when poets vie for the open mike to roast and ridicule each other's work. Most nights, however, jazz is on the menu, beginning around 9pm and winding down just before closing at 4am (5am on Saturday). Tuesday has been locked up for ages by the swingin' retro Mighty Blues Kings, while Thursday is big-band night, and late Sunday is owned by chanteuse Patricia Barber. Get there early to claim one of the plush velvet booths.

○ **Jazz Showcase.** 59 W. Grand St. (at Clark St.). ☎ **312/670-BIRD.** Tickets $10–$20.

Spanning more than 50 years and several locations, founder Joe Segal has become synonymous with jazz in Chicago. His son, Wayne, recently took over running the business, but this latest venue in the River North restaurant and entertainment district is the spiffiest yet, a spacious and handsome room with sharp black-and-white photographs of jazz greats, many of whom have passed through Segal's clubs. There are two shows a night, and reservations are recommended when a big-name headliner is featured. The Segals make an effort to cultivate new generations of jazz lovers, too: The club admits all ages (children under 12 are free), has a no-smoking policy, and offers a Sunday 4pm matinee show that won't keep the kids up late.

The Segal's latest outpost is the new **Joe's Be-bop Cafe and Jazz Emporium** at Navy Pier, 600 E. Grand Ave. (☎ **312/595-5299**), a Southern-style BBQ restaurant with live music nightly.

Pops for Champagne. 2934 N. Sheffield Ave. (at Oakdale Ave.). ☎ **773/472-1000.** Cover $5–$9.50.

A very civilized, elegant way to enjoy jazz, the Pops champagne bar is one of the prettiest rooms in the city, with fine murals, a vaulted ceiling, and a stage rising above the sunken bar. Live jazz is presented 7 nights a week, from 8:30pm to 12:30am Sunday through Thursday, from 9pm to 1am Friday and Saturday. There's also an early set on Friday from 5:30 to 8:30pm. Sunday nights are free.

Underground Wonder Bar. 10 E. Walton St. (at State St.). ☎ **312/266-7761.** Cover $3–$6.

This intimate jazz club on the Near North Side only gets better as the night wears on. Open until 4am (5am on Saturday), look for jazz trios and R&B vocalists playing the quirky, compact, and, yep, below-street-level room. Stick around until the wee hours, which is really when the fun begins—musicians playing in other clubs in town often drop by on their way home to improvise a final set. Tex-Mex and other chow is served late.

BLUES

With a few notable exceptions, Chicago's best and most popular blues showcases are located in the entertainment districts of the Near North Side. As with the jazz venues listed above, most of the blues clubs have cover charges that are well below $10 unless a major act is performing.

Blue Chicago. 736 N. Clark St. (between Chicago Ave. and Superior St.). ☎ **312/ 642-6261.** www.bluechicago.com. E-mail: blues@bluechicago.com. Cover $6–$8.

Blue Chicago pays homage to female blues belters with a strong lineup of the best women vocalists around. The forties-style brick-walled room, decorated with original artwork of Chicago blues vignettes, is open Monday through Saturday, with music beginning at 9pm. Admission allows you to club hop between this venue and a second location, open Tuesday through Sunday, down the street at 536 N. Clark St.

B.L.U.E.S. 2519 N. Halsted St. (between Wrightwood and Fullerton aves.). ☎ **773/ 528-1012.** Cover $5–$10.

On the Halsted strip, look for B.L.U.E.S.—the name says it all. This is a small joint for the serious blues aficionado—you won't miss a single move of the musicians standing on stage only yards away. Shows start at 9:30pm daily. A second club, **B.L.U.E.S. Etcetera,** 1124 W. Belmont Ave. (☎ 773/525-8989), accommodates bigger crowds for big names in blues, Chicago style and otherwise, such as Junior Wells. It looks a bit like a cafeteria or a coffee shop, but then again, you don't go to a blues club for the decor.

Buddy Guy's Legends. 754 S. Wabash Ave. (between Balbo Ave. and 8th St.). ☎ **312/ 427-0333.** http://buddyguy.com. Cover $6–$15.

A legend himself, the gifted guitarist runs one of the more popular and most comfortable clubs in town and is known to hang out there when he's in town. Located on the southern edge of downtown, the club's walls are decorated with blues paraphernalia, from a Koko Taylor dress to a Muddy Waters tour jacket. The kitchen serves Louisiana-style soul food and barbecue.

House of Blues. 329 N. Dearborn St. (at Kinzie St.). ☎ **312/923-2000** for general information, 312/923-2020 for concert information, or 312/559-1212 for Ticketmaster orders. Ticket prices vary depending on the act.

Club owners have nervously watched the arrival of this blues-themed enterprise, a combo nightclub, restaurant, and hotel complex that's breathing new life into the base of the corn-cob-shaped Marina City. The largest outpost in the growing House of Blues chain, this 55,000-square-foot complex, extravagantly decorated with 600 pieces from owner Isaac Tigrett's collection of Mississippi Delta folk art, isn't really a blues club as much as a showcase for rock, R&B, zydeco, reggae, and everything else. Besides the concerts in the beautifully gilded mini-European opera house, there's also a restaurant serving lunch and dinner with hometown blues accompaniment and the requisite gift shop. The popular Sunday gospel brunch, offering a Southern-style buffet, brings a different Chicago gospel choir to the stage each week; the three weekly "services" often sell out, so get tickets in advance.

✪ **Kingston Mines.** 2548 N. Halsted St. (between Wrightwood and Fullerton aves.). ☎ **773/477-4646.** Cover $9–$12.

One of Chicago's premier blues bars, which celebrated its 30th anniversary in 1998, Kingston Mines is where musicians congregate after their own gigs to jam together and to socialize. Celebs have been known to drop by, including recent sightings of George Clooney, Dan Akroyd, and Keanu Reeves. The show begins at 9:30pm daily, with two bands on two stages, and goes until 4am (5am on Saturday). There's also a kitchen open late serving up burgers and ribs.

Lilly's. 2513 N. Lincoln Ave. (between Wrightwood and Fullerton aves.). ☎ **773/525-2422.** Cover $3–$5.

In Lincoln Park, Lilly's still enshrines the old-time blues, featuring blues jams every Thursday night. The rest of the week Lilly's books jazz and blues combos.

New Checkerboard Lounge. 423 E. 43rd St. ☎ **773/624-3240.** Cover $5–$7.

Despite its location in a marginal neighborhood on the South Side, the New Checkerboard Lounge is the "in spot." It's one of the surviving joints on a street once hopping with blues clubs. The music is the real thing here, very close to its Mississippi roots. There are four sets a night, beginning at 9:30pm. Don't take public transit here: It's best to drive and park in the monitored lot across the street.

Rosa's Lounge. 3420 W. Armitage Ave. (at Kimball Ave.). ☎ **773/342-0452.** www. rosaslounge.com. E-mail: tony@rosaslounge. Cover $5–$10.

Rosa's is strictly a neighborhood hangout, but it has live blues every night of the year and all the atmosphere required to fuel its heartfelt lamentations. Most blues groups and music lovers feel right at home here. Rosa's also sponsors a blues cruise on Lake Michigan every July. The doors open at 8pm, and the show starts around 9:30pm and runs until 2am (3am on Saturday). Closed Sunday and Monday.

BASICALLY ROCK

A few years ago Chicago's burgeoning alternative rock scene, which has produced such names as Smashing Pumpkins, Liz Phair, Veruca Salt, and Urge Overkill, attracted the national spotlight. Drawn by the vibrant musical scene and a love for Chicago, several established acts, including Poi Dog Pondering, Syd Straw, and Jon Langford of the Mekons, decided to call the city home. The Bucktown/Wicker Park neighborhood has been the center of the movement. The hype has passed, but there's still plenty to see and hear at tons of small clubs. Scan the *Reader* or *New City* to see who's playing where.

Cubby Bear. 1059 W. Addison St. (at Clark St.). ☎ **773/327-1662.** Cover $5 on band nights, more for special shows.

Across from Wrigley Field, Cubby Bear is a showcase for new rock bands and an occasional offbeat act and draws a scrub-faced postcollegiate crowd. Concerts are staged on weekends and many Wednesday nights. Otherwise there's always billiards, darts, and other distractions.

Double Door. 1572 N. Milwaukee Ave. (at North Ave.). ☎ **773/489-3160.** Tickets $6–$10.

This relatively new club, a biker country/western bar in a former life, has capitalized on the Wicker Park/Bucktown neighborhood's ascendance as a breeding ground for rock and alternative music. Owned by the proprietors of the venerable rock showplace Metro (see below), the club has some of the better acoustics and sight lines in the city and attracts buzz bands and unknowns to its stage. When you need to escape the noise, there's a lounge-type area, the Dirt Room, with pool tables in the basement. Concerts are staged Thursday to Sunday, when the acid-jazz outfit Liquid Soul holds forth.

The Empty Bottle. 1035 N. Western Ave. (between Division St. and Augusta Blvd.). ☎ **773/276-3600.** Cover $5–$10.

This alternative rock club in the Ukrainian Village neighborhood is a haven for young arty scenesters drawn here for camaraderie, obscure bands, and cheap beer. But the club is hardly narrow, with experimental jazz on Tuesday and Wednesday and other nights given over to a deejay's underground improvisations. To get here via public transportation, take the Blue Line to Western, then transfer to bus no. 49.

Fireside Bowl. 2646 W. Fullerton Ave. (between California and Western aves.). ☎ **773/ 486-2700.** Cover usually $5.

Punk rock lives! As many as eight acts take to the makeshift stage each night, from suburban acts young enough to be Johnny Rotten's grandchildren to touring international cult faves. It's certainly one of the more unique settings for live music in town. Doors open at 7pm, and mohawks of all ages are welcome.

✪ **Lounge Ax.** 2438 N. Lincoln Ave. (between Fullerton and Wrightwood aves.). ☎ **773/525-6620.** www.loungeax.com. Tickets $4–$10.

This compact, basementlike Lincoln Park rock club has a reputation among concert-goers for its sharp eye to some of the more interesting and edgy bands around, including the likes of Wilco (one of the co-owners is married to frontman Jeff Tweedy), Superchunk, and the Mekons.

✪ **Metro.** 3730 N. Clark St. (at Racine Ave.). ☎ **773/549-0203,** or 312/559-1212 for Ticketmaster orders. www.metrochicago.com. E-mail: metro@metrochicago.com. Tickets $5–$20.

Metro, located in an old auditorium, is Chicago's premier venue for live alternative/rock acts on the verge of breaking into the big time. Everybody who is any-body has played here over the years, from REM to such local heroes as the Smashing Pumpkins. A new band showcase takes the stage on Tuesday. The Smart Bar—at the same location—is a dance club open 7 nights a week. Some shows are all ages, but most require concert-goers to be 21 and older. Tickets are sold in person through the box office in the attached record shop, **Clubhouse** (sans service charges) or by phone through Ticketmaster.

New World Music Theater. 19100 S. Ridgeland Ave., Tinley Park (Harlem exit off I-80). ☎ **708/614-1616.** Tickets $15–$50.

When the chill of April has subsided, blockbuster mega-acts like the Dave Matthews Band and Garth Brooks touch down for the spring and summer months at this out-door venue, an hour's drive (depending on traffic) south of the city in suburban Tinley Park. Like most open-air amphitheaters, concert-goers have the option to purchase tickets for covered seats or go cheap and lounge on the lawn.

Phyllis' Musical Inn. 1800 W. Division St. (at Wood St.). ☎ **773/486-9862.** Cover $3–$5.

Typical of the neighborhood bars in Wicker Park, Phyllis' is a small, generally uncrowded club booking live rock music (sometimes jazz and blues) 4 to 5 nights a week.

Rosemont Horizon. 6920 N. Mannheim Rd. (between Higgins and Touhy), Rosemont. ☎ **847/635-6601,** or 312/559-1212 for Ticketmaster orders.

On the periphery of O'Hare airport is the 18,000-seat Rosemont Horizon, which holds big events such as rock concerts, the circus, and important college basketball games. By public transportation, take the Blue Line El to the River Road station and connect to the suburban Pace bus no. 222.

Vic Theater. 3145 N. Sheffield Ave. (at Belmont Ave.). ☎ **773/472-0366** (concert line), or 312/559-1212 for Ticketmaster orders. Tickets $12–$20.

A former vaudevillian theater, this Lakeview hall is a frequent host to emerging rock acts. On nonshow nights, the theater screens second-run movies under the auspices of "Brew & View."

COUNTRY, FOLK & ETHNIC MUSIC
The mix of cultures and ethnicities in Chicago's neighborhoods translates into a wealth of music clubs catering to all kinds of musical tastes, from mellow folk and melancholy Irish to suave salsa and spicy reggae.

Abbey Pub. 3420 W. Grace St. (at Elston Ave.). ☎ **773/478-4408.** Cover $3–$10.

Irish brogues abound at this gathering place for rock and folk acts from here and abroad. Besides Guinness and other Emerald Isle beers on tap, there's a full menu. There's an Irish jam every Sunday.

Baby Doll Polka Club. 6100 S. Central Ave. ☎ **773/582-9706.** No cover.

Polka is alive and kicking in Chicago at the Baby Doll Polka Club, located across the street from the runways at Midway airport. Relive those golden memories of Lawrence Welk and skip-step to the magic accordion of the house band, the Merry Makers. It's open daily, with live music on weekends only (Sunday is the day to be here).

Elbo Room. 2871 N. Lincoln Ave. (at George St.). ☎ **773/549-5549.** Cover $5–$6.

Step downstairs into this basement-level Lincoln Park music room for a lineup of nightly musical entertainment that's delightfully schizophrenic: rockabilly, hip-hop, even big band with the legendary drummer Barrett Deems, a one-time player with Louis Armstrong, and his orchestra.

Equator Club. 4715 N. Broadway (between Lawrence and Wilson aves.). ☎ **773/728-2411.** Cover $5 on deejay nights, $20 or more for live bands.

The sounds of Africa and the Caribbean fill this basement-level club, either produced by a deejay spinning lively calypso, high life, and soukous tunes or by international bands from the Congo, Senegal, and other nations. The patrons, some dressed in African garb, dance just the same.

Heartland Cafe. 7000 N. Glenwood Ave. (at Lunt Ave.). ☎ **773/465-8005.** Cover $3–$7.

On the weekends, you'll usually find something happening music-wise at the Heartland Cafe, a neo-hippie restaurant in Rogers Park. The musical menu, scheduled on Friday and Saturday, is eclectic—anything from funky rock to Irish tunes.

Irish Eyes. 2519 N. Lincoln Ave. (between Fullerton and Wrightwood aves.). ☎ **773/348-9548.** Cover $2–$3.

This place showcases Irish music on Friday and Saturday nights beginning after 9pm. Bluegrass music is on tap about once a month.

Kitty O'Sheas. 720 S. Michigan Ave. (between Balbo Ave. and 8th St.). ☎ **312/922-4400,** ext. 4454. No cover.

The Chicago Hilton and Towers is the unlikely home for an authentically appointed Irish pub, with no detail spared, from the carved mahogany bar to the Guinness pints expertly poured by the Irish native bartenders here on a work exchange. Irish duos and trios get the conventioneers—and even a few Irish guys talking about the latest soccer match—to do a jig on the small dance floor. There's also a menu featuring such traditional selections as shepherd's pie and lamb stew.

Old Town School of Folk Music. 4533 N. Lincoln Ave. (between Wilson and Montrose aves.). ☎ **773/525-7793.** Tickets $8–$18.

Country, folk, bluegrass, Latin, Celtic—the Old Town School of Folk Music covers a spectrum of indigenous musical forms. The school, which celebrated its 40th anniversary in 1997, is best known as a training center offering a slate of music classes, but it also hosts everyone from the legendary Pete Seeger to bluegrass phenom Alison Krauss. Last year, the school moved into a spacious new home with a pristine 420-seat concert hall in a former 1930s library in the Lincoln Square neighborhood.

Park West. 322 W. Armitage Ave. (at Clark St.). ☎ **773/929-5959,** or 312/559-1212 for Ticketmaster orders. Ticket prices vary.

With its cabaret seating and sharp acoustics, Park West elevates concert-going from the usual beer-sloshed rock show. This Lincoln Park venue is intimate and dignified (save for the sometimes surly management) and a fine place to see a folk, jazz, or alternative rock show. For an extra charge, you can call ahead for many shows to reserve a table for a party of four.

Schubas Tavern. 3159 N. Southport Ave. (at Belmont Ave.). ☎ **773/525-2508.** Tickets $4–$15.

Country and folk singer-songwriters have found a home in this divine little concert hall located in a former Schlitz tavern. It's a friendly and intimate place, best experienced from one of the wooden booths ringing the room. There's also a bar up front and an attached restaurant, Harmony Grill, where you can grab a pretty good burger and fries after the show.

Wild Hare and Singing Armadillo Frog Sanctuary. 3530 N. Clark St. (between Addison and Roscoe sts.). ☎ **773/327-4273.** Cover $5–$8.

Number one on Chicago's reggae charts is the Wild Hare, in the shadow of Wrigley Field. Grab a Red Stripe and dance to bands from Jamaica and elsewhere: Burning Spear, the Wailers, Yellowman, among the big names. The atmosphere inside the bar—dark and slightly dingy—might have been transported from a side street in Montego Bay, from the part of town tourists seldom wander through, though the crowds are safely suburban and mainstream with a few dreadlocked patrons thrown into the mix. No cover before the scheduled showtime of 9:30pm and for some special shows.

CABARETS & PIANO BARS

The Baton Show Lounge. 436 N. Clark St. (between Hubbard and Illinois sts.). ☎ **312/644-5269.** Cover $10 plus 2-drink minimum.

Catch the city's long-running revue of female impersonators at this River North lounge. Shows are held Wednesday through Sunday at 8:30 and 10:30pm and 12:30am.

Coq d'Or. In the Drake Hotel, 140 E. Walton St. (at Michigan Ave.). ☎ **312/787-2200.** No cover.

Loyal followers of piano stylist Buddy Charles have followed him to the Coq d'Or, the cozy, clubby bar ensconced in the Drake Hotel. Whether you're huddled close around the piano or hanging back on the red Naugahyde banquettes, you're in for a treat when Charles hits the keyboard at this old-time Chicago haunt.

Jilly's. 1007 N. Rush St. (at Oak St.). ☎ **312/664-1001.** Cover $5 weekends.

Named for Frank Sinatra's former manager, Jilly's has brought new life to Rush Street. Music and a lively buzz from the patrons spills into the street during warm weather, and piano stylists and trios play the dark room decorated with photos of the Brat Pack, Steve and Edie, and the like. Downstairs in the basement is the dance club Jilly's Retro, keeping the seventies alive ($10 cover).

Pump Room. 1301 N. State Pkwy. (at Goethe St.). ☎ **312/266-0360.** No cover.

Even if you're not dining at the storied Chicago restaurant, the dark-paneled Pump Room bar operated by a tuxedoed staff offers a good vantage point for soaking up some Gold Coast elegance. Live music gets the dressed-up (jackets are required for men), grown-up patrons on the small, well-worn dance floor.

Toulouse Cognac Bar. 2140 N. Lincoln Park W. (between Webster and Armitage aves.). ☎ **773/665-9071.** Cover $10–$15.

Toulouse Cognac Bar, located across from Lincoln Park, is just right: Some of the best cabaret singers working today play a romantic, intimate room done up with lots of red velvet and art reproductions on the walls.

Zebra Lounge. 1220 N. State Pkwy. (between Division and Goethe sts.). ☎ **312/642-5140.** No cover.

Now that the wonderfully quirky Joann Piano Bar is no more, the Zebra Lounge has stepped up as my favorite wonderfully quirky piano bar. Just as you would expect, black-and-white stripes are the unifying decor theme at this dark, tiny Gold Coast spot, furnished with black vinyl booths, a small mirrored bar, and a keyboardist who leads a nightly sing-along.

4 The Club Scene

Chicago is the hallowed ground where house music was hatched in the 1980s, so it's no surprise to find a few big dance clubs pounding away the big beat with a mostly under-30 crowd. A skeptical Midwestern sensibility has always reined here, so the attitude and fashion required for a big dance club has limited appeal. But there are plenty of other clubs and bars with square footage given over to dancing. You may find spots that specialize in one brand of music and others that offer an ever-changing mix of rhythms and beats that follow the latest deejay-driven trend. A general note about dance clubs: Avoid wearing sneakers, baseball caps, or jeans, or risk the bouncer turning you away at the door.

Berlin. 954 W. Belmont Ave. (at Sheffield Ave.). ☎ **773/348-4975.** Cover $5.

One of the more enduring dance floors in Chicago, Berlin is primarily gay during the week but draws dance hounds of all stripes on weekends and for special theme nights dedicated to new wave, disco, and Prince. The owners are no dummies: The cover charge applies only on Friday and Saturday after midnight, which is about an hour earlier than you ought to show up. (See also below under "The Gay & Lesbian Scene.")

The Clique. 2347 S. Michigan Ave. (at 23rd St.). ☎ **312/326-0274.** Cover $10.

They're "dressed to impress" at this stylish, two-level nightclub on the South Side that has tuxedoed doormen enforcing a dress code for the mostly African-American clientele. There's a comedy club and jazz lounge downstairs, a discotheque upstairs.

Club Inta's. 308 W. Erie St. (at Orleans St.). ☎ **312/664-6595.** Cover $5–$10.

A stylish grown-up club in a River North warehouse, Club Inta's is like a different club every night of the week, from a hub for African-American professionals when a deejay spins R&B tunes to a hot Latin night spot when a live salsa band keeps the sexy crowd flaunting their smoothly choreographed dance moves. Note the dress code (no gym shoes, jeans, or T-shirts) and a minimum age of 23. Closed Monday.

Crobar Night Club. 1543 N. Kingsbury St. (south of North Ave.). ☎ **312/413-7000.** Cover $4–$15.

A youthful hormone-fueled crowd comes to Crobar, located in a warehouse district near Lincoln Park, to dance to the big sounds of hip-hop, techno, and house music on weekends at this epic-size club styled with quasi-religious, postapocalyptic trappings. There are plenty of perches from which to watch the action, as well as a quieter upstairs bar and a VIP room. On Sunday night, Crobar becomes GLEE Club (which stands for Gay Lesbian Everyone's Equal), which counts Dennis Rodman among its regulars.

Drink. 702 W. Fulton St. ☎ **312/733-7800.** Cover after 9pm Thurs–Sat $5.

The rapid loft redevelopment west of downtown pushed Drink to a new warehouse location down the street. The new space is a series of biggie-size environments—a colorful psychedelic room with a stage for live music; a cigar room with a humidor; and a Moroccan-themed room with tenting, mosaic tiling, and antique doors. The high-concept club is co-owned by a guy who has the nightlife business in his blood: His father is famed Chicago restaurateur Arnie Morton and his brother is a Hard Rock Cafe founder. True to its name, Drink specializes in creatively presented libations. You have your choice of imbibing from a mason jar, baby bottle, bucket, or shot glass sculpted out of ice. A vodka bar offers more than 50 types of vodkas, and a tequila bar features 75 variations. Open for lunch, the menu includes sandwiches and pizza. Bands take the stage on many Thursdays; the seventies tribute band, the Afrodisiacs, has been a long-running hit. Drink is closed Monday and Tuesday nights, but is open for lunch weekdays. The club is open until 4am Friday and 5am Saturday.

Elixir. 325 N. Jefferson St. (at Fulton St.). ☎ **312/258-0523.** Cover $3–$10.

All the surfaces are shiny and sleek here, from the sports cars parked indiscreetly out front to the modelish crowd making the scene inside this two-level dance lounge located in a converted warehouse in an increasingly fashionable edge of downtown. Deejays spin hip-hop, house, and acid jazz sounds. Open until 4am Thursday and Friday and 5am Saturday.

Excalibur. 632 N. Dearborn St. (at Ontario St.). ☎ **312/266-1944.** Cover $5–$10.

The Romanesque castle built for the Chicago Historical Society has been reincarnated in its latest form as Excalibur, a multilevel nightclub that anchors the theme-parkish playground along Ontario Street. There's something for everyone here: three dance floors, including the adjacent alternative music Dome Room (with a separate entrance and admission); a restaurant; billiards; and a big game room.

Karma. 318 W. Grand Ave. (at Orleans St.). ☎ **312/321-1331.** Cover $5–$15.

A three-level River North nightspot with two dance floors and a mixed crowd.

Neo. 2350 N. Clark St. (at Fullerton Ave.). ☎ **773/528-2622.** Cover $2–$5.

The cavernlike Neo, located at the end of a long lighted alley in Lincoln Park, is a throwback to the new-wave era of the late seventies and early eighties. Deejays spin everything from electronic dance to dark and gloomy goth. Open Monday, Tuesday, Friday, and Saturday.

✪ **Red Dog.** 1958 W. North Ave. (at Milwaukee Ave.). ☎ **773/278-1009.** Cover $6–$10.

Another spot you have to reach by slipping down an alley, Red Dog is a groovy loft space overlooking the action in Wicker Park. It easily qualifies as one of the most underground nightspots in the city. Clubsters are a diverse lot, and the gay-themed Boom-Boom Room on Monday is hands down the most exotic night on the social calendar with club kids, drag queens, platform dancers, everybody bobbing to a house beat. Besides Monday, the club is open Wednesday and weekends.

Smart Bar. 3730 N. Clark St. (at Racine Ave.). ☎ **773/549-4140.** Cover $1–$7 (free with show at upstairs Metro).

A long-established name on the dance circuit, Smart Bar, tucked in the basement below the rock club Metro, spins the latest musical forms from jungle to "futuristic jazz." The scene starts late and the dancing denizens vary widely depending on which bands are playing upstairs (concert-goers get free admission to the Smart Bar). The club has been spiffed up from its old dark days with a cheerier art-directed interior of trendy light fixtures and super-clubby booths ringing the dance floor. No cover before 11pm during the week.

Tania's. 2659 N. Milwaukee Ave. (at Kedzie Ave.). ☎ **773/235-7120.** Cover $10 (free for women).

Offering the Latin beat and a primarily Latino scene is Tania's, located on the northwest side. A neighborhood institution with a wall of autographed photos of local Latino politicos and sports figures, Tania's serves Cuban and South American cuisine and stays open late with salsa bands getting everybody out of their seats to dance in a dark corner of the restaurant (Friday and Saturday beginning at 10:30pm).

Tropicana d'Cache. 2047 N. Milwaukee Ave. (at Armitage Ave.). ☎ **773/489-0600.** Cover $5–$12.

From the gold lamé curtains backing the stage to the deliciously dressed-up Latin crowd, this two-level nightclub delivers a fun, cosmopolitan evening on the town. Big bands from Chicago and out-of-town oversee the action on a roomy dance floor that fills up fast. There's amateur boxing on Tuesday nights. The space also includes a restaurant and separate bar area. Women are admitted free before 10 or 11pm some nights; the club is closed Wednesday and Sunday.

5 The Bar & Cafe Scene

If you want to soak up the atmosphere of a neighborhood tavern or sports bar, it's best to venture beyond downtown into the surrounding neighborhoods. The Near North Side has a few entertainment zones that are saturated with bright, upscale neighborhood bars. If you're feeling casual, the city also has its share of dives scattered around, and the real no-frills "corner taps" are also well represented in the blue-collar neighborhoods of Chicago.

As for hotel nightlife, virtually every hotel in Chicago has a cocktail lounge or piano bar, and in some cases, more than one distinct environment where you can take an aperitif before dinner or watch an evening of entertainment. The piano bars at the Drake and the Pump Room in the Omni Ambassador East Hotel are standouts.

BARS
THE LOOP & VICINITY

The Berghoff. 17 W. Adams St. (between Dearborn and State sts.). ☎ **312/427-3170.**

Women weren't admitted to the stand-up bar at The Berghoff—a certifiable Chicago institution with claim to the city's post-Prohibition liquor license no. 1—until they protested their way in the door in 1969. The only women's bathroom is in the dining room, but today Loop business types of both genders gather after work in the dark oak-paneled bar for one of The Berghoff's own drafts and a roast beef sandwich.

Big Brasserie and Bar. 151 E. Wacker Dr. (between Michigan Ave. and Columbus Dr.). ☎ **312/565-1234.**

It's no problem bellying up to the bar at the Hyatt Regency's lobby lounge. The Big Bar comes by its name honestly: It spans 228 feet and bartenders must climb 15-foot-high brass rolling ladders to reach the liquor shelves. The drink menu lists one of the most extensive wine and liquor selections in the city, especially single-malt scotches. The bar offers dramatic big-city views, too.

NEAR THE MAGNIFICENT MILE

✪ **Billy Goat Tavern.** 430 N. Michigan Ave. ☎ **312/222-1525.**

Tucked below the Wrigley Building is this storied Chicago hole-in-the-wall, a longtime hangout for newspaper reporters over the years, evidenced by the yellowed clippings and memorabilia papering the walls. But it's the "cheezeburgers, cheezeburgers" served at the grill that gave inspiration to the famous *Saturday Night Live* sketch. Despite all the press, the Goat has endured the hype without sacrificing a thing.

Jay's. 933 N. State St. (at Walton St.). ☎ **312/649-9188.**

One of the few "institutions" remaining on State Street is Jay's, catering to construction worker types by day and businesspeople and the like by night. The TVs on both ends of the bar are usually tuned to some sporting event or movie, and the Italian beef sandwich with hot peppers is a treat to be accompanied by a bottle of Old Style beer. A dartboard completes the picture.

Signature Lounge. 96th floor of the John Hancock Center, 875 N. Michigan Ave. ☎ **312/787-7230.**

The drinks are pricey, but you're not surprised, are you? Anyway, you get a drink and a fabulous view for the price of a trip to the tower's observatory, two floors below. Open until 1am Sunday through Thursday and 2am weekends.

RIVER NORTH & VICINITY

Iggy's. 700 N. Milwaukee Ave. (at Huron St.). ☎ **312/829-4449.**

The unofficial dress code is anything black at this dark, velvet-draped late-night haven for terminally hip insomniacs. Perfectly situated on a desolate strip on the edge of downtown that gives Iggy's an extra edge of mystery, food and drink are served long after (4am most nights) most of the city's other bars have called it a night. On Sunday nights in the summer, movies are screened on the backyard patio.

✪ The Matchbox. 770 N. Milwaukee Ave. ☎ **312/666-9292.**

The owners boast that this hallway-size spot at the intersection of Milwaukee, Chicago, and Ogden avenues is Chicago's "most intimate bar." It's hard to argue with them: Once duffs have planted themselves on the dozen and a half stools, there's not much room for anyone else. But they do it up big at the bar with a smart selection of microbrew beer, wine by the glass or bottle, and expertly mixed drinks (the place is known for its Manhattans and Gimlets).

Narcisse. 710 N. Clark St. (between Superior and Huron sts.). ☎ **312/787-2675.**

The cigar-and-martini virus has wrought this next-generation retro concept: a "champagne salon and caviar bar." Ivana Trump would feel right at home here among all the turn-of-the-century imperial glamour: chandeliers, gilded walls, and yards of plush fabric. A friend said all they needed were mirrors at the tables for the Euro-model crowd to gaze at their own reflections. We looked to an adjacent table, and there they were: mirrors! The thick menu has pages and pages of champagnes (more than 50, with a few bottles topping $300), wine, martinis, and other mixed drinks. Besides about a dozen types of caviar, the kitchen also serves French-Italian tapas and some tasty-sounding desserts.

O'Callaghan's. 29 W. Hubbard St. (at Dearborn St.). ☎ **312/527-1180.**

This friendly River North gathering spot attracts an after-work crowd and has an impressive oak bar and good pub grub.

Rock Bottom Brewery. 1 W. Grand Ave. (at State St.). ☎ **312/755-9339.**

An after-work and out-of-town crowd gathers at this River North brew pub, which serves several lagers and ales produced on the premises, as well as an expansive lunch and dinner menu. There's a large bar area for viewing sports and shooting some pool and a rooftop deck open in the summer.

RUSH & DIVISION STREETS

Around Rush Street are what a bygone era called singles bars—attracting primarily a college-aged contingent. The bars are always crowded on the weekends, making for a frat party feel on the street. Some of the bars maintain the action on weeknights by allowing women free admittance. Rush Street's glory days have long passed, but there are still a few vestiges of the old times. Division Street, with its succession of singles bars, is still the place where, on any given night, pitchmen stand on the sidewalk before their respective establishments trying to attract customers. Most of the bars have special nights when the price of drinks for women is heavily discounted. The bars lining Division Street include the **Alumni Club,** 15 W. Division (☎ **312/337-4349**); **Shenanigan's House of Beer,** 16 W. Division (☎ **312/642-2344**); **Butch McGuire's,** 20 W. Division (☎ **312/337-9080**); the **Lodge,** 21 W. Division (☎ **312/642-4406**); and **Mother's,** 26 W. Division (☎ **312/642-7251**). Because they're so close to downtown hotels and steeped in the city's nightlife history, these taverns attract mostly conventioneers and suburbanites.

OLD TOWN

The center of nightlife in Old Town is Wells Street, home to Second City and other comedy clubs, as well as a string of reliable restaurants and bars. This area also traditionally has appealed to out-of-towners.

Old Town Ale House. 219 W. North Ave. (at Wells St.). ☎ **312/944-7020.**

This is one of Old Town's legendary saloons, a dingy neighborhood hangout since the late fifties with a fading mural that captures the likenesses of a class of regulars from the early seventies. Put some quarters in the jukebox that's filled with an eclectic selection of crooner tunes and just hang out. Open daily from noon to 4am (until 5am on Saturday).

O'Rourke's. 1625 N. Halsted St. (at North Ave.). ☎ **312/335-1806.**

An unpretentious Irish pub, O'Rourke's has long been favored by writers and actors (Steppenwolf is across the street) who still mourn the bar's relocation years ago from its old digs on North Avenue. Large portraits of Irish literary lions (Yeats, Wilde, Joyce) dominate the decor, and bartenders put pints of masterfully poured Guinness into patrons' hands. No TV, no toys, just a place for conversation.

LINCOLN PARK

In Lincoln Park, concentrations of in-spots run along Armitage Avenue, Halsted Street, and Lincoln Avenue.

Burwood Tap. 724 W. Wrightwood Ave. (at Burling St.). ☎ **773/525-2593.**

Your basic neighborhood bar—only this neighborhood is dominated by postcollege singles and young marrieds.

Corner Pocket. 2610 N. Halsted St. (at Wrightwood Ave.). ☎ **773/281-0050.**

Started by a few Ivy League–types who'd rather shoot pool than crunch numbers, the Corner Pocket has become a hangout for the same. There are nine regulation-size tables in two rooms and a bar area with a decent burger and salad menu and a fine offering of microbrews.

The Duke of Perth. 2913 N. Clark St. (at Wellington Ave.). ☎ **773/477-1741.**

A traditional Scottish pub serving one of the city's best selections of single-malt scotch plus baskets of fish-and-chips ($6.95 all you can eat special on Wednesday and Friday).

Espial. 948 W. Armitage Ave. (east of Sheffield Ave.). ☎ **773/871-8123.**

A hip little corner of starched-shirt Lincoln Park, the lounge tucked behind this French-Italian bistro is a stylish place to linger over a martini—of course, make it the house special Cosmopolitan—and enjoy sophisticated conversation. The walls are red, covered with kitschy old movie posters, and the jukebox is stacked with lots of fun tunes (from Eartha Kitt to Earth, Wind & Fire). Closing hours vary during the week so call ahead.

Gamekeepers. 345 W. Armitage Ave. (at Lincoln Ave.). ☎ **773/549-0400.**

This is Lincoln Park's most popular sports bar, with TV monitors galore.

✪ **Glascott's Groggery.** 2158 N. Halsted St. (at Webster Ave.). ☎ **773/281-1205.**

At the top of any self-respecting Lincoln Park yuppie's list of meeting places is Glascott's, an Irish pub that's been in the same family since it opened in 1937. You'll see groups of guys stopping in after their weekly basketball game, couples coming in after dinner to catch up with their friends, and singles hoping to hook up with old college buddies and meet new ones.

Goose Island Brewing Company. 1800 N. Clybourn Ave. (at Sheffield Ave.). ☎ **312/915-0071.**

The first brew pub in the city features its own Honker's Ale on tap, as well as several other beers produced here and at an off-site distillery. Ask for a tasting menu to try them all. Goose Island has the added benefit of a casual full-service restaurant. A free brewery tour is conducted on Sunday at 3pm (including a free sample).

John Barleycorn Memorial Pub. 658 W. Belden Ave. (at Lincoln Ave.). ☎ **773/348-8899.**

"Se habla Beethoven" states the legend beneath the sign of the landmark John Barleycorn Memorial Pub. In contrast to the frat-house craziness on much of the block, this is a tavern for highbrows, who are treated to a background of classical music, a continuous slide show of art masterpieces, and an extensive collection of model ships. The patio is nice in warm weather, and patrons can order a burger from the menu, too.

North Beach. 1551 N. Sheffield Ave. (at North Ave.). ☎ **312/266-7842.**

After the volleyball scene along the lakefront has wrapped up for the summer, players migrate to North Beach's indoor lots, with sun-splashed murals, sand, and all. The sports-minded Lincoln Park bar does its best to help distract you from the reality outdoors: It's a veritable playground outfitted with hoops, bowling, billiards, darts, and a miniature golf course.

Red Lion Pub. 2446 N. Lincoln Ave. (between Fullerton and Wrightwood aves.). ☎ **773/348-2695.**

An English pub in the heart of Lincoln Park, the Red Lion is a comfortable neighborhood place with a mix of old and young DePaul students, actors, and Anglophiles who feel right at home among the Union Jacks and photos of Winston Churchill. The British owner even claims the place is haunted. Old movies are screened on the TV during the day.

River Shannon. 425 W. Armitage Ave. (at Hudson Ave.). ☎ **312/944-5087.**

Another popular Lincoln Park bar, part singles hangout and part sports bar.

Sterch's. 2238 N. Lincoln Ave. (at Webster Ave.). ☎ **773/281-2653.**

Sterch's is one of the many neighborhood bars that dot the Chicago landscape. It's a bit of an oddball on this popular strip of youngster bars. Pictures of carrots on the bar's awnings and on the canvas flaps that flank the doorway apparently refer to a former practice of serving carrot sticks as munchies instead of chips and pretzels.

Webster's Wine Bar. 1480 W. Webster Ave. (between Clybourn and Ashland aves.). ☎ 773/868-0608.

The low-lit, sophisticated decor of Webster's in Lincoln Park is an alternative to the usual beer blast. The wait staff can help you choose from a list of dozens of wines by the bottle or glass, or you can hone your taste buds with a flight of several wines. There's also a tapas-style menu for noshing. Step back into the library area to light up a cigar and recline on the couch.

WRIGLEYVILLE & THE NORTH SIDE

You'll find a mostly postcollegiate crowd partying on Clark Street, across from Wrigley Field.

Ginger Man Tavern. 3740 N. Clark St. (at Racine Ave.). ☎ 773/549-2050.

Ginger Man definitely plays against type on a row of predictable sports bars across the street from Wrigley Field. On game days, the earthy bar has been known to crank classical music in an attempt to calm drunken fans—or at least shoo them away. Pool tables (free on Sunday) are always occupied by slightly bohemian neighborhood 20-somethings who have more than 80 beers to choose from.

✪ **Hopleaf.** 5148 N. Clark St. (south of Foster Ave.). ☎ 773/334-9851.

A hall for 20- and 30-somethings in the Andersonville neighborhood. The appeal here is the chalkboard menu chockful of microbrews and import beers (110 and counting, especially strong on Belgian ales); the booths and tables gathered close; the vintage jukebox loaded with R&B, hillbilly, and jazz; and the shelf of artsy magazines.

Schulien's Restaurant and Saloon. 2100 W. Irving Park Rd. (between Damen and Western aves.). ☎ 773/478-2100.

This is one of the oldest continuously operating bars in the city, which is immediately obvious when you walk in the door and encounter the beautiful old bar, the bartenders dressed in bow ties and white shirts, and the photos and memorabilia lining the walls, including a mug of Al Capone. You may want to opt to dine here: The German restaurant continues its tradition of magicians performing card tricks tableside.

Sheffield's Beer and Wine Garden. 3258 N. Sheffield Ave. (between Belmont Ave. and Roscoe St.). ☎ 773/281-4989.

A neighborhood gathering spot—especially for the theater crowd—is Sheffield's, 1 block north of Belmont, on the corner of School Street. It's particularly popular in the summer, when its large beer garden, furnished with what's got to be the only outdoor pool table in the city, is open. Sheffield's boasts a selection of more than 80 beers, including one featured "bad beer" of the month. The bar opens early on Sunday when a Bears game is on the tube.

WICKER PARK

For an alternative scene, head over to Wicker Park where slackers and some adventurous yuppies populate bars dotting the streets near the confluence of North, Damen, and Milwaukee avenues.

The Note. 1565 N. Milwaukee Ave. (at North Ave.). ☎ 773/489-0011. Live music cover $5–$7.

Located in the historic Flat Iron Building, The Note is a great after-hours bar with the right after-hours music: a jukebox exclusively devoted to blues and jazz. On weekends, this Wicker Park bar is unbelievably packed until closing time (4am, 5am on Saturday) with a cross-section of club crawlers who make this their last stop of the night. The Note has also assembled a pretty strong lineup of live jazz acts, from experimental free form to swing (with dance lessons) to the big band of legendary 80-something drummer Barrett Deems. It's got pool tables, too.

Rainbo Club. 1150 N. Damen Ave. (at Division St.). ☎ **773/489-5999.**

This old Polish social club functions today as a social club for art students, indie-rockers, and the tattooed and pierced set in Wicker Park.

HYDE PARK

Jimmy's Woodlawn Tap. 1172 E. 55th St. (at Woodlawn Ave.). ☎ **773/643-5516.**

One of the few places to hang in Hyde Park, Jimmy's survived neighborhood redevelopment in the sixties that erased what was once a busy strip of bars. Now into his eighties, Jimmy still works behind the bar, a warren of rooms populated by U of C grinds. You shouldn't be surprised to learn that there's a set of encyclopedias behind the bar at the ready to settle intellectual wrangling.

CAFES

☉ Intelligentsia. 3123 N. Broadway (between Belmont Ave. and Diversey Pkwy.). ☎ **773/348-8058.**

Down-to-earth San Francisco marrieds have set up their own coffee-roasting operation in the heart of Chicago's Lakeview neighborhood. Beans are roasted in a French roaster that dominates the cafe, and the owners also make their own herbal and black teas— all of which are sold in bulk. Warm drinks are served in handsome cups nearly too big to get your hands around, and tea sippers are furnished with their own pot and brew timer. Sit in the window or in one of the Adirondack chairs on the sidewalk and watch the world go by, or decamp to the homey seating area in the back.

No Exit Café. 6970 N. Glenwood Ave. (between Morse and Lunt aves.). ☎ **773/743-3355.** Cover $3–$7.

Chicago's original beatnik cafe dates to 1958. It's moved around over the years and finally came to rest here alongside the El tracks. The most recent owners, eager to wash their last coffee-stained mug, retired last year. The place could have disappeared, but taking the reins were some younger regulars who promised, other than freshening up the menu with some more interesting fare, to keep the culture of the place intact. The small, somewhat worn room remains cluttered with bric-a-brac, worn wooden tables and chairs, and a mix of neo-hippies and Rogers Park activists who come to linger over bottomless cups of coffee, take in a folk performance, or engage in serious rounds of the Japanese game Go. Open weekdays (except Tuesday) 4pm to midnight, 1pm to 12:30am Saturday, 11am to midnight Sunday.

Pick Me Up Cafe. 3408 N. Clark St. (at Sheffield and Roscoe sts.) ☎ **773/248-6613.**

A kitsch-laden after-hour spot conveniently located on the strip in Wrigleyville, this cafe is open Sunday through Thursday 5pm to 5am, 24 hours Saturday and Sunday.

Uncommon Ground. 1214 W. Grace St. (at Clark St.). ☎ **773/929-3680.**

When you're looking for refuge from the riotous exuberance of Cubs game days and party nights in Wrigleyville, Uncommon Ground offers an oasis of civility. Not only that, but this two-room cafe commits what some may view as a coffeehouse heresy:

Smoking is not allowed. Located just off busy Clark Street, the cafe has a soul-warming fireplace in winter (when the cafe's bowl—yes, bowl—of hot chocolate is a sight for cold eyes) and a spacious sidewalk operation in more temperate months (where smokes are permitted). Breakfast is served all day, plus there's a full lunch and dinner menu. Music figures strongly at the cafe; ex-Bangle Susanna Hoffs and the late Jeff Buckley are among those who've played the place. The cafe has even issued a CD compilation of favorite performers. Open until 11pm Sunday through Thursday, midnight Friday and Saturday.

6 The Gay & Lesbian Scene

Most of Chicago's gay bars are conveniently clustered on a stretch of North Halsted Street in Lakeview, making it easy to sample many of them in a breezy walk. While men's bars predominate, there are a few places in Chicago exclusively catering to lesbians, and a few gay bars that get a mix of men and women. A couple of helpful free resources published each week are the entertainment guide *Nightlines* and the club rag *Gab*. The bars and clubs recommended below have no cover charge unless otherwise noted.

✪ **Berlin.** 954 W. Belmont Ave. (east of Sheffield Ave.). ☎ **773/348-4975.** Cover after midnight Fri–Sat $5.

Step into this frenetic Lakeview danceteria and you're immediately swept into the mood. The disco tunes pulse, the clubby crowd chatters, and the lighting bathes everyone in a cool reddish glow. Special nights are dedicated to disco, amateur drag, and the eighties new wave; male dancers perform some nights. Don't bother showing up before midnight; the club stays open until 4am Friday and 5am Saturday.

✪ **Big Chicks.** 5024 N. Sheridan Rd. (between Argyle St. and Foster Ave.). ☎ **773/728-5511.** E-mail: bigchick@megsinet.net.

One of the more eclectic bars in the city, Big Chicks is a magnet for the artsy goateed set perhaps a bit weary of the bars on Halsted Street, some lesbians, a smattering of straights, and random locals from the surrounding rough-hewn neighborhood. They come for owner Michelle Fire's superb art collection (hung salon style from the bar walls to the bathrooms to the patio), midnight shots, and the free buffet on Sunday afternoons. Dancing on weekends.

✪ **The Closet.** 3325 N. Broadway (at Buckingham St.). ☎ **773/477-8533.**

The Closet is an unpretentious neighborhood spot with a loud and constant loop of music videos (and sports games when it matters) that draws mostly lesbian regulars, though gay men and straights show up, too. Open until 4am every night, 5am Saturday.

Cocktail. 3357 N. Halsted St. (at Roscoe St.). ☎ **773/477-1420.**

One of the latest additions to the Halsted strip is this corner spot, a less frenzied spot than its neighbors, where it's easy to converse and watch the passing parade from big picture windows. This is one of the few places on the street where men and women congregate.

Fusion. 3631 N. Halsted St. (at Addison St.). ☎ **773/975-0660.** Cover $8–$15.

The late-night dance club known as Vortex has undergone a name change and a slight interior redesign (the dance floor now doubles as the dining room for a new Brazilian restaurant), but the offerings are still about the same: big dance floor, big sound system, big lights. When the other bars close up for the night, Halsted Street habitués wander up to Fusion for a couple of furious hours of dancing and the occasional performer like RuPaul or Thelma Houston. Open weekends only.

The Generator. 306 N. Halsted St. (between Fulton and Kinzie sts.). ☎ **312/243-8889.** Cover $2–$5.

On the fringes of downtown, this sprawling warehouse dance club is packed late into the night with black gay men and a handful of women taking full advantage of the infectious house beat and ample dance floor acreage. Open Sunday and Wednesday through Friday until 4am, Saturday until 5am.

Gentry. 440 N. State St. (between Illinois and Hubbard sts.). ☎ **312/664-1033.**

A gay cabaret, this popular after-work destination moved this year to new digs in River North. The piano bar is overseen by local cheeky chanteuse Honey West and out-of-town headliners, with two shows a night and an open mike on Tuesday. There's also a Boys Town branch at 3320 N. Halsted St. (☎ **773/348-1053**).

Girlbar. 2625 N. Halsted St. (between Diversey Pkwy. and Wrightwood Ave.). ☎ **773/871-4210.** Cover $3–$5.

The women's scene got a boost in 1996 when this lesbian bar opened in the usually straight confines of Lincoln Park. There's a modest dance floor on the first floor, pool tables, pop jukebox, and porch upstairs. Wednesday is "Boy Night" at Girlbar when a youngish gay crowd surrounds the bar for the cheap pitchers of beer. Closed Monday.

GLEE Club at Crobar. 1543 N. Kingsbury St. (south of North Ave.). ☎ **312/413-7000.**

On Sunday night, the sprawling nightclub hosts a long-running gay dance party that draws a young body-conscious crowd dancing to technopop and house.

Manhole. 3458 N. Halsted St. (at Cornelia St.). ☎ **773/975-9244.**

A late-night dance club not for the prude of heart: The decorating motif is a sewer, and access to the back bar and dance floor is granted only by the doffing of shirts or the donning of leather or military dress. Monthly underwear parties are the club's signature.

Roscoe's Tavern. 3356 N. Halsted St. (at Roscoe St.). ☎ **773/281-3355.** Cover after 10pm Sat $2.

The picture windows onto Halsted make Roscoe's, a gay neighborhood bar in business since 1987, an especially welcoming place, and there's plenty of activity to occupy your time, including the large antique-filled front bar, an outdoor patio, a pool table, and a large dance floor. The adjoining cafe serves sandwiches and salads.

✪ Sidetrack. 3349 N. Halsted St. (at Roscoe St.). ☎ **773/477-9189.**

If you make it to Roscoe's, you'll no doubt end up at Sidetrack. The popular bars are across the street from one another, and there's a constant flow of feet between the two. The windowless Sidetrack is a sleek video bar where TV monitors are never out of your field of vision, nor are the preppy professional patrons.

7 Movies & the Spoken Word

MOVIES

Chicago boasts a dozen or so film festivals throughout the year. The **Chicago International Film Festival** is held annually over two weeks beginning in early October (call ☎ **312/425-9400,** or 312/332-FILM for a film schedule). Films by or about gays and lesbians, women, children, and Latinos get their due at respective festivals during the year. Listed below are some of the houses showing unusual, art, or foreign films.

Biograph. 2433 N. Lincoln Ave. (between Fullerton and Wrightwood aves.). ☎ **773/348-4123.**

At the deco-style Biograph, John L. Dillinger saw his last flick before being gunned down in the alleyway next to the theater. Some of those indentations in the telephone pole near the sidewalk end of the alley are said to be bullet holes. History aside, the current-day cinema is nothing special—save for the famous marquee—since it was chopped into three screens showing the latest Hollywood product.

Brew and View. 3145 N. Sheffield Ave. (at Belmont Ave.). ☎ **312/618-VIEW.** www.brewnview.com.

The next best thing to plopping down on a couch and popping a tape in the VCR, this movie hall invites patrons (of legal age) to bring pitchers of beer to their tables, and, if they're so inspired, to ad lib some running commentary to the movies—fun and frivolous fare geared to the tastes of the 20-something audiences. There's a full bar and pizza from Bacino's across the street. Call ahead: The screen is dark on nights when rock concerts are booked here.

Chicago Filmmakers. Office at 1543 W. Division St. (at Milwaukee Ave.). ☎ **773/384-5533.** www.chicagofilmmakers.org. E-mail: info@chicagofilmmakers.org.

Chicago Filmmakers is a nonprofit exhibitor, strictly for shorts and documentaries. Screenings, which are held in a gallery space at the Xoinx Tea Room, 2933 N. Lincoln Ave. in Lincoln Park, present the work of the world's current crop of experimental filmmakers. The group also sponsors the Chicago Lesbian and Gay International Film Festival, held each November at the Music Box Theatre.

Facets. 1517 W. Fullerton Ave. (immediately east of Ashland Ave.). ☎ **773/281-4114** (film info line), or 773/281-9075 (office).

At Facets, another nonprofit, patrons can expect daily screenings that mix a broad selection of old favorites with the work of contemporary independents. Facets also supports an experimental theater company, sponsors an annual international festival of children's films in October, and has one of the largest and most diverse libraries of videotapes, available for both rental and sales.

The Film Center. School of the Art Institute of Chicago, Columbus Dr. and Jackson Blvd. ☎ **312/443-3737** (film info line), or 312/443-3733 (office).

The Film Center screens contemporary feature films unlikely to be exhibited by the city's commercial theaters, as well as the great films of the past, many of them accompanied by lectures and other programs designed to educate.

Fine Arts Theatre. 418 S. Michigan Ave. (between Van Buren St. and Congress Pkwy.). ☎ **312/939-3700.**

This art movie house is appropriately ensconced on the ground floor of the landmark Fine Arts Building, a warren of art and music studios for nearly a century. Two old vaudevillian theaters were remodeled years ago to double the number of screens, but the result is still a notch more charming than the average multiplex. Both foreign and independent films run from 1 week to months on end.

✪ **Music Box Theatre.** 3733 N. Southport Ave. (between Irving Park Rd. and Addison St.). ☎ **773/871-6604** (film info line), or 773/871-6607 (office open after 5pm). www.musicboxtheatre.com.

The cheery pink-neon marquee of this refurbished 1929 movie theater—complete with a Moorish motif, clouds floating across the ceiling, and an operable organ—has outlasted most of the city's vintage movie houses and sparked a dramatic redo of Southport Avenue into a charming place to stroll among the restaurants and eclectic shops. One of the city's real gems, the theater presents an array of offbeat and foreign fare, as well as cult faves at midnight and nostalgic weekend matinees of golden oldies. The Music Box also operates a second shoe-box-size screening room, so it's worth calling ahead to see if your film is playing in the main theater.

Pipers Alley. 1608 W. North Ave. (at Wells St.). ☎ **312/642-7500.**

This Old Town multiplex is the other major first-run movie theater in town presenting independent and offbeat film fare.

3 Penny Cinema. 2424 N. Lincoln Ave. (at Fullerton and Lincoln aves.). ☎ **773/935-5744** (film info line), or 773/935-6416 (office).

Across the street from the Biograph, this modest, slightly dog-eared movie house is popular with Lincoln Park filmophiles. It offers the best in foreign, commercial, and specialized films soon after they've left the other screens in town. At $3.50, you can't beat Monday night at the 3 Penny.

University of Chicago Doc Films. Ida Noyes Hall, 1212 E. 59th St. (at the Midway Plaisance). ☎ **773/702-8575** (film info line), or 773/702-8574 (office). www.docfilms. uchicago.edu.

Located at the university's Max Palevsky Cinema, this film center is the longest continuously operating student film society in country. Second-run movies, often part of a curated series (Hitchcock, "Trouble in the Balkans") are shown 7 nights a week during the academic year, 4 nights a week in the summer.

THE SPOKEN WORD

Guild Complex. Chopin Theater, 1543 W. Division St. (at Milwaukee Ave.). ☎ **773/ 278-2210.** Readings $5–$7.

The Guild Complex, a not-for-profit literary center with a strong emphasis on cross-cultural works, sponsors a steady lineup of poetry and prose readings, storytelling, lectures, and other cultural events.

Museum of Contemporary Art. 220 E. Chicago Ave. ☎ **312/280-2660.**

To go along with its new 300-seat auditorium, the MCA has developed a performance calendar. In addition to music and dance, the theater is a place to hear poets and monologists from Chicago's own lively performance scene, as well as such out-of-town names as Spaulding Gray.

Uptown Poetry Slam. The Green Mill, 4802 N. Broadway (at Lawrence Ave.). ☎ **773/ 878-5552.** Cover $5.

The performance poetry craze of the 1980s can be traced to the popular Poetry Slam held at the Green Mill jazz club in the somewhat gritty Uptown area. For more than a decade, host Marc Smith has been overseeing the development of Chicago poets in the Sunday night "slam" in which aspiring poets give their best original readings. More than a few performance careers have been launched here. The lively scene begins at 7pm with an open mike, followed by a featured performer, and then the competition itself.

Appendix: Useful Toll-Free Numbers & Web Sites

AIRLINES

Air Canada
☎ 800/776-3000
☎ 888/247-2262
www.aircanada.ca

American Airlines
☎ 800/433-7300
www.americanair.com

America West Airlines
☎ 800/235-9292
www.americawest.com

British Airways
☎ 800/247-9297
☎ 0345/222-111 in Britain
www.british-airways.com

Canadian Airlines
☎ 800/426-7000
☎ 800/665-1177 in Canada
www.cdair.ca

Carnival Airlines
☎ 800/824-7386
www.carnivalair.com

Continental Airlines
☎ 800/525-0280
www.flycontinental.com

Delta Air Lines
☎ 800/221-1212
www.delta-air.com

Kiwi International Air Lines
☎ 800/538-5494
www.jetkiwi.com

Midway Airlines
☎ 800/446-4392

Northwest Airlines
☎ 800/225-2525
www.nwa.com

Southwest Airlines
☎ 800/435-9792
iflyswa.com

Trans World Airlines (TWA)
☎ 800/221-2000
www2.twa.com

United Airlines
☎ 800/241-6522
www.ual.com

US Airways
☎ 800/428-4322
www.usair.com

CAR-RENTAL AGENCIES

Alamo
☎ 800/327-9633
www.goalamo.com

Avis
☎ 800/331-1212 in the
continental U.S.
☎ 800/TRY-AVIS in Canada
www.avis.com

Budget
☎ 800/527-0700
www.budgetrentacar.com

Dollar
☎ 800/800-4000

Enterprise
☎ 800/325-8007

Hertz
☎ 800/654-3131
www.hertz.com

National
☎ 800/CAR-RENT
www.nationalcar.com

Rent-A-Wreck
☎ 800/535-1391
rent-a-wreck.com

Thrifty
☎ 800/367-2277
www.thrifty.com

MAJOR HOTEL & MOTEL CHAINS

Best Western International
☎ 800/528-1234
www.bestwestern.com

Clarion Hotels
☎ 800/CLARION
www.hotelchoice.com/
  cgibin/res/webres?clarion.html

Comfort Inns
☎ 800/228-5150
www.hotelchoice.com/
  cgibin/res/webres?comfort.html

Courtyard by Marriott
☎ 800/321-2211
www.courtyard.com

Days Inn
☎ 800/325-2525
www.daysinn.com

Doubletree Hotels
☎ 800/222-TREE
www.doubletreehotels.com

Embassy Suites
☎ 800/EMBASSY
www.embassy-suites.com

Four Seasons Hotels & Resorts
☎ 800/332-3442
www.fshr.com

Hampton Inn
☎ 800/HAMPTON
www.hampton-inn.com

Hilton Hotels
☎ 800/HILTONS
www.hilton.com

Holiday Inn
☎ 800/HOLIDAY
www.holiday-inn.com

Howard Johnson
☎ 800/654-2000
www.hojo.com/hojo.html

Hyatt Hotels & Resorts
☎ 800/228-9000
www.hyatt.com

Inter-Continental Hotels & Resorts
☎ 800/327-0200
www.interconti.com

ITT Sheraton
☎ 800/325-3535
www.sheraton.com

Marriott Hotels
☎ 800/228-9290
www.marriott.com

Motel 6
☎ 800/4-MOTEL6 (800/466-8536)

Omni Hotels
☎ 800/THE-OMNI
www.omnihotels.com

Radisson Hotels International
☎ 800/333-3333
www.radisson.com

Ramada Inns
☎ 800/2-RAMADA
www.ramada.com

Residence Inn by Marriott
☎ 800/331-3131
www.residenceinn.com

Swissôtel
☎ 800/63-SWISS
☎ 800/73-SWISS
www.swissotel.com

Westin Hotels & Resorts
☎ 800/228-3000
www.westin.com

Index

See also separate Accommodations and Restaurants indexes, below.
Page numbers in italics refer to maps.

FROMMER'S® COMPLETE TRAVEL GUIDES

Alaska
Amsterdam
Arizona
Atlanta
Australia
Austria
Bahamas
Barcelona, Madrid & Seville
Belgium, Holland &
  Luxembourg
Bermuda
Boston
Budapest & the Best of
  Hungary
California
Canada
Cancún, Cozumel &
  the Yucatán
Cape Cod, Nantucket &
  Martha's Vineyard
Caribbean
Caribbean Cruises & Ports
  of Call
Caribbean Ports of Call
Carolinas & Georgia
Chicago
China
Colorado
Costa Rica
Denver, Boulder &
  Colorado Springs
England
Europe
Florida
France

Germany
Greece
Greek Islands
Hawaii
Hong Kong
Honolulu, Waikiki & Oahu
Ireland
Israel
Italy
Jamaica & Barbados
Japan
Las Vegas
London
Los Angeles
Maryland & Delaware
Maui
Mexico
Miami & the Keys
Montana & Wyoming
Montréal & Québec City
Munich & the Bavarian Alps
Nashville & Memphis
Nepal
New England
New Mexico
New Orleans
New York City
New Zealand
Nova Scotia, New Brunswick
  & Prince Edward Island
Oregon
Paris
Philadelphia & the
  Amish Country
Portugal

Prague & the Best of the
  Czech Republic
Provence & the Riviera
Puerto Rico
Rome
San Antonio & Austin
San Diego
San Francisco
Santa Fe, Taos &
  Albuquerque
Scandinavia
Scotland
Seattle & Portland
Singapore & Malaysia
South Pacific
Spain
Switzerland
Thailand
Tokyo
Toronto
Tuscany & Umbria
USA
Utah
Vancouver & Victoria
Vermont, New Hampshire
  & Maine
Vienna & the Danube Valley
Virgin Islands
Virginia
Walt Disney World &
  Orlando
Washington, D.C.
Washington State

FROMMER'S® DOLLAR-A-DAY GUIDES

Australia from $50 a Day
California from $60 a Day
Caribbean from $60 a Day
England from $60 a Day
Europe from $50 a Day
Florida from $60 a Day

Greece from $50 a Day
Hawaii from $60 a Day
Ireland from $50 a Day
Israel from $45 a Day
Italy from $50 a Day
London from $75 a Day

New York from $75 a Day
New Zealand from $50 a Day
Paris from $70 a Day
San Francisco from $60 a Day
Washington, D.C.,
  from $60 a Day

FROMMER'S® PORTABLE GUIDES

Acapulco, Ixtapa &
  Zihuatanejo
Alaska Cruises & Ports of Call
Bahamas
California Wine Country
Charleston & Savannah
Chicago

Dublin
Las Vegas
London
Maine Coast
New Orleans
New York City
Paris

Puerto Vallarta, Manzanillo
  & Guadalajara
San Francisco
Sydney
Tampa & St. Petersburg
Venice
Washington, D.C.

FROMMER'S® NATIONAL PARK GUIDES

Family Vacations in the
  National Parks
Grand Canyon

National Parks of the
  American West
Yellowstone & Grand Teton

Yosemite & Sequoia/
  Kings Canyon
Zion & Bryce Canyon

FROMMER'S® MEMORABLE WALKS

Chicago
London

New York
Paris

San Francisco
Washington D.C.

FROMMER'S® IRREVERENT GUIDES

Amsterdam
Boston
Chicago

London
Manhattan

New Orleans
Paris

San Francisco
Walt Disney World
Washington, D.C.

FROMMER'S® DRIVING TOURS

America
Britain
California

Florida
France
Germany

Ireland
Italy
New England

Scotland
Spain
Western Europe

THE COMPLETE IDIOT'S TRAVEL GUIDES

Boston
Cruise Vacations
Planning Your Trip to Europe
Hawaii

Las Vegas
London
Mexico's Beach Resorts
New Orleans

New York City
San Francisco
Walt Disney World
Washington D.C.

THE UNOFFICIAL GUIDES®

Branson, Missouri
California with Kids
Chicago
Cruises
Disney Companion

Florida with Kids
The Great Smoky &
  Blue Ridge
  Mountains

Las Vegas
Miami & the Keys
Mini-Mickey
New Orleans

New York City
San Francisco
Skiing in the West
Walt Disney World
Washington, D.C.

SPECIAL-INTEREST TITLES

Frommer's Britain's Best Bike Rides
The Civil War Trust's Official Guide
  to the Civil War Discovery Trail
Frommer's Caribbean Hideaways
Frommer's Gay & Lesbian Europe
Israel Past & Present
Monks' Guide to California
Monks' Guide to New York City
New York City with Kids
New York Times Weekends
Outside Magazine's Adventure Guide
  to New England
Outside Magazine's Adventure Guide
  to Northern California

Outside Magazine's Adventure Guide
  to Southern California & Baja
Outside Magazine's Adventure Guide
  to the Pacific Northwest
Outside Magazine's Guide
  to Family Vacations
Places Rated Almanac
Retirement Places Rated
Washington, D.C., with Kids
Wonderful Weekends from Boston
Wonderful Weekends from New York City
Wonderful Weekends from San Francisco
Wonderful Weekends from Los Angeles

www.frommers.com

Arthur Frommer's | OUTSPOKEN ENCYCLOPEDIA OF TRAVEL

You've Read our Books, Now Visit our Website...

With more than 6,000 pages of the most up-to-date travel bargains and information from the name you trust the most, Arthur Frommer's Outspoken Encyclopedia of Travel brings you all the information you need to plan your next trip.

Register to Win free tickets, accommodations and more!

Arthur Frommer's Daily Newsletter

Bookmark the daily newsletter to read about the hottest travel news and bargains in the industry or subscribe and receive it daily on your own desktop.

Hot Spot of the Month

Check out the Hot Spot each month to get the best information and hottest deals for your favorite vacation destinations.

200 Foreign & Domestic Destinations

Choose from more than 200 destinations and get the latest information on accommodations, airfare, restaurants, and more.

Frommer's Travel Guides

Shop our online bookstore and choose from more than 200 current Frommer's travel guides. Secure transactions guaranteed!

Bookmark www.frommers.com for the most up-to-date travel bargains and information—updated daily!

MACMILLAN
DIGITAL PUBLISHING USA
A VIACOM COMPANY

WHEREVER YOU TRAVEL, *H*ELP IS NEVER FAR AWAY.

From planning your trip to

providing travel assistance along

the way, American Express®

Travel Service Offices

are always there to help

you do more.

American Express Travel Service
Offices are found in central locations
throughout Chicago.